A HISTORY

OF

MEDIÆVAL POLITICAL THEORY

A HISTORY

OF

MEDIÆVAL POLITICAL THEORY
IN THE WEST

BY

SIR R. W. CARLYLE, K.C.S.I., C.I.E.

AND

A. J. CARLYLE, M.A., D.LITT.

LECTURER IN POLITICS AND ECONOMICS (LATE FELLOW)
OF UNIVERSITY COLLEGE, AND OF LINCOLN COLLEGE,
OXFORD

VOL. I.

THE SECOND CENTURY TO THE NINTH

BY A. J. CARLYLE, M.A., D.LITT.

FOURTH IMPRESSION

New York

BARNES & NOBLE, INC.

4578

VOL. I.

A HISTORY OF POLITICAL THEORY

FROM

THE ROMAN LAWYERS OF THE SECOND CENTURY
TO THE POLITICAL WRITERS OF THE NINTH

BY

A. J. CARLYLE.

PREFACE.

PREFACE.

In bringing out the first volume of a History of Mediæval
Political Theory, it may be well to indicate briefly the character
of the work which we hope to carry out. In this volume
we deal with the elements out of which the more developed
theory of the Middle Ages arose; we hope to carry on the
work to the political theorists of the sixteenth and early
seventeenth centuries—that is, to the time when, as it is
thought, the specific characteristics of modern political theory
began to take shape.

The subject with which we are endeavouring to deal is
strictly a history of theory, not of institutions. We believe,
indeed, that in the Middle Ages, as at other times, the two
things are closely related to each other,—that theory never
moves very far away from the actual conditions of public
life; but yet the two things are distinct, if not separate.
The principles which lie behind the development of political
institutions are sometimes the subject of careful reflection,
sometimes are hardly apprehended; but in either case they
are to be distinguished from any particular concrete forms
in which they may be embodied. We have, indeed, been
compelled frequently to examine the institutions of the Middle
Ages, but we have done this only in order to draw out more
clearly the character of the theories which were actually

current among those who reflected on the nature of political
life.

We are very conscious of the fact that in the attempt to
deal with a subject which extends over so many centuries
it is probable that we have made many mistakes, and have
been guilty of many omissions. We can scarcely hope that
we have succeeded in discovering or understanding every
important reference to political theory, and we shall be very
grateful to any one who may enable us to supplement or
correct our judgment upon any aspect of the subject.

PREFACE TO VOLUME I.

WHILE I am alone responsible for the judgments which are expressed in this volume, it would have been impossible for me to prepare it without the work which my brother has already completed on the political literature of the eleventh, twelfth, and thirteenth centuries. I must express my indebtedness first of all to my friend the Rev. J. M. Schulhof, M.A., of Clare College, Cambridge, and Exeter College, Oxford, who has read through the whole of the proofs, and to whose learning and careful correction I owe the removal of many serious mistakes. But I must also express my most sincere gratitude to Mr A. J. Greenidge, Lecturer in Ancient History at Brasenose and Hertford Colleges, Oxford, who has read the proofs of Parts I. and II. of this volume; to the Rev. F. E. Brightman, Fellow of Magdalen College, Oxford, who has read most of Part III.; to Mr H. W. C. Davis, Fellow and Tutor of Balliol College, Oxford, who has read Part IV.; and to the Rev. J. N. Figgis, formerly Chaplain and Lecturer of St Catharine's College, Cambridge, who has read a large part of the work. These gentlemen are not responsible in any degree for the judgments expressed in this volume, but I am under great obligations to them for many important corrections and suggestions.

A. J. CARLYLE.

CONTENTS OF THE FIRST VOLUME.

PART I

INTRODUCTION.

CHAPTER I.

THE POLITICAL THEORY OF CICERO.

CHAPTER II.

THE POLITICAL THEORY OF SENECA.

PART II.

THE POLITICAL THEORY OF THE ROMAN LAWYERS.

CHAPTER III.

THE THEORY OF THE LAW OF NATURE.

PART III.

THE POLITICAL THEORY OF THE NEW TESTAMENT AND THE FATHERS.

CHAPTER VIII.

THE POLITICAL THEORY OF THE NEW TESTAMENT.

CHAPTER IX.

NATURAL LAW.

CHAPTER X.

NATURAL EQUALITY AND SLAVERY.

CHAPTER XI.

NATURAL EQUALITY AND GOVERNMENT.

CHAPTER XII.

THE THEORY OF PROPERTY.

CHAPTER XIII

THE SACRED AUTHORITY OF THE RULER.

CHAPTER XIV.

AUTHORITY AND JUSTICE.

CHAPTER XV.

THE THEORY OF THE RELATION OF CHURCH AND STATE.

PART IV.

THE POLITICAL THEORY OF THE NINTH CENTURY.

CHAPTER XVI.

NATURAL EQUALITY AND SLAVERY.

CHAPTER XVII.

THE DIVINE AUTHORITY OF THE KING.

CHAPTER XVIII.

THE THEORY OF THE KING AND JUSTICE.

CHAPTER XIX.

THE KING AND THE LAW.

CHAPTER XX.

THE THEORY OF THE SOURCE AND CONDITIONS OF AUTHORITY IN THE STATE.

CHAPTER XXI.

THE RELATION OF THE AUTHORITIES OF CHURCH AND STATE.

TEXTS OF AUTHORS REFERRED TO
IN VOLUME I.

Ado of Vienne, Migne Patrologia Latina, vol. 123.
St Agobard of Lyons, Monumenta Germaniæ Historica, Epistolæ, v.
Alcuin, Opera, Migne Patrologia Latina, vols. 100, 101.
—— Epistolæ, Monumenta Germaniæ Historica, Epistolæ, iv.
Alexander of Hales. Coloniæ Agrippinæ, 1622.
St Ambrose, Migne Patrologia Latina, vols. 14-17.
Ambrosiaster, Commentaries on St Paul's Epistles, in St Ambrose, Migne Patrologia Latina, vol. 17.
—— Quæstiones Veteris et Novi Testamenti, Pseudo-Augustine. Ed. A. Souter, 1908.
Apostolical Canons, Canones Apostolorum et Conciliorum. Ed. H. T. Bruns.
St Augustine, Opera, Migne Patrologia Latina, vols. 32-47.
—— De Civitate Dei. Ed. B. Dombart (Teubner).
Pseudo-Augustine, in St Augustine, Migne Patrologia Latina, vol. 39.

St Barnabas, Patrum Apostolicorum Opera. Ed. O. Gebhardt, A. Harnack, and T. Zahn.

Cassiodorus, Opera, Migne Patrologia Latina, vols. 69, 70.
—— Varia, Monumenta Germaniæ Historica, Auctorum Antiquissimorum, xii.
Cathulfus, Monumenta Germaniæ Historica, Epistolæ, iv.
Cicero. Ed. C. F. W. Mueller (Teubner).
Clement of Alexandria, Migne Patrologia Græca, vols. 8, 9.
St Clement of Rome, Patrum Apostolicorum Opera. Ed. O. Gebhardt, A. Harnack, and T. Zahn.
Codex Ecclesiæ Africanæ, Canones Apostolorum et Conciliorum. Ed. H. T. Bruns.
Codex of Justinian, Corpus Juris Civilis. Ed. P. Krueger.
Council of Arles, Mansi, Councils, vol. xiv.

Council of Frankfort, Mansi, Councils, vol. xiii., and Monumenta Ger-
maniæ Historica Legum, sect. ii. vol. 1.
Council of Gangræ, Canones Apostolorum et Conciliorum.   Ed. H. T.
Bruns.
Councils of Toledo, Canones Apostolorum et Conciliorum.   Ed. H. T.
Bruns.
St Cyprian.   Ed. G. Hartel.

De Duodecim Abusivis Sæculi.   Ed. S. Hellmaun, 1908.
Digest of Justinian, Corpus Juris Civilis.   Ed. Th. Mommsen.
Diogenes Laertius.   Ed. G. C. Corbet.

Felix II., Epistolæ Romanorum Pontificum . . . A. S. Hilaro usque ad
Pelagium II.   Ed. Thiel.
Florus Diaconus, Migne Patrologia Latina, vol. 119.

Gaius, Institutes.   Ed. P. Krueger et G. Studemund, 1900.
Gelasius I., Epistolæ Romanorum Pontificum . . . A. S. Hilaro usque ad
Pelagium II.   Ed. Thiel.
Gratian, Decretum, Corpus Juris Canonici.   Ed. A. Friedberg.
St Gregory the Great, Opera Migne Patrologia Latina, vols. 75-79.
——— Epistolæ, Monumenta Germaniæ Historica, Epistolæ, i. and ii.

Hadrian I., Migne Patrologia Latina, vol. 96.
——— Monumenta Germaniæ Historica, Epistolæ, iii. Codex Carolinus.
St Hilary of Poitiers, Migne Patrologia Latina, vols. 9, 10.
Hincmar of Rheims, Opera, Migne Patrologia Latina, vols. 125, 126.
——— De Ordine Palatii, Monumenta Germaniæ Historica, Legum, sect.
ii. vol. 2.
Hosius of Cordova, in St Athanasius, Opera, Migne Patrologia Græca, vol. ii.
Hrabanus Maurus, Opera, Migne Patrologia Latina, vols. 107-112.
——— Epistolæ, Monumenta Germaniæ Historica, Epistolæ, v.

Institutes of Justinian, Corpus Juris Civilis.   Ed. P. Krueger.
St Irenæus, Migne Patrologia Græca, vol. 7.
St Isidore of Seville Etimologiæ.   Ed. W. M. Lindsay, 1910.
——— Sententiæ, Migne Patrologia Latina, vol. 83.
Pseudo-Isidore, Decretales Pseudo-Isidorianæ.   Ed. P. Hinschius.

St Jerome, Migne Patrologia Latina, vols. 22-30.
Jonas of Orleans, Migne Patrologia Latina, vol. 106.
Justin Martyr, Migne Patrologia Græca, vol. 6.

Lactantius, Migne Patrologia Latina, vols. 6, 7.
St Leo I., Migne Patrologia Latina, vols. 54-56.
Leo III., Monumenta Germaniæ Historica, Epistolæ, v.
Leo IV., Monumenta Germaniæ Historica, Epistolæ, v.
Liber Pontificalis.   Ed. L. Duchesne.
Lucifer of Cagliari, Migne Patrologia Latina, vol. 13.

Marculfus, Formulæ, Monumenta Germaniæ Historica, Legum, sect. v.
Minucius Felix, Octavius, Migne Patrologia Latina, vol. 3.
Monumenta Germaniæ Historica, Auctores Antiquissimi, quarto.
—— Diplomata, quarto.
—— Epistolæ, quarto.
—— Leges, quarto.
—— Scriptores, folio

New Testament, Revised Version.
Novels of Justinian, Corpus Juris Civilis. Ed. R. Schoell and G. Kroll.

St Optatus of Milevis, Migne Patrologia Latina, vol. 11.
Origen, Migne Patrologia Græca, vols. 11-17.

Plato. Ed. M. Wohlrab (Teubner).
Pliny. Ed. H. Keil (Teubner).
Plutarch. Ed. G. N. Bernardakis (Teubner).
Polybius. Ed. T. Büttner-Wobst (Teubner).

Rufinus of Aquileia, Migne Patrologia Latina, vol. 21.

Salvian, Monumenta Germaniæ Historica, Auctorum Antiquissimorum, i. 1.
Sedulius Scotus, Migne Patrologia Latina, vol. 103.
Seneca, Opera. Ed. F. Haase (Teubner).
—— Epistolæ. Ed. O. Hense (Teubner).
Smaragdus Abbas, Migne Patrologia Latina, vol. 102.
Stobæus. Ed. A. Meineke (Teubner).

Teaching of the Twelve Apostles, or Didache. Ed. A. Harnack, 1886.
Tertullian, Migne Patrologia Latina, vols. 1-3.
Theophilus of Antioch, Migne Patrologia Græca, vol. 6.
St Thomas Aquinas, Summa Theologica. Romæ, Ex Typographia Senatus,
    1886.

St Zeno of Verona, Migne Patrologia Latina, vol. 11.

PART I.

INTRODUCTION.

CHAPTER I.

THE POLITICAL THEORY OF CICERO.

BETWEEN the active and profound political thought of Plato and Aristotle and the energetic political speculation of modern times there lies a great interval of time and an almost equally great interval of character. It has often been thought that between these periods there was no such thing as a living and active political theory. It has been thought that with the disappearance of the free Greek communities political speculation became wholly abstract and lifeless; that the freedom of men's political thought was first crushed by the weight of the great empires, and then lost in the confusion of the barbaric invasions in which the ancient civilisation perished, and that in the sixteenth century political theory arose suddenly and without any immediate antecedents, being grounded in part upon original reflection, abstract or related to actual political conditions, and in part on the recovery of ancient philosophy.

Such judgments, we are aware, have long ceased to be held by those who have any acquaintance with the characteristics of mediæval thought, and have been corrected by the work of several writers, especially in England by Mr R. L. Poole in his 'Illustrations of Mediæval Thought'; but they still continue to affect the judgment of many, and even those who are aware that in the Middle Ages political thought was both active and closely related to the actual conditions of society have yet no very clear conception of the relations of the mediæval theory to the ancient, or of the dependence of modern theory upon the mediæval.

We think that the conception of the disappearance of a living political theory in the Middle Ages is fundamentally wrong, and that the more closely the political conceptions of the Middle Ages are examined, the more clear will it become that there is no such gulf between ancient and modern political thought as has been imagined. There are, no doubt, profound differences between the ancient mode of thought and the modern,—the civilisation of the ancient world is very different from that of the modern; but, just as it is now recognised that modern civilisation has grown out of the ancient, even so we think it will be found that modern political theory has arisen by a slow process of development out of the political theory of the ancient world,—that, at least from the lawyers of the second century to the theorists of the French Revolution, the history of political thought is continuous, changing in form, modified in content, but still the same in its fundamental conceptions.

We are indeed conscious of the fact that between Aristotle and the Roman Lawyers there are profound differences, and we would suggest that if there did exist anywhere a real break in the continuity of political thought, it would be found to lie here. We feel, indeed, that the inquiry on which we are setting out should have begun with the successors of Aristotle and Plato, and that there is thus an important omission in our discussion. But the subject of the later forms of Greek Philosophy is one which can only be adequately handled by those who are intimately acquainted with the greater philosophic literature of Greece, and we can scarcely pretend to this knowledge. We hope that some philosophic scholar will before long undertake this task; and we anticipate that under such a careful investigation much which is at present obscure in the transitions of thought will be explained, and that, while the fact of a great change in political theory during these centuries will remain clear, the process of thought by which these changes came about will be found capable of explanation.

The political theory of the Middle Ages is founded upon the theory represented by the Roman Lawyers from the second to the sixth century, and by the Christian Fathers from the second to the seventh century, while it is modified by the constitutional traditions and customs of the Teutonic races. We therefore have to begin our work with an examination of the political theory of the Roman Lawyers. We shall next consider the political theory of the Fathers, endeavouring to estimate the influence of distinctively Christian conceptions upon this. But before dealing with these subjects we must make some inquiry as to the antecedents of these political conceptions. A complete examination of these would involve that careful study of the character of the post-Aristotelian philosophy of which we have spoken. In the absence of this we must content ourselves with an examination of one or two Latin writers in whom we can, as it appears to us, trace the development of a good many of the characteristic conceptions of the Lawyers and the Fathers. Cicero has left to us in the fragments of the 'De Republica' and in his treatise 'De Legibus' a very interesting and significant account of the political theory fashionable in the first century before our era; while Seneca's writings serve to illustrate some general tendencies of political thought one hundred years later. With the assistance of these writers we can in some measure reconstruct the general outlines of the political conceptions which influenced the Lawyers and the Fathers. We can at least learn from them the commonplaces of political philosophy in their days, the notions current among the educated men of the period.

Cicero is a political writer of great interest, not because he possesses any great originality of mind, or any great power of political analysis, but rather because, in the eclectic fashion of an amateur philosopher, he sums up the commonplaces of the political theory of his time. We feel in reading him that, while he has no special contribution of his own to make to philosophy, he is really as interesting to us as if he had been able to do

this. For, when we read him, we feel that we learn not so
much what Cicero thought as what was generally current in
his time; we learn how the honourable and right-minded and
reasonably intelligent politician of his time tended to think,
what were the conceptions which the public of that time would
have applauded as being just and edifying with regard to the
nature of society and the principles underlying social relations.
We find these ideas expressed not in any very profound fashion,
but with grace, with considerable clearness at least on the
surface, and with an abundant and often impressive rhetorical
eloquence.

Among the fragments of Cicero's 'Republic' which St
Augustine has preserved for us in the 'De Civitate Dei' none
is more important than a passage which comes, he says, from
the end of the second book of the 'Republic.'[1] He tells us
that in Cicero's Dialogue Philus requests that the subject
of justice should be carefully discussed, especially because it
was a common saying of the time that injustice was necessarily involved in the administration of the commonwealth.
Scipio agrees to do this, and lays it down that no progress can
be made with the discussion of the nature of the State until
it is recognised, not only that the popular saying is false, but
rather that the truth is that it is impossible for the State to
have any existence at all unless it is founded upon and represents the highest justice. It is this conception which is expressed in the definition of the State propounded by Scipio:[2]
"Res publica, res populi, populus autem non omnis hominum
coetus quoquo modo congregatus, sed coetus multitudinis juris
consensu et utilitatis communione sociatus." The commonwealth is the affair of the people, but the people is not any
assemblage of men, gathered together in any fashion, but a
gathering of the multitude united together under a common
law and in the enjoyment of a common wellbeing.

Augustine in another passage comments on this definition,
and asserts that Cicero defines the meaning of "juris consensu"
when he says that the State cannot exist without justice:

---

[1] De Civ. Dei, ii. 21 ; Cicero, De Rep., ii. 43. 44.
[2] De Rep., i. 25. 39.

where there is no justice there can be no *jus*, and therefore no
populus, but only a multitude which is not worthy of the name
of *populus*.[1]   On these grounds, he elsewhere says, Cicero maintained that when the government is unjust, whether a tyranny,
an oligarchy, or a democracy, there is no *res publica* at all; an
unjust government is not merely evil and injurious, but destroys the very being of the State.[2]

Justice is, then, the foundation of law and of organised
society, and Cicero is concerned to explain that he means by
justice something which is wholly independent in its character
of the consent of man.   Cicero appears to have cited Carneades
as maintaining that laws only arise out of the experience of
utility, and that thus they continually vary in different places
and times; that there is no such thing as *jus naturale;* that,
properly speaking, there is no such thing as justice, or else
that justice is mere foolishness, and the only source of virtue
is human agreement.[3]   Cicero is as much shocked at these
sentiments as any modern politician of respectable character
would be, and denounces the theory of utility as the foundation
of justice with much warmth and eloquence.   It is not utility
but nature which is the source of justice and law.[4]   Cicero is
clearly maintaining the same view of justice as that of Chrysippus and the other Stoics as cited by Stobæus[5] and Plutarch,[6]
in opposition to the theory of Epicurus[7] and such thinkers as
Carneades, who maintained that justice was the name for a
convention devised among men for the advancement of their
own utility.

Justice is a principle of nature, a principle which lies behind
all the order of the world, the expression of a universal principle or law of nature—the ultimate principle behind all law.
Lactantius has preserved for us a passage from the 'De Republica,' in which Cicero has with some real eloquence described this.   There is a law which is the same as true reason
accordant with nature, a law which is constant and eternal,

[1] De Civ., xix. 21.   ii. 18.
[2] De Civ., ii. 21.   [5] Stobæus, Ecl., ii. 184.
[3] Lactantius, Div. Inst., v. 17;   [6] Plutarch, De Stoic. Rep., 9.
Cicero, De Rep., iii. 12. 21.   [7] Diog. Laert., x. 150.
[4] De Leg., i. 14.-16.   Cf. De Finibus,

which calls and commands to duty, which warns and terrifies men from the practice of deceit. This law is not one thing at Rome, another at Athens, but is eternal and immutable, the expression of the command and sovereignty of God.[1] In his treatise on laws, Cicero carefully points out that all civil law is but the expression or application of this eternal law of nature. That which is not derived from it may have the formal character of law but not its true character. The people or the prince may make laws, but they have not the true character of *jus* unless they are derived from the ultimate law. The original source and the foundation of *jus* must be studied in that supreme law which came into being ages before any State existed.[2]

It is important, we think, to observe with some care this emphatic exposition of the principle and character of the law of nature. Cicero's treatment may leave a good deal to be desired in point of clear analysis,—we may indeed doubt whether Cicero had himself a clear conception of the subject with which he is dealing. But we think that we have said enough to show both the importance of the theory of natural law in the current philosophical system with which Cicero was in sympathy, and also the close relation of this conception to the theory of justice. The theory of natural law is to Cicero the form of the theory of justice in society, and it is also the groundwork upon which the whole structure of human society rests. Human society is founded upon nature; its cause is "naturalis quædam hominum quasi congregatio."[3]

We may feel that while Cicero's treatment of the law of nature represents a stronger emphasis upon the conception than that which is characteristic of older thinkers, he does not do much more than develop conceptions which belonged to them. It is very different with the subject which we must next consider, Cicero's theory of human nature and its relation to the institutions of society.

---

[1] Lactantius, Div. Inst., vi. 8 ; De Rep., iii. 22.
[2] De Leg., i. 6. 19, 20 ; 10. 28 ; 15.

42 ; 16. 45. Cf. De Leg., ii. 4.
[3] De Rep., i. 25. 39.

There is no conception which is more fundamental to the Aristotelian theory of society than the notion of the natural inequality of human nature. Upon this turns not only his theory of slavery but also his theory of Government. To Aristotle the institution of slavery is a necessary condition of civilised life and of a civilised social order, and it is natural, because there are some men so inferior to their fellows as to be naturally servile. And again, to Aristotle the government of civilised society is always the expression of the superiority of some men over others. The most ideal government is that of the best man over his inferiors, next to that is the government of the aristocracy ; but even his ideal commonwealth is the rule of a small body of citizens, approximately equal in capacity and education, over a great unenfranchised multitude of inferiors, mechanical persons and slaves. It is a presupposition of his commonwealth that there should be a reasonable equality of virtue and capacity among all the citizens, or at least such a measure of it as, under a careful system of public education, will render every citizen moderately competent for the discharge of public duties. But this equality is confined to the small body of the citizens: the great majority of the persons included in the commonwealth are wholly inferior to the citizens and incompetent for the responsibilities of public duty. By nature some men are fit for rule, others only for subjection. There is a naturally servile class, possessing only a small share of reason, enough only to render obedience to the developed reason of others. True excellence or virtue is not within the reach of all, but belongs only to a few.

These presuppositions of the Aristotelian theory arose naturally from the circumstances of Greek civilisation, though they had been questioned by some writers before Aristotle. In general culture, and perhaps even more in political culture, the Greek belonged to a different world from the races which surrounded him. The distinction between the Greek and the barbarian might be exaggerated by the Greek, but the difference was real and profound. In art, in letters, in philosophy the Greek was not merely different from those who surrounded him, but belonged to another order. And in political matters

the subjects of the barbaric despotisms of the East might well
seem to the Greek citizen to confess their naturally servile
character, for they did not even possess or desire to possess the
political responsibility of the Greek citizen. Centuries afterwards we find a citizen of the Roman Commonwealth laying
it down that the Roman Emperor was the lord of free men,
while the barbarian ruler was the master of slaves.[1] What
Gregory the Great could say in the decline of the Roman
Empire with truth of sentiment the citizen of the free Greek
state felt as true in every fibre of his being.

There is no change in political theory so startling in its completeness as the change from the theory of Aristotle to the
later philosophical view represented by Cicero and Seneca.
Over against Aristotle's view of the natural inequality of
human nature we find set out the theory of the natural equality
of human nature. There is no resemblance in nature so great
as that between man and man, there is no equality so complete.
There is only one possible definition for all mankind, reason
is common to all ; men differ indeed in learning, but are equal
in the capacity for learning. There is no race which under the
guidance of nature cannot attain to virtue. The same virtues
are pleasing, the same vices are detestable to all nations ; all
men can be made better by learning the true conception of life.
It is only the perversions which depraved habit and foolish
conceptions have brought, which cause men to differ so much
from each other. Nature has given to all men reason, that is,
true reason, and therefore the true law, which is right reason
commanding and forbidding.[2] We shall see later how these

[1] St Gregory the Great, Ep. xiii. 34.
[2] De Leg., i. 10. 28-12. 33 :
"*M.* Sunt hæc quidem magna,
quæ nunc breviter attinguntur, sed
omnium, quæ in hominum doctorum
disputatione versantur, nihil est profecto præstabilius quam plane intellegi
nos ad justitiam esse natos, neque
opinione, sed natura constitutum esse
jus. Id jam patebit, si hominum inter
ipsos societatem conjunctionemque per-
spexeris. Nihil est enim unum uni tam
simile, tam par, quam omnes inter

nosmet ipsos sumus. Quodsi depravatio
consuetudinum, si opinionum vanitas
non inbecillitatem animorum torqueret
et flecteret, quocumque cœpisset, sui
nemo ipse tam similis esset, quam
omnes essent omnium. Itaque, quæcumque est hominis definitio, una in
omnis valet ; quod argumenti satis est
nullam dissimilitudinem esse in genere ;
quæ si esset, non una omnis definitio
contineret ; etenim ratio, qua una
præstamus beluis, per quam conjectura
valemus, argumentamur, refellimus,

sweeping generalisations recur in Seneca, and it can scarcely
be doubted that we have here presented to us the foundation
of those dogmatic statements of the lawyers like Ulpian and
Florentinus,[1] in which all men are presented to us as being by
nature free, by nature equal. We are indeed at the beginnings
of a theory of human nature and society of which the " Liberty
Equality, and Fraternity " of the French Revolution is only the
present-day expression. To complete the parallelism of the
conception, we may observe that the " Fraternity " of the Revolution is only a later form of Cicero's phrase,[2] " By nature we
are disposed to love men ; this is the foundation of law."

We have ventured to suggest that the dividing-line between
the ancient and the modern political theory must be sought,
if anywhere, in the period between Aristotle and Cicero. We
think that this cannot be better exemplified than with regard
to the theory of the equality of human nature. Further on we
shall have occasion to examine the relation of Christianity to
this conception, but in the meanwhile it must be noticed that the
appearance of this conception is not consequent upon Christ-

disserimus, conficimus aliquid, con-
cludimus, certe est communis, doctrina
differens, discendi quidem facultate par.
Nam et sensibus eadem omnia compre-
henduntur, et ea, quæ movent sensus
itidem movent omnium, quæque in
animis imprimuntur, de quibus ante
dixi, inchoatæ intellegentiæ, similiter
in omnibus inprimuntur, interpresque
mentis oratio verbis discrepat sententiis
congruens ; nec est quisquam gentis
ullius, qui ducem nactus ad virtutem
pervenire non possit.

"Nec solum in rectis, sed etiam in
pravitatibus insignis est humani generis
similitudo. . . . Quæ autem natio non
comitatem, non benignitatem, non
gratum animum et beneficii memorem
diligit ? quæ superbos, quæ maleficos,
quæ crudeles, quæ ingratos non asper-
natur, non odit ? Quibus ex rebus
quom omne genus hominum sociatum inter se esse intellegatur, illud extremum
est, quod recte vivendi ratio meliores
efficit. Quæ si adprobatis, pergam

ad reliqua ; sin quid requiritis, id ex-
plicemus prius. Att. Nos vero nihil,
ut pro utroque respondeam.
"M. Sequitur igitur ad participan-
dum alium communicandumque
inter omnes jus nos natura esse factos.
Atque hoc in omni hac disputatione
sic intellegi volo, jus quod dicam,
natura esse, tantam autem esse cor-
ruptelam malæ consuetudinis, ut ab ea
tamquam igniculi extinguantur a
natura dati exorianturque et con-
firmentur vitia contraria. Quod si,
quo modo est natura, sic judicio
homines ' humani,' ut ait poëta, ' nihil
a se alienum putarent,' coleretur jus
æque ab omnibus. Quibus enim ratio
a natura data est, isdem etiam recta
ratio data est, ergo etiam lex, quæ est
recta ratio in jubendo et vetando ; si
lex, jus quoque ; et omnibus ratio ; jus
igitur datum est omnibus."
[1] Dig., i. 1. 4 ; i. 5. 4 ; l. 17. 32.
[2] De Leg., i. 15. 43.

ianity, however true it may be that the progressive translation of this great abstract conception into such measure of practical reality as it may now possess has been largely carried out under its influence.

Cicero already speaks with the cosmopolitan accent of modern civilisation; to him the older conception of an absolute natural difference between the civilised man and the barbarian has become impossible. It is not difficult to recognise the historical circumstances which probably were in the main instrumental in producing this change. With the rise of the Macedonian Empire, the intense but restricted culture of the Greeks became the culture of the world, losing much no doubt in intensity as it gained in expansion. The Greek went out into the world, and found that the barbarian whom he had thought to be incapable of rational cultivation was at least capable of reproducing his own culture. The conquest of the world by Hellenism had the necessary effect of changing the Hellenic conception of the world. The literature, the art, the philosophy of the Hellenic world might be on a lower plane than that of the Hellenic city, but it was Hellenic. If the Greek himself was thus compelled to admit that the barbarian was capable of entering into the commonwealth of Greek civilisation, if the Macedonian Empire convinced the philosophers of the homogeneity of the human race, this was necessarily and even more definitely the consequence of the Roman Empire. The Latin conqueror indeed was himself, to the Greek, one of the barbarians, and more or less the Latin recognised this,—more or less he was compelled to recognise that his intellectual and artistic culture came to him from the Greek. The Latin brought indeed, in his genius for law and administration, his own contribution to the cosmopolitan culture of the world, but that was all he brought. It was impossible for him to imagine himself to be the man possessed of reason and capable of virtue and to deny these qualities to others. The Roman Empire continued and carried on the work of the Macedonian Empire in welding the countries of the Mediterranean basin into one homogeneous whole. The homogeneity of the human race was in the Roman Empire no mere theory of the philosophers, but an actual fact of experience, a reality in political and social conditions. If the philosopher had learned to believe in the homogeneity of mankind under the Macedonian Empire, he was confirmed and strengthened in his belief by the experience of the Roman.

When we turn to Cicero's theory of government we may find what we think are indications of the influence of this conception. In the meantime we may point out that while in Cicero's writings the relation between the theory of equality and the theory of slavery is not drawn out, it is still worth noting that in one passage at least Cicero refers to the condition of the slave in a fashion different, at least in some respects, from earlier writers. We must, he says, act justly even to those of the lowest condition—that is, the slaves—of whom it has been well said that they should be treated as hired labourers; they should be required to work, but should receive just treatment.[1] The suggestion that the slave should be regarded in the same light as a hired labourer comes from the Stoic Chrysippus, and suggests an important contrast with Aristotle's conception of the inferiority of the position of the mercenary labourer as compared with that of the slave. It is certainly worth noting that the slave is recognised to have his just rights; he is looked upon as a man with some independent personality. When we turn to Seneca we shall find that the relations of the theory of human equality to the independent personality of the slave is more fully drawn out.

There are indeed two fragments of the 'De Republica' which would seem to represent a somewhat different attitude to slavery from that which we have described. In the first of these, described by St Augustine, the question is raised as to the justice of the conquest of one nation by another, and, as St Augustine reports, it is maintained that such conquest is just because subjection (*servitus*) is useful for some men, as tending to check the tendency to licence. In the second passage, Cicero, as quoted by Nonius, seems to have been distinguishing between the unjust form of slavery, where those who are capable of being *sui* are *alterius*, and some just form, presumably when those are slaves who are incapable of governing themselves.[2]

[1] De Off., i. 13. 41.   [2] De Rep., iii. 24; De Civ. Dei, xix. 21; De Rep., iii. 25.

There can be little doubt that in these passages we find Cicero to be speaking under the influence partly at least of the Aristotelian principle of the fundamental distinction in human nature ; we find him thinking of mankind as capable of being divided into those who are able to govern themselves and those who are not. But we venture to think that such passages do not in any serious measure weaken the effect of those which we have already discussed. It must be remembered that Cicero's eclecticism is in part the expression of a certain incoherence in his philosophical conceptions, and that it is not a matter for any great surprise that we should find him holding together opinions hardly capable of reconciliation.

It must be observed that the first quoted passage may also be taken as indicating a tendency to one particular solution of some of the difficulties of social theory, which became in the course of time of the greatest importance. It will be observed that Cicero speaks of subjection as being a remedy for the tendencies to licence and evil, and this conception may be connected with Cicero's theory of the actual condition of human nature. In a passage which we have already quoted, Cicero points out that men would all be like each other, were it not for the perversion caused by depraved habit and foolish thoughts. Cicero at the same moment that he dogmatically maintains the fundamental similarity of human nature, admits that this is affected by the fact that human nature is constantly corrupted,—that this corruption brings into human life conditions and distinctions which are not truly natural. Cicero, that is, draws a distinction between the true or ideal character of man and the actual. Human nature is actually often corrupt and depraved, the fire of life, of truth, is extinguished, and the contrary vices grow and flourish under the influence of evil custom.[1] St Augustine represents Cicero as describing men as coming into being not only bare and fragile in body, but with a soul prone to terror, weak in will to labour, prone to lust, while yet a certain divine fire dwells in them.[2] Cicero's treatment of the subjection of man to man seems to anticipate the attitude of Seneca and the Fathers to

[1] See p. 8, note 2.   [2] De Rep., iii. 1.

the institution of slavery and to the other institutions of civilised society. We can see the germs of a theory of human society which was ultimately to trace the great institutions of mankind to the necessity of checking the faults of human nature,—which would tend to look upon the organisation of the State as the necessary consequence of the depravity of human nature and as its true remedy. The inadequacy of this conception of the organisation of society is to our own mind sufficiently obvious, and indeed since the "Contrat Social" the tendency of political philosophy is obviously to return to the larger view of the great thinkers who look upon the organisation of society rather as the method of progress, both negative and positive, than as merely the barrier to vice and disorder. But for eighteen centuries political theorists were governed in large measure by this conception. Cicero, then, maintains the theory of natural human equality, but is partly conscious that this theory has to take account of the actual facts of human diversity and corruption.

We go on to consider his theory of the origin and character of the State. It would appear that Cicero was familiar with two theories: the one, that men were by nature solitary and had no inclination to the society of their fellows, but were driven by the dangers of life to seek each other out and to join together for mutual defence ; the other, which Cicero puts in the mouth of Scipio Africanus, who emphatically repudiates this conception, and maintains that men are naturally inclined to the society of each other.[1] We shall probably not be far wrong in supposing that the first view had been maintained by Carneades and probably by the Epicureans, while the view of Cicero himself is that of Aristotle and of the Stoics. We shall see that Seneca illustrates very clearly a great divergence between the attitude of the Stoics and the Epicureans towards the State.

Society to Cicero is a natural institution, and the organisation of society in the State is the greatest work to which a man can set his hand: human excellence never comes so near

[1] De Rep., i. 25. 39, 40 ; Lactantius, Div. Inst., vi. 10.

to the divine as when it applies itself to the foundation or preservation of states.[1] Man is naturally made for society, and the great society of the State has grown up gradually on the foundation of the elementary form of human association, the family.[2] Cicero evidently follows the same tradition as Aristotle. We also find in him a conception of the development of the State which is worthy of notice, though its importance in political theory was scarcely perceived until the historical movement at the end of the eighteenth century, when Burke recognised its profound significance. We mean the conception of the constitution of a State as an organic growth in contradistinction to the conception of it as a mechanical product. At the beginning of the second book of the 'Republic'[3] Cicero says that he will rather discuss the actual constitution of the Roman Commonwealth than create one out of his own imagination, and mentions with approbation the opinion of Cato that the reason why the Roman constitution was superior to all others was that it had not been devised by one man's wisdom or created by one man's labours, but rather by the wisdom and efforts of many generations. It is interesting to observe this judgment, though it does not appear that it had any direct and immediate results in political thought.

Cicero, then, conceives of the State as being the natural method of human life. But he is careful to point out with all the emphasis that he can command that the State is not any chance association of men, whatever the methods and objects of the association. The State to be a State must be founded upon justice, upon law, and it must exist for the promotion of the common wellbeing of all its citizens. This is the significance of that definition of the State which we have already quoted.[4] The Commonwealth is the affair of all the people, but the people is not any assembly of men gathered together in any fashion, but is a gathering of the multitude associated together under a common law and in the enjoyment of a common wellbeing. The form of the government may vary, but the foundation of the State is

[1] De Rep., i. 7. 12.
[2] De Off., i. 17. 54.
[3] De Rep., ii. 1. 1-3.
[4] De Rep., i. 25. 39. See p. 4.

always this bond of justice and the common good.   There
must be government that the State may have continuance,
but this government must always be founded upon, and express,
the first principles of the association.   Government may be
in the hands either of one person or of a chosen few or of
the whole people, and it will be legitimate if that first bond
of association is preserved, the bond of justice and the common
good, if the State is well and justly governed.   But if the
government is unjust, whether it is that of the king or of
the few or of the people, then Cicero maintains that the
State is not to be called corrupt, but rather that it is no
State at all.[1]   Who can call that a commonwealth (*res publica*)
where all are oppressed by the authority of one, and where
there is no bond of law, no true agreement and union?[2]   So
far Cicero would seem to follow the same general line of
thought as Aristotle, the legitimacy of a form of government
is determined by its end; so long as this is the wellbeing of
all, the form of the government is comparatively immaterial.
But we find also in Cicero traces of a conception not perhaps
strictly new, but receiving a new emphasis.   The three forms
of government, he says, are only tolerable; he is not really
satisfied with any of them.   The least satisfactory form to
him is that in which the whole power is in the hands of
the people.   The very equality of this is, in his judgment,
unjust, since there are no grades of dignity.   But he is
equally dissatisfied with the mere aristocracy or monarchy;
and it is here that his conception assumes a new significance.
The most just aristocracy, such as that of the Massilians, or
the most just monarchy, such as that of Cyrus, is to him
unsatisfactory, for under such forms of government there is
at least an appearance of slavery, and the multitude in such
a State can scarcely possess liberty.[3]

Cicero's identification of liberty with a share in political
power is another of the indications of the essentially modern

---

[1] De Rep., i. 26. 41, 42; De Rep.,
iii., in St Aug., De Civ., ii. 21.
[2] De Rep., iii. 31.
[3] De Rep., i. 26 and 27; "inest

tamen in ea conditione similitudo quædam servitutis," and "vix particeps
libertatis potest esse multitudo."

character of his political thought. We seem to be at the commencement of that mode of thought which has been so characteristic of modern democracy, that political liberty is identical with the possession of the franchise, that even the best government is unsatisfactory which is not directly controlled by the people as a whole. We are not here discussing the value of this conception in political philosophy, but it is interesting to observe its appearance in Cicero. When we go on to consider the theories of the Roman Lawyers, we shall have to observe the fact that they knew of no other foundation of political authority than the consent of the whole people, and we shall have to consider the relation of this to the development of the theory of consent or contract as the foundation of the State. The conceptions of the Roman Lawyers and of Cicero are both related to the traditions of the Roman Government, to the constitutional theory which had grown up under the Republic; but we think that they are also related to that conception of the natural equality of men with which we have already dealt. Indeed it is obvious enough that Cicero's objection to monarchy and aristocracy rests upon this basis, that every citizen has in him some capacity for political authority, some capacity which ought to find a means of expression. Cicero is, in truth, dissatisfied with all the three simple forms of government, both on account of their inherent character and because they all have a dangerous tendency to perversion: monarchy easily passes into tyranny, aristocracy into oligarchy, and democracy into the rule of the mob.[1] He is therefore himself in favour of a fourth form of government, compounded of the three simple elements, possessing some of the virtues of each, and possessing in greater degree the quality of stability.[2] His conception of this is, we have little doubt, in large measure drawn from the history of Rome, and it is not very materially different from that of earlier writers.[3]

Cicero, then, looks upon the true order of the State as being founded upon the principle of justice, which is expressed in the law, and secures the common wellbeing. It should give to every citizen some share in the control of the public life, and

[1] De Rep., i. 28. 44.   [2] De Rep., i. 45. 69.   [3] Cf. Polybius, vi. 11.

provide room for the exercise and recognition of the varying qualities and capacities of the citizens. The commonwealth is an organic development out of the natural association of the family, and at the same time it is the expression of the common will and consent, for every citizen has his share in its control. There is one passage in the 'De Republica' in which this conception seems to be drawn out in a manner which nearly approaches the theory of a contract.[1] This judgment seems to be placed in the mouth of a defender of that theory, which, as we have said, reduced justice and virtue to a matter of agreement. It is, however, interesting to observe the presence of this conception in the political theory of the time; it has antecedents in such a description of the contract as that which Plato gives in the "Laws." [2]

We have thus seen how important in the political theory of Cicero are the three related conceptions of natural law, natural equality, and the natural society of men in the State. Nature is the test of truth and validity in law, in social order, in organised society. We do not mean that Cicero has a very clear and precise conception of the meaning of nature; generally he seems to use it as expressing the true order of things, though once at least he seems to use it as equivalent to the primitive, undeveloped order.[3] But generally his conception of natural law is sufficiently distinct. Behind all actual laws and customs of men there exists a supreme and permanent law, to which all human order, if it is to have any truth or validity, must conform. This ultimate principle is the law and will of the power which lies behind all the external forms of the universe, and it is by it that all things live, while it also manifests itself, at least in part, to the rational consciousness of men. His conception of natural equality is clear enough. All men have reason, all men are capable of virtue. His conception is clear, but the relation of his conception to actual social conditions is not

---

[1] De Rep., iii. 13 : "Sed cum alius alium timet, et homo hominem, et ordo ordinem, tum quia nemo sibi confidit, quasi pactio fit inter populum et po-

tentes, ex quo existit id quod Scipio laudabat, conjunctum civitatis genus."
[2] Plato, Laws, iii. 684.
[3] De Off., i. 7. 21.

developed. He has repudiated the traditional philosophical justification of slavery, but he has not considered the consequences of his own judgment. He has not drawn out in this connexion that distinction between the original condition of things and the conventions of human society which is, as we venture to think, the first meaning of the distinction made by Ulpian and the other lawyers of his school between the *jus naturale* and the *jus gentium*. On the other hand, his conception of organised society in relation to nature is well developed and clearly applied. He conceives of society as being natural to man, and of social organisation as needing to conform itself to certain principles of justice and certain characteristics of human nature, if it is to be legitimate. The State must be just and must also provide for liberty.

Cicero's conception of nature and natural law has then its ambiguities and perhaps its incoherencies, but it is evident that it is round this conception of nature that his philosophy of society revolves. "Ex natura vivere summum bonum," to live according to nature is the highest good, he says;[1] nature is the guide of man, the true test of justice and goodness. But nature is not found by man in solitude or in misanthropy, but in the society and the love of his fellow-man.

[1] De Leg., i. 21. 56.

CHAPTER II.

THE POLITICAL THEORY OF SENECA.

WHEN we turn from Cicero to Seneca we find ourselves in an atmosphere of a somewhat new kind. The change from the Republic to the Empire necessarily brought with it certain changes in the idea of the State, but, what is perhaps more than this, we find in Seneca a professed philosopher of one definite school, who tries to adjust his views of life and of society to the general conceptions of that school. Seneca may not be a very profound philosopher; it is very possible to feel that he often mistakes rhetorical sentiment for profound ethical emotion, and that he has little of that power of critical analysis which might have given seriousness and force to his opinions: he is too much pleased with the fine sound of his own sentiments to examine them very carefully, and carry them out to their conclusions. But still, he does represent to us in a literary form, always interesting and sometimes forcible, the theory of life and society of the Stoic schools of his time, and he presents them with a certain coherence and consequence which differs not a little from Cicero's expression of the preferences of a well-mannered and honourable-minded philosophical amateur. And yet, after all, while there are important differences between Cicero and Seneca in political theory, we think that they are governed by the same general conceptions, that they illustrate different forms of the same attitude to the theory of society.

It is somewhat curious to find that Seneca rarely if at all refers to natural law, that he nowhere discusses the conception of law as related to some general principle of life and the world. We think that this does not mean that he has a conception of things different in this respect from Cicero. For while he does not use the phrase "natural law," the phrase "nature" seems to occupy much the same place in his mind. To live according to his nature is the command of reason to man.[1] It is nature which teaches a man the true method of life.[2] Anger is foolish, for it is not natural.[3] Nature is the test of goodness, everything which is good is according to nature, though there may be things in nature too trifling to deserve the name of good.[4] Nature is that which is perpetual, unchanging: that which is variable cannot be truly natural.[5]

We may at least gather from these phrases that Seneca looks upon nature as being or containing a principle which is the test of truth and goodness, to which man must conform himself if he would find the true method and quality of life. In the main he seems to conceive of it as the permanent principle and end of life, not as identical with its primitive forms. We shall have to consider the question presently in relation to his conception of the primitive character of society, and we shall see then that while he may occasionally at least use the word "nature" as representing the primitive,[6] yet his general tendency is to look upon the completest perfection of human nature in a developed society as being the true "nature" in man.

The conception of human nature in Seneca's writings is very similar to that which we have studied in Cicero. The conception of the equality of human nature is continued and developed in greater detail, but on the same lines as in Cicero's writings. The slave is of the same nature as his master, Seneca says, and he draws out this theory with real eloquence in the De Beneficiis. Some, he says, have denied that a slave can confer a benefit upon his master. Those who think

---

[1] Ep. iv. 12.
[2] De Otio, v. 8.
[3] De Ira, i. 6.
[4] Ep. xx. 1.

[5] Consol. ad Marciam, vii. 3.
[6] Ep. xiv. 2. 44, "non enim dat natura virtutem : ars est bonum fieri."

thus are ignorant of the true principles of human nature. It is a man's intention, not his position, which gives the quality of a benefit to his action. Virtue can be attained by all, the free, the freedman, the slave, the king, the exile : virtue cares nothing for house or fortune, but only seeks the man. A slave can be just, brave, magnanimous.[1] Again, we all have the same beginnings, the same origin; no one is in truth nobler than another, except so far as his temper is more upright, his capacities better developed. We are all descended from one common parent, the world; to this we must all trace our origin, whether by splendid or by humble steps.[2] It is fortune that makes a man a slave.[3] Slavery is hateful to all men; the kindliness of a slave towards his master is therefore only the more admirable.[4] And, finally, slavery is after all only external, only affects the body of a man : he errs greatly who thinks that the condition of slavery affects the whole man; his better part has nothing to do with it. The body may belong to a master, the mind is its own (*sui juris*): it cannot be given into slavery.[5]

These phrases may no doubt be said to be rhetorical, and it would be foolish to overpress their practical significance, but at the same time they seem to complete the impression which Cicero's writings have given to us, of the great change which had come over the philosophical conception of human nature. It may indeed be urged that Aristotle not only indicates that, even in his time, a conception of the unnatural character of slavery was already current, but even that Aristotle himself is somewhat uneasy in his judgment as to the institution. Still, Aristotle's conception of the profound differences in human nature had, as we have said, its basis in what might well appear to the Greek mind the actual facts of life. Seneca's treatment of human nature shows us again how completely the Aristotelian view had gone; his view of human nature is in all essentials the view of modern times. Nothing indeed could be more significant than the stress

---

[1] De Ben., iii. 18.   [4] De Ben., iii. 19.
[2] De Ben., iii. 28.   [5] De Ben., iii. 20.
[3] De Ben., iii. 20.

Seneca lays upon the freedom of the soul. It is just where Aristotle found the ground and justification of slavery that Seneca finds the place of unconquerable freedom; the body may be enslaved, the soul is free.

It must not be thought that this speculation upon slavery is wholly abstract, and has no practical significance. When we consider the theories of the lawyers, we shall have occasion to compare the development of their theory with the actual legal modifications of the condition of the slave. It is worth while to compare Seneca's theory of slavery with his conception of the relations of master and slave in actual life. In one of his letters he deals with the question in detail. He represents himself as having heard with pleasure from his friend that he lived on intimate terms with his slaves : he finds that such conduct is eminently worthy of his good sense and learning. He bids him remember that if they are slaves, they are humble friends, nay, rather, they are fellow-slaves. This man whom you call your slave is sprung from the same source, dwells under and rejoices in the same heaven, breathes the same air, lives the same life, dies the same death as you : you might be the slave, he the freeman. He is a slave, but perchance he is free in his soul. Who is not a slave ? one man is in bondage to his lusts, another to avarice, another to ambition, all men to their fears. Live with your slaves kindly and courteously, admit them to your conversation, to your counsels, to your meals; let your slave reverence you rather than fear you. Some may argue that your slaves will become your clients rather than slaves, that the masters will lose their dignity; surely it is enough that the master should receive the same honour as God, who is reverenced and loved.[1] We may find much of merely rhetorical sentiment in all this, but sentiment is only the reflection of the actual conditions and tendencies of life. It has often been observed that, as Roman society lost its primitive vigour and moral quality, it also grew more humane. Certainly the development of the humane sentiment is very clear. Seneca then looks upon human nature as fundamentally the same in

[1] Ep. v. 6.

all : we again find that we are close to the legal theory of
the original and natural equality and liberty of men.

So far Seneca illustrates the same position as Cicero. But
in his case these conceptions are related to others, which Cicero
either passes over or rejects.   Behind the conventional institutions of society there lay a condition in which these institutions
had no place.   Before the existing age there was an age when
men lived under other conditions, in other circumstances, an age
which was called the golden.   In this primitive age men lived
in happiness and in the enjoyment of each other's society.
They were uncorrupt in nature, innocent, though not wise.
They were lofty of soul, newly sprung from the gods, but
they were not perfect or completely developed in mind and
soul.   They were innocent, but their innocence was rather the
result of ignorance than of virtue ; they had the material out of
which virtue could grow rather than virtue itself, for this
properly only belongs to the soul trained and taught and
practised : men are born to virtue but not in possession of it.
It is important to notice these points in Seneca's theory, for
they serve to differentiate his position from that of some later
theorists of the state of nature.   In this primitive state men
lived together in peace and happiness, having all things in
common ; there was no private property.   We may infer that
there could have been no slavery, and there was no coercive
government.   Order there was and that of the best kind, for
men followed nature without fail, and the best and wisest men
were their rulers.   They guided and directed men for their good,
and were gladly obeyed, as they commanded wisely and justly.
The heaviest punishment they could threaten was expulsion
from their territories.[1]
We have here a statement of that theory of the state of
nature, which was to exercise a great influence upon the whole
character of political thought for nearly eighteen centuries.
It is true that the conception of the state of nature in Seneca
is not the same as in some other writers ; but the importance of
the theory for our inquiry lies not so much in the particular

[1] Ep. xiv. 2.

forms in which men held it, as in the fact that in all forms it
assumed a distinction between primitive and conventional
institutions which largely influenced the ideal and sometimes
even the practical tendency of men's thoughts.

Seneca does not regard this primitive condition as one of perfection, rather as one of innocence—we may say that he regards
it as representing the undeveloped, not the developed, "nature"
of man—and he is thus in sharp contradiction to those who
look upon this as the "natural" condition in the full sense of
the word. But still it was a state of happiness, of at least
negative virtue and goodness. Men passed out of it, not
through the instinct of progress, but through the growth of
vice. As time passed, the primitive innocence disappeared;
men became avaricious, and, dissatisfied with the common enjoyment of the good things of the world, desired to hold them
in their private possession. Avarice rent the first happy
society asunder. It resulted that even those who were made
wealthy became poor; for desiring to possess things for their
own, they ceased to possess all things. The rulers grew dissatisfied with their paternal rule; the lust of authority seized
upon them, and the kingship of the wise gave place to tyranny,
so that men had to create laws which should control the rulers.

Seneca thus looked upon the institutions of society as being
the results of vice, of the corruption of human nature: they are
conventional institutions made necessary by the actual defects
of human nature rather than the natural conditions of ideal
progress. This point is so important in relation to later theory
that it will be well to notice his conception of human nature
somewhat more fully. In another of his letters he discusses
the proper characteristics of human nature. Man, he says, is
a rational animal; that is his peculiar quality, and reason
bids man live according to this his true nature, a thing
which ought to be most easy, but is made difficult by that
universal madness which possesses mankind.[1] And in another
letter we find him carrying out this idea in sentences which
remind us forcibly of Christian theology. It was a true judgment, he says, of Epicurus, that the beginning of salvation

[1] Ep. iv. 12.

(*salutis*) is the recognition of sin. If a man does not recognise his faults, he will not be corrected; it is idle to think of improvement while a man confuses his evil with good. Therefore let a man accuse himself, judge himself.[1]

We have already seen in Cicero some traces of this theory of the corruption or faultiness of human nature; in Seneca it is more clearly and explicitly drawn out. And if we now put this together with his theory of primitive human life, we see that Seneca's view is, in all important points, the same as that of the Christian Fathers, that man was once innocent and happy, but has grown corrupt. And, further, we find that what Cicero only suggests as the cause of the subjection of man to man, Seneca holds of the great institutions of society, property and coercive government, namely, that they are the consequences of and the remedies for vice. Private property is a necessary condition of a social order in which few men can rival Diogenes in his contempt for all wealth, and the best thing is that a man should have enough to keep him from poverty, but not so much as to remove him far from it.[2] And in the same way organised government and law is a necessary protection against tyranny. Seneca, that is, seems clearly to draw a sharp distinction between the conditions suitable to man, had he continued innocent, and those which are adapted to the actual facts of the perversion and corruption of human nature. The great institutions of organised society are conventions adapted to the latter conditions, good as remedies, but not properly to be called good in themselves. The coercive state is a great institution to which, as we shall presently see, men owe their service; but its actual form is not so much a consequence of man's true nature as a remedy for his corrupted nature.

So far Seneca's view is on the whole clear, perplexed only by the intrusion of the perpetual paradox of the promotion of good through evil; for it must be carefully borne in mind that Seneca's primitive man, though innocent and happy, had no true virtue, while man as we know him is oppressed by vice and misery, but is yet capable of virtue. But here we come to a point in Seneca's theory which requires careful notice, if we are not to

[1] Ep. iii. 7.   [2] De Tranquillitate, viii.

misapprehend him, and in which also we find interesting matter for comparison with certain tendencies in the theory and practice of Christianity. Seneca uses phrases of great force and plainness to emphasise the conception of the self-sufficiency of the truly wise man. No one can either injure or benefit the wise man; there is nothing which the wise man would care to receive. Just as the divine order can neither be helped nor injured, so is it with the wise man: the wise man is, except for his mortality, like to God Himself.[1] It is only in some general, outward, and loose sense that it may be said that the wise man can receive a benefit.[2]

The conception of the self-sufficiency of the wise man had apparently developed in the later schools of philosophy, and at first sight it would seem as though this conception would necessarily greatly affect the conception of the relation of the individual to society. It seems clear that Epicurus and his school had applied it so as to destroy the notion of the necessary duty of the individual to society; but it is also quite clear that the Stoic writers had very clearly and emphatically repudiated the Epicurean view upon the latter point, and that, while generally maintaining the conception that the philosopher was independent of the help of society, they taught the imperative duty of serving society.

We should venture to suggest that this fact is closely connected with the character of the Stoic ethical ideas, at least as they are represented by Seneca. In one of his letters Seneca, discussing the nature of liberal studies, seems to deny any value to those which are not related to the moral life;[3] his tone indeed is curiously like that of many religious writers on education. Seneca seems undoubtedly to look upon knowledge as advantageous only so far as it tends to make man better. He looks upon the philosophic life of meditation as the highest life; but he justifies the view by the argument that in the long-run it is the philosopher with his contemplation of nature and goodness who does most for the service of mankind. Nature, he says, meant that man should both act and contemplate, and

---

[1] Ad Serenum, "Nec injuriam," &c., viii.   [2] De Ben., vii. 4, &c.
[3] Ep. xiii. 3.

indeed men do both, for there is no contemplation without action.[1]

The wise man, therefore, in Seneca's view may give his time to contemplation, but this does not mean that he is exempt from the obligation to the service of society. There is in Seneca's mind no real inconsistency between his view of the self-sufficiency of the wise man and his general theory of the relation of man to society. He has given ample expression to this theory in several treatises. Man is by nature drawn to love his fellow-man : man is born to mutual service or helpfulness.[2] The Stoic doctrine is that man is a social animal, born to serve the common good ;[3] and in his definition of the highest good in his treatise on the Blessed Life it is interesting to observe that the temper of mind which constitutes this includes the qualities of humanity and helpfulness. The highest good is a temper which despises the accidents of life, which rejoices in virtue, or, the unconquerable temper of a man experienced in life, tranquil in action, of a great humanity and care for those with whom he is concerned.[4] Seneca is clear in maintaining that man is born to live in society and to serve it: his necessities may not drive him to this, but the true disposition of soul will do so.

The wise man, therefore, is driven to take his share in the work of society and, if it is possible, of the State. Part of a treatise which he devoted to this subject, the 'De Otio,' has come down to us, and furnishes us with a fairly complete picture of the current opinions on the subject. There was evidently a very clear difference between the Stoics and Epicureans upon the subject. Epicurus had said, "The wise man will not take part in the business of the commonwealth, unless some special cause should arise." Zeno, on the other hand, had said, "The wise man should take part in the business of the commonwealth, unless some special cause should prevent him." Seneca admits that there may be conditions of public life which make it impossible for the wise man to do any good in public affairs, and in such a case he will

---

[1] De Otio, v. 8.
[2] De Ira, i. 5.
[3] De Clementia, i. 3, 2.
[4] De Vita Beata, iv.

withdraw from them.[1] But even this does not mean that he will cease to serve the State. The philosopher and moral teacher serve the commonwealth as well as the politician; even under the thirty tyrants Socrates was able to be of use to the Republic.[2] The true rule of man's life is that he should be of use to his fellow-men, if possible to many; if this cannot be, then to a few at least of his neighbours. If even this is impossible, then let a man improve himself, for in doing this he is really working for the public good, for just as a man who depraves himself defrauds others of the good he might have done them, so a man who studies his own improvement really serves others, because he is rendering himself capable of being of use to them.[3]

Seneca then clearly maintains that the wise man is constantly bound to the service of society, and even if possible to that of the State. But he bids men remember, if it seems impossible to serve the State, that there are after all two commonwealths, the one that of the State in which we are born, the other the greater commonwealth of which the gods are members as well as men, a commonwealth whose bounds are only to be measured with the circuit of the sun; and he doubts whether the greater commonwealth may not be best served in retirement, in philosophic meditation upon virtue, upon God and the world.[4] Such philosophic meditation is itself action; nature calls us both to act and to contemplate, and this contemplation cannot be without action.[5] Zeno and Chrysippus worked more for mankind than if they had led the armies of a nation or held its offices or made its laws: they made laws not for one state but for mankind.[6] This conception of the universal commonwealth is interesting and suggestive, in its relation to the theory of human nature, which we have already considered. We may perhaps feel that Seneca's mode of handling the subject suggests to our minds some doubt whether his hold upon the conception of the organic relation of human nature and progress to the organised society of the State is quite certain. Had the

---

[1] De Otio, iii.
[2] De Tranquillitate, v.
[3] De Otio, iii.
[4] De Otio, iv.
[5] De Otio, v. 8.
[6] De Otio, xxxii.

materials been more abundant, it would have been interesting
to consider its relation to such a conception as that of Origen,
who defends the Christians against Celsus, who blamed them
for their reluctance to take office and bear arms: he urges
that they are members of another society (σύστημα πατρίδος),
and that their service in the Church of God is directed towards
the salvation of mankind.[1]   There have, no doubt, been always
traceable in the political theory of mediæval and modern times
two tendencies of thought, the one national, the other cosmopolitan, and though it is perfectly true that these ideas are not
incompatible with each other, yet historically they have sometimes come into conflict.

Seneca, then, has a very clear general view as to the necessity
of the State, of its fundamental importance in human life: he
is even anxious to clear the philosophers of his time of the
charge which seems to have been commonly made against
them, that they were disloyal, or at least indifferent, to the
State; he urges that no men are more grateful to the State
than the philosophers, for it is under its protection that they
are able to enjoy leisure for philosophic meditation.[2]   He
fully recognises that the State is necessary under the actual
conditions of human nature, if only as a remedy for the corruption of human nature.

With regard to the conception of liberty and the best form
of government Seneca seems to waver and hesitate.   If Lactantius is correct in attributing to Seneca a fragment which
he has preserved, he gives an account of the expulsion of the
Tarquins, representing it as due to the hatred of slavery, and
says that the Roman people determined to make the law rather
than the king supreme.   The Roman Commonwealth reached
its maturity under this free government; but at last, when it
had conquered the world, it turned its arms upon itself and
finally returned as to a second childhood under the rule of
one man.   Rome lost its liberty, and its old age was so infirm
that it could not stand without the support of a master.[3]   The

[1] Contra Celsum, viii. 73. 75.   [3] Lactantius, Div. Inst., vii. 15.
[2] Ep. ix. 2.

same conception of the end of the Republic is presented in another place, where Seneca praises Cato, who, when his sword could not give his country liberty, turned it upon himself and so liberated himself;[1] and again, when he speaks of the same Cato as having struggled to maintain the tottering commonwealth, and when it fell, as falling with it—for Cato did not survive liberty, nor liberty Cato.[2] In these passages Seneca seems to think of liberty as being related to a certain form of government, and that this government is the only one suited to the character of a mature nation.

But in another treatise Seneca's tone is markedly different. He speaks indeed in praise and admiration of Brutus; but adds that in slaying Cæsar he greatly erred, both as a philosopher and as a practical statesman. Brutus had forgotten the Stoic doctrine when he allowed himself to be terrified by the mere name of king, for the best form of State is the just monarchy. And he showed himself a man of little insight into the actual conditions of Roman Society, when he refused to recognise that the ancient character of the Roman people was gone, and that men were contending not as to whether they should be subjected to some one man, but only as to whom they should serve.[3] Seneca gives us to understand that the technical Stoic doctrine of government, like the Aristotelian, treated the form of government as being a matter of indifference so long as its end was just; and the contrast with Cicero's view is at least worth noting.

His acquiescence in the practical necessities of Roman life is also worth observing, and we may reasonably connect with this a very interesting treatment of the place of the Emperor in the State, which we find in the 'De Clementia.' Seneca is recommending clemency to the Emperor, and appeals to his sense of responsibility, to the magnanimity of soul which so great an office requires. The Prince should show himself such towards his subjects as he would wish the gods to be towards himself.[4] He should remember that he out of all mankind has

---

[1] "Quare aliqua incommoda," &c., ii.
[2] Ad Serenum, "Nec injuriam," &c., ii.
[3] De Ben., ii. 20.
[4] De Clementia, i. 7.

been chosen to act in the place of the gods : the life and death, the fate and lot, of all men are in his hands.[1] He is the source of the laws which he has drawn out of darkness and obscurity, and he will keep himself as though he were to render an account to those laws.[2] The ruler, whether he is called prince or king, or by whatever other name he is known, is the very soul and life of the commonwealth. He is the bond which keeps the State together, and to his protection, therefore, all the people will devote themselves.[3] Nothing can check his anger, not even those who suffer under his sentences will resist; how great then will be his magnanimity if he restrains himself and uses his power well and gently.[4]

These phrases are evidently rhetorical, and it would be unwise to insist too much upon them; but their recognition of absolutism, and their tendency to think of this as resting in some sense upon the divine providence, are at least worth noticing. When we come to discuss the theories of the Christian Fathers, we shall have to consider very carefully this theory of the divine source of government and the divine authority of the ruler. It would be going too far to say that Seneca has any clearly defined conception of this kind in his mind; but it is at least interesting to observe his tendency towards this, and it may very well be compared with a similar tendency in Pliny's Panegyricus.[5]

When we look back and try to sum up the general results of our examination of Seneca's political theory, we see that the most important difference between him and Cicero is to be found in his developed theory of the primitive state of innocence, the state before the conventional institutions of society existed, and the consequent theory that these institutions are only the results of, and the remedies for, the vices of human nature. In the course of our investigation we shall have to consider the history of this theory, to pursue it through many forms. We must again observe that, in Seneca's judgment, the fact that the innocent and unconventional state was

---

[1] De Clementia, i. 1., "qui in terris deorum vice fungerer ?"

[2] De Clementia, i. 1.

[3] De Clementia, i. 3. and 4.

[4] De Clementia, i. 5.

[5] Pliny, Panegyricus, 1.

primitive does not at all mean that it was the complete
expression of the true nature of man; on the contrary, while
we must admit such an occasional ambiguity in his use of the
phrase "nature" as we have pointed out, it is quite evident that
Seneca conceived of the primitive state as being one in which
man was yet undeveloped and imperfect, and that, while the
actually existing conditions of society may be unnatural in so
far as they arise from the vices and perversions of human
nature, yet they are natural in so far as they are the methods
by which man may, under the actual conditions of life, go
forward and advance towards perfection.

PART II.

THE POLITICAL THEORY OF THE ROMAN LAWYERS.

CHAPTER III.

THE THEORY OF THE LAW OF NATURE.

We have in the previous chapters attempted to examine the general character of political theory in the first century before Christ, and the first century after, in order that we may be better able to understand the historical position and significance of the conceptions of the Roman Lawyers of the Digest and the Institutes of Justinian, and the Christian Fathers from the first to the seventh century. It will not be doubted by any one who is acquainted with the political theory of the mediæval writers that their conceptions are based in large measure upon the Lawyers and the Fathers. They may often cite these in a very external and mechanical fashion, and, as we hope to show later, their political theory is as much affected by, and as closely related to, the actual conditions of their own times, as any other living system of political thought, yet the descent of their theories from those of the Lawyers and Fathers is unmistakable.

In this section of our work we propose to examine the general character of the political theory of the lawyers. We cannot usefully approach the Fathers until we have done this, for it is clear that the theory of the Fathers is primarily derived from that current in their time. We shall have to consider how far these general conceptions of their time are modified under the influence of strictly Christian or Jewish conceptions, but we think it is certain that the general structure of their theory is in no way original. How much they may have derived directly from the lawyers it may be difficult to say, but we must study the lawyers in order that we may come to some conclusion as to the general character of the political theory of the Empire apart from Christian influence. The Digest and the Institutes of Gaius and Justinian are the best guides which we have for this inquiry, while it may be true that there are a good many points in which the Fathers may be thought to be nearer the general opinion of their time than the lawyers.

It has been sometimes supposed that the jurists are in the main disciples of one philosophical school—that they do more or less consistently adhere to the Stoic tradition. We venture to think that there is no sufficient evidence for such a judgment, that there is no sufficient reason for saying of the lawyers as a body that they belong quite distinctively to any one philosophical school. It is indeed possible that some of the lawyers came nearer to this position than others; the obvious divergence among the lawyers on the great question of the *jus naturale* may have some relation to disputes which are rather philosophical than legal. But in the main it would seem that it is best to regard the lawyers not as professed philosophers but rather as intelligent and able men, who when they turned from the sufficiently engrossing practical work of the interpretation and application of law to the changing conditions of Roman Society and speculated upon the foundations of Society and social life, took up the conceptions current among educated men without very carefully inquiring how far these were the doctrines of one school of philosophers rather than of another. Indeed one is more than half disposed to think that Ulpian, who, if any jurist, might be thought to show a speculative turn, intends to depreciate philosophy, when he somewhat pointedly contrasts the true philosophy of the lawyer as such, the study of justice, of the lawful and the unlawful, of the method of deterring men from evil and drawing them to good, with some feigned and presumably unprofitable system, which he does not further define.[1] At the same time, it is true that in some very important points the Jurists seem to follow a tradition which is the same as that of the Stoics, that their conception of justice and of the nature of law is obviously related to that of the Stoics and opposed to such views as those of Epicurus and the later Academics.

The lawyers, then, are not, properly speaking, philosophers, or even political philosophers. There is little or no trace in their work of original reflection upon the nature of Society and its institutions; they seem to use the commonplaces of the political thought of their time just as any intelligent man might use those of the present day : natural law and natural equality do not perhaps mean much more to them than evolution or progress mean to the modern politician. But it must at the same time be recognised that the use which they made of certain conceptions not only serves to show us the general tendencies of political thought in their time, but did much to give those conceptions a clearness and precision which hitherto they had scarcely possessed.

We are fortunate in being able to examine the political theory of the Roman Lawyers at two distinct periods, widely separated from each other in time. In Justinian's Digest are preserved fragments of the work of the great lawyers of the second and the early years of the third century, and in the Institutes of Justinian we have a handbook of law drawn up by the lawyers of Justinian's Court in the sixth century. In the Code we have a collection of the most important Imperial constitutions belonging to the period from Hadrian to Justinian, which serve in some measure to illustrate the principles of law expounded in the Digest and Institutes. We are thus able to study the political theory of the lawyers, not as a thing fixed and unalterable, but as living and changing; we are able to some extent to discover which of the various legal theories of the second century did as a matter of fact dominate the general course of thought: for though it is true that the writers of the Institutes seem almost nervously anxious to combine the most

---

[1] Dig., i. 1. 1.

divergent views of the great lawyers of the second and third centuries into one whole, yet they are unable to prevent us from concluding with some reasonable confidence as to the character of their own opinions.   We are also able within the second and third centuries to trace in some measure the course of political theory and to study the conflict of opinion between various legal schools.   The selections of which the Digest is made up are fortunately always cited with the names of the authors, and though Justinian [1] warns us that by his authority the compilers of the Digest were empowered to omit, and even alter, anything that seemed to them unwise or erroneous in the ancient writers, yet we have no reason to think that this power was very largely exercised.   We are able in a few cases, especially in that of Gaius, whose Institutes have been preserved for us, to compare the original work of the great lawyers with the selections of the Digest; and though, as we shall have occasion to notice, some changes seem to have been made, yet our impression is that the compilers of the Digest did not avail themselves greatly of this authority to alter the selections which they made, at least on those matters with which we are here concerned.

The first subject which requires our attention when we approach the political theory of the lawyers is their theory of natural law, its relation to the law of nations and to the civil law.   The subject is certainly perplexed and difficult, for we may doubt whether any of the lawyers had very clear conceptions upon the matter, and it has been rendered even more obscure by the attempt of the compilers of Justinian's Institutes to combine conceptions of the subject which are really incoherent, if not contradictory.   There is no doubt that we find in the great lawyers of the second and third centuries not one view, but two.   There can be no reasonable doubt that Gaius in the middle of the second century recognised no opposition between the *jus naturale* and the *jus gentium;* while Ulpian at the end of the second century sharply distinguishes the one from the other.   We shall endeavour to point out what we

---

[1] Cod., i. 17. 1, 7.   (Prefixed to Digest.)

think to be the significance of this change of view and the reasons which convince us that the view of Ulpian is that which ultimately prevailed and so became the foundation of the mediæval theory upon the subject.

We cannot approach the subject better than by examining the views of Gaius upon the *jus gentium*. In the first words of his Institutes, which are also embodied in the Digest, there are two propositions which are of the greatest importance: the first, that the *jus gentium* is universal, embodies principles which are recognised by all mankind; the second, that these principles have been taught men by *naturalis ratio*.[1] We must turn to other passages for additional details with regard to the *jus gentium*. In a section of the Digest taken from a work of Gaius which has not been preserved, and in which Gaius discussed the origin of property in various things, we have the important statement that the *jus gentium* is coeval with the human race,—embodies those principles which from the first beginnings of human life were taught to mankind by their natural reason.[2] In a third passage Gaius connects with the *jus gentium* another quality of great importance. Property by "tradition," he says, belongs to the *jus gentium*, and is clearly consistent with natural equity.[3]

When we put together these various conceptions which Gaius connects with the *jus gentium*, we see that he conceives of it as that body of principles or laws which men have always learned from their reason to recognise as useful and just. The *jus gentium* is primitive, universal, rational, and equitable.

[1] Gaius, Inst., i. 1; Dig., i. 1. 9: "Omnes populi qui legibus et moribus reguntur, partim suo proprio, partim communi omnium hominum jure utuntur; nam quod quisque populus ipse sibi jus constituit, id ipsius proprium est, vocaturque jus civile, quasi jus proprium civitatis; quod vero naturalis ratio inter omnes homines constituit, id apud omnes populos peræque custoditur vocaturque jus gentium, quasi quo jure omnes gentes utuntur."

[2] Dig., xli. 1. 1: "Quarundam rerum dominium nanciscimur jure gentium, quod ratione naturali inter omnes homines peræque servatur, quarundam jure civili, id est jure proprio civitatis nostræ. Et quia antiquius jus gentium cum ipso genere humano proditum est, opus est, ut de hoc prius referendum sit."

[3] Dig., xli. 1. 9, 3: "Hæ quoque res quæ traditione nostræ fiunt jure gentium nobis adquiruntur: nihil enim tam conveniens est naturali æquitati quam voluntatem domini volentis rem suam in alium transferre ratam haberi."

Gaius does not often use the phrase *jus naturale*, but from those passages in his writings where it occurs we conclude that it has much the same meaning to him as *ratio naturalis*. In his Institutes he speaks in one sentence of property as being alienated and transferred by "tradition" under the *jus naturale*, and in the next, refers to this as agreeable to *naturalis ratio*.[1] There is no trace in any writing of Gaius which has survived to us of any opposition between the *jus gentium* and the *jus naturale*; such an opposition would indeed seem to be wholly incompatible with the character of the *jus gentium* as he conceives it.

It would seem, then, that the *jus gentium* of Gaius is not greatly different from natural law as we have seen that Cicero understood it, except that, as we may perhaps say, Cicero is thinking of this as a part of the eternal law of God, while Gaius is only thinking of law in relation to the world. But they agree in thinking of law as a rational and just principle of life which is not enacted by men, but is the expression of the universal and natural reason and sense of justice. The theory of law which is held by Gaius, then, is not limited to the conception of the positive law of any one state, but is founded upon a conception of law, universal, primitive, and rational. We shall see later that the civil law of any particular state is at least in some measure dominated by this general principle of law.

We may infer that Gaius is, like Cicero, a follower of the Stoic theory of law and justice, regarding them not as something which men create for their own utility, but as something which they learn. Law in its general sense does not express the will of man, but is rather that which he rationally apprehends and obeys. The conception of the *jus gentium* which we derive from an examination of these passages of Gaius is the same as that expressed in the definition of the *jus naturale*, which Paulus, a lawyer of somewhat later date, gives us.[2] We have no reason to think that Paulus drew any distinction be-

---

[1] Gaius, Inst., ii. 65 and 66.

[2] Dig., i. 1. 11 : "Jus pluribus modis dicitur : uno modo, cum id quod semper æquum ac bonum est jus dicitur, ut est jus naturale. Altero modo, quod omnibus aut pluribus in quaque civitate utile est, ut est jus civile."

tween the *jus naturale* and the *jus gentium*,—we have no evidence that he did so; and in any case this definition does not seem to take any such distinction into account, and indeed seems clearly, at least for the purpose in hand, to exclude it.

Gaius then recognises no distinction between the *jus naturale* and the *jus gentium*. In the beginning of the third century we find three lawyers who do clearly oppose the *jus gentium* to the *jus naturale* or *natura*. Tryphoninus says that liberty belongs to the *jus naturale*, and that lordship was introduced from the *jus gentium*.[1] Florentinus asserts that slavery is an institution of the *jus gentium*, by which one man is, contrary to nature, subjected to another.[2] Ulpian expresses the same opposition when he says that the manumission of slaves belongs to the *jus gentium*, for by the *jus naturale* all men were born free and slavery was unknown; but when slavery came in by the *jus gentium*, then manumission also came in.[3] Ulpian has also drawn out the distinction between the *jus gentium* and the *jus naturale* in set terms. Private law, he says, is tripartite—it is gathered from natural precepts, or those of nations, or civil laws; there are three kinds of *jus*, the *jus naturale*, the *jus gentium*, and the *jus civile*. And he goes on to define their several characters. The *jus naturale* is that which nature has taught all animals; it is not peculiar to the human race, but belongs to all animals. From this law springs the union of male and female, the procreation and bringing up of children. The *jus gentium*, on the other hand, is that law which the nations of mankind observe: this is different from natural law, inasmuch as that belongs to all animals, while this is peculiar to men.[4]

[1] Dig., xii. 6. 64 : "Ut enim libertas naturali jure continetur et dominatio ex gentium jure introducta est." (I owe this reference to an article on the "History of the Law of Nature: a preliminary study," by Sir F. Pollock.)

[2] Dig., i. 5. 4 : "Servitus est constitutio juris gentium, qua quis dominio alieno contra naturam subicitur."

[3] Dig., i. 1. 4 : "Manumissiones quoque juris gentium sunt . . . quæ res a jure gentium originem sumpsit, utpote cum jure naturali omnes liberi nascerentur nec esset nota manumissio, cum servitus esset incognita : sed posteaquam jure gentium servitus invasit, secutum est beneficium manumissionis."

[4] Dig., i. 1. 1, 2, 3, and 4 : "Privatum jus tripertitum est; collectum etenim est ex naturalibus præceptis aut gentium aut civilibus. Jus naturale est, quod natura omnia animalia docuit : nam jus istud non humani generis proprium, sed omnium animalium, quæ in terra, quæ in mari nas-

In considering this subject we must be careful to keep clearly apart the two points suggested by these phrases of Ulpian : first, the definite separation of the *jus naturale* from the *jus gentium*, which is common to the three jurists ; and secondly, Ulpian's definition of the *jus naturale*, which is peculiar to himself. The first is clear and distinct ; whatever may be the character of the difference, the fact of the difference is something quite unambiguous. We cannot say the same with regard to his definition of the *jus naturale*.

As Ulpian presents this here, the *jus naturale* would seem to be something of the nature of the general instinct of animals, not properly speaking rational or ethical ; while he does not actually contrast the rational character of the *jus gentium* with the irrational instinct of the *jus naturale*, at least he says that it is peculiar to men. To consider the definition fully, we must notice Ulpian's use of the phrases Natural Law and Nature in other places. The first passage where the phrase recurs is that to which we have already referred, in which he tells us that manumission is an institution of the *jus gentium*, for by natural law all men were born free.[1] Another passage which may very well be compared with this we find in the fiftieth book of the Digest. In this Ulpian says, that as far as concerns the civil law slaves are held *pro nullis ;* but this is not so by natural law, for as far as natural law is concerned all men are equal.[2] In another place he says that a man seems "naturaliter" to possess that of which he has the usufruct ;[3] and again, that nothing is so natural as that an agreement should be dissolved by the same method as that by which it was made ;[4] and in another

---

cuntur, avium quoque commune est. Hinc descendit maris atque feminæ conjunctio, quam nos matrimonium appellamus, hinc liberorum procreatio, hinc educatio : videmus etenim cetera quoque animalia, feras etiam istius juris peritia censeri. Jus gentium est, quo gentes humanæ utuntur. Quod a naturali recedere facile intellegere licet, quia illud omnibus animalibus, hoc solis hominibus inter se commune sit."

[1] Dig., i. 1. 4.
[2] Dig., l. 17. 32 : "Quod attinet ad jus civile, servi pro nullis habentur : non tamen et jure naturali, quia, quod ad jus naturale attinet, omnes homines æquales sunt."
[3] Dig., xli. 2. 12 : "Naturaliter videtur possidere is qui usum fructum habet."
[4] Dig., l. 17. 35 : "Nihil tam naturale est quam eo genere quidque dissolvere, quo colligatum est."

passage still he says that it is by nature just that a man should enjoy another man's liberality only so long as the donor wishes.[1]

We do not feel very clear as to the judgment which ought to be pronounced on the meaning of natural law and nature in these passages: they are not perhaps absolutely inconsistent with the character of the precise definition we have already quoted, but yet they leave with us the impression that they do not quite correspond with it. When Ulpian says that by natural law men were once free and are still equal, it scarcely seems adequate to explain this as meaning that as far as their animal instinct was concerned they were free and equal, but by a rational system of order they are unequal and some are slaves of others. We doubt whether Ulpian had really arrived at a complete and coherent conception of the law of nature: it would rather seem that he had for some reason judged that some distinction between the law of nature and the law of nations should be made, but that he was not very clear as to the nature of the distinction.

We do not get much help towards understanding this distinction from the other jurists. We have seen that Florentinus and Tryphoninus make the same distinction as Ulpian, but we do not possess any definition either of the *jus naturale* or the *jus gentium* written by them. We can only say that the character of the opposition between the *jus gentium* and the *jus naturale* or *natura*, as they present it, does not suggest that they understood *jus naturale* or *natura* to be equivalent to an animal instinct. Of the other jurists of the second century, as far as the fragments of their work enable us to judge, some appear to make no distinction between the *jus naturale* and the *jus gentium*, while others give us no indication of their view. Marcianus[2] and Paulus[3] seem to know nothing of the distinction; Pomponius uses the phrase *jus naturæ*, but does not define it.[4]

So far, then, as the lawyers of the second and third centuries are concerned, we cannot say that we can get a clear light upon the nature of the distinction between the Law of Nature

[1] Dig., xliii. 26. 2 : " Est enim natura æquum tamdiu te liberalitate mea uti, quamdiu ego velim."

[2] Dig., i. 8. 2 and 4.
[3] Dig., i. 1. 11.
[4] Dig., l. 17. 206.

and the Law of Nations: the fact of the distinction is clear,
the ground of the distinction remains somewhat uncertain.
We think that we can find an explanation of this with the
help of a passage cited in the Digest from the writings of a
jurist of the fourth century, a passage in the Institutes of
Justinian, and the definition of the *jus naturale* and the *jus
gentium* given by St Isidore of Seville, a Christian writer of
the beginning of the seventh century.

There is preserved in the Digest a passage from the writings
of Hermogenianus, a jurist of the time of Constantine, which
is undoubtedly interesting, though not free from ambiguities.
We have here a list of institutions which come under the
jus gentium,[1] and we have the strong impression that Hermogenianus is contrasting these with other institutions which
belong to the *jus naturale* or giving an account of the origin of
institutions which had no existence under the *jus naturale*. This
impression is difficult to resist when we compare with Hermogenianus the other passages to which we have just referred.

In the first of these the compilers of the Institutes, after
giving an account of the *jus naturale*, the *jus gentium*, and the
jus civile, come back to the subject of the *jus gentium* and
explain that it is a system of law common to all mankind
and represents the experience of the human race, for in process
of time wars, captivities, and slavery arose, and these are contrary to the *jus naturale*.[2] We cannot say that the writers of
the Institutes had the passage of Hermogenianus immediately
before them, but there is certainly a considerable correspondence of thought between their words and his.

St Isidore also defines the *jus naturale* and the *jus civile*, and

---

[1] Dig., i. 1. 5 : "Ex hoc jure gentium introducta bella, discretæ gentes,
regna condita, dominia distincta, agris
termini positi, ædificia collocata, commercium, emptiones venditiones, locationes conductiones, obligationes institutæ : exceptis quibusdam quæ jure
civili introductæ sunt."

[2] Inst., i. 2. 2 : "Jus autem gentium
omni humano generi commune est.
Nam usu exigente et humanis necessitatibus gentes humanæ quædam sibi
constituerunt: bella etenim orta sunt et
captivitates secutæ et servitutes, quæ
sunt juri naturali contrariæ. Jure
enim naturali ab initio omnes homines
liberi nascebantur. Ex hoc jure gentium et omnes pæne contractus introducti sunt, ut emptio venditio, locatio
conductio, societas, depositum, mutuum et alii innumerabiles."

then comes to the *jus gentium,* and gives us a list of the institutions which belong to this, such as wars, captivities, slavery, treaties of peace, &c.[1] Again, we cannot say that St Isidore's definition is founded upon the passage from Hermogenianus, but at least it seems to us clearly to belong to the same tradition and to be closely related to the passage in the Institutes.

The impression which these passages leave upon us is this: that the writers have present to their minds some primitive circumstances, some primeval or natural institutions of the human race, as distinguished from even the oldest and most universal conventional institutions of human society. St Isidore indeed describes the *jus naturale* as that which is held "instinctu naturæ, non constitutione aliqua."[2] We think that the position of Ulpian, Florentinus, and Tryphoninus may legitimately be interpreted with their assistance. We should suggest that the cause which produced the theory of a law behind the universal law of all nations was a judgment, that some at least of the institutions which were as a matter of fact universal, and were reckoned to belong to the *jus gentium,* could not be looked upon as, properly speaking, primitive or natural in the full sense of the word. We venture to think that here we trace the influence of that mode of thought about the primitive conditions of human life which we have seen in Seneca, and which we may gather was representative of the general character of at least some Stoic theories.

Ulpian clearly conceived of man as having originally been free, and maintained that slavery only came in later.[3] That is, with respect at least to the institution of slavery he has in his mind some primitive state, before this conventional institution was introduced. Florentinus[4] and Tryphoninus[5] do not throw any clear light on the subject, but they seem to agree with Ulpian. There are no direct references, so far

---

[1] St Isidore of Seville, Etymologies, v. 6: "Jus gentium est sedium occupatio, ædificatio, munitio, bella, captivitates, servitutes, postliminia, fœdera pacis, induciæ, legatorum non violandorum religio, connubia inter alienigenas prohibita: et inde jus gentium, quod eo jure omnes fere gentes utuntur."

[2] St Isid., Etym., v. 4.
[3] Dig., i. 1. 4.
[4] Dig., i. 5. 4.
[5] Dig., xii. 6. 64.

as we have been able to see, in the lawyers of the Digest to a primitive state of nature; but we think that this is really implied in the attitude of Ulpian, Florentinus, and Tryphoninus to slavery. We should suggest that it is in connexion with this that the distinction between the *jus naturale* and the *jus gentium* arose. The passage from Hermogenianus which we have already cited seems to us to belong to a further development of the same theory. We shall see in a later chapter that there can be no doubt that the Christian Fathers generally accept the theory of the primitive state of nature in which the conventional institutions of society did not yet exist, while they give this theory a peculiar turn by bringing it into connexion with the theory of the fall.

We think therefore that the distinction made by Ulpian between the *jus naturale* and the *jus gentium* is really connected, though Ulpian may not have been fully conscious of the fact, with a tendency to conceive of some state of nature as lying behind the actual conditions of human life. Ulpian's definition of the *jus naturale* is not governed by this mode of thought; but we would suggest that this should be taken mainly as illustrating the fact that he had not arrived at any very clear conception of the whole subject. At least, whatever doubt we may continue to feel as to the true significance of Ulpian's distinction and definition, there can be little doubt that the tendency of legal theory was towards the distinction between the primitive and the conventional of which we have spoken. The Institutes of Justinian not only reproduce Ulpian's tripartite definition of *jus*, but in the passage we have already cited [1] they more or less definitely give us an account of the process through which the institutions of the *jus gentium* came into existence.

What the ultimate significance of this theory of natural law, as embodying the primitive principles of human life, was to be, we shall have occasion to consider later: we shall see in the Christian Fathers that the natural law represents a body of principles more or less ideal and adapted to a state of innocence, but not therefore related to the actually existing condition of imperfection.

[1] Inst., i. 2. 2.

CHAPTER IV.

SLAVERY AND PROPERTY.

IN considering the subject of natural law and the law of nations we have cited many of the passages which relate to the theory of slavery and equality. But the subject is one of such importance that even at the risk of some repetition we must examine some of these over again. We have seen that there is no point in which the Aristotelian mode of thought is more sharply contrasted with that of Cicero and Seneca than in the treatment of the equality of human nature. We have suggested that this change in the conception of the actual conditions of human nature can be accounted for in large measure by the new experience of the cosmopolitan Empires, by the fact that the Greeks in impressing their culture upon the countries of the Mediterranean seaboard discovered that after all the barbarian was possessed of reason and capable of virtue and of culture. However the change of conception may have taken place, there is no doubt that it did come about, there is no doubt that both Cicero and Seneca bear evidence to the fact that the older view was disappearing. It is of great importance to make ourselves clear upon the position of the Roman lawyers with regard to this matter: we may well imagine that the technical lawyers would be the last to yield to the new views, the most conservative of conceptions relating to so great and fundamental a social institution as that of slavery.

When we examine the writers of the 'Digest' in their chronological order, we discover that the appearance of the distinction, which we have been considering, between the natural law and the law of nations corresponds in point of time with the appearance of certain new phrases about human nature, with the dogmatic assertion of natural liberty and equality. It must not be supposed, however, that the older jurists of the Digest show us any trace of a belief that slavery is founded upon natural inequality. If they are silent on the theory of natural equality, they are equally silent, so far as we have found, on the opposite theory.

Gaius nowhere gives us any complete account of the origin of slavery. He assumes the distinction between the slave and the freeman as being one of primary importance in the classification of the law of persons,[1] and he gives us an account of the legal position of the slave and says that the slave is *in potestate*, and that this condition of slavery exists under the *jus gentium*, that everywhere the masters have the power of life and death over their slaves, and that whatever the slave acquires belongs to his master.[2] In another passage of the Digest he is cited as laying it down that slavery arises from capture in war.[3] This is the only explanation of the origin of slavery which Gaius gave, so far at least as the evidence of his remains goes. Marcianus, a later jurist, is cited in the Digest as laying it down that slaves come into our possession by the *jus gentium* when they are captured in war or are born of our slave women.[4] We may conjecture that his statement would represent the views of Gaius as well as of himself. These jurists then look upon slavery as an institution of the *jus gentium*, and taking into account what Gaius meant by the *jus gentium*, we infer that they looked upon the institution as rational and just; but they must not therefore be understood to hold the same views with regard to the inequality of human nature as Aristotle. Indeed it is noticeable enough that they have no explanation to offer of the origin of the institution, except as connected with war.

When we come to Ulpian, Tryphoninus, and Florentinus at the close of the second century, we find that remarkable turn of theory whose expression we have already noticed in con-

---

[1] Gaius, Inst., i. 9 ; Dig., i. 5. 3.
[2] Gaius, Inst., i. 52.   Dig., i. 6. 1.
[3] Dig., xli. 1. 5, 7 : "Item quæ ex hostibus capiuntur jure gentium statim capientium fiunt . . . adeo quidem ut et liberi homines in servitutem deducantur."
[4] Dig., i. 5. 5, 1.

sidering the meaning of "natural law." It will be as well to put together these phrases in this new connexion. In the first place we may perhaps put the famous phrase of Ulpian : "Quod ad jus naturale attinet, omnes homines æquales sunt."[1] It is just possible that this phrase is a little more technical than might at first sight appear, for Ulpian is evidently discussing the legal position of the slave, and the equality of which he speaks may conceivably have had primarily a technical signification, as equal in position before the law. Still, the phrase is very noteworthy in its bold and direct character. The impression it makes is not weakened but rather confirmed when we turn to his equally famous phrase, "cum jure naturali omnes liberi nascerentur."[2] Slavery had no place under the *jus naturale*, but came in under the *jus gentium*. By the law of nature men were free and equal.

When we turn to Florentinus we feel that this conception of the natural freedom of man is again confirmed. Slavery is an institution of the *jus gentium* and contrary to nature. We even seem to trace a half-apologetic tone in the famous explanation of the name "servus" which Florentinus adds. The slave is called so because he is preserved alive and not slain as he might be by the laws of war.[3] Tryphoninus, again, expresses the same judgment with great clearness, when he says that liberty belongs to natural law, lordship was introduced by the *jus gentium*.[4]

---

[1] Dig., 1. 17. 32 : "Quod attinet ad jus civile, servi pro nullis habentur : non tamen et jure naturali, quia, quod ad jus naturale attinet, omnes homines æquales sunt."

[2] Dig., i. 1. 4 : "Manumissiones quoque juris gentium sunt. Est autem manumissio de manu missio, id est datio libertatis : nam quamdiu quis in servitute est, manui et potestati suppositus est, manumissus liberatur potestate. Quæ res a jure gentium originem sumpsit, utpote cum jure naturali omnes liberi nascerentur nec esset nota manumissio, cum servitus esset incognita : sed posteaquam jure gentium servitus invasit, secutum est beneficium manumissionis. Et cum

uno naturali nomine homines appellaremur, jure gentium tria genera esse cœperunt : liberi et his contrarium servi et tertium genus liberti, id est hi qui desierant esse servi."

[3] Dig., i. 5. 4 : "Libertas est naturalis facultas ejus quod cuique facere libet, nisi si quid vi aut jure prohibetur. Servitus est constitutio juris gentium, qua quis dominio alieno contra naturam subicitur. Servi ex eo appellati sunt, quod imperatores captivos vendere ac per hoc servare nec occidere solent."

[4] Dig., xii. 6. 64 : "Ut enim libertas naturali jure continetur et dominatio ex gentium jure introducta est."

It may be urged that these are meaningless phrases, illustrating only the progress of an unpractical, sentimental speculation, which had no relation to the actual conditions of life. We think that this would be an exaggerated mode of speaking. These sentiments, just as those of Cicero and Seneca, were indeed held by men of whom we may fairly say that they never dreamed of overturning the actually existing conditions of society which were founded upon the institution of slavery, but that is not the same thing as to say that their phrases were meaningless and had no relation to the actual facts of life. We have seen that the sentiment of human equality was the result of the actual experience of the Mediterranean world,—that it only represents in theory an experience in fact. We venture to think that the theory of equality could not but react upon the theory of slavery, could not but alter the judgment of men as to its origin; and when we turn to examine the actual conditions of slavery as they are illustrated in the Roman Jurisprudence, we see that the change of theory was at least parallel with a change in the conditions of slavery.

If we turn back to that phrase of Gaius in which, as we have already seen, he describes the legal condition of the slave, we shall find it useful to notice that the words to which we have referred are followed by a sentence in which he tells us that the unrestricted power of the master over his slave, of which he has just spoken, did not any longer exist within the Roman Empire, and that all excessive cruelty on the part of the master was prohibited.[1]   In the Digest, where these words are quoted, the compilers seem to have inserted "legibus cognita" after

[1] Gaius, Inst., i. 53 : "Sed hoc tempore neque civibus Romanis, nec ullis aliis hominibus qui sub imperio populi Romani sunt, licet supra modum et sine causa in servos suos sævire : nam ex constitutione sacratissimi imperatoris Antonini, qui sine causa servum suum occiderit non minus teneri jubetur, quam qui alienum servum occiderit. Sed et major quoque asperitas dominorum per ejusdem principis constitutionem coercetur : nam consultus a quibusdam præsidibus provinciarum de his servis, qui ad fana deorum vel ad statuas principum confugiunt, præcepit ut, si intolerabilis videatur dominorum sævitia, cogantur servos suos vendere ; et utrumque rectefit : male enim nostro jure uti non debemus ; qua ratione et prodigis interdicitur bonorum suorum administratio."

"sine causa" and to have read "puniri" for "teneri,"[1] changes which are interesting as exhibiting the tendency to a growing strictness.

It is certainly worth noticing that the Roman Law had thus begun to limit the strict rights of the master and to interfere in the condition of the slave. In other references in the Digest we can trace this tendency back to the middle of the first century. Modestinus tells us that, by an edict of the Emperor Claudius, if a slave were deserted by his master on account of his suffering from severe illness, he was to receive his freedom ;[2] and that Vespasian decreed the liberation of slave women whose masters prostituted them, when they had been sold under the condition that they should not be prostituted.[3] Ulpian says that Hadrian had banished for five years a certain lady, who on the very slightest grounds had outrageously ill-treated her slave women.[4]

Ulpian gives us at length a rescript of Antoninus Pius which, as he understands it, defines the law in the case of a master outrageously ill-treating his slaves or driving them to un-chastity. The Emperor is anxious not to interfere with the rights of masters, but he judges that it is to their interest that those who are unjustly ill-treated should be protected, and he therefore, in a particular case referred to, orders that the slaves who had fled to the Emperor's statue—if it was found that they had been treated with greater severity than was just, or had been infamously injured—should be sold, and not restored to their masters.[5]

It is natural and reasonable to connect these tendencies of

[1] Dig., i. 6. 1, 2
[2] Dig., xl. 8. 2.
[3] Dig., xxxvii. 14. 7.
[4] Dig., i. 6. 2.
[5] Dig., i. 6. 2 : "Si dominus in servos sævierit vel ad impudicitiam turpemque violationem compellat, quæ sint partes præsidis, ex rescripto divi Pii ad Ælium Marcianum proconsulem Bæticæ manifestabitur. Cujus re-scripti verba hæc sunt : 'Dominorum quidem potestatem in suos servos illi-batam esse oportet nec cuiquam hom-inum jus suum detrahi : sed domin-orum interest, ne auxilium contra sævitiam vel famem vel intolerabilem injuriam denegetur his qui juste deprecantur. Ideoque cognosce de querellis eorum, qui ex familia Julii Sabini ad statuam confugerunt, et si vel durius habitos quam æquum est vel infami injuria affectos cognoveris, veniri jube ita, ut in potestate domini non revertantur. Qui si meæ consti-tutioni fraudem fecerit, sciet me ad-missum severius exsecuturum.'"

the Roman jurisprudence to regulate and ameliorate the condition of the slave with that great change in the conception of human nature of which we have spoken. It will be remembered that Cicero urges that the slave should be treated with justice, and that Seneca exhorts men to live with their slaves as friends and companions: the tendency of the Roman law to recognise certain elementary claims of humanity is naturally to be related to the recognition of the fact that the slave was essentially of the same nature and possessed of the same powers of reason and virtue as his master. We are well aware that the great changes in the position of the slave and the gradual disappearance of slavery in Europe must be traced in large measure to the operation of economic forces, just as is the case with the disappearance of villeinage in later times; but it is not therefore necessary to overlook the influence of the sentiment of human nature on social conditions. The economic and ethical foundations of society are not to be separated from each other, nor will historical truth be best served by insisting exclusively on one aspect of human life alone.

Whatever may be our judgment upon the matter, it is at least of importance to observe the fact that the lawyers, as well as those writers whom we have already examined, clearly indicate that the theory of natural inequality had disappeared, and that at least by the end of the second century the theory of a natural equality and natural liberty of human nature was firmly established. In later chapters we shall have to consider the relation of these theories to Christianity, but in the meantime we must make it clear to ourselves that Christianity did not produce these theories of human nature, but rather brought the same theories with it, whether derived from the same general sources or having antecedents of their own we shall have to consider. It may with much force be urged that in this matter Christianity turned what was to some extent an abstract theory into something which is continually tending to make itself real in outward fact; but when this is urged, those practical tendencies of the Roman Jurisprudence, of which we have spoken, must not be overlooked.

Our examination of the theory of slavery has then resulted

in our finding that at least with regard to this institution
we may very well conjecture that the tendency of Ulpian,
Tryphoninus, and Florentinus is to contrast the actual conditions of society with some primitive state in which such an
institution did not exist. We have seen that in Seneca's
theory this primitive condition is contrasted with the actual,
with special reference to the absence of the institutions of
property and coercive government. With regard to that particular form of property called slavery, we may feel that
Ulpian, Tryphoninus, and Florentinus tend to the same
opinion.

We must now consider the legal view of the origin of the
institution of private property. We do not discuss the legal
conception of property,—such a discussion would take us far
away from our subject,—and we endeavour to confine ourselves
to an inquiry into the view of the jurists as to the origin of
property and its relation to natural law.

The earliest writers whom we have observed to be cited
in the Digest on the subject are Labeo and Nerva Filius, two
jurists of the first century. Paulus quotes both these
writers, and we gather that Labeo and Nerva Filius treat of
property as arising naturally from the occupation or capture
of that which previously had belonged to no one.[1] We may
compare a passage from Neratius, a jurist of the time of
Trajan, from which we gather that some things are brought
forth by nature which are not in the dominion of any one,
and that these, as fishes and wild beasts, become the property
of any one who captures them.[2] This is the foundation of
the treatment of the origin of property by Gaius. In that
passage to which we have already referred this is drawn out
with much detail. It is by the law of nations that we
acquire the possession of many things, such as wild animals and

---

[1] Dig., xli. 2. 1 : "Possessio appellata est, ut et Labeo ait, a sedibus
quasi positio, quia naturaliter tenetur
ab eo qui ei insistit, quam Græci
κατοχήν dicunt. Dominiumque rerum ex naturali possessione cœpisse

Nerva filius ait ejusque rei vestigium
remanere in his, quæ terra mari cœloque capiuntur : nam hæc protinus
eorum fiunt, qui primi possessionem
eorum adprehenderint."
[2] Dig., xli. 1. 14, 1.

the property of our enemies; and it is by the same law of
nations that we acquire things by "tradition": other things
we acquire by the civil law.[1]

If we turn now to Marcianus we find that he maintains
the same view and tells us in set terms that some things
are by natural law common to all, some are private property.[2]
We have already seen that the *jus naturale* of this passage
seems to be the same as the *jus gentium* of other passages
from Marcianus,—that he does not distinguish between the
two. Paulus also tells us that certain methods of acquiring
private property belong to the law of nations and are natural.[3]
It would seem clear, then, that those writers who make no distinction between the *jus naturale* and the *jus gentium* looked
upon the institution of private property as being primitive,
rational, and equitable.

We turn now to those writers who make this distinction.
It must be observed that we have very little information as
to their conception of the origin of the institution of property.
We have only noticed two passages from their writings which
seem to bear on this. The first of these is contained in a definition of Precarium by Ulpian.[4] This definition does not help
us very much; it would be quite improper to conclude from
it that he looked upon all forms of private property as belonging to the *jus gentium*. The other passage, which is from

---

[1] Dig., xli. 1. 1: "Quarundam rerum dominium nanciscimur jure gentium, quod ratione naturali inter omnes
homines peræque servatur, quarundam
jure civili, id est jure proprio civitatis
nostræ. . . . Omnia igitur animalia,
quæ terra, mari, cœloque capiuntur, id
est feræ bestiæ et volucres pisces capientium fiunt. . . ."
    xli. 1. 3: "Quod enim nullius est
id ratione naturali occupanti con-
ceditur. . . ."
    xli. 1. 5, 7: "Item quæ ex hostibus
capiuntur, jure gentium statim capientium fiunt. . . ."
    xli. 1. 9, 3: "Hæ quoque res, quæ
traditione nostræ fiunt, jure gentium
nobis adquiruntur: nihil enim tam con-

veniens est naturali æquitati quam
voluntatem domini volentis rem suam
in alium transferre ratam haberi."
Cf. Gaius, Inst., ii. 65-69.
    [2] Dig., i. 8. 2: "Quædam naturali
jure communia sunt omnium, quædam
universitatis, quædam nullius, pleraque singulorum, quæ variis ex causis
cuique adquiruntur."
    [3] Dig., xviii. 1. 1, 2: "Est autem
emptio juris gentium." Dig., xix. 2. 1:
"Locatio et conductio cum naturalis
sit et omnium gentium."
    [4] Dig., xliii. 26. 1: "Precarium est,
quod precibus petenti utendum con-
ceditur tamdiu, quamdiu is qui con-
cessit patitur. Quod genus liberali-
tatis ex jure gentium descendit."

Florentinus,[1] seems to show that his general theory of the origin of private property was much the same as that of the writers whom we have before examined. We should conjecture that Florentinus is describing one of the forms of appropriation of things which were before *nullius.* However this may be, one thing is clear, that Florentinus treats of one form of private property as belonging to the *jus naturale.* The institution of private property, then, to Florentinus is primitive and natural, and not like that of slavery, which is contrary to nature. So far then as our evidence goes, we can only say that Florentinus agrees with the other writers in looking upon property as a natural institution, even though he differs from them on the relation of the *jus gentium* to nature; and that with respect to the position of Ulpian we have no information.

It only remains again to consider that passage from Hermogenianus [2] which we have already had occasion to examine in connexion with the question of the contrast between the institutions of the *jus gentium* and those of the *jus naturale.* Again we have to lament our ignorance of the general position of Hermogenianus. We cannot but retain the impression that he is contrasting these institutions with others which belong to the *jus naturale* or to the *jus civile.* We have at least to notice the description of the *dominia distincta* as belonging to the *jus gentium,* and we have the impression that he looks upon this form of property as belonging to a condition of things not perhaps entirely primitive. Our interpretation of Hermogenianus is naturally affected, as we have already said, by a comparison with the Institutes of Justinian [3] and the Etymologies of St Isidore;[4] but we have already cited these and we need not again go over the ground.

Our examination of the Roman Lawyers with regard to the origin and character of private property has yielded us the following results. Those lawyers who, like Gaius, make no

---

[1] Dig., i. 8. 3 : "Item lapilli, gemmæ ceteraque, quæ in litore invenimus, jure naturali nostra statim fiunt."

[2] Dig., i. 1. 5 : "Ex hoc jure gentium introducta bella, discretæ gentes, regna condita, dominia distincta, agris termini positi," &c.

[3] Inst., i. 2. 2.

[4] St Isidore, Etym., v. 6

distinction between the *jus naturale* and the *jus gentium* clearly look upon the institution of private property as rational, just, and primitive. They know nothing of any condition of human life where private property did not exist. It is likewise clear that Florentinus, although he distinguishes between nature and the *jus gentium*, also holds that private property is natural, belonging to the *jus naturale*, and therefore primitive as well as rational. The position of Ulpian and Hermogenianus is uncertain. We have no means of arriving at any confident conclusion with regard to their views, although we may incline to think that Hermogenianus very possibly reckoned private property as belonging to the *jus gentium* and not to the *jus naturale.*

The Lawyers, then, do not, so far as the theory of property is concerned, give us much help in studying the development of the theory of a state or condition of nature. We have seen that with regard to the institution of slavery Ulpian, Tryphoninus, and Florentinus certainly seem to incline to contrast the primitive with the actual, but there is no evidence of any tendency to develop this with reference to other institutions. We have seen that this theory was current among the Stoic thinkers; we shall find it again in the Fathers, and we shall see that Ulpian's distinction of the *jus naturale* from the *jus gentium* is one of the conceptions which ultimately gave it clearness and precision. But, except with reference to slavery, it does not appear that even the school (if we may call it so) of Ulpian developed the theory of the state of nature with any clearness, or indeed that the conception is very distinctly present to their minds at all, for even their treatment of slavery tends rather to fall in with such a theory than to be definitely and consciously, by them, related to it.

CHAPTER V.

THE THEORY OF THE CIVIL LAW.

WE have seen with what emphasis Cicero maintains that all
law is derived from the one eternal law of God, which is the
same as the principle of justice and reason in man's heart; we
have seen how indignantly and scornfully he repudiates the
notion that unjust laws are true laws (*jura*), how emphatically
he maintains that neither kings nor people can make that to
be law which is not the expression of the eternal principles of
justice. We have now to consider what is the principle and
definition of the civil law in the great jurists. We must adopt
the chronological method in examining our subject, for though,
as we think, there is little trace of variation among the lawyers
on this subject, yet we cannot but recognise the fact that there
are some ambiguities in their statements, and at any rate we
cannot arrive at the same certainty with regard to some of
them as with regard to others.

We commence our inquiry with Gaius, and, indeed, a sentence
of his Institutes indicates the legal conception of the relation
between the positive law of the State and the principles of
reason, as clearly as any passage we can find. He is speaking
of the guardianship or tutelage of those who are under age, and
says it ought to be a principle of the law of every State that
those under age should be under guardianship, for this is agreeable to natural reason.[1] Natural reason is the guide and director
of all civil legislation ; this natural reason is itself the source of

---

[1] Gaius, Inst., i. 189: "Impuberes
quidem in tutela esse omnium civitatum jure contingit, quia id naturali
rationi conveniens est, ut is qui per-
fectæ ætatis non sit alterius tutela
regatur."

the *jus gentium,* and therefore controls both the general law of mankind and the particular law of any one State. The conception of law as necessarily conformed to some general principle apart from the caprice of any individual or group of individuals is sufficiently indicated in this phrase.

The matter is, however, much more completely developed by Marcianus early in the third century. He cites two most important Greek definitions of law, whose significance for our purpose is very great. He first cites a definition of law put forward by Demosthenes and then one of Chrysippus, whom he describes as "philosophus summæ stoicæ sapientiæ." Marcianus makes no comment on these two definitions, and we may take it that he accepted them as representing his own conception of the subject. It is evident enough that the standpoint of the two writers is not by any means the same; but, at the same time, there is a very substantial agreement between them on some of the most important points of the conception of law. In the first place, they both of them regard law in the general sense as being something which is related to the divine or universal order as well as to the regulation of any particular State. Every law, Demosthenes says, is discovered and given by God; while Chrysippus treats law as the ruler of all things both divine and human. Law, according to Demosthenes, is intended for the correction of offences; while Chrysippus says that it is the norm or standard of things just and unjust. Both Demosthenes and Chrysippus bring their definitions into relation with civil law, by defining law, in the sense in which they are using the term, as being that which all in the State must obey and as belonging to all living creatures which are by nature political. To these more general conceptions Demosthenes adds certain specific conditions of the civil law—namely, that it should be set forth by the wise man, and should be agreed to by the whole State: to these we shall have to return when we consider the nature and source of authority in the State.[1]

---

[1] Dig., i. 3. 2: "Nam et Demosthenes orator sic definit: τοῦτὸ ἐστι νόμος, ᾧ πάντας ἀνθρώπους προσήκει πεί- θεσθαι διὰ πολλὰ, καὶ μάλιστα ὅτι πᾶς ἐστὶ νόμος εὕρημα μὲν καὶ δῶρον θεοῦ, δόγμα δὲ ἀνθρώπων φρονίμων ἐπανόρθωμα

These definitions of Demosthenes and Chrysippus bring out very clearly what we have already seen is indicated by Gaius, that civil law is to be regarded, not primarily as expressing the will of any community or person in a community, but as the particular application in any community of the principles of the universal reason and justice. This is indeed substantially the same view as that of Cicero. We do not suggest that Marcianus is to be considered as a strict disciple of the Stoic school; but clearly enough he, like Cicero, follows the Stoic conception of justice and law, as contrasted with that of the Epicureans or the later Academics.

So far we have examined the opinions of those to whom the distinction between the *jus naturale* and the *jus gentium* had no special meaning, and we have seen that this does not in the least affect their view of the relation between the civil law and the general or universal principles of justice. We turn to the view of Ulpian, as representing the new theory, and we find him maintaining the same view with greater detail, but on the same general lines.

The compilers of the Digest open that work with a very significant and important statement by Ulpian on this subject.[1] Nothing could well be clearer than the general tendency of these sentences. The jurist must understand that law is the art of the good and just, that it is his duty to study the meaning of this, to distinguish the just from the unjust, to draw men to do what is good. The law, that is, which the jurist has to deal with, is not to be looked at simply as a

δὲ τῶν ἑκουσίων καὶ ἀκουσίων ἁμαρτημά-
των, πόλεως δὲ συνθήκη κοινή, καθ' ἣν
ἅπασι προσήκει ζῆν τοῖς ἐν τῇ πόλει.
Sed et philosophus summæ stoicæ sapientiæ Chrysippus sic incipit libro, quem
fecit περὶ νόμου: ὁ νόμος πάντων ἐστὶ
βασιλεὺς θείων τε καὶ ἀνθρωπίνων πραγ-
μάτων· δεῖ δὲ αὐτὸν προστάτην τε εἶναι
τῶν καλῶν καὶ τῶν αἰσχρῶν καὶ ἄρχοντα
καὶ ἡγεμόνα, καὶ κατὰ τοῦτο κανόνα τε
εἶναι δικαίων καὶ ἀδίκων καὶ τῶν φύσει
πολιτικῶν ζῴων, προστακτικὸν μὲν ὧν
ποιητέον, ἀπαγορευτικὸν δὲ ὧν οὐ ποιητέον."

[1] Dig., i. 1. 1 : "Juri operam da-
turum prius nosse oportet, unde nomen
juris descendat. Est autem a justitia
appellatum : nam ut eleganter Celsus
definit, jus est ars boni et æqui. Cujus
merito quis nos sacerdotes appellet :
justitiam namque colimus, et boni et
æqui notitiam profitemur, æquum ab
iniquo separantes, licitum ab illicito
discernentes, bonos non solum metu
pœnarum, verum etiam præmiorum
quoque exhortatione efficere cupientes,
veram nisi fallor philosophiam, non
simulatam affectantes."

series of positive regulations of any particular society, but rather as the expression of the perpetual principles of justice and goodness.

These views are further illustrated in the well-known phrases in which Ulpian attempts to define the nature of justice, the main principles of law (*jus*), and the true character of juris-prudence.[1] These famous phrases, repeated constantly through-out the Middle Ages and later, may suggest to us that Ulpian was rather a facile and rhetorical than a profound thinker upon law : we may feel that these sentences, for all their admirable sound, carry us little further, and that we do not know much more about the nature of justice than we did. But regarded historically, these words are of the greatest importance, not merely as assuring us of Ulpian's position, but as forming one of the most important links in the chain by which the theory of law of the ancient world was handed down to mediæval and so to modern thinkers. The general view of Ulpian, then, is obviously the same as that of Marcianus and that which is indicated in the sentence of Gaius which we have already quoted.

We have, however, another statement of Ulpian's in which the relation between the civil law and the natural law is more specifically, but also more ambiguously, dealt with.[2] We cannot but regret that the compilers of the Digest have not preserved for us a more detailed explanation of these some-what ambiguous phrases. They are obviously capable of a meaning in harmony with the conclusions which we have drawn from the statements we have already examined, but they might also bear a somewhat different construction. It is easy enough to understand what Ulpian means when he speaks of the civil law as being something added to the *jus commune*, a phrase which seems to mean simply the *jus naturale* and *·us gentium*, as being universal in their application, but it is not so

[1] Dig., i. 1. 10 : "Justitia est con-stans et perpetua voluntas jus suum cuique tribuendi. Juris præcepta sunt hæc; honeste vivere, alterum non lædere, suum cuique tribuere. Juris prudentia est divinarum atque humanarum rerum notitia, justi atque injusti scientia."

[2] Dig., i. 1. 6 : "Jus civile est, quod neque in totum a naturali vel gentium recedit, nec per omnia ei servit : itaque cum aliquid addimus vel retrahimus juri communi, jus proprium, id est civile efficimus."

easy to understand what he means by the *jus civile* as something which may take away from the *jus commune.*

The first phrase which suggests itself as possibly furnishing us with the means of comment on Ulpian's words is that phrase of Florentinus which we have so frequently cited,[1] slavery is an institution of the *jus gentium* and contrary to nature. It is true that Florentinus is here speaking of the relation of the *jus gentium* to nature, but it would seem that the words might be applied to the relation of the *jus civile* to nature. Ulpian has expressed the same opposition, with ref- erence to the same institution. By the *jus naturale,* he says, men were born free; by the *jus gentium* they are enslaved;[2] and in another place, as we have seen, he has contrasted the relation of the *jus civile* with that of the *jus naturale* on the subject of the equality of men.[3]

We seem to find in these phrases of Florentinus and Ulpian illustrations of what Ulpian may mean by the civil law as taking away something from the *jus naturale;* but we are still far from clear as to how this is to be explained in conformity with the general conception of law which he seems to maintain. The word *jus* is, he has told us, taken from *justitia; jus* is the "ars boni et æqui"; of the lawyers he has said, "justitiam namque colimus et boni et æqui notitiam profitemur." Jus- tice, then, must reside either in the *jus naturale* or the *jus gentium* or the *jus civile,* or in all of them. It is possible to maintain that Ulpian does not connect it specially with the *jus naturale.* We have seen that his definition of that system of law leaves us very uncertain whether he had any clearness of conception about it; but it is very difficult to suppose that in that case he did not find justice in the *jus gentium,* where, as we have seen, it would appear that the lawyers who take the same view as Gaius, found it.

We should suggest that the explanation may again be found in the relation of the conceptions of Ulpian and Florentinus to the theory of a natural state antecedent to the conventions of organised society; and that, just as Seneca looks upon the institutions of property and organised government as the

---

[1] Dig., i. 5. 4.   [2] Dig., i. 1. 4.   [3] Dig., l. 17. 32.

result of the progress of vice among men, and yet regards them as adapted to, and therefore justifiable under, the actual conditions of human life, so Ulpian and Florentinus may conceive of the *jus civile* as differing from the *jus naturale*, as the conditions of the conventional life differ from those of the natural, and yet as being just under the actual conditions of human life. We shall see that this is the explanation which the Christian Fathers furnish of the contrast between the primitive or natural conditions of human life and the actual; and the fact that in this matter Seneca seems to represent a current Stoic tradition encourages us to think that the lawyers, like Ulpian and Florentinus, may have been influenced by some such ideas, even though they were not very clearly conscious of their influence.

There remains to be considered a sentence of Paulus, a contemporary of Ulpian. We have already mentioned this phrase, and must now reconsider the passage with relation to the subject we have in hand. Paulus says that we may define law in different fashions : in one way when we speak of that which is always just and good, this is *jus naturale ;* in another way when we speak of that which is useful to all or the majority in any State, this is *jus civile.*[1] At first sight we seem here to have a frank recognition of the utilitarian and interested character of civil law, and might feel inclined to think that Paulus must represent that tradition which so much angered Cicero, that law is merely that which is convenient to those who have power in any State. It is of course possible, though not probable, that this may be the case. We do not know that there is any reason to maintain that such opinions were not current at the time when Paulus wrote, and that he might not have been influenced by them. At the same time, in the absence of any other clear trace of such a view in the Digest and Institutes, we feel rather disposed to think that Paulus used these words without any great care, and that we therefore must

---

[1] Dig., i. 1. 11 : "Jus pluribus modis dicitur, uno modo, cum id quod semper æquum ac bonum est jus dicitur, ut est, jus naturale. Altero modo, quod omnibus aut pluribus in quaque civitate utile est, ut est jus civile."

not press their significance to those conclusions which might be drawn from them. We think that he very probably intended nothing more than a contrast between the perpetual principles of justice embodied in, or represented by, what he calls the *jus naturale*, and the temporary and changing application of those principles as adapted to the varying circumstances and varying desires of the members of any State.

We have seen then, that, except so far as there may be some doubt about the position of Paulus, the Roman Jurists of the second century hold a clear view of the relation of the civil law to the principles of justice; whether these are looked upon as embodied in the *jus naturale* or the *jus gentium*. They hold with Cicero that the civil law is organically related to the ultimate law of reason and justice; that it is not merely the expression of the capricious will of the lawgiver, but constantly tends, at least, to embody, to apply to the actual conditions of life, principles which are of perpetual obligation. We have seen that it is possible that the judgment of some of these may have been perplexed by their own distinction between the *jus naturale* and the *jus gentium*, that they may have felt that actually existing or universal institutions could not be considered to belong to the primitive and perpetual principles of life, while they were not prepared to condemn them. This only illustrates a perplexity of mind, which was indeed a natural result of the perpetual ambiguity in the conception of social justice in relation to the ideal justice, whether this is regarded as belonging to the past or to the future. The regulations of society ought to be just, and yet we are constantly compelled to amend them. Their claim to the obedience of man is founded upon the fact that they represent justice, and yet they never are in the complete sense of the word just. The perplexity with regard to the past found a solution for many centuries in the theory of a change in the condition of human nature, in the judgment that principles of perfect justice which were adapted to a condition of perfect innocence cannot well be adapted to a condition of vice and imperfection. In the eighteenth century, when many thinkers understood very imperfectly the social significance of the faultiness of human nature, the difficulty resulted in the revolutionary bias given to the conception of the return to nature. Gradually men have turned back to the conception of perfect justice as belonging to the future, as being the ideal towards which the institutions of society tend, the principle which governs their development; but the difficulties of the actual condition have not therefore been completely solved. It is a thing worthy of note how few have recognised the significance of the most resolute modern attempt to suggest a solution, the attempt made by Rousseau in his theory of the "General Will." In England Professor T. H. Green and, recently, Mr Bosanquet are among the very few who have recognised the real importance of that theory.

CHAPTER VI.

THE SOURCE OF POLITICAL AUTHORITY.

WE have still to consider the theory of the Roman Lawyers with regard to one very important subject, the source of authority in the State. It will be remembered that we found in Cicero a very interesting tendency towards a conception of liberty, as identified with a share in the control of the State. The Roman Lawyers of the second century and onwards deal briefly indeed, but very distinctly, with the question of the ultimate source of authority in the State, and we think that, so far, they do very clearly carry on the tradition represented by Cicero. They do not conceive of the Roman citizen as having any direct share in the actual administration of the Commonwealth, but in their view the Roman citizens are the sole ultimate source of authority, whether legislative or administrative. The relation of their view to that of Cicero is interesting, but much more important is the connexion between their theory and the democratic theory of mediæval and modern times. The mediæval theory of the social contract, which, so far as we know, was first put forward definitely in the end of the eleventh century, may have relations with such ancient forms of the theory as are perhaps suggested by Cicero [1] and had been developed by Plato,[2] and perhaps by authors whose works have now disappeared. We shall see that the mediæval theory is related primarily to the traditional ideas of the Teutonic races on government, and to the course of the history of the Teutonic empire and kingdoms. But at the same time, the theory of the Roman Lawyers with respect to the people as the

---

[1] Cicero, De Rep., iii. 13.　　　　[2] Plato, Laws, iii. 684.

sole ultimate source of authority in the State seems to us to be clearly an undeveloped form of the theory of contract. We might call it the theory of consent, which is not the same thing as the theory of contract in any of its forms, but is the germ out of which the theory of contract might very well grow. When we discuss the theories of the mediæval writers in detail we shall have to consider what traces there are of the direct influence of this aspect of the legal view, we shall certainly recognise that they were acquainted with it. In the meanwhile we consider the Roman Lawyers as expressing one aspect of the theory out of which the mediæval and modern democratic conception of the State has grown.

Few phrases in the Digest are more familiar than that of Ulpian, " Quod principi placuit, legis habet vigorem ";[1] sometimes at least it has been forgotten that Ulpian continues, " utpote cum lege regia, quæ de imperio ejus lata est, populus ei et in eum omne suum imperium et potestatem conferat." Few phrases are more remarkable than this almost paradoxical description of an unlimited personal authority founded upon a purely democratic basis. The Emperor's will is law, but only because the people choose to have it so. Ulpian's words sum up in a single phrase the universal theory of the lawyers ; so far as we have seen, there is no other view known to the Roman jurisprudence. From Julianus, in the earlier part of the second century, to Justinian himself in the sixth, the Emperor is the source of law, but only because the people by their own legislative act have made him so. The matter is of such importance that we must justify this judgment by an examination of all the writers of the Digest who, so far as we have found, refer to the question.

The earliest discussion, in the Digest, of the authority which lies behind the civil law of Rome is, so far as we have seen, contained in a citation from Julianus, a jurist of the period of Hadrian and the Antonines. He is cited to illustrate the place of custom in law, and says that custom has rightly the force of law, inasmuch as law derives its authority from the people, and it is immaterial whether the people declares its will by vote or

[1] Dig., i. 4. 1.

by custom.[1] It is certainly interesting to observe this uncompromising and dogmatic statement of the authority of the people in making and unmaking laws (*leges*). It might indeed be urged that *lex* is the distinctive name for the legislation of the *populus,* and that we must not therefore press the phrases of Julianus to mean that *leges* are the only forms of law. We shall presently see that Gaius, in his classification of law, distinguishes the *lex* from other forms of law: whether this distinction is here present to the mind of Julianus may perhaps be doubted; but if it is, we shall also probably judge that Julianus, like Gaius, looks upon the *lex* of the whole people as the original form of law, from which all other forms are descended.

Gaius has furnished us with a general definition of the nature of the civil law in that passage which we have had occasion to quote several times.[2] We must now examine the words with which he carries out the definition in detail, with regard to the Roman State.[3] It might seem at first sight that there are here as many authorities as there are forms of law, but a closer

[1] Dig., i. 3. 32 : "Inveterata consuetudo pro lege non immerito custoditur, et hoc est jus quod dicitur moribus constitutum. Nam cum ipsæ leges nulla alia ex causa nos teneant, quam quod judicio populi receptæ sunt, merito et ea, quæ sine ullo scripto populus probavit tenebunt omnes : nam quid interest suffragio populus voluntatem suam declaret an rebus ipsis et factis ? Quare rectissime etiam illud receptum est, ut leges non solum suffragio legis latoris, sed etiam tacito consensu omnium per desuetudinem abrogentur."

[2] Gaius, Inst., i. 1. ; Dig., i. 1. 9 : "Quod quisque populus ipse sibi jus constituit, id ipsius proprium est, vocaturque jus civile, quasi jus proprium civitatis."

[3] Gaius, Inst., i. 2 -7.: "Constant autem jura populi Romani ex legibus, plebiscitis, senatus - consultis, constitutionibus principum, edictis eorum

qui jus edicendi habent, responsis prudentium. Lex est quod populus jubet atque constituit. Plebiscitum est quod plebs jubet atque constituit. . . . Unde olim patricii dicebant plebiscitis se non teneri, quia sine auctoritati eorum facta essent : sed postea lex Hortensia lata est, qua cautum est ut plebiscita universum populum tenerent ; itaque eo modo legibus exæquata sunt. Senatus-consultum est quod senatus jubet atque constituit, idque legis vicem obtinet, quamvis fuerit quæsitum. Constitutio principis est quod imperator decreto, vel edicto, vel epistola constituit, nec umquam dubitatum est, quin id legis vicem obtineat, cum ipse imperator per legem imperium accipiat. Jus autem edicendi habent magistratus populi Romani. . . . Responsa prudentium sunt sententiæ et opiniones eorum quibus permissum est jura condere."

observation shows us that ultimately these come back to the
authority of the whole *populus*. It is they and they alone who
have the power of making a *lex*, and all other authority is
derived from this. Thus the *plebiscitum*, or law made by the
plebs alone, without the other classes, only has the force of law
because this was decreed by the *lex Hortensia*. The constitution
of the prince, in the same way, has the force of law because the
emperor receives his *imperium, per legem*. The magistrates have
the *jus edicendi*, but this no doubt is derived from their election.
The *Responsa Prudentium*, if they all agree, have the force of
law, but this is because such an authority is given to the juris-
consults. The only form of law of which we cannot definitely
conclude, from this statement of Gaius, that its authority can
be traced back to the people, is the *Senatus consultum*. Gaius
does not define the mode in which this form of law came to be
recognised as such. Pomponius suggests that it was due to the
growing difficulty of getting together the *populus* as the Roman
population increased :[1] both he and Gaius seem to look upon the
legislative authority of the Senate as tacitly recognised, though,
as Gaius seems to indicate, at first there was hesitation about it.

The same theory of the source of authority is put before
us in that very interesting account of the origin and development of the Roman legal system, by Pomponius, a contemporary of Gaius, to which we have just referred.[2] In this
we have a succinct history of the Roman law from the time
of Romulus down to the organisation of the Imperial system.
The most important points in this are as follows. At first
there was no certain *lex* or *jus* in the State, and all things were
directed by the kings. Romulus first began to propose definite
laws (*leges*) to the people. After the expulsion of the kings
these laws went out of use, and for some time the Roman
people was governed rather by uncertain usages and customs
than by definite laws. At last ten men were appointed to pro-
cure laws from the Greek cities, that the State might be founded
on laws (*leges*), and they were given supreme authority in the
State for a year, to put these into order and to correct them if
necessary, and to interpret them with such authority that there

---

[1] Dig., i. 2. 2, 9.   [2] Dig., i. 2. 2.

should be no appeal from them. These laws, to which the name of the laws of the Twelve Tables was given, were finally adopted. They needed to be interpreted by the great lawyers, and out of this interpretation grew up that form of *jus* connected with the *prudentes*, the *jus* which is " proprium jus civile, quod sine scripto in sola prudentium interpretatione consistit." Then on the basis of these laws were founded the " legis actiones." Later it came about that there was a dispute between the *plebs* and the *patres*, and the *plebs* made laws for themselves which were called *plebiscita*.[1] When the *plebs* had been brought back and much discord had arisen with respect to these *plebiscita*, it was finally agreed that they should be recognised as *leges*, and this was sanctioned by the lex Hortensia.[2] Then, the people growing so numerous that it was difficult to gather together the *populus*, or even the *plebs*, the very necessity of the case made it necessary that the Senate should be charged with the care of the State, and the Senate began to issue decrees : this form of law was known as *Senatus consultum*.[3] At the same time the magistrates who declared the law issued their edicts, that the citizens might know exactly the *jus* under which cases would be decided. Finally it became necessary that one man should be charged with the care of the State ; a prince was created, and he was given the authority, that whatever he should ordain should have the force of law.[4]

It is interesting to observe the laborious care with which Pomponius explains each new development in the legal system. By his presentation of the subject we see again that, with the exception of the *Senatus consultum*, every form of law derives

[1] Dig., i. 2. 2, 8 : " Evenit ut plebs in discordiam cum patribus perveniret et secederet sibique jura constitueret quæ jura plebiscita vocantur."

[2] Dig., i. 2. 2, 8 : " Pro legibus placuit et ea observari lege Hortensia : et ita factum est, ut inter plebiscita et legem species constituendi interesset potestas autem eadem esset."

[3] Dig., i. 2. 2, 9 : " Necessitas ipsa curam reipublicæ ad senatum deduxit ; ita cœpit senatus se interponere et

quidquid constituisset observabatur, idque jus apellabatur senatus consultum."

[4] Dig., i. 2. 2, 11 : " Novissime, sicut ad pauciores juris constituendi vias transisse ipsis rebus dictantibus videbatur per partes, evenit. ut necesse esset reipublicæ per unum consuli (nam senatus non perinde omnes provincias probe gerere poterat) : igitur constituto principe datum est ei jus ut quod constituisset, ratum esset."

its authority ultimately from the *populus*. This is especially important with respect to the Imperial power, and here indeed Pomponius's phrases are almost apologetic in their anxiety to account for the legislative authority of the Emperor. The historical value of Pomponius's account is of course a very different matter from its interest to us: so far, indeed, as we are concerned, this is quite immaterial; we are only concerned with his narrative as illustrating the political theory of the second century, and for that purpose it is invaluable.

Early in the third century we come to Marcianus, whose citations from Demosthenes and Chrysippus we have already examined in another connexion. We must return to the first of these in relation to our present inquiry. His words are as follows: "This is law which all men should obey for many reasons, and especially because every law is a thing found and given by God, a judgment ($\delta\acute{o}\gamma\mu a$) of wise men, a correction of voluntary and involuntary transgressions, a common agreement of the State, in accordance with which all those who are in the State should live."[1] We have already discussed the significance of the first part of this definition: for our present purposes the important phrases are two—that a law is something decreed or advised by wise men, and something adopted by the common agreement of the State. This latter part of the definition is adopted by Papinian, a contemporary of Marcianus: his definition is, with slight modification, evidently taken from that of Demosthenes.[2] In this definition, then, it is clear that the immediate source of the authority of the law of any State is the agreement of the whole State, and we may take it that it governs the short general description of the civil law given by Papinian in another place, where he deals with it in very much the same terms as Gaius:[3] we are entitled to interpret this classification by the definition to which we have just referred.

We have, then, come down to the time of Ulpian, with whose

---

[1] Dig., i. 3. 2.   See p. 56, note 1.

[2] Dig., i. 3. 1 : "Lex est commune præceptum, virorum prudentium consultum, delictorum quæ sponte vel ignorantia contrahuntur coercitio, communis reipublicæ sponsio."

[3] Dig., i. 1. 7 : "Jus autem civile est quod ex legibus, plebis scitis senatus consultis, decretis principum, auctoritate prudentium venit."

sentence on the Imperial authority we commenced our inquiry. We are now in a position to recognise that his statement, that the authority of the prince is derived from the fact that the people have by the *lex regia* conferred on him all their authority, is strictly in harmony with the political theory of all the earlier jurists. But we can trace the same theory down to the time of Justinian himself. In a rescript of Theodosius and Valentinian of the year 429, the relation of the Imperial authority to the law is expressed in very clear and forcible terms. Theodosius and Valentinian say that the prince is bound by the laws, for his authority is drawn from the authority of the law.[1] Nothing could well be plainer than this statement, nothing could show more clearly that the theory of Ulpian is still the theory of the fifth century. And, finally, in the rescript which is prefixed to the Digest, we find Justinian himself referring in explicit terms to the ancient law by which the Roman people transferred all their authority and power to the Emperor.[2]

It is true that in Justinian we also find some trace of a conception out of which there grew another theory of the authority of the ruler. The first words of the rescript we have just quoted are, "Deo auctore nostrum gubernantes imperium, quod nobis a cælesti majestate traditum est."[3] In another rescript, also prefixed to the Digest, we read, "quia ideo imperialem fortunam rebus humanis deus præposuit, ut possit omnia quæ noviter contingunt et emendare et componere et modis et regulis competentibus tradere."[4] In another place still, he speaks of God subjecting all laws to the Emperor, whom He has given to men as a living law.[5] These phrases may be compared with those of Seneca and Pliny, to which we have already referred,[6]

---

[1] Codex, i. 14. 4 : "Digna vox majestate regnantis legibus alligatum se principem profiteri : adeo de auctoritate juris nostra pendet auctoritas. Et re vera majus imperio est submittere legibus principatum. Et oraculo præsentis edicti quod nobis licere non patimur indicamus."

[2] Cod., i. 17. 1, 7 : "Cum enim lege antiqua, quæ regia nuncupabatur, omne jus omnisque potestas populi Romani in imperatoriam translata sunt potestatem."

[3] Cod., i. 17. 1.

[4] Cod., i. 17. 2, 18.

[5] Novel., cv. 4 : Πάντων δὲ δὴ τῶν εἰρημένων ἡμῖν ἢ βασιλέως ἐξηρήσθω τύχη, ᾗ γε καὶ αὐτοὺς ὁ θεὸς τοὺς νόμους ὑπέθηκε νόμον αὐτὴν ἔμψυχον καταπέμψας ἀνθρώποις.

[6] See p. 31.

and with the patristic conception of the relation between God
and the ruler, which we shall presently have to examine; but
in themselves the words of Justinian can hardly be pressed to
mean more than that the providence of God rules even over
the matters of the State.

From the second century, then, to the sixth, we have seen
that the Roman law knows one, and only one, ultimate source of
political power, and that is the authority of the people. It
may of course be said that this is the merest abstract theory,
that during this time the Imperial power was obtained by
every method, but never by that of popular appointment; that
the legislative authority of the people was only a name and a
pretence, and it must be noticed that Justinian seems even to
speak of the Emperor as the sole[1] *legis lator*, as though, in
fact, the legislative action of the Roman *populus* had wholly
ceased. But still the theory of the ultimate authority of the
people subsisted, and so came down till it touched the new
Teutonic theory of law and political authority, a theory which
again knew nothing of any legislative authority in the State
apart from the whole body of the State.

We think that the legal theory, that all political power is
derived from the people, is at least one of the sources from
which the theory of the social contract sprang. It is far from
being the same theory, but it seems to us to represent an elementary form of the same conception. The Roman lawyers
indeed usually deal with the matter only from the point of
view of the Roman Commonwealth, but this is not always the
case. Papinian, and Marcianus in his citation from Demosthenes,[2] define law in terms of universal application. And, after
all, the Empire was to the Roman much the same as the world.
The principles which belonged to it were at least the principles
of the civilised world, and their application to the conditions of
the world at large was natural and easy.

---

[1] Cod., i. 14. 12, 3 and 4.   [2] See p. 68.

CHAPTER VII.

THE POLITICAL THEORY OF JUSTINIAN'S INSTITUTES.

WE have so far examined mainly the jurists of the second and third centuries, and have endeavoured to make ourselves clear as to the general character of the political theory which they represent. We have observed that their theory is not something fixed, but that we can trace the changes of legal opinion, in the course of these centuries, with regard at least to some subjects. It is for our purpose important that we are able to compare these views with those of the lawyers of the sixth century as embodied in the Institutes of Justinian. From such a comparison we are able to arrive at some conclusions with regard to the permanent tendencies of the legal traditions, to judge, with respect to certain of them, which ultimately tended to predominate. It must at the same time be confessed that the compilers of the Institutes were so anxious to express themselves in the phrases of the great lawyers of the second and third centuries that it is often difficult to be quite certain as to their own opinions. It is difficult to imagine that the compilers were not aware that the passages they quote from different writers often represent views inconsistent with each other, and yet they do actually sometimes join together in the same passage citations which are completely out of harmony.

This carelessness of construction is nowhere more noticeable than it is with reference to the theory of the law of nature. We think that the opinion of the authors of the Institutes on the subject is clear and distinct, but it must be admitted that occasionally they embody in their work phrases which belong to another view. Their general position will be sufficiently shown by a few sentences: "Dicendum est igitur de jure privato, quod est tripertitum; collectum est enim ex naturalibus præceptis aut gentium aut civilibus."[1] This dogmatic statement of the threefold character of law is followed by the definition of the *jus naturale* which is cited in the Digest from Ulpian, and then by the definition of the *jus gentium* from Gaius's Institutes, and a description of the *jus civile;*[2] they add that account of the *jus gentium* which we have had occasion to notice before.[3]

The fact that the compilers of the Institutes follow Ulpian in distinguishing the *jus gentium* from the *jus naturale* is certainly clear enough. It is true that the first two passages we have just mentioned are quoted directly from Ulpian, but the last mentioned is not taken from any known source (with the exception of the words, "Jure enim naturali ab initio," &c.) We have already suggested that it may be related to that passage from Hermogenianus[4] which we have already mentioned, but the explanation of the origin of the institutions is not contained in the passage from Hermogenianus, as we have it in the Digest. At any rate, whether these phrases are wholly borrowed or partly original, they do very clearly show that the compilers of the Institutes distinguished between the *jus naturale* and the *jus gentium,* and the last passage gives us some indication of their conception of the nature of the distinction.

Before we discuss the meaning of the *jus naturale* in the Institutes, we must examine one passage which seems directly to contradict those which we have just considered. This passage is contained in the first title of the Second Book of the Institutes, a title which deals with certain general questions of property.[5] This passage is evidently founded upon those words

[1] Inst., i. 1. 4.

[2] Inst., i. 2.

[3] Inst., i. 2. 2 : "Jus autem gentium omni humano generi commune est. Nam usu exigente et humanis necessitatibus gentes humanæ quædam sibi constituerunt : bella etenim orta sunt et captivitates secutæ et servitutes, quæ sunt juri naturali contrariæ. Jure enim naturali ab initio omnes homines liberi nascebantur. Ex hoc jure gentium et omnes pæne contractus introducti sunt, ut emptio venditio, locatio conductio, societas, depositum, mutuum et alii innumerabiles."

[4] Dig., i. 1. 5. See p. 42, note 1.

[5] Inst., ii. 1. 11 : "Singulorum autem hominum multis modis res fiunt : quarundam enim rerum dominium nanciscimur jure naturali,

of Gaius's in the Digest, which we have already several times had occasion to quote,[1] but the compilers of the Institutes have made several important changes. In the first place, they have substituted the words "jure naturali, quod sicut diximus appellatur jus gentium" for Gaius's words, "jure gentium, quod ratione naturali inter omnes homines peræque servatur." Next, they have written "Palam est autem vetustius esse naturale jus, quod cum ipso genere humano rerum natura prodidit" in place of Gaius's " Et quia antiquius jus gentium cum ipso genere humano rerum natura proditum est"; and finally, they have added the last clause. The two latter points are interesting, but the real difficulty is raised by the first sentence.

We have just seen that the authors of the Institutes separate the *jus naturale* from the *jus gentium*. It is difficult to understand what they can mean by saying that the law of nature is called the *jus gentium*: they not only say this, but add that they have said it already, while we can find no trace of any such statement in the earlier parts of the Institutes. The form of the statement suggests that we may have here a quotation from some otherwise unknown source. We can only conjecture either that this is the explanation of the phenomenon, or that this is to be found in the fact that the passage forms part of a title which deals with the theory of property, consisting for the most part of citations from Gaius, Marcianus, and other jurists who identify the *jus naturale* and the *jus gentium*, and that the editors have adapted their language to this fact. The statement is certainly perplexing, but it seems impossible to allow this phrase to change the conclusion which we derive from the clear and repeated statements which we have already examined. There can be no doubt that normally the authors of the Institutes did distinguish the *jus naturale* from the *jus gentium*.

Their formal definition of the *jus naturale*[2] is, as we have

---

quod sicut diximus appellatur jus gentium, quarundam jure civili. Commodius est itaque a vetustiore jure incipere. Palam est autem vetustiore esse naturale jus, quod cum ipso genere humano rerum natura prodidit : civilia

enim jura tunc cœperunt, cum et civitates condi et magistratus creari et leges scribi cœperunt."

[1] Dig., xli. 1. 1. See p. 37, note 2.
[2] Inst., i. 2.

seen, the same as that of Ulpian, — that is, they reproduce that definition which suggests that the *jus naturale* means little more than the instincts common to all animals. But whatever may be the case with Ulpian, this definition does not appear to present at all a complete account of the view of the authors of the Institutes. At the close of the same title they use phrases descriptive of the *jura naturalia* which seem to convey quite another conception, the conception of their divine and immutable character.[1] The matter may be illustrated from other passages. In the Third Book of the Institutes we find a phrase of much significance.[2] The "natural laws" here are equivalent to permanent and divine principles of life which are superior to the civil law, and to which the civil law ought to be conformed. In the same title we find the action of the prætor, in admitting emancipated children to a share in the inheritance of their parents, described as being due to the sense of "naturalis æquitas."[3] Again, the same title and the next, in dealing with the changes of the law of succession in relation to females and their representatives, describe certain changes in the civil law as being due to the feeling that the old law was contrary to nature and to the inspiration of a humaner sense.[4] Natural laws are divine and ought to govern and correct all other forms of law, for they represent the permanent principles of justice and humanity. This is evidently quite another view of the *jus naturale* from that which may seem to be expressed in the formal definition of Ulpian which the Institutes cite. It would appear, then, that whatever uncertainty we may feel as to the meaning attached to the *jus naturale* by Ulpian and his contemporaries, by the sixth century the phrase was certainly taking that meaning which

[1] Inst., i. 2. 11: "Sed naturalia quidem jura, quæ apud omnes gentes peræque servantur, divina quadam providentia constituta semper firma atque immutabilia permanent: ea vero, quæ ipsa sibi quæque civitas constituit, sæpe mutari solent vel tacito consensu populi vel alia postea lege lata."

[2] Inst., iii. 1. 11: "Naturalia enim jura civilis ratio peremere non potest."

[3] Inst., iii. 1. 9: "Sed prætor naturali æquitate motus dat eis bonorum possessionem."

[4] Inst., iii. 1. 15: "Divi autem principes non passi sunt talem contra naturam injuriam sine competenti emendatione relinquere." Inst., iii. 2. 3a, "humano proposito," and 7, "humanitate suggerente."

it has throughout the Middle Ages and later—that is, that the *jus naturale* means that body of principles of justice and reason which men can rationally apprehend, and which forms the ideal norm or standard of right conduct and of the justice of social institutions.

We do not mean that the authors of the Institutes had arrived at any perfectly clear judgment on the matter,—on the contrary, the fact of their reproducing Ulpian's definition shows us sufficiently clearly that this was not the case,—but we think that the tendency of their thought is clear enough, that they show us the development of a conception which in the second century was still unformed and indistinct. We have seen that the *jus gentium* was by Gaius conceived as embodying the principles of justice and reason, that indeed the *jus gentium* in Gaius is practically the same thing as the *jus naturale* in Cicero. The conception, therefore, of a principle of law, apprehended by reason as lying behind all positive law and embodying the principles of justice and reason, was not new. The new thing was simply the distinction between this ultimate law and the *jus gentium*.

We have already considered the question of the causes which led to this distinction. We think that in the main it must have arisen from the judgment that certain institutions, which were actually universal, could not be looked upon as having been primitive or natural in the full sense of the word. It is round the question of slavery that this distinction, as far as our evidence goes, seems to take shape in the legal writings, and this, again, seems to be related to the question of natural equality. But the conception could be extended easily to other conditions and circumstances of life. The distinction between the *jus naturale* and the *jus gentium* seems, then, to be very clearly related to the distinction between the primitive state of nature and the conventional organisation of society. The writers of the Institutes do not deal with this directly and explicitly, but in two passages at least they seem to come a good deal nearer to it than any writer cited in the Digest, with the possible exception of Hermogenianus. We have already quoted these passages, but must do so again. The first comes after the definition of the tripartite law, and resumes the description of the *jus gentium* which had been first given in the words of Gaius. This passage, which, as we have already mentioned, is not drawn from any known source, though it reminds us of Hermogenianus, seems quite clearly to imply a contrast between the primitive conditions of human life and the time when the conditions and institutions referred to came into existence.[1] The other phrase comes at the end of that passage which we have already mentioned in discussing the relation of the *jus naturale* and the *jus gentium*.[2] In this passage, as we have already seen, the authors of the Institutes have spoken of the *jus naturale* and the *jus gentium* as being identical, and therefore the primitive condition is not thought of under terms which belong in any exclusive sense to the *jus naturale*. But the writers of the Institutes do seem clearly to conceive of a time when States did not exist, nor magistrates, nor written laws. That is, they seem to contrast the primitive conditions of human life, in which such institutions as those mentioned did not exist, with the later time when they did.

The treatment of slavery in the Institutes is the same as that in Ulpian, Tryphoninus, and Florentinus; indeed, with the exception of the words, "bella etenim orta sunt, et captivitates secutæ, quæ sunt juri naturali contrariæ," [3] they simply reproduce the phrases of Ulpian and Florentinus, "Jure enim naturali ab initio omnes homines liberi nascebantur," [4] and "Servitus autem est constitutio juris gentium, qua quis dominio alieno contra naturam subjicitur." [5]

We need not say anything as to the theory of property in the Institutes: it does not seem to differ in any way from that presented in the Digest. The compilers simply put together in shorter form the same views as those which we have seen to

---

[1] Inst., i. 2. 2 : "Jus autem gentium omni humano generi commune est. Nam usu exigente et humanis necessitatibus gentes humanæ quædam sibi constituerunt : bella etenim orta sunt et captivitates secutæ et servitutes quæ sunt juri naturali contrariæ."

[2] Inst., ii. 1. 11 : "Palam est autem vetustius esse naturale jus, quod cum ipso genere humano rerum natura prodidit : civilia enim jura tunc cœperunt, cum et civitates condi et magistratus creari et leges scribi cœperunt."

[3] Inst., i. 2. 2.

[4] Inst., i. 2. 2.   Cf. Dig., i. 1. 4.

[5] Inst., i. 3. 2.   Cf. Dig., i. 5. 4,

be generally held by the jurists of the second and third centuries. They throw no further light on that interesting passage from Hermogenianus on which we have commented.

And again we find the same thing to be the case with regard to the theory of the relation of the civil law to the general principles of law : the writers of the Institutes begin their own treatise with Ulpian's definition of justice and of the general character of jurisprudence,[1] but they add nothing. And so, again, with regard to the source of the authority of the civil law. They define the varieties of the civil law and the source of their authority mainly in the words of Gaius and of Ulpian.[2] They represent the same tradition which we have seen to be characteristic of all the legal theory of Rome from the second century to Justinian, that the Roman people are the ultimate source of the authority of the civil law of Rome.[3]

The Institutes then furnish us with valuable information as to the development of the theories of natural law and the natural state between the second century and the sixth, and seem to show us that, with regard to the other subjects into which we have inquired, the legal theory continues during these centuries unchanged.

Looking back now on our examination of the political theory of the Roman lawyers, we feel it in the first place important to observe how very small a place such theory occupies in their work. We have been compelled to take up a considerable space in our discussion of this, but that is simply due to the fact that the subject is obscure, and that there are many points whose interpretation presents some difficulties. The references of the lawyers to the theory of politics are few in number, and somewhat slight, if not superficial, in character. We cannot pretend to think that the lawyers contributed much to the philosophy of the State by their own reflections, but in reproducing the theories current among intelligent men they probably did much to give them a precise and definite character, and the mere fact of the embodiment of such theories in the technical law-books could not but give them a new importance and influence. The

---

[1] Inst., i. 1. 1.   Cf. Dig., i. 1. 10.   [2] Inst., i. 2. 3-8.   [3] Inst., i. 2. 6.

influence of the lawyers in the development of political theory was probably quite out of proportion to their actual capacity as political thinkers. Their importance for our purpose is obviously very great : the period to which they belong is one in which there seems to have been very little formal writing on political theory, or else the works which may have dealt with this have disappeared. The lawyers furnish us with the best materials for estimating what was the general tendency of political theory during these centuries, apart from the Christian influences. When we turn to the Christian Fathers we shall find that they provide us with much information on our subject, but if we were to go to them without first examining the views of the lawyers, we should have some difficulty in discriminating between conceptions which belong to the Christian tradition and those which were the common property of the Roman world. The influence of the jurists upon mediæval political thought is very great, certainly very obvious, and while, as we shall see, the relations between mediæval thought and the Roman jurisprudence may often be somewhat superficial, yet its influence is so constant, both directly and through the gradually growing and developing body of the Canon Law, that some study of the Roman law is necessary as a preliminary to any complete examination of mediæval ideas.

If now we consider what are historically the most important elements in the political theory of the Roman lawyers, we shall be inclined to say that first in order of significance comes their contribution to the theory of the natural law and the natural state. We have seen how these conceptions take shape or are implied in the writings of the jurists of the second century, and are by them transmitted to those of the sixth. We have seen that these conceptions seem to be related to some judgment, instinctive perhaps rather than fully reasoned, that some actual institutions of society cannot be thought of as being strictly in harmony with the primitive conditions of human life, which are also conceived of as representing some ideal system of justice. We have seen that through Ulpian, Tryphoninus, and Florentinus the theory of the natural equality and liberty of mankind passed into the system of the Roman law, and it can hardly be doubted that this fact was not without a powerful influence upon the course of speculation on the theory of human institutions.

Secondly, we think it is probable that the influence of the lawyers on future times was greater than we might at first think with respect to the theory of the relation of law and the ultimate principle of justice. They contributed at least to fix for many centuries in the minds of men the conviction that the civil law of any State represents the practical application of the principles of justice and reason. Cicero and the Stoics indeed had maintained this view with clearness and conviction; but whether it would have become predominant apart from the influence of the jurists may perhaps be doubted. When we come to discuss the theory of St Augustine, we may have occasion to observe some signs of another view.

And, finally, we think that in the conception of the Roman lawyers as to the source of authority in the State we probably have one foundation of the mediæval and modern theory of democracy. We shall have to study the immediate sources of this in later chapters of this volume, and in the next volume we shall have to examine the mediæval conception in detail, and shall then be in a position to estimate more precisely the importance of the contribution of the Roman lawyers to the development of modern democratic theory. But in the meanwhile it is at least well worth observing that, if the ancient civilisation ended in a system of monarchical though legal absolutism, yet the theory of government which the jurists of the old world handed down to the new was a theory in which all authority in the State is conceived of as coming from the people.

PART III.

THE POLITICAL THEORY OF THE NEW TESTAMENT
AND THE FATHERS.

———

CHAPTER VIII.

THE POLITICAL THEORY OF THE NEW TESTAMENT.

WE have so far been engaged upon an inquiry into the political theory of the ancient world, in its last stages indeed, but as un-affected by any of those new conceptions which may have come into it with Judaism and Christianity. We have now to con-sider the leading features of the political theory of the West as we find it in the Christian writers of the first six centuries of our era. We have to consider what contributions the new mode of thought actually made to the general stream of political and social ideas, how far it simply coincided with these, how far it may have changed them, and how far, even when it did in the main correspond with them, it may have tended to give these ideas a new form or a new force.

Historians have often spoken in general terms of the far-reaching effects of Christianity in changing men's conceptions with regard to the character, the purpose, and the ruling prin-ciples of human society, and no doubt the influence of Christi-anity upon these has been profound and far-reaching, but we think that we have already said enough to show that if we are to arrive at any just and well-grounded judgment upon this question, we must be at pains to discriminate very carefully those elements of the theory of Christian writers which are really original to them, and those in which they do but reproduce the opinions already current in the civilised world. There are, no doubt, certain elements of political and social theory which are distinctive of the Christian writers, but we shall have to recognise a little more distinctly than has always been done that very often they are simply drawing from the common stock of ideas current in their times.

We must begin by considering the significance and scope of the references to the theory of human nature and society in the New Testament. But behind the New Testament there lies the literature of the Old Testament, whether belonging to the earlier history of Israel or to the period between the Exile and the advent of our Lord. It is especially in the literature, whether canonical or apocryphal, of this later period, that we have to look for the explanation of many of the phenomena of New Testament theory: unhappily the field is as yet but very imperfectly explored. The obscurity of the period indeed corresponds in time and in importance with the parallel obscurity of the period between Aristotle and Cicero, and until more light has been thrown upon these centuries, much in the New Testament will remain difficult to understand, and still more difficult to explain with reference to sources and origins. Among the many obscurities of our subject, perhaps the most obscure and perplexing are the questions which arise as to the contact between Jewish and Hellenic ideas, and the influence which the latter exercised upon the former. The importance of the subject has long been recognised with regard to the interpretation of St Paul's conception of religion and the world, but it may be much more important with regard to the whole of the New Testament than we yet understand.

We find in the New Testament matter of importance with regard to the theory of natural law, the theory of human equality, the theory of property, and the theory of government. We begin by examining the theory of natural law.

The references to this theory in the New Testament are very scanty—indeed we have not observed any distinct reference to the subject, except in one passage in St Paul's letter to the Romans; but this reference is very clear and distinct, and may be taken as presenting a conception which is constantly assumed by St Paul as true and important. The passage occurs in a very important and indeed fundamental discussion of the relation to God of the Gentiles who have not received a revealed law from God: "For as many as have sinned without law shall also perish without law: and as many as have sinned under law shall be judged by law; for not the hearers of a law are just before God, but the doers of a law shall be justified: for when Gentiles which have no law do by nature the things of the law, these, having no law, are a law unto themselves; in that they show the work of the law written in their hearts, their conscience bearing witness therewith."[1]

There can be little doubt that St Paul's words imply some conception analogous to the "natural law" in Cicero, a law written in men's hearts, recognised by man's reason, a law distinct from the positive law of any State, or from what St Paul recognised as the revealed law of God. It is in this sense that St Paul's words are taken by the Fathers of the fourth and fifth centuries like St Hilary of Poitiers, St Ambrose, and St Augustine,[2] and there seems no reason to doubt the correctness of their interpretation. It would be an interesting question to discuss the source of this conception in St Paul; how far it came to him from the presumably Hellenic culture of his youth at Tarsus, how far from the general stock of ideas current among the more educated Jews. For our purpose it is sufficient to observe that we find the conception in the New Testament. We have already considered its character in the writings of Cicero, and the development of the conception among the jurists of the second and third centuries. We shall have to consider it again in the Christian Fathers.

We turn to the theory of human nature and equality in the New Testament, and first to this as presented in the teaching of

[1] Rom. ii. 12-14.
[2] St Hilary of Poitiers, Comm. on Ps. cxviii. 119; St Ambrose, De Jacob et Vita Beata, vi., and Ep. lxxiii. 2; St Augustine, contra Faustum Manichæum, xix. 2.

ɔur Lord in the Gospels. Whatever questions may be raised as
to the universalist and particularist aspects of the Gospels, it will,
we think, now be admitted by all critics that the doctrine of our
Lord must have contained the germs of that universalism which
ultimately predominated in the Christian Church. It is evident
that more or less clearly our Lord must have taught the doctrine of the universal fatherhood of God, that in His eyes the
distinctions of Jew and Gentile were not fundamental nor permanent. The Jewish people are warned that " many shall come
from the east and from the west, and shall sit down in the
kingdom of heaven with Abraham, and Isaac, and Jacob," while
the children of the kingdom, the people of Israel, are shut out.[1]
This is only one example of a conception which is continually
making itself felt in warnings to the Jews, and in the expression
of the universal compassion and mercy of God.

The same conception is expressed in set terms by St Paul,
"There can be neither Jew nor Greek, there can be neither
bond nor free, there can be no male and female: for ye all are
one man in Christ Jesus";[2] but this aspect of St Paul's
teaching is too well known to need any detailed exposition.
It is perhaps interesting and worth while to notice that the
author of the Acts of the Apostles represents St Paul as expressing the conception of the universal fatherhood of God in
the terms of a Stoic philosopher and poet, "For in him we live,
and move, and have our being; as certain even of your own
poets have said, For we are also his offspring."[3] The doctrine
of St Paul with regard to the common relation of all mankind
to God is the same as that of the later philosophers.

We find, then, as characteristic of the Christian faith, that
same conception of the identity of human nature over all the
world which we have already considered in Cicero and Seneca.
We cannot here enter into the question of the history of this
conception in the later Judaism. We can see that among the
Palestinian Jews there was still in St Paul's time a strong conservative party which looked upon these sentiments with suspicion. Apart from all the critical disputes as to the relation

[1] Matt. viii. 11, 12.   and Col. iii. 11.
[2] Gal. iii. 28. Cf. 1 Cor. xii. 13;   [3] Acts xvii. 28.

of St Paul to Jewish Christians, there can be little doubt that it was the form of his universalism which, more than any other cause, tended to concentrate upon him the anger of the Jews.

There are indeed traces in Hebrew literature from an early date of a tendency to transcend the national principle in religion. Both in the first and the second parts of Isaiah, in connection with the expectation of the deliverer and restorer, there is expressed, however vaguely, the sense that his work will transcend the limits of the people of Israel, that it will be his work to establish righteousness and equity for all mankind, and to extend the knowledge of God over all the world.[1] How far these ideas grew and developed during that most obscure period which followed the return from the great captivity, how far the nationalism of the Jews may have revived under the stress of the resistance to Hellenism under the Maccabees, how far the contact with Hellenism, even when resisted, may have yet actually tended to break down the Judaic isolation,—all this is a subject still obscure and perplexed. That our Lord took up again the tradition of the great prophets, and, translating it into a new form, gave it a profound and permanent life, seems clear, as is also the fact that St Paul carries on the doctrine of our Lord. The Christian Church then set out on its history with a conception of human nature which had outgrown the sense of national limitations, a conception which coincided very closely with the conception of the contemporary philosophy.

We shall therefore not be surprised to find that the treatment of slavery, and its relation to human nature, in the New Testament, is very closely analogous to that of the writers whom we have hitherto considered. We have a series of interesting passages which deal with the subject in St Paul's writings, and while these leave a good deal obscure, yet they enable us to form a fairly clear conception of the principles which from the first dominate the attitude of the Christian Church towards the institution of slavery.

The earliest reference to the subject by St Paul is contained in that passage which we have already considered,[2] in which St

---

[1] Cf. especially Isa. xi. 9-12 and xlii. 1-6.   [2] Gal. iii. 28.

Paul speaks of the distinction between slave and freeman as one which has no meaning in relation to God. This evidently does not mean that Christianity has made the institution of slavery unlawful, but simply that it has no significance in God's sight,—that the slave, just as much as the freeman, is capable of the religious life, capable of knowing God and of the life of the child of God. We might translate St Paul's phrase into other terms,—the slave is possessed of reason and capable of virtue. St Paul would obviously have emphatically repudiated the notion that there is a natural or inherent distinction in human nature, which renders some men capable of the higher life, while others must remain upon a lower level. The passages in the Corinthian and Colossian [1] letters to which we referred are strictly parallel, but add nothing further.

In the letter to Philemon we have a practical commentary on this conception, and we have a further development of St Paul's principles with regard to slavery. St Paul sends a certain Onesimus back to his master Philemon, from whom he had apparently escaped. He had fallen in with St Paul and been converted to Christianity. It is very noteworthy that St Paul felt it right to send Onesimus back to his master, and does not even suggest that Philemon should set him at liberty. On the other hand, St Paul expects Philemon to receive Onesimus not as a mere slave, a runaway to be punished, but as a beloved brother. The epistle seems to illustrate clearly two principles: that slavery is not in St Paul's mind unlawful, but that the condition of slavery is only external—that it has no existence in the moral and spiritual life.

We have another reference to the subject in the first letter to the Corinthians, which would be extremely interesting if we could be more confident as to its meaning: "Let each man abide in that calling wherein he was called. Wast thou called being a bond-servant? care not for it: but if [2] thou canst become free, use it rather. For he that was called in the Lord, being a bond-servant, is the Lord's freedman: likewise he that was called, being free, is Christ's bond-servant. Ye were bought with a price; become not bond-servants of men. Brethren, let

---

[1] 1 Cor. xii. 13; Col. iii. 11.　　　[2] Or, "Nay, even if."

each man, wherein he was called, therein abide with God."[1] One general conclusion can clearly enough be founded upon this passage, namely, that in relation to Christ it is completely indifferent whether a man is a slave or a freeman. But when we ask ourselves, Does St Paul in this passage advise a man to get his freedom if he can, or does he rather urge upon him that the whole thing is so unimportant that it is not worth while taking steps to obtain his freedom ? we find ourselves in much uncertainty, and can hardly express any decided opinion.

Another aspect of St Paul's conception of slavery is presented to us in two passages, obviously parallel to each other, but not identical. We may take first that in the letter to the Ephesians : "Bond-servants, be obedient unto them that according to the flesh are your masters, with fear and trembling, in singleness of your heart, as unto Christ; not in the way of eyeservice, as men-pleasers ; but as bond-servants of Christ, doing the will of God from the heart; with good will doing service, as unto the Lord, and not unto men. . . . And, ye masters, do the same things unto them, and forbear threatening: knowing that both their Master and yours is in heaven, and there is no respect of persons with Him."[2] St Paul's phrases are very general in their character, but three conclusions may be drawn from them. First, that he looks upon the performance of his work by the slave as a duty in the sight of God. Secondly, that before God the master and the slave are on the same level. Thirdly, it is probably safe to interpret St Paul's injunctions to the masters, "do the same things unto them," as meaning that they are to behave towards their slaves with fairness. Perhaps we may find the best commentary on these words in the parallel passage in the letter to the Colossians: "Bond-servants, obey in all things them that are your masters according to the flesh : not with eye-service, as men-pleasers, but in singleness of heart, fearing the Lord : whatsoever ye do, work heartily, as unto the Lord, and not unto men ; knowing that from the Lord ye shall receive the recompense of the inheritance : ye serve the Lord Christ. For he that doeth wrong shall receive again

[1] 1 Cor. vii. 20-24.   [2] Eph. vi. 5-9.

for the wrong that he hath done: and there is no respect of
persons. Masters, render unto your bond-servants that which
is just and equal; knowing that ye also have a Master in
heaven."[1] The first part of this passage is substantially the
same as that in the Ephesian letter, but in the last sentence
there is a change of phrase of some interest. Instead of
"Masters, do the same things unto them," we have, "Masters,
render unto your bond-servants that which is just and equal" (τὸ
δίκαιον καὶ τὴν ἰσότητα). The words are a little vague, but at
least they seem clearly to express the principle that justice and
fairness is a quality which ought to belong to the relation of
master and slave, that a man's actions in this relation ought to
have the same quality as that which belongs to the other relations of life. We are reminded of Cicero's phrase, "Meminerimus
autem etiam adversus infimos justitiam esse servandam. Est
autem infima condicio et fortuna servorum."[2]

St Paul's attitude to the question of slavery is obviously
founded upon his conviction that all men are at least morally
and spiritually equal in character. To him all men are in
God's sight equal, distinctions of condition belong only to the
outer man, men are to each other brothers. The conduct of
masters towards their slaves must be governed by the same
principles of equity and fairness as those which govern their
relations to other men. We can hardly say that St Paul goes
beyond the position of Cicero or Seneca as to the natural
similarity and equality of human nature, or beyond Seneca in
his judgment that slavery is a condition which only affects the
outer character of the man. His theory of human nature is
indeed very similar to theirs, and his attitude towards slavery is
much the same. Seneca indeed goes somewhat further than St
Paul when he recognises that slavery is to all men hateful and
burdensome;[3] as we have seen, St Paul's attitude towards the
question of the advantages of emancipation is uncertain. If St
Paul's conception of slavery was to have a greater influence on
the future of that institution, we must probably conclude that
this was due to the fact that St Paul's judgment dominated the

---

[1] Col. iii. 22, iv. 1.   [3] Seneca, De Beneficiis, iii. 19.
[2] Cicero, De Officiis, i. 13. 41.

thought and the practical tendencies of the Church, while Seneca's was but the sentiment of an individual, representative probably of a very general judgment, but not enforced by an organised common judgment.

There are two references to the subject of slavery in the "Pastoral" epistles, but they illustrate not so much the theory of slavery as the relation of the writers of the New Testament to anarchical and disorderly elements in the primitive Church, which were probably of much greater importance than we have hitherto recognised. We shall have to deal with the matter immediately in connection with the theory of government in the New Testament. The passages are in the first letter to Timothy, and in the letter to Titus.[1] The writer of the letters exhorts the slaves to honour and obey their masters, and particularly not to despise their masters if they also were Christians. We may probably infer that the writer felt that there was some danger lest the new sense of spiritual dignity, and of spiritual relation between Christians of all conditions, should tend violently to destroy the old social order: he is afraid lest the conduct of Christian men should bring discredit or suspicion upon the religion of Christ.

We turn to the theory of the institution of government, and here we find certain conceptions whose importance in the history of later political thought is very great indeed. The most important passage in the New Testament which is connected with this subject is that in the thirteenth chapter of St Paul's epistle to the Romans. "Let every soul be in subjection to the higher powers : for there is no power but of God ; and the powers that be are ordained of God. Therefore he that resisteth the power withstandeth the ordinance of God : and they that withstand shall receive to themselves judgment. For rulers are not a terror to the good work, but to the evil. And wouldest thou have no fear of the power ? do that which is good, and thou shalt have praise from the same : for he is a minister of God to thee for good. But if thou do that which is evil, be afraid ; for he beareth

[1] 1 Tim. vi. 1, 2 ; Titus ii. 9, 10. Cf. 1 Peter ii. 18.

not the sword in vain : for he is a minister of God, an avenger
for wrath to him that doeth evil.   Wherefore ye must needs
be in subjection, not only because of the wrath, but also for
conscience' sake.   For for this cause ye pay tribute also; for
they are the ministers of God's service, attending continually
upon this very thing.   Render to all their dues : tribute to
whom tribute is due; custom to whom custom; fear to whom
fear; honour to whom honour." [1]

This passage, which is of the greatest importance throughout
the whole course of mediæval political thought, being indeed
constantly quoted from the second century onwards, is indeed
pregnant and significant in the highest degree.   It defines in
the profoundest way the Christian theory of the nature of
political society, while it furnishes us with the most interesting
evidence with regard to the condition of the Christian societies
of the apostolic period.

St Paul's general meaning is plain and distinct.   The order
of civil government is of divine institution, a thing deriving its
authority and sanction from God Himself; to refuse to submit
to it is to refuse to submit to God; obedience to the State is
not merely a political necessity, but a religious obligation.
But, we may ask, why is this so ?   Why are we to take the
civil order of the State to be a divine institution, to which
we must render obedience as to God Himself ?   Here also
St Paul's answer is clear and distinct; it is because the end
and purpose of civil government is to repress the evil and
to encourage the good.   The civil ruler is God's servant for a
good purpose ; the good man need have no fear of the civil
ruler, but only the evil man.   To put this into the more
technical phrases of political theory, St Paul means that we
must obey the civil order, as having a divine authority, because it exists for the maintenance of justice.   It is the
just end of the civil State which gives it a sacred character.

There are some other passages of importance which should
be considered along with this one.   In the letter to Titus [2]
we have an exhortation in general terms to obedience to
authorities, and in the first letter to Timothy Christian men

---

[1] Rom. xiii. 1-7.   [2] Titus iii. 1, 2.

are exhorted to pray "for kings and all that are in high place; that we may lead a tranquil and quiet life in all godliness and gravity."[1] The position of the ruler is defined clearly, along with the ground of the attitude of Christian men towards him, namely, that it is his function to secure order and peace for society.

In the first letter of St Peter we have a more complete parallel to the phrases of St Paul in the Roman letter. "Be subject to every ordinance of man for the Lord's sake: whether it be to the king, as supreme; or unto governors, as sent by him for vengeance on evil-doers and for praise to them that do well. For so is the will of God, that by well-doing ye should put to silence the ignorance of foolish men: as free, and not using your freedom for a cloke of wickedness, but as bond-servants of God. Honour all men. Love the brotherhood. Fear God. Honour the king."[2] We have here the same conception as that of St Paul, that the authority of the ruler is divine, that obedience is to be rendered to him for the Lord's sake; and the same explanation of this, as resting upon the fact that the function of the ruler is to punish the evil and to reward the good. But the passage is also interesting as suggesting to us some explanation of the urgency with which St Paul and the writer of this letter deal with the matter: for our purposes it is immaterial whether the author is, as we should judge probable, St Peter, or some other and later writer.

We might very well at first sight wonder what it is that leads St Paul and St Peter to insist upon such an obvious truism as that the honest man should respect and obey the civil power. The first explanation which offers itself is, that they are anxious to counteract some Jewish antipathy to the Roman rule, and the explanation is consistent with the character of the persons to whom the letter to the Romans and the letter of St Peter are addressed. It is fairly clear that the Roman Church, when St Paul wrote, consisted partly of Jewish, partly of Gentile Christians, and it would seem that the letter of St Peter may be addressed mainly to Jewish Christians.[3] It is indeed most

---

[1] 1 Tim. ii. 2.
[2] 1 Peter ii. 13-17.

[3] Cf. 1 Peter i. 1: ἐκλεκτοῖς παρεπιδήμοις διασπορᾶς.

probable that the Christian teachers were compelled at an early date to deal with this question of the relation of the Church to the Roman Government. The Jewish religious and political leaders had evidently tried to entangle our Lord in the difficult questions relating to the Jewish nationality and the Roman Empire. There can be no mistake about the purpose of the question with regard to paying tribute to Cæsar;[1] it was obviously intended to involve our Lord in a charge either of want of patriotism, or of disloyalty to the Roman Government. The apparent failure of the attempt evidently did not prevent the Jewish authorities from bringing the latter charge against our Lord. It is true that only St Luke's gospel actually records the definite form of the charge, "We found this man perverting our nation, and forbidding to give tribute to Cæsar, and saying that he himself is Christ a king;"[2] but it is clear from all the accounts of the trial before Pilate that some such charge must have been made. The common tradition of all the narratives represents Pilate as asking our Lord whether he claimed to be the King of the Jews,[3] and there seems therefore to be nothing improbable in St John's statement that it was by pressing the charge of disloyalty that the Jewish leaders were able to coerce Pilate into ordering our Lord's crucifixion.[4] Our judgment is confirmed by the account of the inscription placed upon the cross.[5] There is some evidence that this same charge of disloyalty was brought against the Christians in the later part of the first century. According to the author of the Acts of the Apostles, the Jews at Thessalonica tried to embroil the newly founded Christian community in that city with the authorities, by bringing against them a charge closely connected with that brought against our Lord. "These that have turned the world upside down are come hither also ; whom Jason hath received : and these all act contrary to the decrees of Cæsar, saying that there is another king, one Jesus."[6] There may be some trace of charges of the same kind in the narrative of the incidents

---

[1] Mark xii. 13-17, and parallels.
[2] Luke xxiii. 2.
[3] Matt. xxvii. 11 ; Mark xv. 2 ; Luke xxiii. 3 ; John xviii. 33.
[4] John xix. 12-16.
[5] Matt. xxvii. 37, and parallels.
[6] Acts xvii. 6, 7.

at Philippi,[1] and in the charges brought against St Paul at Cæsarea.[2]

The Apocalypse also furnishes us with clear evidence that, as a matter of fact, the Jewish hatred of the Roman Government was at one time, and in some circles, common among Christian men, when Rome first turned from its early indifference and careless protection, and became the violent enemy of the Christian societies. Without entering into any discussion of the interpretation of the Apocalypse as a whole, or any criticism of its sources, it is at least obvious that we have in it an expression of the most intense hatred of the Roman oppressor, which, even if it were Jewish in its original form, has been adopted by a Christian writer. It may of course be urged that this represents the feelings of one section only of the Christian community ; but even if this is so, the fact that such sentiments were current in any section of the Christian societies must be taken into account in considering the position of their leaders.

It is thus very possible that these leaders were compelled at a very early date to deal with the question of the relation of their converts to the Roman Government, and the suggestion is a reasonable one, that we might interpret the passages whose significance we are discussing, as being primarily intended to check any tendency on the part of the members of the Christian communities to adopt the national Jewish attitude towards the Roman Government.

But we do not think that this explanation is really adequate to the interpretation of these passages. They seem to have some more general significance ; there is no trace in them of any special reference to a Jewish attitude towards the Roman Government, such as we might reasonably expect to find were they intended primarily to detach Christian men from a Jewish nationalism. We think that the full explanation of these phrases must be found in a characteristic of the early Christian societies, of which there are numerous traces in the apostolic letters, and which St Peter seems to indicate in the passage we have quoted : "For so is the will of God, that with well-doing ye should put to silence the ignorance of foolish men : as free,

---

[1] Acts xvi. 20, 21.   [2] Acts xxiv. 5.

and not using your liberty for a cloke of wickedness, but as bond-servants of God." [1]

The freedom of the Christian man is one of the most important of the conceptions of St Paul: "With freedom did Christ set us free: stand fast therefore, and be not entangled again in a yoke of bondage." [2] We have just seen that St Peter's epistles also recognise freedom as a true characteristic of the Christian. Even St James uses the name of freedom, whatever may be the precise meaning which he attaches to the phrase.[3] But it is also evident that the doctrine of the freedom of the Christian man was attended in the primitive Church with the same difficulties as in later times; indeed we venture to think that it was precisely in primitive times that the difficulties and dangers attending upon the conception made themselves most urgently felt.

It requires only a slight study of the apostolic writings to perceive that if the early Christian teachers had hard work to overcome the traditional legalism of the Jew, they were confronted with an almost equally dangerous tendency to anarchism, especially no doubt among their Gentile converts. The tendency shows itself first in a disposition to slight the ordinary duties of life, to refuse submission to the discipline of the common life. "We exhort you, brethren," St Paul says in his first letter to the Thessalonians, "that ye abound more and more [in works of love]; and that ye study to be quiet, and to do your own business, and to work with your own hands, even as we charged you." [4] And again, "We exhort you, brethren, admonish the disorderly." [5] And so again in the second letter, "Now we command you, brethren, in the name of our Lord Jesus Christ, that ye withdraw yourselves from every brother that walketh disorderly, and not after the tradition which they received of us. For yourselves know how ye ought to imitate us: for we behaved not ourselves disorderly among you; neither did we eat bread for nought at any man's hand, but in labour and travail, working night

---

[1] 1 Peter ii. 15, 16.
[2] Gal. v. 1. Cf. 2 Cor. iii. 17.
[3] James i. 25, ii. 12.
[4] 1 Thess. iv. 10, 11.
[5] 1 Thess. v. 14.

and day, that we might not be a burden to any of you. . . . For even when we were with you, this we commanded you, If any will not work, neither let him eat. For we hear of some that walk among you disorderly, that work not at all, but are busybodies. Now them that are such we command and exhort in the Lord Jesus Christ, that with quietness they work, and eat their own bread." [1] It would appear that in the Thessalonian church a number of persons had so interpreted the Christian spirit of freedom, and the Christian consciousness of the dignity of the spiritual relation of man to God, that they were disinclined to submit to the ordinary duties of life, and to any kind of human authority.

The same tendencies, if under slightly different forms, exhibit themselves in the Corinthian church. It is clear from any examination of the letters to this church that St Paul had a very real difficulty, especially with his own Gentile converts, to persuade them that the liberty of the Christian man did not mean a complete emancipation from all discipline and order in life. It is clear that some at least of the Corinthian Christians were inclined to press the principle of the indifference of external rules and forms to the point of a complete disregard of the principle of that mutual subordination of desires and actions which alone makes social life possible. "All things are lawful" [2] seems to have been the catchword of this tendency. St Paul argues that, while it is quite true that the Christian man is free from the legal principle in life, he must remember that his conduct must be governed by the fundamental principles of society, the principles of mutual love and consideration. "All things are lawful; but all things are not expedient. All things are lawful; but all things edify not. Let no man seek his own, but each his neighbour's good." [3] And so with regard to those spiritual gifts which St Paul and the Corinthian Christians firmly believed that they possessed, St Paul tries to persuade them that not the more remarkable and conspicuous, or the more abstractly

[1] 2 Thess. iii. 6-12. (The importance of the passage is independent of any question that may be raised as to the authorship of the letter.)
[2] 1 Cor. vi. 12, x. 23.
[3] 1 Cor. x. 23, 24.

spiritual gifts were the most valuable, but rather the gifts of service and counsel, and that the greatest gift was that of love.[1] Even in writing to the Galatian churches, when St Paul was stirred to the very depths of his nature by the necessity of counteracting the legal spirit which threatened to take possession of them, St Paul warns his converts against the misinterpretation and perversion of the conception of liberty, "For ye, brethren, were called for freedom; only use not your freedom for an occasion to the flesh, but through love be servants one to another."[2] There can, we think, be little doubt that the early Church was troubled with anarchical tendencies, very similar to those of some of the Anabaptist movements of the sixteenth century, and that these sprang from the same source. The reaction against the legal spirit carried men off their feet, and St Paul has to take the greatest pains to counteract the possible effects of his own teaching, just as Luther had to do when he wrote his treatise on 'The Liberty of the Christian Man.'

There is indeed no direct evidence in the New Testament, nor, as far as we have seen, in the early Fathers, of an explicit repudiation of the principle of civil government in the early Church, though such a charge may have been brought against the Church; but it is at least very easy to conjecture that the enthusiastic spirit of the freedom of the sons of God, of the members of the true kingdom of Christ, might easily pass into a contempt for all government, especially when that government was in the hands of unspiritual persons. In a later volume we shall have to consider the significance of Wycliffe's doctrine of civil lordship: it is possible that his view may have been anticipated in primitive times. There are even not wanting some germs out of which such sentiments might grow, both in the Gospels and in St Paul's own writings. Our Lord had very sharply contrasted the spirit of the Gentiles with the spirit of His kingdom, when he said: "Ye know that they which are accounted to rule over the Gentiles lord it over them; and their great ones exercise authority over them. But it is not so among you: but whoso-

[1] 1 Cor. xii. and xiii.　　　　[2] Gal. v. 13.

ever would become great among you, shall be your minister: and whosoever would be first among you, shall be servant of all." [1] It is not difficult to understand how such a conception might lead men of a rash and impulsive disposition into a contempt for all secular authority. In St Paul's first letter to the Corinthians we have a reference to the relation of Christians to the law-courts, which might quite possibly be understood as indicating a certain tendency to slight the ordinary machinery of the secular power. "Dare any of you, having a matter against his neighbour, go to law before the unrighteous, and not before the saints? Or know ye not that the saints shall judge the world? and if the world is judged by you, are ye unworthy to judge the smallest matters?" [2] No doubt St Paul's words are aimed at the contentious unbrotherly spirit which prevailed in the Church, but there is, probably unintentionally and unconsciously, a slightly depreciatory accent in the reference to the secular courts, perhaps a slight confusion with regard to the nature of civil justice.

It seems most probable, then, that St Paul's vindication of the authority of the civil ruler, with the parallel expressions of St Peter's epistle, were intended to counteract some anarchical tendencies in the early Christian societies, were intended to preserve the Christian societies from falling into an error which would have destroyed the unity of human life, and would have tended to put them into a ruinous opposition to the general principles of human progress. We shall have occasion to see how this question is developed in the writings of the Fathers, and we shall then recognise both how important it was that St Paul had so clearly laid down the true principles of the religious conception of the state, and also how even the clearness of his treatment failed to save later Christian thinkers from a perversion of this conception.

When we now consider the relation of this theory of the nature of government to the contemporary philosophical conception of the state, we find that it is both old and new. It is

---

[1] Mark x. 42-44. Cf. Matt. xx. 25, 26 ; Luke xxii. 25, 26.
[2] 1 Cor. vi. 1-8.

essentially the same theory as that of the Stoics, that man is by nature a social creature, that government is an institution necessary to the proper development of human life.   St Paul is translating the philosophical conception into the Christian conception of the divine order, and the translation has its real importance, but fundamentally the conception is the same.   It is new in expression but the same in substance, and even the expression is, as we have already seen, to be found in such contemporary writers as Seneca and Pliny.[1] We shall have presently to consider the theories that grew up on this translation, but we shall see throughout our work that the translation was necessary if Christian civil- isation was to inherit the philosophical tradition of Aristotle and the Stoics.   We must remember that clearly enough the Epicurean tradition was not the same as the Stoic, that the attitude of the philosophers of that school towards the organised State was at least one of indifference, and, as we have just seen, there were elements in the Christian concep- tions which might have tended towards a similar position.   It is therefore a matter of the greatest importance that St Paul should have recognised the gravity of the question, and should have set forth his views with such distinctness and penetration.

We have still to consider the theory of property in the New Testament.   A great deal has been said about what has been called the communism of the early Church, and it has been thought that we see the beginnings of this in the condition of the Church of Jerusalem as described in the first chapters of the Acts.   We must begin by examining the exact nature of the accounts of this which are given to us.   The first refer- ence is at the end of the second chapter: "And all that believed were together, and had all things common; and they sold their possessions and goods, and parted them to all, according as any man had need." [2]   The next reference is in the fourth chapter: "And the multitude of them that believed were of one heart and soul: and not one of them said that aught of the things

[1] See p. 31.   [2] Acts ii. 44, 45.

which he possessed was his own; but they had all things common. . . . For neither was there among them any that lacked: for as many as were possessors of lands or houses sold them, and brought the prices of the things that were sold, and laid them at the apostles' feet: and distribution was made unto each, according as any one had need." [1]

There is no doubt that if these words stood alone we should conclude that a complete communistic system was established in the Church of Jerusalem, and we might almost conclude that conformity to this was one of the regular tests of membership. But we must look at the general narrative a little more carefully, and our first impression will then be a good deal modified. One of the most dramatic incidents in the story of the primitive Church is the narrative of the falsehood and death of Ananias and Sapphira, and in this narrative we observe phrases which materially affect our judgment of the condition of the Church. " A certain man named Ananias, with Sapphira his wife, sold a possession, and kept back part of the price, his wife also being privy to it, and brought a certain part, and laid it at the apostles' feet. But Peter said, Ananias, why hath Satan filled thy heart to lie to the Holy Ghost, and to keep back part of the price of the land? Whiles it remained, did it not remain thine own? and after it was sold, was it not in thy power? How is it that thou hast conceived this thing in thy heart? thou hast not lied unto men, but unto God." [2]

It is at least clear from this narrative that there was no compulsory system of communism in the Church, that submission to it was not a condition of membership of the Christian society in Jerusalem, and we are compelled to reconsider the judgment which we might be inclined to found upon the passages first quoted. It would seem safest to conclude that the first wave of enthusiasm in the Christian society in Jerusalem led to a sudden development of the charitable impulses of the community to such a point that at least for the time the Christian society might well have appeared to be living in a complete community of goods, but that this condition of things was never developed into a complete system, and that

[1] Acts iv. 32-35. [2] Acts v. 1-4.

the surrender of individual property was never a condition of church membership.

The narrative of the Acts throws no light upon the continuance of this state of things in Jerusalem. There are many traces in the letters of St Paul of great poverty in the Church of Jerusalem, a poverty probably due mainly to the crowds of Jews, many of them doubtless of very small resources, who from time to time made their way to Jerusalem, from all parts of the Empire, to attend the great festivals; and we find St Paul engaged in collecting money in the churches which he visited, for the relief of this poverty, but there is nothing to show us whether the Church in Jerusalem itself continued to be under the same conditions as at first or not.

It may perhaps be said that there are traces in the Gospels, and especially in the Epistle of St James, of a tendency to look upon the rich as being, by the very fact of their riches, evil, and the poor as being, by reason of their poverty, good. It is certainly noteworthy at least that St James represents the true disciple as being poor, and oppressed by the rich, and that he proclaims the coming judgment of God upon the rich.[1] And in the Gospels there is more than one trace of a tendency to regard the condition of the rich as being, normally at least, full of danger,[2] and the condition of the poor as being one of blessedness.[3] (In St Matthew's gospel this poverty is explained in a spiritual sense.) In one well-known passage our Lord tells the rich young ruler that for him the way of perfection lies in the renunciation of all his wealth.[4] It is of course true that the interpretation of the passage has been the subject of much dispute: we shall see presently in what very various fashions the Fathers deal with it, but the general impression which we derive from the Gospels is certainly that wealth is at least a difficulty in the spiritual life.

When we consider the condition of the Christian Church outside of Judæa, we find no trace of any such system of the common life as may have existed in some loose fashion in

---

[1] James ii. 5, 6 ; v. 1-6.
[2] Mark x. 25 ; Luke xviii. 24.
[3] Luke vi. 20.
[4] Mark x. 21 ; Matt. xix. 21 ; Luke xviii. 22.

Judæa. St Paul, in his various letters, constantly exhorts his disciples to liberality, especially towards the poor Christians in Jerusalem,[1] but also in more general terms;[2] but there is little trace of a community of goods in the churches to which he writes, unless we may conjecture that the idle and disorderly life of some of the Christians at Thessalonica may be related to a somewhat indiscriminate system of almsgiving in that community. St Paul's emphatic words, "If any will not work, neither let him eat,"[3] may imply that the benevolence of the brethren was encouraging a certain number of Christians in idle and thriftless ways. We have discussed the traces of certain anarchical tendencies in the primitive Christian societies, and it is quite possible that this spirit was fostered by a charity which may sometimes have been almost reckless. But in all this there is no trace of any strict community of goods, any notion that the ownership of property was something illegitimate.

So far as the New Testament is concerned, we can hardly say that there is any theory of property of a strict kind: the Gospels and St James may tend to represent the sense of the dangerous responsibilities and temptations which wealth brings; the Acts and the Epistles show us that the Christian societies, from the outset, felt the imperious claims of the brotherhood, and interpreted them as meaning that it was the duty of a Christian man to see that his brother was not in want.[4] We shall return to the subject again when we deal with the theory of property as it is presented in the early Fathers.

---

[1] 1 Cor. xvi. 1 ; 2 Cor. viii. Cf. Rom. xv. 26 ; Gal. ii. 10.

[2] 1 Tim. vi. 17-19.

[3] 2 Thess. iii. 10. Cf. 1 Thess. iv. 9-12.

[4] 1 John iii. 17.

CHAPTER IX.

NATURAL LAW.

WHEN we consider the character of the political theory of the Christian Fathers we find ourselves in face of a considerable difficulty in arranging our materials. The writings which we have to consider extend over a period of some six centuries, from St Clement of Rome and the 'Teaching of the Twelve Apostles' in the first century to St Isidore of Seville in the beginning of the seventh, and they represent very various standpoints. Some of them are written by men who have nothing of a philosophical habit of thought; while others represent the more or less reasoned reflections of men who might be good or bad philosophers, but who were at any rate thinkers. Some of them, that is, simply seem to show us what notions were current among Christian men, others must be taken also to represent the particular turn given to these by the individual writers. We are compelled to recognise considerable diversities of opinion among these writers, and we have endeavoured to note these when they occur, and to discuss the relations of the different views to each other : at the same time, we think that it is true to say that in the main the Fathers represent a homogeneous system of thought, and we have therefore usually arranged our materials under the same general system which we have so far followed, not under the names of the individual writers, while we have usually endeavoured to present their opinions in some roughly chronological order.

We have seen the importance of the development of the theory of natural law in the Roman jurists, we have seen how at the close of the second century the law of nations is distinguished from the law of nature, and how this distinction is fixed with more or less complete definiteness in the sixth century. We must now consider the treatment of this subject in the Christian writers of these centuries. We have observed the general characteristics of the theory of Cicero with respect to the natural law, that there is a law behind all the positive ordinances of human society, a law which is written in the hearts of all men, drawing them to good, forbidding them to do evil, a law which is itself the expression of the reason and nature of God Himself, and that from this all the true laws of men are derived. We have also seen that at least in one great passage St Paul indicates that he also conceives of such a principle as existing in the heart of every man—that every man does in his heart know the law of God, which forbids man to sin, and commands him to do what is right. Whether St Paul's conception should be traced to the natural development of Jewish thought, or to the influence of that Hellenic culture which had already strongly affected Judaism, or to the special circumstances of his own education at Tarsus, is, as we have said, difficult to determine. For our purpose, indeed, we may suppose that it was derived from any or all of these sources. It will be obvious to any one who studies the phenomena, that here is one of the many points where the Christian conception and that of the Western world at large coincided. The theory of natural law became one of the commonplaces of Christian thought.

In Origen's treatise against Celsus there is an interesting sentence which may be taken as characteristic of the attitude of the Christian thinkers. Celsus had urged that "Law is king of all things," and Origen, after expressing a necessary qualification of the phrase as liable to misunderstanding, agrees that that which is law in the proper sense of the word is by nature king of all things, even though there may be some who have like robbers abandoned the law and deny its validity. The Christians, he says, have come to the knowledge of this law which is by nature king of all things, for it is the same as the law of God, and they endeavour to live in accordance with it.[1] This frank admission of the truth of the conception and the identification of the law of nature with the law of God— an identification already made, at least in terms, by Cicero— is representative of the common attitude of Christian writers towards this conception.

Even Tertullian, who, if any man, represents the extreme opposition to the ideas of the Greek world, uses language which is the same as that of the philosophers. Nature, he says, is our first school: we know God first by nature. Nature is the teacher, the soul the disciple. Whatever nature taught, it was taught by God.[2] Lactantius, with his usual somewhat captious way of dealing with ancient philosophy, when discussing Zeno's principle of living according to nature, complains at first that this is too vague: there are many varieties of nature, he says, and the phrase might mean that men are to live like beasts; but finally he admits that, if the principle means that man, who is born to virtue, is to follow his own nature, it is a good principle.[3] These Fathers, that is, admit that there is a law written by nature in men's hearts which is the true rule of human life and conduct.

The view of the later Fathers is the same. The writer known as "Ambrosiaster," in his commentary on St Paul's Epistle to the Romans, gives us an interesting tripartite definition of law, and a statement of the relation of the law of nature to the law of Moses.[4] The definition is interesting, but more significant is the conception of the relation of the Mosaic Law to the natural law, as being something intended to supplement as

[1] Origen, Contra Celsum, v. 40.

[2] Tertullian, De Corona, v. and vi. De Test. An., 5. (From Dr Fairbairn's 'Christ in Modern Theology,' p. 96.)

[3] Lactantius, Div. Inst., iii. 8.

[4] Ambrosiaster, Com. in Ep. ad Rom., iii. 20: "Triplex quidem lex est, ita ut prima pars de sacramento divinitatis sit Dei: secunda autem quæ congruit legi naturali, quæ interdicit peccatum: tertia vero factorum, id est, sabbati, neomeniæ, circumcisionis, etc. Hæc est ergo lex naturalis, quæ per Moysen partim reformata, partim auctoritate ejus firmata in vitiis cohibendis, cognitum fecit peccatum." We should refer our readers who wish to know more about this writer and his identity with the author of the "Quæstiones Veteris et Novi Testamenti," formerly attributed to St Augustine, to an article by Dom. Morin in the 'Revue d'Histoire et de Littérature religieuse,' 1899; and to Prof. A. Souter's edition of the "Quæstiones Veteris et Novi Testamenti," and to the same author's "Study of Ambrosiaster."

well as to confirm it. The same conception is expressed in a
letter of St Ambrose : The Mosaic law was given because men
had failed to obey the natural law.[1] Again, St Ambrose says,
Law is twofold, natural and written. The natural law is in
man's heart; the written laws in tables. All men are under
the law—that is, under the natural law.[2] And again : The law
of God is in the heart of the just man. Which law ? Not the
written but the natural law, for law is not set for the just, but
for the unjust man.[3] The natural law, says St Jerome, speaks
in our heart, telling us to do what is good and to avoid what
is evil; and, again, he says that the whole world received
the natural law, and the Mosaic law was given because the
natural law was neglected or destroyed.[4]

It is interesting to notice that the Fathers frequently, as we
have before said, connect their treatment of the natural law
with St Paul's phrases in Romans. St Ambrose, for instance,
says that it is the Apostle who teaches us that the natural
law is in our hearts.[5] St Augustine also refers to St Paul's
words in a passage in which he divides law into three species ;[6]
and St Hilary of Poitiers does the same in describing the general
scope of the natural law. He defines this as being that a man
must not injure his fellow-man, must not take that which
belongs to another, must keep himself from fraud and per-

---

[1] St Ambrose, Ep. lxxiii. 10 : " Accipe
aliud. Non fuit necessaria lex per
Moysen. Denique subintravit, quod
utique non ordinarium sed velut furtiv-
um significare videtur introitum ; eo
quod in locum naturalis legis intra-
verit. Itaque si illa suum servasset
locum, hæc lex scripta nequaquam esset
ingressa."

[2] Id., De Fuga Sæculi, iii.

[3] Id., Enarr. in Ps. xxxvi. 31.

[4] St Jerome, Com. on Gal. iii. 2, and
on Isaiah xxiv. 6.

[5] St Ambrose, Ep. lxxiii. 2 : " Esse
autem legem naturalem in cordibus
nostris etiam apostolus docet, qui scrip-
sit quia plerumque 'et gentes naturaliter ea, quæ Legis sunt, faciunt, et
cum Legem non legerint, opus tamen
Legis scriptum habent in cordibus suis '
(Rom. ii. 14, 15). Ea igitur lex non

scribitur, sed innascitur : nec aliqua
percipitur lectione, sed profluo quodam fonte in singulis exprimitur, et
humanis ingeniis hausitur." Cf. 'De
Jacob et Vita Beata,' vi.

[6] St Augustine, Contra Faustum Manichæum, xix. 2 : "Sunt autem legum
genera tria : unum quidem Hebræ-
orum, quod peccati et mortis Paulus
appellat (Rom. viii. 2). Aliud vero
Gentium, quod naturale vocat : ' Gentes
enim,' inquit, 'naturaliter quæ legis
sunt faciunt ; et ejusmodi legem non
habentes, ipsi sibi sunt lex ; qui ostend-
unt opus legis scriptum in cordibus
suis' (Rom. ii. 14, 15). Tertium vero
genus legis est veritas, quod perinde
significans, apostolus dicit : Lex enim
spiritus vitæ in Christo Jesu liberavit
me a lege peccati et mortis " (Rom.
viii. 2).

jury, must not plot against another man's marriage.[1] It is interesting to compare this with the definitions of the natural law by St Ambrose [2] and by St Augustine.[3] It is clear that these are derived from Cicero and other ancient writers.

It is unnecessary to multiply quotations. There seems to be no division of opinion among the Fathers upon the subject. Practically they carry on the same conceptions as those of Cicero and the later philosophers, and while they bring these into connection with the suggestion of St Paul, they cannot be said either to modify these inherited conceptions or to carry them any farther.

The treatment of the law of nature in the Fathers is not complete till we come to St Isidore of Seville at the beginning of the seventh century. Then we find that distinction which we have considered in Ulpian, Tryphoninus, and Florentinus, and in the Institutes of Justinian, restated with great direct-ness, and defined in a method which is interesting and to some extent novel. The importance of the treatment of the natural law by St Isidore is, however, not only due to the fact that he furnishes us with interesting evidence as to the general prevalence of the theory of law in this form, and shows us that it was adopted by an important Christian writer. His importance in the history of the theory of natural law is much greater than this. His definitions were finally embodied, in the twelfth century, in Gratian's Decretum, and so passed into the structure of the Canon Law, and furnished the form of

[1] St Hilary of Poitiers, Tract. on Ps. cxviii. 119 : " Lex enim veluti naturalis est, injuriam nemini inferre, nil alienum præripere, fraude ac perjurio abstinere, alieno conjugio non insidiari. Novit et hanc Apostolus legem, dicens. ' Cum enim nationes, quæ legem non habent, naturaliter secundum legem faciunt,' etc."

[2] St Ambrose, De Off., iii. 3 : " Hæc utique lex naturæ est, quæ nos ad omnem astringit humanitatem, ut alter alteri tanquam unius partes corporis invicem deferamus. Nec detra-hendum quidquam putemus, cum

contra naturæ legem sit non juvare." St Ambrose, De Off., iii. 24 : " Nihil-que judicandum utile, nisi quod in commune prosit. . . . Etenim si una lex naturæ omnibus, una utique utilitas universorum, ad consulendum utique omnibus naturæ lege constring-imur."

[3] St Augustine, De Diversis Questioni-bus xxxi. : " Natura jus est quod non opinio genuit, sed quædam innata vis inseruit, ut religionem, pietatem, gra-tiam, vindicationem, observantiam, veritatem."

all the mediæval ecclesiastical treatment of the subject; and though, no doubt, with the reviving study of the Roman jurisprudence, the same conceptions would probably have appeared, yet the fact that they were already embodied in St Isidore's Etymologies secured the unanimity of mediæval theory upon the subject.

The position of St Isidore in the development, especially of the political theory of the Middle Ages, is indeed out of all proportion to the intrinsic merits or pretensions of his work. His 'Origins,' or 'Etymologies,' is really the seventh-century equivalent of a modern encyclopædia. He suggests the derivation of each word with which he deals, and gives a brief account of the thing which it describes. It would be extremely interesting, were it not here out of place, to trace the history and origin of such an encyclopædic work as that of St Isidore. It is evident enough that in most points and in general conception it is not original. It seems to belong to the same class of work as Martianus Capella's 'De Nuptiis Philologiæ.' How much farther back this encyclopædic form of literature can be traced we are not competent to say. It will be seen in the course of our inquiries that St Isidore furnishes the model of a variety of works of the same kind in the Middle Ages, of which the nearest is Hrabanus Maurus's 'De Universo,' which belongs to the ninth century.

St Isidore's work has therefore little of the character of an original production, and indeed makes no claim to this. For our purpose, indeed, this fact rather increases than diminishes its importance. We feel convinced in reading St Isidore's definitions that he is giving us not merely his own judgments but the generally current conceptions of his time. It may of course be urged that St Isidore, writing as he did in Spain, was rather far removed from the centre of the culture of his time, and that we must be prepared to admit the influence of the new barbarian circumstances upon his mode of thought. With regard to some aspects of his political ideas this may be quite true, and indeed may be a fact of some importance. But with regard to the subject which we are at present considering, his treatment of the theory of Natural Law, there seems no reason to think that any such special influences are at work upon him. We should indeed be glad, if it were possible, to trace more clearly the sources of his theories, for much remains, to us at least, very obscure; but we see no reason at all why we should look for these outside of the limits of the Latin culture.

St Isidore of Seville deals with the definition of law in the following terms:[1] "Jus autem naturale est aut civile aut gentium." That is, he begins by laying down the tripartite character of law as Ulpian and the Institutes do. He then defines natural law, "Jus naturale est commune omnium nationum, et quod ubique instinctu naturæ, non constitutione aliqua habetur; ut viri et feminæ conjunctio, liberorum successio et educatio, communis omnium possessio, et omnium una libertas, adquisitio eorum quæ cœlo, terra, marique capiuntur. Item depositæ rei vel commendatæ pecuniæ restitutio, violentiæ per vim repulsio. Nam hoc, aut si quid huic simile est, numquam injustum, sed naturale, æquumque habetur."

It will be evident that the definition is related to that of Ulpian and the Institutes,[2] and yet that there are considerable differences between them, and these of some significance. The statement that the *jus naturale* is common to all animals has disappeared, and in its place we read that it is common to all nations, and that men follow it "instinctu naturæ non constitutione aliqua." We have already had occasion to deal with this change, but we must again point out that it seems to represent the fact that while Ulpian's definition suggests that the *jus naturale* was something of the nature of the animal instinct, the general tendency of thought was to look upon it as a body of principles rationally apprehended. It is true that St Isidore says that men follow it "instinctu naturæ," but this is con-

[1] St Isidore, Etymol., v. 4.

[2] Ulpian's definition is: "Jus naturale est, quod natura omnia animalia docuit: nam jus istud non humani generis proprium, sed omnium animalium, quæ in terra, quæ in mari nascuntur, avium quoque, commune est. Hinc descendit maris atque feminæ conjunctio, quam nos matrimonium appellamus, hinc liberorum procreatio, hinc educatio: videmus etenim cetera quoque animalia, feras etiam istius juris peritia censeri." (Dig., i. 1. 1. 3.) The definition in Inst., i. 2., is practically the same.

trasted, not with reason, but with "constitutio aliqua," and it should be observed that under the definition is included an ethical habit, such as the "depositæ rei vel commendatæ pecuniæ restitutio." This has no place in Ulpian's definition. St Isidore defines the *jus gentium* in the following terms : "Jus gentium est sedium occupatio, ædificatio, munitio, bella, captivitates, servitutes, postliminia, fœdera pacis, indutiæ, legatorum non violandorum religio, conubia inter alienigenas prohibita. Et inde jus gentium, quia eo jure omnes fere gentes utuntur."[1] We have already compared this definition with a fragment of Hermogenianus contained in the Digest, and with one part of the discussion of this question in the Institutes of Justinian.[2] It is difficult to say whether St Isidore's definition is directly related to these, but there seems to be a general agreement of character between them all. In passing we may point out that there is the same contrast between the natural liberty of all, under the *jus naturale,* and the slavery which belongs to the *jus gentium,* in St Isidore and in the Institutes ; but we shall have to return to this point later. The *jus civile* is defined by St Isidore as follows : "Jus civile est, quod quisque populus, vel civitas sibi proprium, humana divinaque causa constituit."[3] This is practically the same as the definition of the civil law as distinguished from the *jus gentium* and the *jus naturale* in the Institutes of Gaius and Justinian.[4]

St Isidore of Seville has obviously reproduced with certain changes of detail the theory of the tripartite character of law which we have already seen in the works of Ulpian and in the

---

[1] St Isid., Etym., v. 6.

[2] Hermog., in Dig., i. 1. 5 : "Ex hoc jure gentium introducta bella, discretæ gentes, regna condita, dominia distincta, agris termini positi, ædificia collocata, commercium, emptiones venditiones, locationes conductiones, obligationes institutæ : exceptis quibusdam quæ jure civili introductæ sunt." Inst., i. 2. 2 : "Jus autem gentium omni humano generi commune est. Nam usu exigente et humanis necessitatibus gentes humanæ quædam sibi constituerunt : bella etenim orta sunt, et

captivitates secutæ et servitutes, quæ sunt juri naturali contrariæ. Jure enim naturali ab initio omnes homines liberi nascebantur. Ex hoc jure gentium et omnes pæne contractus introducti sunt, ut emptio venditio, locatio conductio, societas, depositum, mutuum et alii innumerabiles."

[3] St Isid., Etym., v. 5.

[4] Gaius, i. 1 : "Nam quod quisque populus ipse sibi jus constituit, id ipsius proprium est, vocaturque 'jus civile,' quasi jus proprium civitatis." Cf. Inst., i. 2. 1.

Institutes of Justinian. With his work the conception passes into the common stock of mediæval tradition on political theory. The distinction would, however, have had little or no meaning if it had not been closely connected with that theory of the natural condition, or state of nature, the state antecedent to the conventional institutions of society, which we have already studied in Seneca, and whose influence we have recognised in the lawyers. We must examine this theory as it is exhibited to us in the Fathers, but we shall find it best to approach the subject by considering their theory of human nature and human institutions. We shall find that there is continually implied in this a reference to a condition of life precedent to and other than that which now exists. We shall see that the conception of the state of nature is in the Fathers identified with the conception of the condition of mankind in the unfallen state.

CHAPTER X.

NATURAL EQUALITY AND SLAVERY.

WE have seen that in the New Testament writings we find a conception of human nature which is very clear and distinct as to the essential and inherent equality of mankind; we find that in the teaching of our Lord Himself men are regarded as all equally the children of God, and that in St Paul's writings we have the more technical expression of this conception as signifying the capacity of all men for the spiritual and moral life. Whether a man is slave or free he is still capable of the same moral and spiritual life, capable of knowing God and serving Him. If he is a slave he must be treated fairly and reasonably by his master, who is no dearer to God than is the slave.

This conception is carried on with eloquence and force in the writings of the early Fathers—is indeed implied in all that they say. We may refer to one or two passages which deal with the matter directly: the first is in the little work known as the 'Octavius,' written by Minucius Felix. He says that all men, without difference of age, sex, or rank, are begotten with a capacity and power of reason and feeling, and obtain wisdom, not by fortune, but by nature.[1] It is interesting to observe how close these phrases, in spite of certain differences, are to those of Cicero and Seneca; indeed it might be difficult to say whether the author derives his method of expression from the New Testament or from the philosophers. Another passage is contained in Lactantius's work, the 'Divine Institutes.' He is discussing the nature of justice, and after having given the first place in the conception of this to *pietas* he goes on to urge

[1] Octavius, xvi.

that the second part of justice is *æquitas*—that is, the temper which teaches a man to put himself on an equality with his fellow-men, the quality which Lactantius says Cicero had called *æquabilitas*. God, who brings forth and inspires men, wished them all to be equal. He made them all for virtue, promised them all immortality. No one, in God's sight, is a slave or a master; He is the Father of all men, we are all therefore His children. Lactantius finds fault with Roman and Greek institutions as not recognising these principles of equality sufficiently, but it does not appear that he is really attacking the institutions so much as what he considers the wrong temper with which men regard these institutions; for when he considers the objection which some one might make, that the same differences of rank and condition exist also among Christian people, he replies not by denying that the differences exist, nor by condemning their existence, but by urging that Christian people do really recognise each other as brothers and equals, that they estimate all things by their spiritual and not by their material value.[1]

Lactantius's phrases are well-meaning and no doubt sincere, but they scarcely justify his attempt to censure the Greek and Roman spirit, and his somewhat inexcusable forgetfulness of the fact that writers like Cicero and Seneca had taken up much the same position towards the inequalities of human condition as his own. Lactantius does not really condemn the existence of the great inequalities of society, only he wishes them to be corrected by the sense of the fundamental equality of human nature, just as Seneca had done.

In the later Fathers this conception of the intrinsic and primitive equality of human nature is discussed with much fulness, but almost always in direct connection with the treatment of the institution of slavery: they assert that this equality is primitive, and also that in some sense it always continues, while they also develop with great clearness a theory which is to account for the existence of this unprimitive and, in one sense, unnatural institution of slavery.

We do not know that any passage in the writings of the Fathers represents the general character of their theory better

[1] Lact., Div. Inst., v. 15 and 16.

than a discussion of the subject by "Ambrosiaster," in his commentary on St Paul's Epistle to the Colossians. He begins by warning masters lest they be puffed up with pride and forget that God made, not slaves and free men, but all men free. Slavery is the consequence of man's sin; man, making war upon his fellow-man, makes captives, and chance determines whether these are to remain slaves or to be redeemed. Before God the sinner is the slave; Ham is an example of this, and the ancient writers who maintain that the wise were free and the foolish slaves, really recognised this principle. Masters must remember that their lordship extends only over the body; they have no authority over the soul, God only is the master of that: let them remember this, and only exact just service from their slaves, who are still their equals, not to say their brethren.[1]

It will be noticed that there are really four distinct propositions with regard to human nature and slavery contained in this passage. First, that men as God made them were free; second, that this still continues in some sense, the condition of slavery is very largely one determined by fortune, and this condition does not extend beyond the body; thirdly, that slavery is the result of man's sin and sinfulness, the true slavery is that of the soul, for the foolish are the true slaves;

---

[1] Ambrosiaster, Com. on Coloss. iv. 1: "'Domini quod justum est et æquum servis præbete, scientes quod et vos dominum habetis in cœlis.' Ne domini temporales superbia extollantur, præsumentes de dominatu, mitigat et cohibet animos illorum, ut adhibita consideratione humani generis animadvertant auctorem Deum non servos et liberos sed omnes ingenuos condidisse. Sed hoc mundi iniquitate factum est, ut dum alter alterius fines invadit tunc captivos ducit ingenuos; unde et manu capti dicti sunt a veteribus inde mancipia. Hic casus et conditio etiam nunc apparet; alii redimuntur, alii remanent servi; apud Deum autem hic servus habetur qui peccaverit. Denique peccati causa, Cham servus audivit: 'Maledictus puer Chanaam, servus servorum erit fratribus suis.' Cui sententiæ veteres assensere, ita ut definirent omnes prudentes esse liberos, stultos autem omnes esse servos. . . . Ostendit ergo dominis, quia non vere sunt domini sed quasi per imaginem; corporum enim non animorum sunt domini. Solus enim dominus, et auctor rerum invisibilis Deus, tam corporibus quam animis dominatur: ut hæc considerantes justa ab eis exigant servitia: talia utique qualia et a se exigi volunt a Domino communi. Nam cum ipsi non ut dignum est, Deo serviant, quem non negant omnium potestatem habere, cujusque quotidiana dona per ministeria creaturæ humanis usibus exhiberi, a paribus suis (ut non dicam fratribus) tam gravia exigunt servitia, ut ferri non possint: non ponentes in animo, quia et ipsi velint nolint, servi sunt; et viderint cujus meriti."

fourthly, that masters must treat their slaves with consideration and forbearance.   All these points can be amply illustrated
from the works of the Fathers.

All the Fathers maintain that in their original nature men
were free and equal.   Salvian speaks of that human nature
and condition which makes masters and slaves equal.[1]   St
Augustine, in a very notable passage, to which we shall have
to return, lays it down that God did not make rational man
to lord it over his rational fellows, but only to be master of
the irrational creatures, and that no one in that nature in
which God first made man is the slave either of man or of sin.
In the original order of things men would have been free and
equal.[2]   Gregory the Great insists upon the same conception.
Masters are admonished that they should remember that their
slaves are of the same nature as themselves, lest they should
cease to recognise that those whom they hold in bondage are
equal with them, through their share in one common nature.[3]
In a passage in his work on Job, a passage which is frequently referred to in mediæval literature, and some of whose
phrases have become almost classical, Gregory admonishes great
men to remember that by nature we are all equal, that nature
brought forth all men equal, that it is only by a secret
dispensation of God that some men are set over or are inferior
to others.[4]   St Gregory's phrase, " Omnes namque natura
æquales sumus," is strictly parallel to Ulpian's " Quod ad jus
naturale attinet, omnes homines æquales sunt."   We have just
seen how St Isidore of Seville says that under the natural law
there is " omnium una libertas."[5]

[1] Salvian, De Gubernatione Dei, iii.
28.

[2] St Aug., De Civ. Dei, xix. 15.

[3] Gregory the Great, Liber Pastoralis Curæ, Part iii. 5.

[4] Gregory the Great, Expositio
Moralis in Beatum Job, xxi. 15:
"Potentibus viris magna est virtus
humilitatis, considerata æqualitas conditionis.   Omnes namque homines
natura æquales sumus, sed accessit
dispensatorio ordine, ut quibusdam
prælati videamur. . . . Si enim apud

semetipsam mens descendit de vertice
culminis, citius planitiem invenit naturalis æqualitatis.   Nam ut præfati
sumus, omnes homines natura æquales
genuit, sed variante meritorum ordine,
alios aliis dispensatio occulta postponit.
. . . Sancti autem viri cum præsunt,
non in se potestatem ordinis, sed æqualitatem conditionis attendunt, nec
præesse gaudent hominibus, sed prodesse."

[5] St Isidore of Seville, Etym., v. 4.
See p. 108.

But, further, this equality is not a thing wholly of the past: the inequalities of condition and life only affect the body, they have no relation to the mind and soul. The slave, St Ambrose says, may be the superior, in character, of his master; no condition of life is incapable of virtue, the flesh can be enslaved, the mind is free. The slave may really be more free than the master. It is sin which renders a man truly a slave, innocence is free. He is free under any outward form of slavery who is not governed by the love of the world, by avarice, by fear. The free man is he who can look out with confidence on his actual life and for whom the future has no terrors.[1] St Ambrose's words remind us very forcibly of those of Seneca, and indeed so far the theories we are considering do not seem essentially to differ from those with which we have already dealt. But they are reinforced by the emphatic assertion that in Christ we are all one. St Ambrose in another treatise puts this very forcibly. Neither family nor rank affect the true position of men. Slaves or freemen, we are all one in Christ; slavery can take nothing from man's character, nor can freedom add anything to it.[2] This is expressed in another and perhaps more technical fashion by the author of one of the sermons attributed to St Augustine, who protests against the harsh treatment of Christian slaves by Christian

[1] St Ambrose, De Joseph Patriarcha, iv.: "Cæterum quod ad moralem pertinet locum, quia omnes vult salvos fieri Dominus Deus noster, dedit per Joseph etiam iis qui sunt in servitute solatium: attribuit magisterium; ut discerent etiam in ultima conditione posse mores esse superiores, nec ullum statum immunem esse virtutis, si animus se uniuscujusque cognoscat; carnem servituti subditam esse, non mentem, multosque servulos esse dominis liberiores, si in servitute positi a servilibus putent operibus abstinendum. Servile est omne peccatum, libera est innocentia. Unde et Dominus ait: Omnis qui facit peccatum, servus est peccati. . . . Ille vero in quavis conditione servitii semper liber, qui mundi amore non capitur, avaritiæ vinculis non tenetur, metu criminis non alligatur, qui securus spectat præsentia, quem futura non terrent."

[2] St Ambrose, Exhortatio Virginitatis, i. 3: "Nullum ergo ad commendationem hominis condicio affert impedimentum; nec dignitas prosapiæ meritum, sed fides affert. Sive servus, sive liber, omnes in Christo unum sumus. . . . Nec servitus derogat nec libertas adjuvat. . . . Apud Christum enim servitus et libertas æqua lance penduntur, nec ullo discerniculo bonæ servitutis et libertatis merita dividuntur: quia nulla major est dignitas quam servire Christo."

masters, and upbraids them for not considering that the slave is their brother by grace, has equally with them put on Christ, partakes of the same sacraments, has the same Father, God, and should find in his master a brother.[1]   These Christian conceptions do not perhaps add anything in strict theory to the philosophic conception of the equality of man's nature, but they represent to us a mode of apprehending this which has probably had a very great and continuous influence on the development of the practical consequences of this theory of human nature.

Man, then, as God made him was free and equal. The subjection of man to man is something which belongs not to his original nature but to his present condition; and more than that, this equality and freedom is in one sense indestructible and inalienable: even now, though his body may be in subjection, his mind and soul are free, he is still capable of reason and virtue, he may even now be superior to the man to whom he is enslaved, and in his relation to God all differences of condition are meaningless. Men, whether slaves or freemen, are called to one common life in Christ and God, called to know God as the common Father and to hold each other as brethren. We may stay for a moment to notice once again how far we have travelled from the Aristotelian mode of thought, how clearly we are in presence of what we may call the modern conception, the fundamental idea upon which the modern democratic theory of society depends. The Christian Fathers are clearly restating in their own fashion the same conceptions as those which we already met with in Cicero, in Seneca, and in the lawyers.

But slavery is not, in the judgment of the Christian Fathers, unlawful or improper: they recognise its existence, they acquiesce in its presence, and they furnish a complete theory of its origin and a new justification of its continuance. Slavery, they say, had no place in the primitive condition of life; man, as God

---

[1] Pseudo Augustine, Sermones, cxlvi. 3: "Et quod magis dolendem est, christianus dominus christiano in his diebus servo non parcit, minime respiciens quod etsi servus est conditione, gratia tamen frater est. Etenim similiter Christum induit, iisdem participat sacramentis, eodem quo et tu, utitur Deo Patre; cur te non utatur ut fratre?"

created him, was not made to be either the slave or the lord of his fellow-man; but, they add, man has long ago passed out of that primitive condition, and lives now under other circumstances. He was once innocent and harmless, now he is vicious and inclined to attack and injure his fellow-man. Under the primitive conditions, he needed no coercive discipline to train him to goodness and to restrain his evil desires; he lived in freedom, and under conditions of equality, for he had no tendency to abuse his freedom to the injury of his neighbours, and therefore he did not need to be under the domination of his fellow-man, lest he should do wrong.

The Fathers conceive of the state of man before the Fall much as Seneca conceives of the Golden Age,[1] and they account for the disappearance of the primitive conditions of that age by the theory of the Fall. By the Fall man passed out of the state of nature into the state in which the conventional institutions of society are necessary. Slavery did not exist in the state of nature when men were free, and in some very large sense equal. But the Fall brought with it the need of new conditions, of a new discipline, by which the new and evil tendencies of human nature should be corrected. Slavery is a consequence of the coming of sin into the world, and is also a disciplinary system by which the sinful tendencies of man may be corrected.

We have already seen how this conception is stated by "Ambrosiaster." In general terms he puts the universal theory of the Fathers, that slavery came into the world with sin. This conception is drawn out with greater completeness by St Augustine, St Ambrose, and St Isidore of Seville. The passage to which we have already referred in the 'De Civitate Dei,' as illustrating the conception of the equality and primitive liberty of mankind, also contains one of the best statements of the patristic theory of the origin and rationale of slavery.[2]

---

[1] See p. 23.

[2] De Civ. Dei, xix. 15 : "Rationalem factum ad imaginem suam noluit (Deus) nisi irrationabilibus dominari; non hominem homini, sed hominem pecori. Inde primi justi pastores pecorum magis quam reges hominum constituti sunt, ut etiam sic insinuaret Deus quid postulet ordo creaturarum, quid exigat meritum peccatorum. Condicio quippe servitutis jure intellegitur imposita peccatori. Proinde nusquam scripturarum legimus

Man, who was made in the image of God, and endowed with reason, was made to be the lord of all irrational creatures, but not of his fellow-men. Slavery has been imposed by the just sentence of God upon the sinner: it is a consequence not of man's nature but of man's sinfulness; by nature man is the slave neither of sin nor of his fellow-man. Slavery is intended to preserve the true order of life, which is threatened with destruction by sin. St Augustine looks upon slavery partly as a punishment of sin, but also as a remedy for sin, as one of those institutions, unnatural in one sense, as being contrary to the primitive conditions of human nature, but necessary under the actual circumstances of society. St Ambrose urges more than once that sin and vice and ignorance do in themselves make a man a slave. Sin is always servile, innocence alone is free. "Every one who commits sin is a slave of sin."[1] It is really better for a vicious man to be a slave; a man who cannot rule himself is better under the authority of a wise man. When Isaac put Esau into subjection to Jacob, he was really conferring upon him a benefit.[2] The same conception is drawn out with precision and clearness by St Isidore of Seville. Slavery is a punishment for sin, but a remedial punishment; it is intended

---

servum, antequam hoc vocabulo Noe justus peccatum filii vindicaret. Nomen itaque istud culpa meruit, non natura. . . . Prima ergo servitutis causa peccatum est, ut homo homini condicionis vinculo subderetur; quod non fit nisi Deo judicante, apud quem non est iniquitas et novit diversas pœnas meritis distribuere delinquentium. Sicut autem supernus Dominus dicit: 'Omnis qui facit peccatum, servus est peccati.' Ac per hoc multi quidem religiosi dominis iniquis non tamen liberis serviunt: 'A quo enim quis devictus est, huic et servus addictus est.' Et utique felicius servitur homini quam libidini, cum sævissimo dominatu vastet corda mortalium, ut alias omittam, libido ipsa dominandi. Hominibus autem illo pacis ordine, quo aliis alii subjecti sunt, sicut prodest humilitas servientibus, ita nocet superbia dominantibus. Nullus autem

natura, in qua prius Deus hominem condidit, servus est hominis aut peccati. Verum et pœnalis servitus ea lege ordinatur, quæ naturalem ordinem conservare jubet, perturbari vetat; quia si contra eam legem non esset factum, nihil esset pœnali servitute cohercendum. Ideoque apostolus etiam servos monet subditos esse dominis suis et ex animo eis cum bona voluntate servire; ut scilicet, si non possunt a dominis liberi fieri, suam servitutem ipsi quodam modo liberam faciant, non timore subdolo, sed fideli dilectione serviendo, donec transeat iniquitas et evacuetur omnis principatus et potestas humana et sit Deus omnia in omnibus."

[1] St Ambrose, De Joseph Patriarcha, iv. See p. 115, note 1.

[2] St Ambrose, Ep. xxxvii., and Ep. lxxvii. 6.

to correct the evil tendencies of original sin in human nature. It is necessary that the evil dispositions of some men should be restrained by terror, and yet God is equally careful for men whether they are slaves or free, and it may chance that a good man may be enslaved to an evil master while he is really his superior.[1] St Isidore seems to mean that slavery is one of those disciplinary institutions which are necessary under the actual conditions of human nature, which do, in the general, tend to correct the result of men's depravity, though he is evidently compelled to recognise that the dispensation of Providence is not always adjusted correctly to the individual case.

This theory of the Fathers deserves careful attention. We have seen that they use phrases which illustrate the sincere conviction with which they, like the later philosophers and the lawyers, maintained the natural equality and liberty of mankind. Clearly they all continue to hold firmly to the view that human nature is fundamentally equal, that there is no reality in such a distinction as that which Aristotle had made between the naturally free man and the man who was naturally a slave. Men are all possessed of reason and capable of virtue; they are all the children of God. But it is also quite clear that the Christian writers were no more prepared to condemn the actual institution of slavery as unlawful than were the jurists or the philosophers. In the writings of the jurists we have

[1] St Isidore of Seville, Sententiæ, iii. 47: "Propter peccatum primi hominis humano generi pœna divinitus illata est servitutis ita ut quibus aspicit non congruere libertatem, his misericordius irroget servitutem. Et licet peccatum humanæ originis per baptismi gratiam cunctis fidelibus dimissum sit, tamen æquus Deus ideo discrevit hominibus vitam, alios servos constituens, alios dominos, ut licentia male agendi servorum, potestate dominantium restringatur. Nam si omnes sine metu fuissent, quis esset qui a malis quemquam prohibeat. Inde et in gentibus principes regesque electi sunt, ut terr-ore suo populos a malo coercerent, atque ad recte vivendum legibus subderent. Quantum attinet ad rationem "non est personarum acceptio apud Deum," qui mundi elegit ignobilia et contemptibilia, et quæ non sunt ut ea quæ sunt destrueret : ne glorietur omnis caro, hoc est carnalis potentia coram illo. Unus enim Dominus æqualiter et dominis fert consultum et servis. Melior est subjecta servitus quam elata libertas. Multi enim inveniuntur Deo libere servientes sub dominis constituti flagitiosis, qui et si subjecti sunt illis corpore, prælati tamen sunt mente."

the apparent contradiction stated, without explanation, that slavery is contrary to nature and yet that it exists. Seneca, at least, among the philosophers, suggests an explanation of the apparent contradiction.   Institutions which were not necessary in the age of innocence became necessary as men's vices increased.   The Fathers, bringing to their consideration of society a dogmatic theory of the Fall, are able to apply the same considerations as those which Seneca urges, with completeness and coherence. Had Adam not sinned and brought sin into human nature such an institution as slavery would have been unnecessary ; but the Fall, in bringing corruption into the world, made necessary institutions which should correct and control the sinfulness of human nature.

Here we have the explanation of what at first sight seems a paradoxical contradiction between the principles of the natural law and the actual conditions of human life.   The later Roman jurists had looked upon the natural law as divine and unchangeable,[1] and, almost in the same breath, had spoken of slavery as an institution actually existing and yet contrary to the natural law.   Directly at least they suggest no explanation of the apparent contradiction.   Seneca had suggested, and the Fathers developed completely, an explanation which was in its own way profound and philosophical.   The law of nature in its completeness is only adapted to the state of nature.   In the condition of innocence and simplicity men needed no coercion to make them obey the principles of this law.   But once this innocence had disappeared man needed discipline and coercion to make him obey even the more general principles of justice and right, and hence much which is contrary to nature in the primitive condition is necessary in the actual condition of human life.

Slavery is then, in the view of the Fathers, a lawful institution, and they constantly urge upon the slave the duty of obedience and submission.   St Ambrose, after admonishing masters to remember that they are of the same nature as their slaves, bids the slaves serve their masters with good will ; a man must patiently accept the condition in which he is born,

[1] Inst., i. 2. 11.

and must obey harsh as well as good masters.[1] St Augustine, in one interesting passage which is also of some importance in connection with the theory of government, argues that Christ makes good slaves of bad ones; that, when they turn to Him, He teaches them, not that it is improper that the righteous should serve the wicked, but rather that slaves should follow His example in rendering service.[2] In another place, with still greater emphasis, he repudiates the notion that the precedent of the liberation of the Hebrew slaves in every seventh year might be applied to the case of the Christian slave: the apostle, he says, had admonished slaves to obey their masters, lest Christian slaves should demand such a manumission.[3] The author of one of the sermons attributed to St Augustine puts the matter very forcibly when he bids the slaves love and obey their masters from the heart, because it is God who has made these to be masters and the others to be their servants.[4] But perhaps the most emphatic assertion of the propriety of slavery is to be found in one of the canons of the Council of Gangræ, held in the year 362. In the third canon the anathema of the Church is laid upon any one who under the pretence of godliness should teach a slave to despise his master, or to withdraw himself from his service.[5]

The Church, then, so far from repudiating the institution of slavery, accepted the fact, and framed its own canonical regulations in accordance with it. The history of the canonical

---

[1] St Ambrose, Ep. lxiii. 112: "Domini servis imperate non quasi conditione subditis, sed ita ut naturæ ejusdem cujus vos estis, consortes eis esse memineritis. Servi quoque dominis servite cum voluntate; etenim unusquisque quod natus est, patienter debet suscipere: nec solum bonis, sed etiam asperis obedite dominis.

[2] St Aug., Enarr. in Ps. cxxiv. 3.

[3] St Aug., Quæstionum in Hept. ii. 77: "Quæ de servo Hebræo præcipiuntur, ut sex annos serviat, et dimittatur liber gratis, ne servi Christiani hoc flagitarent a dominis suis,

apostolica auctoritas jubet servos dominis suis esse subditos, ne nomen Dei et doctrina blasphemetur."

[4] Pseudo Augustine, Sermone, cxvii. 12: "Obedite (servi) dominis vestris, diligite ex corde, non ad oculum servientes, sed ministerium ex amore facientes; quia et illos Deus constituit ut vobis dominentur, et vos ut serviatis."

[5] Concilium Gangrense, Canon iii.: Εἴ τις δοῦλον προφάσει θεοσεβείας διδάσκοι καταφρονεῖν δεσπότου, καὶ ἀναχωρεῖν τῆς ὑπηρεσίας καὶ μὴ μετ' εὐνοίας καὶ πάσης τιμῆς τῷ ἑαυτοῦ δεσπότῃ ἐξυπηρετεῖσθαι, ἀνάθεμα ἔστω.

and secular legislation with regard to the slave who entered a
monastery, or procured ordination, is long and intricate, and it
is not necessary here to deal with it in detail; still some
points in this should be observed. At an early date it had
become the Church rule that a slave could not be ordained
unless he were first set at liberty. St Leo expressly prohibits
this,[1] and a little later the matter is treated with considerable
detail by Pope Gelasius I. In one of his letters he orders
a certain bishop to restore a slave, who had been made a
"clericus," to his mistress; but with regard to another slave
who had been ordained to the priesthood he orders that he
should be sent back to his mistress, not as a slave but as
a priest at the church on her estates.[2] In another letter he
forbids the reception of any slave into a monastery without
the permission of his master.[3] This does not, however, represent the universal character of Christian legislation on the
subject. In Justinian's fifth Novel the question of the entrance
of slaves into monasteries is handled in a somewhat different
spirit. Justinian prefaces his judgment on the subject by
the recognition of the fact that the divine grace makes no
distinction with regard to human conditions; that in the
worship of God all distinctions of male or female, slave or
free, disappear; and he goes on to lay it down that every one,
whether free or a slave, must undergo a probation of three
years before being accepted as a monk. If within that time
a master come to reclaim his slave, and can prove that the
slave had stolen something, or had committed a crime of

---

[1] St Leo, Ep. iv. Cf. Canones Apost.,
81, and Concil. Tolet., iv. 19, 73, 74.

[2] St Gelasius I., Ep. xxi. : "Nuper
etenim actores illustris feminæ Placidiæ
petitorii oblatione conquesti sunt,
Sabinum Marcellianensis sive Casilinatis
urbis Antiochum servum juris patronæ
suæ, absentis dominæ occasione captata,
ad presbyterii honorem usque produc-
tum, ejusque fratrem Leontium cleri-
calis officii privilegio decorasse. Et ideo,
fratres carissimi, inter supradictos
actores et eos, qui conditionis extremæ
repetuntur, objectam cognitionem vobis

nostra auctoritate deputamus : et omni
veritate discussa, si revera objectam sibi
maculam justitiæ refragationis non
potuerit ratione diluere, Leontium
clericum, quem gradus præfinitus legibus non defendit, ad sequendam cognationis suæ necessitatem modis omnibus redhibete. Antiochum vero, quia
propter sacerdotium non jam potest
retolli, si in suam ecclesiam in hoc, in
quo est, honore desiderat collocare, non
veluti redditum sibi, sed habeat pro
mysteriorum celebratione susceptum."

[3] St Gelasius I., Ep. xiv. 4.

some kind, and had therefore fled to the monastery, the slave is to be restored to him, on the promise that he will not injure him. But if he cannot prove the charge, the slave is not to be surrendered to him, even if the master's demand is made within the three years : after that, no demand can be made even on the ground of any crime committed by the slave before his coming to the monastery. Only, if the slave leave the monastery to return to the secular life, then the master can reclaim him.[1] We shall have to recur to this question of the position of the slave or serf with respect to ordination or entering a monastery in later chapters. We here refer to the matter only as illustrating the fact that the Christian Church acquiesced in the institution of slavery, and even formed its own internal regulations in accordance with the fact.

Slavery, then, in the judgment of the Fathers, is a legitimate and useful institution. But the Fathers are very careful to urge upon the masters that they must show their slaves consideration and kindness, and even that they are responsible for the spiritual welfare of their slaves. St Augustine urges upon the masters of slaves that while with respect to temporal matters they may well distinguish between their children and their slaves, with regard to the worship of God they should take equal thought for both : the true Pater familias will try to bring up his whole household in the service of God.[2] St Gregory the Great, in a letter addressed to the nobles and proprietors of Sardinia, warns them that they will have to give account to God for all those who are in subjection to them ; it is true that these are to serve the temporal interests of their lords, but the lords are responsible for their eternal wellbeing.[3]

We must not be understood to be discussing the question of the complete influence of Christianity on ancient slavery : our work here is concerned with the theory of the subject. So far as we should venture an opinion on this matter, we should say that Christianity was one of the many influences which were gradually tending to bring the slavery of the ancient world to an end. It would appear evident that the

[1] Novel v. 2.   [2] De Civ. Dei, xix. 16.   [3] St Gregory the Great, Ep. iv. 23.

influence of Christianity tended to promote the mitigation of the hardships of slavery, not only by its exhortations to the master to remember that the slave was his brother, but also by promoting legislation for the protection of the slave and by actually encouraging manumission.   The laws of the Christian Emperors carry on from the older legislation, and seem to develop further, regulations for the protection of slave women and children from prostitution[1] and exposure,[2] and it is very noticeable that one of the earliest laws enacted by Constantine after his conversion was that by which it was permitted to perform the ceremony of manumission in the Christian Churches.[3]   The theory of the Church may have looked upon slavery as legitimate, but it is clear enough that the practical influence of the Church was in favour of manumission.   In later centuries we find references to the manumission of slaves which imply that this was considered to be a pious work, likely to profit the souls of the persons who perform it.[4]   We do not doubt that the general influence of the Church tended towards the mitigation of the hardships of slavery, and even towards the disappearance of the institution.   But the more clearly we may recognise this the more necessary is it to recognise also that the theory of the Church is somewhat different: we think that it must be admitted that the influence of the theory may have had considerable effect both in defending the actually existing slavery of the ancient world, and in assisting in its revival in the fifteenth century when Europeans came into contact with the negro races.

[1] Cod. i. 4. 12, 14, vi. 4. 4. 2.
[2] Cod. i. 4. 24.
[3] Cod. i. 13. 1 and 2.   Cf. Cod. Eccl.

Africanæ, 64 and 82.
[4] Cf. the "Formulæ" of Marculfus, xxxii. and xxxiv.

CHAPTER XI.

NATURAL EQUALITY AND GOVERNMENT.

IN dealing with the question of slavery we have anticipated a good deal of what we have to say about the relation of the theory of natural equality to the theory of organised society and government. That natural equality which is, in the judgment of the Fathers, contrary to slavery, is also contrary to the subjection of man to man in government.

The Fathers maintain that man is made for society, that he is by nature sociable and inclined to love his fellow-men. Lactantius, in commenting on a passage from Cicero's De Republica, which we have already discussed, denies that they were ever apart.[1] It is indeed possible that Lactantius is a little confused in his judgment of human nature. In another place he seems to mean that man does indeed desire society, but it is on account of the weakness of his body, which makes him incapable of defending himself in solitude.[2] Still, even so, he maintains that men are by nature driven to the social life. A clearer conception is very forcibly stated by St Augustine in several passages. Human nature is, he says, sociable, and men are held together by the bond of kinship.[3] He approves of the conception that the life of the wise man is a social life.[4] Man, he says, is driven by the very laws of his nature to enter into society and to make peace with

---

[1] Lact., Div. Inst., vi. 10.

[2] Lact., De Opificio Dei, iv.

[3] St Aug., De Bono Conjugali, i.: "Quoniam unusquisque homo humani generis pars est, et sociale quiddam est humana natura, magnumque habet et naturale bonum, vim quoque amicitiæ; ob hoc ex uno Deus voluit omnes homines condere, ut in sua societate non sola similitudine generis, sed etiam cognationis vinculo tenerentur."

[4] St Aug., De Civ., xix. 5.

men.[1] It is of some importance to observe this judgment, for, as we have already said, it must be remembered that ancient philosophy had spoken with a twofold voice on the matter. The Epicurean had plainly tended to think of political life as at the most a necessity, perhaps an unfortunate necessity, arising from the infirmities of human nature, while the conception of the obligation of political life even for the wise man had been carried on by the Stoics, although, as we have already seen, it requires a little care to recognise how emphatically they held this. Lactantius may perhaps waver between two opinions, perhaps scarcely recognising the significance of the question; but St Augustine, at least, is clear in his judgment, and he is, as far as we see, the representative of the normal type of thought of Christian writers.

Man is by nature made for society. But it is not by nature that man is the lord of man, it is not by nature that man is in subjection to man. We must recur again to that most important treatment of the question by St Augustine, to which we have already referred in dealing with slavery. God made rational beings in His own image, not to be lords over each other, but to be lords of the irrational creatures; the primitive good men were rather shepherds of their flocks than kings of men.[2] The government of man by man is not part of the natural order of the world. In another place St Augustine speaks in the severest terms of the desire of domination, and treats it as arising from an intolerable pride which forgets that men are each other's equals.[3] Gregory the Great represents precisely the

[1] St Aug., De Civ., xix. 12: "Quanto magis homo fertur quodam modo naturæ suæ legibus ad ineundam societatem pacemque cum hominibus, quantum in ipso est, omnibus obtenendum."

[2] St Aug., De Civ., xix. 15: "Rationalem factum ad imaginem suam noluit nisi irrationalibus dominari : non hominem homini, sed hominem pecori. Inde primi justi pastores pecorum magis quam reges hominum constituti sunt, ut etiam sic insinuaret Deus, quid postulet ordo creaturarum, quid exigat meritum peccatorum."

[3] St Aug., De Doctr. Christ., i. 23: "Magnum autem aliquid adeptum se putat, si etiam sociis, id est aliis hominibus, dominari potuerit. Inest enim vitioso animo id magis appetere, et sibi tanquam debitum vindicare, quod uni proprie debetur Deo. . . . Cum vero etiam eis qui sibi naturaliter pares sunt, hoc est, hominibus, dominari appetat, intolerabilis animi superbia est."

same attitude towards the primitive order of human life. In the passage already quoted in relation to slavery, he points out the immense profit that great men will derive from the consideration of the equality of human nature, the great benefit they will gain if they will recollect that in the beginning man was set over the other animals, not over his fellow-man.[1] It is probable that Gregory the Great is here following St Augustine, but the general source of the theory can hardly be mistaken : it is that same Stoic theory of a primitive state in which the conventional institutions of society did not yet exist, of which we have already spoken so often. The primitive state of man was to these Fathers, as it had been to the Stoics like Posidonius and Seneca, a state without any coercive government : in the state of nature men did not need this.

It must be noticed that, at least in St Gregory the Great, this does not mean that in the state of innocence there was no order of society or distinction of authority. In a letter addressed to the bishops of the kingdom of Childebert, in ratifying the authority of Virgilius, the Bishop of Arles, as representing the Roman See, St Gregory urges that some system of authority is necessary in every society—that even the angels, although they are free from sin, are yet ordered in a hierarchy of greater and less.[2] St Gregory's conception is very similar

---

[1] St Gregory the Great, Exp. Mor. in Job, xxi. 15 : "Sancti autem viri cum praesunt, non in se potestatem ordinis sed aequalitatem conditionis attendunt, nec praeesse gaudent hominibus sed prodesse. Sciunt enim quod antiqui patres nostri non tam reges hominum quam pastores pecorum memorantur. . . . Homo quippe animalibus irrationabilibus, non autem ceteris hominibus natura praelatus est." Cf. xxiv. 25.

[2] St Gregory the Great, Ep. v. 59 : "Ad hoc dispensationis divinae provisio gradus diversos et ordines constituit esse distinctos, ut, dum reverentiam minores potioribus exhiberent et potiores minoribus dilectionem impender-

ent, una concordiae fieret ex diversitate contextio et recte officiorum gereretur administratio singulorum. Neque enim universitas alia poterat ratione subsistere, nisi hujusmodi magnus eam differentiae ordo servaret. Quia vero creatura in una eademque aequalitate gubernari vel vivere non potest, caelestium militiarum exemplar nos instruit, quia dum sunt angeli, et sunt archangeli, liquet, quia non aequales sunt, sed in potestate et ordine, sicut nostris, differt alter ab altero. Si ergo inter hos qui sine peccato sunt ista constat esse distinctio, quis hominum abnuat huic se libenter dispositioni submittere, cui novit etiam angelos obedire ?"

to that of Seneca and Posidonius, who, while they think that there was no organised coercive government in the primitive age, think that in that time men freely obeyed the wise.

To return, it seems clear that both St Augustine and St Gregory look upon the institution of coercive government as not belonging to the primitive state of man; they do not think that government of this kind is a natural institution; but this does not mean that the Fathers look upon the ordered government of society among men as they actually are, as a thing improper or illegitimate. We have already, in considering their attitude to the institution of slavery, recognised that they conceive of the conditions proper to human life as having been completely altered by the entrance of sin into the world. Slavery was contrary to the natural law of the primitive condition of human innocence, but is proper and even useful under the actual conditions of human nature. It is the same with the institution of government. Coercive government has been made necessary through sin, and is a divinely appointed remedy for sin.

It is interesting to find this conception developed by the Christian writers from a very early date. We have already considered St Paul's treatment of the institution of government and the sanctity which belongs to it. He affirms its sanctity and explains this as arising from the fact that its purpose is to repress the evil and to reward the good. St Clement of Rome, in the great liturgical prayer which forms a concluding part of his letter, does not go beyond St Paul's conception of the sanctity of government: he prays to God for the rulers of mankind, as those to whom God has given authority and glory, that God will give them wisdom.[1]

Towards the end of the second century we have in the writings of St Irenæus a detailed discussion of the origin of government, of the circumstances which have made it necessary, and of the purpose which it is intended to serve. The passage occurs with that apparent irrelevance which is so characteristic of the writings of the Fathers, in a discussion of the mendacity of the devil. Irenæus begins by asserting

[1] St Clement of Rome, 61.

that the devil was, as always, a liar, when in the temptation he said to our Lord that all the kingdoms of the earth were his, to give to whom he would. It is not the devil at all, Irenæus says, who has appointed the kingdoms of the world, but God, and he establishes this by a reference to the passage in the Proverbs, "By me kings reign and princes administer justice," and the saying of St Paul, already discussed (Rom. xiii. 1, &c.) Authority came from God, not from the devil. So far we have nothing new; but Irenæus then proceeds to discuss the causes which made government necessary, and urges that this is due to the fact that men departed from God and hated their fellow-men, and fell into confusion and disorder of every kind, and so God set men over each other, imposing the fear of man upon men, and subjecting men to the authority of men, that by this means they might be compelled to some measure of righteousness and just dealing.[1] We have here an explicit statement that the institution of government has been made necessary by sin and is a divinely appointed remedy for sin.

The Christian writers of the same period as Irenæus do not indeed draw out the relation of government to the existence of evil, as Irenæus has done, but they agree with him in asserting its divine origin. Justin Martyr lays great stress upon the fact that Christians had been taught by Christ Himself to pay taxes to the ruler, to "render to Cæsar the things which are Cæsar's," and urges that, while Christians can only worship God, in all other ways they gladly serve their rulers.[2] Theophilus of Antioch, another writer of the second century, while also refusing to worship the king, says that he should be honoured and obeyed, for at least in some sense it may be said of him that he has received his authority from God.[3] No doubt these emphatic assertions of the divine authority of the ruler, while they may have been partly intended to allay any suspicions of disloyalty, were also intended to counteract those tendencies to anarchy in the Christian societies, to whose existence the New Testament bears witness. The Christian writers of the second century, then, clearly carry on the tradition of the New Testa-

[1] Irenæus, Adv. Hær., v. 24.
[2] Justin Martyr, First Apology, 17.
[3] Theophilus of Antioch, Ad Autolycum, i. 11.

ment that the principle of authority is a divine principle, while in the case of Irenæus at least we see that this means that government is a divinely instituted remedy for the sin and wickedness of men.

The great writers of the fourth, fifth, and sixth centuries carry on precisely the same conceptions. Most of them indeed only deal with the divine character of government, but St Ambrose, St Augustine, St Gregory the Great, and St Isidore develop the conception of St Irenæus that government is the necessary divine remedy for sin. St Ambrose speaks of the authority of rulers as being imposed upon foolish peoples, to compel men even though unwillingly to obey the wise.[1] St Augustine, as we have already seen, looks upon the government of men by men as being contrary to the primitive condition of human nature, but as being a necessary and divinely appointed consequence of and remedy for sin.[2] We give below another passage from his writings in which his conception of government is very clearly drawn out.[3]

St Gregory the Great echoes the sentiments of St Augustine: we need only refer the reader to the passage which we have already quoted in part, but we may draw attention to some phrases in this which were not specially germane to the subject

---

[1] St Ambrose, Ep. xxxvii. 8.

[2] St Aug., De. Civ. Dei, xix. 15.

[3] St Aug., Quar. Prop. ex Ep. ad Rom., 72 : "Quod autem ait, Omnis anima potestatibus sublimioribus subdita sit : non est enim potestas nisi a Deo, rectissime jam monet ne quis ex eo quod a Domino suo in libertatem vocatus est, factusque Christianus, extollatur in superbiam, et non arbitretur in hujus vitæ itinere servandum esse ordinem suum, et potestatibus sublimioribus, quibus pro tempore rerum temporalium gubernatio tradita est, putet non se esse subdendum. Cum enim constemus ex anima et corpore, et quamdiu in hac vita temporali sumus, etiam rebus temporalibus ad subsidium degendæ hujus vitæ utamur ; oportet nos ex ea parte, quæ ad hanc vitam pertinet, subditos esse potestatibus, id

est, hominibus res humanas cum aliquo honore administrantibus. Ex illa vero parte qua credimus Deo, et in regnum ejus vocamur, non nos oportet esse subditos cuiquam homini, idipsum in nobis evertere cupienti, quod Deus ad vitam æternam donare dignatus est. Si quis ergo putat quoniam Christianus est, non sibi esse vectigal reddendum aut tributum, aut non esse exhibendum honorem debitum eis quæ hæc curant potestatibus ; in magno errore versatur. Item si quis se putat esse subdendum, ut etiam in suam fidem habere potestatem arbitretur eum qui temporalibus administrandis aliqua sublimitate præcellit ; in majorem errorem labitur. Sed modus iste servandus est quam Dominus ipse præscribit, ut reddamus Cæsari quæ Cæsaris sunt, et Deo quæ Dei sunt."

which we were then dealing with. Men, he says, are indeed by nature equal, but they are different in condition as a consequence of sin: as all men do not live equally well, one man must be ruled by another; there is a bestial tendency in the human race which can only be kept down by fear.[1]

St Isidore of Seville, in the same passage in which he deals with slavery as a consequence of and a remedy for sin, also deals with government in the same fashion. The just God, he says, has so ordered life, in making some men slaves and some men lords, that the tendency to evil may be restrained by the fear of punishment; and to the same end princes and kings are appointed, that by fear of them and by their laws the people may be restrained from evil and encouraged to good.[2]

It is unnecessary to multiply quotations from the Fathers to show that they all accept the theory of St Paul, that Government is a divine institution. We shall have to recur to the matter again when we discuss their conception of the character of the authority of Government, the question of its absolute or limited nature, and the propriety or impropriety of resistance to it. So far we are only concerned to make it clear how it is that we find the Fathers at the same time maintaining that Government is not natural and primitive, and yet that it is a divine institution. We have tried to make it clear that this apparently self-contradictory position is really a perfectly intelligible, and, on its own terms, rational one. For man is not now in the condition in which God made him: once he was innocent and harmless, now his nature is depraved and corrupted, and conditions which would have been wholly contrary to his primitive nature are now necessary and useful.

[1] St Gregory the Great, Exp. Mor., in Job xxi. 15 : " Nam ut præfati sumus, omnes homines natura æquales genuit, sed variante meritorum ordine, alios aliis dispensatio occulta postponit. Ipsa autem diversitas, quæ accessit ex vitio recte est divinis judiciis ordinata, ut quia omnis homo iter vitæ æque non graditur, alter ab altero regatur. . . . Nequaquam ergo præpositi ex hoc quæsito timore superbiant, in quo non suam gloriam, sed subditorum justitiam quærunt. In eo enim quod metus sibi a perverse viventibus exigunt, quasi a non hominibus, sed brutis animalibus dominantur, quia videlicet ex qua parte bestiales sunt subditi, ex ea etiam debent formidine jacere substrati."

[2] St Isidore of Seville, Sentent., iii. 47. See p. 119.

CHAPTER XII.

THE THEORY OF PROPERTY.

WE must turn to the theory of property in the Christian writers. We have already seen that the New Testament does not seem to contain any definite theory of property: it may contain traces of a theory that the perfect man has little to do with wealth, but the general tendency of the New Testament writers seems to be to assume the existence of the institution, while they enjoin upon Christian men the duty of using their property especially for the benefit of all the members of the Christian societies.

The earliest Fathers carry on these conceptions very much as we find them in the New Testament: on the one hand they do not seem to have any dogmatic theory of the community of Christian men's goods; on the other hand they continue to insist that the Christian man is bound to use his property to relieve the wants of his fellow-man, and especially of his fellow-Christian. The 'Teaching of the Twelve Apostles' and the so-called Epistle of Barnabas reproduce from some common source very emphatic exhortations to liberality in giving, which in one phrase echo the words of the Acts of the Apostles: "Thou shalt not turn away from him that hath need, but shalt share all things with thy brother, and shalt not say that they are thine own: for if ye are sharers in that which is immortal, how much more in those things which are mortal."[1] The phrase, "Thou shalt not say that they are thine own" ($o\dot{v}\kappa$ $\dot{\epsilon}\rho\epsilon\hat{\iota}\varsigma$ $\ddot{\iota}\delta\iota\alpha$ $\epsilon\hat{\iota}\nu\alpha\iota$), is very near the phrase of the Acts, "No one of them said that ought of the things which he possessed was his

---

[1] 'Teaching of the Twelve Apostles,' iv. 8.   Cf. Ep. of Barnabas, xix. 8.

own" (οὐδὲ εἶς τι τῶν ὑπαρχόντων αὐτῷ ἔλεγεν ἴδιον εἶναι, ἀλλ᾽ ἦν αὐτοῖς ἅπαντα κοινά).

The same conception is represented by Justin Martyr in the second century. In his first 'Apology' he contrasts the covetousness and greed of the ordinary man with the liberality of the Christian. He says of the Christians, that they brought what they possessed into a common stock and shared with every one in need.[1] Justin Martyr again suggests the phrase of the Acts. In the third century St Cyprian quotes the narrative of the Acts, and commenting on it says, that such conduct is that of the true sons of God, the imitators of God. God's gifts are given to all mankind, the day enlightens all, the sun shines upon all, the rain falls and the wind blows upon all, to all men comes sleep, the splendour of the stars and the moon are common to all. Man is truly an imitator of God when he follows the equal beneficence of God by imparting to all the brotherhood the good things which he possesses.[2] Cyprian does not say that the Christian man must share his goods with all the brethren, but clearly he looks on this as the most perfect way. This gradually became the common view of many Christian writers.

But before considering the later Fathers we must observe that other early Christian writers present us with a somewhat different view of the subject. One of the short treatises of Clement of Alexandria discusses the Gospel story of the rich young ruler,[3] and it is both interesting and important to observe that Clement treats our Lord's injunction to the young man to go and sell all that he had and to give to the poor as being a metaphorical saying, and as really referring to the passions of the soul. He maintains that there is no advantage in poverty unless it is incurred for some special object.[4] Destitution is distracting and harassing, and it is much better to have such a competence as will suffice for oneself and enable a man to help those who are in need.[5] Riches, therefore, are

---

[1] Justin Martyr, First Apol., xiv. Cf. lxvii., and Tertullian, Apol., 39. I owe the last two references to an article by Dr Cobb in the 'Economic Review' for April 1895.

[2] St Cyprian, De Op. et Eleem., 25.

[3] Clem. of Alex., Quis Dives Salvetur, 5-14.

[4] Id., 11.

[5] Id., 13.

things which may, if rightly used, be serviceable to the posses-
sor and to others, and are not to be thrown away.[1] Clement's
interpretation of our Lord's words is not, so far as we know, a
common one, but it is of considerable importance.

The same general conception is very strongly held by Lactantius. He discusses Plato's theory of community of property,
and very emphatically repudiates it as impossible and unjust,
and urges that justice is not a matter of external condition
but of the soul.[2] It is not property that must be abolished, but
pride and insolence. If the rich would lay these aside it would
make no difference though one man were rich and another poor.[3]
In another passage he discusses the poetical conception of the
Golden or Saturnian Age. He looks upon this as no poetical
fiction, but a condition of things which really existed and out
of which men passed by reason of sin and the loss of the true
religion. Lactantius, that is, formally accepts that theory of
the state of nature which we have already considered ; but it is
very noticeable that he refuses to accept the poetical conception of a complete community of goods in that age. He maintains that we must take this as a poetical metaphor. He
cannot think that even in that age there was no such thing as
private property, but only that men were so generous and
kindly that no one was in want.[4]

What are we to conclude as to the position of the earlier
Fathers with respect to the institution of property ? We must
first observe that their whole thought is dominated by the
sense of the claims of the brotherhood. Whatever may be the
further significance of the narrative of the Acts and the phrases
of ' Barnabas ' and the ' Teaching of the Twelve Apostles,' this
at least is clear, that the Christian societies recognised that
every member had a claim upon the others for that which was
necessary for his maintenance. Behind this, however, there
lies a question more difficult to answer, Did the first Christian
teachers and societies, or any of them, think that property was
in itself unlawful or improper for the true Christian ? It
should, perhaps, be observed here that the very important
phrases of ' Barnabas ' and the ' Teaching ' are drawn from a

---

[1] Clem. of Alex., 14.   [2] Lact., Div. Inst., iii. 21.   [3] Id., iii. 22.   [4] Id., v. 5.

common source, to which the name of 'Two Ways' has been given, and that it has been argued that this work was a Jewish manual of moral discipline. The phrases in the Acts have a very similar ring. It may be suggested, then, that the notion that the perfect life was that of a society in which all shared equally with their brethren all that they had, was one which belonged to some form of the later Judaism,[1] and so passed into the Church.

It is just possible that there may have existed within the Church a tendency to think that among Christian men there should be no private property. But what we know of the historical conditions of the early Christian societies compels us also to recognise that this conception was not carried out into practice, so far as we know, in any community, not even in the community at Jerusalem. It would, however, seem as though there may very early have grown up in the Christian societies a theory that, while it was perfectly lawful for the Christian man to hold property, to give all that one had to the common funds of the society was the more perfect way. This is not, indeed, a view which was universally held. Clement of Alexandria and Lactantius, as we have seen, exhibit no special inclination towards it, but it seems to underlie the phrases of St Cyprian, it was developed by two of the most influential of Western Christian writers, St Jerome[2] and St Augustine,[3] commenting on our Lord's words to the rich young ruler, and it formed part of that theory of the ascetic life as the more perfect way which dominates so much of Western thought in the Middle Ages.

When we turn to the later Fathers we find that their theory of property is closely connected with the same general philosophical system as that which governs the rest of their political theories. In the first place, it seems quite clear that they recognise that private property is in no way evil if it is rightly used. St Augustine maintains this dogmatically against the Manichæans. Who does not understand, he says, that it is not blameworthy to have such things (*i.e.*, property of various kinds), but only to love them, to put one's hope in them, to prefer

---

[1] It may be conjectured that this was connected with Essene principles.

[2] St Jerome, Ep. cxxx. 14.

[3] St Augustine, Ep. clvii. iv.

them to, or even to compare them with truth, justice, wisdom, faith, a good conscience, with love to God and our neighbours.[1] The same view could be illustrated from the other Christian writers, as being the normal judgment of the Christian Church.[2] Whatever doubt may be entertained as to some primitive Christians, there is no doubt about the formal judgment of the developed society. But when we have recognised this fact, we must also observe that this merely means that the Church accepted the institution of property as being in accordance with the actual conditions of life, just as it accepted the institution of slavery or coercive government: it does not mean that the Church considered private property to belong to the natural or primitive condition of human life. It is true that the Fathers deal with this question in the most incidental and partial manner, and that it is therefore difficult to express ourselves very dogmatically about the theory which lies behind their references, but we think that the best interpretation of these is that they thought that in the primitive state all things were common,—that it is not the law of God but that of the State which directly gives this thing to one man and that to another.

This view is more clearly expressed by St Ambrose than by any other writer. We may first consider a very interesting and well-known passage in his treatise 'De Officiis.' St Ambrose roundly says that private property is not by nature; nature only produced a common right, use and habit produced private right; nature gave all things to all men.[3] We must

---

[1] St Augustine, Contra Adimantum Manichæi Discipulum, xx. 2: "Quis hic non intelligat non esse culpabile habere ista, sed amare et spem in eis ponere, et ea præferre aut etiam conferre veritati, justitiæ, sapientiæ, fidei, bonæ conscientiæ, charitati Dei et proximi, quibus omnibus anima pia dives est in secretis suis coram oculis Dei."

[2] Cf. St Hilary of Poitiers, Com. on Matt. xix. 9; St Ambrose, Ep. lxiii. 92; Salvian, Ad Ecclesiam, i. 7; St Aug., De Moribus Eccl. Cath., i. 35.

[3] St Ambrose, De Off., i. 28, "Deinde formam justitiæ putaverunt, ut quis communia, id est, publica pro publicis habeat, privata pro suis. Ne hoc quidem secundum naturam, natura enim omnia omnibus in commune profudit. Sic enim Deus generari jussit omnia ut pastus omnibus communis esset, et terra foret omnium quædam possessio. Natura igitur jus commune generavit, usurpatio jus fecit privatum. Quo in loco aiunt placuisse Stoicis, quæ in terris gignantur, omnia ad usus hominum creari; homines autem hominum causa esse generatos, ut ipsi inter se aliis prodesse possint.

not understand this as meaning that property is unlawful, but only that it is not a natural or primitive institution. St Ambrose here, as throughout his treatise, is largely dependent òn Cicero's treatise of the same name, and we may be fairly certain that Cicero's words, "Sunt autem privata nulla natura,"[1] are the text which he is amplifying. It is not very easy to give any very definite meaning to Cicero's phrase: that of St Ambrose is a good deal easier, for, as we have seen, by his time the theory of the state of nature as contrasted with the state of conventional institutions had become a commonplace of Christian political theory.

Another passage from St Ambrose will perhaps make the matter clearer. God meant, he says, the world to be the common possession of all men, and to produce its fruits for all; it was avarice which produced the rights of property. It is only just, therefore, that a man should support the poor with some share of that which was meant for all mankind.[2] St Ambrose here comes very near indeed to the form of Seneca's statement of the origin of property, namely, that it arose from avarice,[3] and we feel that we can hardly be wrong in looking upon the foundation of St Ambrose's theory of property as being the same as that of Seneca. With St Ambrose's view may be very well compared that of Ambrosiaster. In one passage he treats charity as St Ambrose does, as being an act of justice,—for God, he says, gives all things in common to all men.[4]

---

[1] Cicero, De Off., i. 7.

[2] St Amb., Com. on Ps. cxviii. 8. 22: "Cum præsertim Dominus Deus noster terram hanc possessionem omnium hominum voluit esse communem, et fructus omnibus ministrare; sed avaritia possessionum jura distribuit. Justum est igitur ut si aliquid tibi privatum vindicas, quod generi humano, immo omnibus animantibus in commune collatum est, saltem aliquid inde pauperibus aspergas; ut quibus juris tui consortium debes, his alimenta non deneges." Cf. also St Amb., De Off., i. 11.

[3] Sen., Ep. xiv. 2. See p. 24.

[4] Ambrosiaster, Com. on 2 Cor. ix. 9, &c.: "Misericordia ergo hæc (i.e., almsgiving to the poor), justitia appellata est; quia sciens qui largitur, omnia Deum communiter omnibus dare, quia sol enim oritur, et pluit omnibus; et terram omnibus dedit; idcirco dividit cum eis, qui copiam terræ non habent; ne beneficiis Dei privati videantur. Justus ergo est, qui sibi soli non detinet, quod scit omnibus datum; et justus non solum hoc in tempore, sed et in æternum; quia in seculo futuro hanc habebit

St Zeno of Verona, a writer of the latter part of the fourth century, might perhaps be taken to illustrate an almost dogmatic theory of the propriety of some system of communism: he is, indeed, speaking mainly of a community of goods among Christians, founding this upon the passage in the Acts which we have already examined, but it must be observed that the latter words of the passage extend his conception to mankind at large.[1] We think, however, that St Zeno is speaking primarily in a practical sense—that he wishes to put in the strongest possible way the obligation of charity and active benevolence: he certainly puts the matter in a very strong way, for he continues, after the passage we have quoted in the note, to say that the obligation to give to those who need is not to be limited even by the duty of providing for a man's own family.

With these views we must compare those of St Gregory the Great. In one passage he deals with private property in much the same spirit as St Ambrose and Ambrosiaster. He treats the earth and its products as the gifts of God to all men, and therefore regards almsgiving as an act of justice, not of charity. It is evident that he does not regard private property itself as wrong, but, on the other hand, he does not seem to regard it as an absolute right. On the contrary, if a man uses it only for himself, he regards his action as unjust.[2]

secum in perpetuum. . . . Omnia Dei sunt, et semina et nascentia Dei nutu crescunt, et multiplicantur ad usus hominum ; Deus ergo qui hæc dat, ipse et jubet de his communicari eis qui indigent. . . . Hæc est justitia, ut quia Deus dat, retribuat ex eo et homo ei, cui deest."

[1] St Zeno of Verona, Tractatus, i. 3. 6 : " Sed, inquies, justum est, ut mea servem, aliena non quæram. Hoc etiam Gentes dicere consueverunt. Cæterum apud Deum quam sit injustum, mox videbimus. Nunc primo omnium, optime Christiane, scire cupio, quæ sunt tua cum sint timentibus Deum universa communia, sicut scriptum est : 'Turba autem eorum, qui crediderant, animo ac mente una agebant ' (Acts iv.

32), nec fuit inter illos discrimen ullum, ' nec quidquam suum ex bonis putabant, quæ eis erant ; sed erant illis omnia communia,' sicut dies, sol, nox, pluvia, nascendi atque moriendi conditio ; quæ humano generi, sine personarum aliqua exceptione, æquabiliter justitia est divina largita. Cum hæc ita sint, procul dubio non est a Tyranno dissimilis, qui solus habet, quod potest prodesse commodis plurimorum."

[2] St Gregory the Great, Liber Regulæ Pastoralis, iii. 21 : ' Admonendi sunt qui nec aliena appetunt, nec sua largiuntur, ut sciant sollicite quod ea de qua sumti sunt, cunctis hominibus terra communis est, et idcirco alimenta quoque omnibus communiter profert. Incassum ergo se innocentes putant,

We should suggest that in this conception we have the beginnings of a distinction which became very important in the Middle Ages, and is very carefully drawn out by St Thomas Aquinas—the distinction between property as a right of distribution, and property as a right of personal use.   St Thomas holds that private property is not an institution of natural but of positive law, and that the right of property only extends to the acquisition and distribution of things : so far as their use is concerned, men are bound to treat them as things pertaining to all.   A man has the right to use what he needs, and St Thomas does not take this in any narrow sense, but beyond this a man only holds his property for the common use.[1]   We should suggest that the passages of the Fathers which we have just examined show us the germs out of which this theory grew. Property is not primitive but conventional ; it is not therefore illegitimate, but, on the other hand, it is not an unrestricted right : the circumstances of the world and of human nature may make it necessary that men should take things to themselves from the common stock, but they do this subject to the responsibility of using all that they do not themselves need, for the common benefit.

St Augustine does not deal directly with the question of the primitive conditions with regard to property.   But he furnishes us with a number of very important observations on the immediate source of this right.   His theory of property is for the most part developed somewhat incidentally in his defence

qui commune Dei munus sibi privatum vindicant ; qui cum accepta non tribuunt, in proximorum nece grassantur ; quia tot pene quotidie perimunt, quot morientium pauperum apud se subsidia abscondunt.   Nam cum quælibet necessaria indigentibus ministramus, sua illis reddimus, non nostra largimur ; justitiæ debitum potius solvimus, quam misericordiæ opera implemus.   Unde et ipsa Veritas cum de misericordia caute exhibenda loqueretur, ait, 'Attendite ne justitiam vestram faciatis coram hominibus.'   Cui quoque sententiæ etiam Psalmista concinnens dicit : ' Dispersit dedit pauperibus, jus-

titia ejus manet in æternum.'   Cum enim largitatem impensam pauperibus præmisisset, non hanc vocare misericordiam sed justitiam maluit ; quia quod a communi Domino tribuitur, justum profecto est, ut quicunque accipiunt, eo communiter utantur. Huic etiam Salomon ait, 'Qui justus est, tribuet et non cessabit.' "

[1] Cf. Notes in Econ. Review, January 1894, by R. W. Carlyle, "Some Economic Doctrines of St Thomas Aquinas."

Cf. especially St Thos. Aquinas "Suma Theologica" 2.2.66.2.

of the confiscation of the churches and other possessions of
the Donatists in Africa by the Imperial Government. It
would seem, from his allusions to their complaints, that they
protested that these confiscations were unjust, and perhaps
even that they were outside the powers of the Government.
His reply to their contentions is founded upon the following
arguments. Property, he says, may be considered as an institution of the divine law or of the human law. By the divine
law property is either all in the hands of God, for " the earth
is the Lord's and the fulness thereof," or else all things belong
to the righteous, and the Donatists are not righteous. By
human law property belongs to this or that individual, but
what human law has given human law can take away. St
Augustine also maintains that the right of property is limited
by the use to which it is put: the man who does not use his
property rightly has no real claim to it.[1]

[1] St Augustine, Epist., xciii. xi.: " Et
quamvis res quæque terrena non recte
a quoquam possideri possit, nisi vel jure
divino, quo cuncta justorum sunt, vel
jure humano, quod in potestate regum
est terræ; ideoque res vestras falso ap-
pelletis, quas nec justi possidetis, et
secundum leges regum terrenorum
amittere jussi estis, frustraque dicatis
' nos eis congregandis laboravimus,' cum
scriptum legatis, ' Labores impiorum
justi edent ' " (Prov. xiii. 22).

Tract. vi. in Joannis Evangelium, 25:
"Ecce sunt villæ : quo jure defendis
villas ? divino an humano ? Respon-
deant : Divinum jus in Scripturis
habemus, humanum jus in legibus
regum. Unde quisque possidet quod
possidet ? Nonne jure humano ? Nam
jure divino, Domini est terra et pleni-
tudo ejus : pauperes et divites Deus
de uno limo fecit, et pauperes et
divites una terra supportat. Jure
tamen humano dicit, Hæc villa mea
est, hæc domus mea, hic servus
meus est. Jure ergo humano, jure
imperatorum. Quare ? Quia ipsa jura
humana per imperatores et reges
sæculi Deus distribuit generi humano.

Vultis legamus leges imperatorum, et
secundum ipsas agamus de villis. Si
jure humano vultis possidere, recitemus
leges imperatorum : videamus si voluerunt aliquid ab hæreticis possideri.
Sed quid mihi est imperator ? Secundum jus ipsius possides terram. Aut
tolle jura imperatorum, et quis audet
dicere : mea est illa villa, aut meus est
ille servus, aut domus hæc mea est ?
Si autem ut teneantur ista ab hominibus, jura acceperunt regum, vultis
recitemus leges, ut gaudeatis quia vel
unum hortum habetis, et non imputetis
nisi mansuetudini columbæ, quia vel
ibi vobis permittitur permanere ?
Leguntur enim leges manifestæ, ubi
præceperunt imperatores, eos qui præ-
ter Ecclesiæ Catholicæ communionem
usurpant sibi nomen Christianum, nec
volunt in pace colere pacis auctorem,
nihil nomine Ecclesiæ audeant possidere.

26 : "Sed quid nobis et imperatori ?
Sed jam dixi, de jure humano agitur.
Et tamen Apostolus voluit serviri reg-
ibus, voluit honorari reges, et dixit
' Regem reveremini.' Noli dicere :
Quid mihi et regi ? Quid tibi ergo

It is clear from these statements that St Augustine regards property as normally an institution of human and positive law. His distinction between the *jus divinum* and the *jus humanum* is not indeed the same as that between the *jus naturale* and the *jus civile*, but at least it is parallel to it, and it suggests to us very strongly that St Augustine recognises no proper right in things except that which is given by the State. This view is by no means on the same lines as that of the lawyers, who regarded some form of private property as being by natural law: he does not indeed contradict the legal theory of " occupation " and the right which can be acquired in the *res nullius* by him who " occupies " it,[1] but his phrases suggest that this theory is not at all in his mind. Incidentally it is interesting to observe in the passage first quoted that the Donatists are represented as urging an argument very analogous to that on which Locke founds his theory of property, namely, that they had acquired their property by labour. St Augustine brushes this aside unsympathetically by an appeal to the Scripture, which says that the just shall devour the labour of the wicked.

et possessioni ? Per jura regum possidentur possessiones. Dixisti, quid mihi et regi ? Noli dicere possessiones tuas ; quia ad ipsa jura humana renuntiasti, quibus possidentur possessiones. Sed de divino jure ago, ait. Ergo Evangelium recitemus : videamus quo usque Ecclesia Catholica Christi est, super quem venit columba quæ docuit : ' Hic est qui baptizat.' Quomodo ergo jure divino possideat qui dicit, Ego baptizo : cum dicat columba ' Hic est qui baptizat,' cum dicat Scriptura ' Una est columba mea, una est matri suæ.' Quare, laniasti columbam ? Imo laniastis viscera vestra : nam vobis laniatis, columba integra perseverat. Ergo fratres mei, si ubique non habent quod dicant, ego dico quod faciant : veniant ad Catholicam, et nobiscum habebunt non solum terram, sed etiam illum qui fecit cœlum et terram."

Epist., cliii. 6 : " Jamvero si pru-

denter intueamur quid scriptum est. ' Fidelis hominis totus mundus divitiarum est, infidelis autem nec obolus ; ' nam omnes qui sibi videntur gaudere licite conquisitis, eisque uti nesciunt, aliena possidere convincimus ? Hoc enim certe alienum non est, quod jure possidetur ; hoc autem jure quod juste, et hoc juste quod bene. Omne igitur quod male possidetur, alienum est ; male autem possidet qui male utitur. (Cf. St Isid. of Seville, Etym., v. 25.)

Sermo, L. c. 2. : "Aurum ejus proprium est, qui illo bene utitur, adeoque verius est Dei. Illius est ergo aurum et argentum, qui novit uti auro et argento. Nam etiam inter ipsos homines, tunc quisque habere aliquid dicendus est, quando bene utitur. Nam quod juste non tractat, jure non tenet. Quod autem jure non tenet, si suum esse dicerit, non erit vox justi possessoris, sed impudentis incubatoris improbitas."

[1] Cf. Digest, xli. 1. 3, &c. See p. 52

We think that when we consider St Augustine's treatment of property alongside of that especially of St Ambrose, we may feel fairly confident that they represent a tradition which differs materially from that of the jurists, a tradition probably derived from the same sources as the view of Seneca—that is, that they would, with Seneca, have classed the institution of property as one of those which belong to the conventions of organised society, and not to the primitive conditions of the human race.

At the same time, it must be observed that St Augustine's views on the limitation of the rights of property, by the use to which it is put, finds a parallel in a phrase of Gaius, treating of the limitation of the rights of masters over their slaves : " Male enim nostro jure uti non debemus," [1]—a phrase repeated in slightly different terms by the compilers of Justinian's Institutes : "Expedit enim reipublicæ, ne quis re sua male utatur." [2]   St Augustine's phrases, however, are much wider in scope, and indicate a much more developed theory than those of the lawyers.   We think that this is to be connected with the theory of St Ambrose and other Fathers, that the things of the world do not cease to be held for the common good, because it is now lawful for particular persons to hold them as their own private property, and that this conception finally takes a definite form in the distinction between the right of property as an authority in distribution and the right of property as one of unlimited use.

We are now in a position to examine the meaning and significance of the references to the theory of property in St Isidore of Seville.   We have already discussed his definition of the *jus naturale ;* we must now recall the words of this : " Jus naturale est commune omnium nationum, et quod ubique instinctu naturæ, non constitutione aliqua habetur; ut viri et feminæ conjunctio, liberorum susceptio et educatio, communis omnium possessio, et omnium una libertas, adquisitio eorum quæ cœlo terra marique capiuntur.   Item depositæ rei vel commendatæ pecuniæ restitutio, violentiæ per vim repulsio.   Nam hoc aut si quid huic simile est, numquam injustum, sed naturale æquumque habetur." [3]   What does St Isidore mean by "communis

<hr />

[1] Gaius, Inst., i. 53.   [2] Inst., i. 8. 2.   [3] St Isidore of Seville, Etym., v. 4.

omnium possessio"? In the Middle Ages he was no doubt taken as meaning the common possession of all things;[1] and if that interpretation is correct, St Isidore sets forth in technical language the theory that by natural law all things were common, and there was no private property. But it is not quite certain whether this is the correct interpretation of the phrase. The words can be taken to mean simply that by the law of nature there is a form of property common to all men. This would not necessarily exclude forms of property belonging to groups of men or to individuals.

It is not very easy to determine which interpretation is the correct one. The nearest parallels to St Isidore's phrase are to be found in the Digest and the Institutes; in the former we have Marcianus's phrase: " Quædam naturali jure communia sunt omnium, quædam universitatis, quædam nullius, pleraque singulorum."[2] Here the phrase itself makes it clear that the genitive *omnium* is possessive; certain things are common to all. In the Institutes[3] we have Marcianus's phrase repeated with a few variations, and throughout the discussion of property we find the genitive case used in the same sense—*e.g.*, "Communia sunt omnium hæc"; "Singulorum autem hominum multis modis res fiunt." As far, then, as the grammatical construction is concerned, the precedents in legal phraseology seem to point to the genitive case in St Isidore's phrase as being possessive. It must be observed, however, that the legal phrases are not absolutely parallel: *communis* is not connected with *possessio.* But, further, St Isidore goes on to mention certain methods of acquiring property, "Acquisitio eorum quæ cœlo, terra, marique, capiuntur,"[4] and certain moral rules which only exist in a condition of things where private property exists, "Depositæ rei vel commendatæ pecuniæ restitutio," and all, it must be noticed, as belonging to the *jus naturale.* It is difficult to understand this, if St Isidore means to say that by natural law all property is common to all: at the most, it may

---

[1] Cf. Gratian, Decretum, Dist. i. and viii., and Alexander of Hales, Summa, part iii. Quæst. xxvi. ; Memb. iii., Art. 2.

[2] Digest, i. 8. 2.
[3] Inst., ii. 1.
[4] Cf. St Isidore on " Possessiones, Etym., xv. 13.

be suggested that St Isidore is inconsistent with himself, and that it is idle to expect a thorough and completely thought-out explanation of the subject from him. It must also be observed that St Isidore in his definition of the *jus gentium* does not indicate that private property belongs to it, as he does, for instance, with regard to slavery, and that there is no reference to property in his definition of the *jus civile*.[1]

It seems to us that for the present we must take it as uncertain whether St Isidore follows the tradition of the Fathers and the Stoics in thinking that private property is not an institution of the natural law, or the general tradition of the lawyers that even by the natural law some things belonged to individuals. The general tendency of the Fathers is, we think, clear, and in the history of political theory this is the important point, for we are thus able to discover the origin of the dogmatic and developed mediæval theory.

We can now look back over certain general characteristics of patristic political theory, and we think it has become plain that this turns upon the distinction between the primitive or natural state, with its natural law and institutions, and the actual state, with its conventional institutions adapted to the new characteristics and circumstances of human nature and life. With regard to the theory of human equality and the institution of slavery, the theory of coercive government, and the theory of property, we have seen that the patristic view turns upon this distinction between the natural and primitive, and the conventional and actual. Neither slavery, nor government, nor property are institutions of the natural law, and they did not exist in the natural state. There was a time when men were innocent—when, therefore, these institutions did not exist, when they were not needed. Out of those conditions men passed through sin, their nature was changed and corrupted, avarice, hatred, and the lust of domination possessed them. New institutions, founded in some measure upon these vices, were needed to correct these same vices. Slavery and government and

---

[1] St Isidore of Seville, Etym., v. 6 and 5.

private property are institutions arising from the vicious tendencies of human nature, as it is, but they are also the instruments by which these vices are corrected. The state and condition of nature is by the Fathers identified with the state and condition of unfallen man.

It is evident, we think, that under some difference of phraseology the Fathers are really carrying on the same theory as that of the Stoics as represented by Seneca. The relation of this to the political theory of the lawyers is more complex, but it is clear that they are related, and that, in some measure at least, it is justifiable to explain the two systems by comparing them with each other. We think that the fact that the entire patristic theory turns upon the distinction between the natural and the conventional state, expressed indeed under the terms of the theological conception of the Fall, but obviously reflecting, not any exclusively Christian conception, but rather some widespread assumption of popular philosophy, encourages us in thinking that the same type of thought lies behind the obscurer references of the lawyers.

It appears to us that it is correct to say that in considering the meaning of justice in human life these thinkers found themselves compelled to recognise that there was an apparent inconsistency between some of the great institutions of society and that natural or essential equality of human nature which they had learned from their experience of the universal empires. Slavery, therefore, which Aristotle could explain by a theory which was at least in many respects reasonable, to them was a real difficulty, and what they thought of slavery would naturally extend itself to government. On the other hand, they recognised instinctively, if we may use such a phrase, that human life, as it actually is, needs discipline, needs an order enforced by coercion. And thus they came to make a distinction between an ideal, which they think of as also the primitive condition of man, and the actual. Ideally, man, following his truest nature, obeying the laws of reason and justice, which he always, in some measure, recognises, would have needed no such coercive discipline. But, being what he is, a creature whose true instincts and nature are constantly overpowered by his lower nature, it is only by means of a hard discipline that he can be kept from an anarchy and disorder in which all men would be reduced to an equal level of misery and degradation. Their theory is properly a justification of coercive government, but, naturally enough, the institution of slavery being actually in existence, and appearing, as it must naturally have done to them, to be essential to the whole fabric of civilised life, they interpreted it as another form of discipline. Private property also, with its enormous inequalities, they could not accept as a primitive and natural institution. In a primitive or natural state the rights of property could have been nothing more than the right to use that which a man required. But again, in face of the actual condition of human nature, in view of the avaricious and covetous tendencies of human nature as it actually is, they found that a formal regulation of the exercise of the right to use was necessary. Private property is really another disciplinary institution intended to check and counteract the vicious dispositions of men.

The thinkers of this philosophical tendency, then, find a just meaning in the great institutions of human society, human nature being what it actually is, but they conceive of these institutions as being dominated by the end which they serve. They are intended to correct the vicious dispositions of men. They are only justified as far as they actually do this. The equality of human nature still dominates all just order. All institutions must be reconciled with this in some sense. Government is intended to correct the evil tendencies of man, but should respect his true qualities. Slavery is justifiable as a necessary discipline of human life, but the man continues in the slave. The institution of private property is necessary to reduce the contradictory claims of men to some order, but the good things of the world are still intended for the use of all. The theory of Natural Law and the Natural State is then partly a theory of the origin of human life and institutions, but it is also a theory of the principles of justice, by which all the actual institutions of life are to be tested and corrected.

CHAPTER XIII.

THE SACRED AUTHORITY OF THE RULER.

WE have now to consider the theory of the nature and immediate source of authority in the Christian writers. We have
seen that in their view the institution of Government is not
primitive, but is made necessary by the vices of human nature.
But Government is a divine institution, a divine remedy for
man's sin, and the ruler is the representative of God, and must
be obeyed in the name of God. It will be easily understood
that the conception was capable of a development which should
make the king or ruler the absolute and irresponsible representative of God, who derives his authority directly from God, and is
accountable to God alone for his actions. This conception,
which in later times became the formal theory of the Divine
Right of the monarch, was, as we think, first drawn out and
stated by some of the Fathers, notably by St Gregory the
Great. It must at the same time be observed that such a
conclusion was not necessary, nor was it at first actually developed. The actual tendencies of the patristic theories are
very complex; we can very clearly see how the theory of the
Divine Right arose out of the general theory of the sacred
character of the civil order, but there are many other tendencies in the political theory of the Fathers, and some of their
phrases and theories became in later times of the greatest
importance in counteracting the arguments of the absolutist
thinkers.

We begin by examining the development in the Christian
writers of the theory of the authority of the civil ruler, as the
representative of God. We have already mentioned some of

the strong phrases used by the early Christian writers to express their sense of the duty of obedience to the civil ruler. We referred to the words of Theophilus of Antioch, in which, while repudiating the worship of the king, he acknowledges that Government is in some sense committed to him by God, and that Christian men will therefore honour and obey him.[1] We should observe that Irenæus, with whose discussion of the origin and object of Government we dealt fully, makes a statement with regard to civil rulers which is of great importance in relation to certain developments of the later theory. He has pointed out that God has given men rulers as a remedy for man's sin and vice, but he adds that often God gives men evil rulers to punish their wickedness.[2] The ruler is not only the minister of God's remedy for sin, but the instrument of His punishments. We may doubt whether Irenæus had in his mind the conclusions which might be and ultimately were connected with this view, but it is at least important to observe its appearance thus early in Christian theory. St Optatus of Milevis, in his treatise on the Donatist schism in North Africa, expresses the conception, that the ruler is the representative of God, in a still more explicit fashion. It appears from a passage in this treatise that when the Imperial authority interfered on behalf of the Catholic party, the leader of the Donatists indignantly protested that the Emperor had no concern with Church affairs. St Optatus replies by urging St Paul's commands to Christian men, that they should offer up prayers for kings and those in authority, and asserts that the Empire is not in the Church, but the Church in the Empire, and that there is no one over the Emperor but God only, who made him Emperor.[3]

---

[1] Theophilus of Antioch, Ad Aut., i. 11.

[2] Irenæus, Adv. Hær., v. 24.

[3] St Optatus of Milevis, 'De Schisma Donatistarum,' iii. 3 : "Qui cum ad Donatum, patrem tuum, venirent, et quare venerant indicarent, illo solito furore succensus, in hæc verba prorupit : 'Quid est imperatori cum ecclesia ?'

. . . Jam tunc meditabatur, contra præcepta apostoli Pauli, potestatibus et regibus injuriam facere, pro quibus, si apostolum audiret, quotidie rogare debuerat. Sic enim docet beatus apostolus Paulus : 'Rogate pro regibus et potestatibus, ut quietam et tranquillam vitam cum ipsis agamus.' Non enim respublica est in Ecclesia, sed Ecclesia

This theory of the ruler as the representative of God is most clearly expressed in a phrase used for the first time, as far as we have been able to see, by Ambrosiaster, if we may assume the correctness of the identification of the author of the ' Quæstiones Veteris et Novi Testamenti,' once attributed to St Augustine, with the author of the commentaries on St Paul's Epistles, once attributed to St Ambrose.[1] In one passage he says that the king is reverenced on earth as the "Vicar of God," and in another passage he draws out his conception in a very curious distinction. The king has "the image of God as the Bishop has that of Christ."[2] We shall find this distinction again in Cathulfus in the ninth century :[3] it is very interesting and curious, but we do not pretend to be able to interpret it. The title of " Vicar of God " is important, as summing up the conception that the authority of the ruler is derived from God Himself. In the Middle Ages it might mean much more than this, but it would be improper to read later conceptions into a writer of the fourth

in republica est, id est, in imperio Romano ; quod Libanum appellat Christus in Canticis Canticorum, cum dicit : ' Veni, sponsa mea, inventa de Libano,' id est, de imperio Romano : ubi et sacerdotia sancta sunt, et pudicitia, et virginitas, quæ in barbaris gentibus non sunt ; et si essent, tuta esse non possent. . . .

" Carthaginis principatum se tenuisse crediderat : et cum super imperatorem non sit nisi solus deus, qui fecit imperatorem, dum se Donatus super imperatorem extollit, jam quasi hominum excesserat metas, ut prope, se Deum, non hominem æstimaret, non reverendo eum, qui post Deum ab hominibus timebatur."

[1] See p. 104, note 4.

[2] Ambrosiaster, Quæstiones Veteris et Novi Testamenti, xci. 8 : " Rex enim adoratur in terris quasi vicarius Dei. Christus autem post vicariam impleta dispensatione adoratur in cœlis et in terra."

xxxv. : " Qua ratione David Saul, postquam Deus ab eo recessit. Christum

Domini vocat, et defert ei ? Non nescius David divinam esse traditionem in officio ordinis regalis, idcirco Saul in eadem adhuc traditione positum honorificat, ne Deo injuriam facere videretur, qui his ordinibus honorem decrevit. Dei enim imaginem habet rex, sicut et episcopus Christi. Quamdiu ergo in ea traditione est, honorandus est, si non propter se, vel propter ordinem. Unde Apostolus omnibus inquit, ' Potestatibus sublimioribus subditi estote. Non est enim potestas, nisi a Deo : quæ enim sunt, a Deo ordinatæ sunt.' Hinc est Gentilem, in potestate tamen positum, honorificamus, licet ipse indignus sit, qui Dei ordinem tenens gratias agit diabolo. Potestas enim exigit, quia meretur honorem. Nam ideo Pharaoni futuræ famis somnium revelatum est : et Nabuchodonosor, aliis secum adstantibus, solus filium Dei vidit in camino ignis, non utique merito suo, qui in idolo se adorari voluit, sed merito ordinis regalis."

[3] Cathulfus in M. G. H. Epist., vol. iv. ; Ep. var. Car. Regn. Script., 7.

century. In the last passage he also discusses the question of the conduct of David towards Saul, and there is considerable significance in his discussion. He evidently thinks that the divine character of the office of kingship cannot be lost owing to any misconduct of the ruler. The sanctity of the office gives sanctity to any ruler, even though an idolater. It is clear that the writer is much influenced by the Jewish conception of kingship, but of this we shall have more to say presently.

We must, however, observe that in another of these "Questions" the author seems to take up a somewhat different position. He evidently believes that there may be a wholly evil form of authority which is not from God, but it is extremely difficult to say what he understands this to be, and what is the test of its character. It does not appear to consist in its unjust character or actions, for the writer says expressly that a man sitting on the throne or chair of God may oppress the innocent; and that we must then say that the judgment, but not the throne, is unjust.[1] The phrases are very obscure, but may tend in some measure to qualify the judgment which we might have founded on the preceding passages.

We have then a theory that the ruler is the representative of

---

[1] Ambrosiaster, Quæst. Vet. et Novi Test., cx. 5 : "Hanc dicimus cathedram pestilentiæ quæ extra Dei ordinationem est, quæ ad hoc utique inventa est, ut inde iniqua exeant judicia : propterea pestilentiæ cathedra dicta est, quæ est corruptio quæ parit mortem, sicut et iniquitas damnationem. Non est ergo a Deo quæ est cathedra mortis. Nam Moyses accepit cathedram vitæ. Ad hoc enim data est, ut auctoritas in ea sit justi judicis vel creatoris Dei. Unde dicit Dominus, 'Super cathedram Moysi sederunt Scribæ et Pharisæi' : et Apostolus, 'non est' inquit 'potestas nisi a Deo : quæ enim sunt, a Deo ordinatæ sunt." Unde dicit ad principem plebis : 'Tu quidem sedes iudicans secundum legem et contra legem jubes me percuti.' Quod dixit, 'secundum legem,' justam et salutarem cathedræ auctoritatem significavit. Illud autem quod ait, 'contra legem jubes me percuti' illum ipsum injustum judicem ostendit, ut in Dei cathedra sedens judicaret injuste. Hinc est unde et Daniel 'Dei est' ait 'regnum, et cui vult dabit illud.' Sicut ergo terreni imperatoris auctoritas currit per omnes, ut in omnibus ejus sit reverentia ; ita Deus instituit, ut ab ipso rege Dei auctoritas incipiat, et currat per cunctos : quamvis frequenter mundus hoc non intelligat, et alii se subjiciat in postestate positus quam debet, tamen institutio est ut unus sit qui timeatur. Ubi ergo hæc institutio non est, ibi cathedra pestilentiæ reperitur. . . .

Itaque si in Dei cathedra sedentes, innocentes opprimant, injustum erit judicium non cathedra. Ubi enim cathedra pestilentiæ est, non potest judicium non esse iniquum."

God, and that whatever his conduct may be, he does not cease in some sense to have this character. St Augustine expresses the same conception with a certain added emphasis. He mentions Nero as an example of the worst type of ruler, but adds that even such rulers receive their power through the providence of God, when he judges that any nation may require such governors.[1] St Isidore of Seville expresses the same view, and even thinks it necessary to explain away a passage of Scripture which, as it appeared to him, might be interpreted as contradicting the theory. The prophet Hosea, as he quotes him, had said of certain kings that they reigned, but not by the appointment of God. St Isidore explains that this means that God had given them to their people in His anger. He quotes the same prophet as saying, " I shall give them a king in my wrath," and concludes that a wicked ruler is appointed by God just as much as a good ruler. The character of the ruler is adapted to the character of the people: if they are good, God will give them a good ruler; if they are evil, He will set an evil ruler over them.[2] How far St Augustine and St Isidore foresaw the conclusions that might be founded upon such statements it is difficult to say. St Augustine does not, so far as we have seen, discuss the question in detail; and St Isidore, as we shall see presently,

---

[1] St Aug., De Civ. Dei, v. 19 : " Etiam talibus tamen dominandi potestas non datur nisi summi Dei providentia, quando res humanas judicat talibus dominis dignas. Aperta de hac re vox divina est loquente Dei sapientia : ' Per me reges regnant et tyranni per me tenent terram.' Sed ne tyranni non pessimi atque improbi reges, sed vetere nomine fortes dicti existimentur (unde ait Virgilius : ' Pars mihi pacis erit dextram tetigisse tyranni '), apertissime alio loco de Deo dictum est : ' Qui regnare facit hominem hypocritam propter perversitatem populi.' Cf. De Civ., v. 21.

[2] St Isidore of Seville, Sententiæ, iii. 48 : " Dum Apostolus dicat ; non est potestas nisi a Deo,' quo modo Dominus per Prophetam de quibusdam potestatibus dicit : ' Ipsi regnaverunt, sed non ex me.' Quasi diceret, non me propitio sed etiam summe irato. Unde et inferius per eumdem prophetam addidit : ' Dabo,' inquit, ' tibi regem in furore meo.' Quo manifestius elucet bonam malamque potestatem a Deo ordinari ; sed bonam propitio, malam irato. Reges, quando boni sunt, muneris est Dei, quando vero mali, sceleris est populi. Secundum enim meritum plebium disponitur vita rectorum, testante Job, ' Qui regnare facit hypocritam propter peccatum populi.' Irascente enim Deo, talem rectorem populi suscipiunt, qualem pro peccato merentur. Nonnunquam pro malitia plebium etiam reges mutantur, et qui ante videbantur esse boni, accepto regno fiunt mali."

evidently held, along with this view, others which have a somewhat different tendency.

The conclusions, however, which are not drawn out by St
Augustine and St Isidore are drawn out and stated with the
greatest emphasis by St Gregory the Great.   We may notice
first that he treats the relation of the evil ruler to God
in the same manner as St Augustine and St Isidore, and
argues like them that a good ruler is God's reward to a good
people, an evil ruler God's punishment on an evil people.
Whether, therefore, the ruler is good or evil, he must be reverenced as one who derives his authority from God.[1]   But
Gregory the Great goes much further than this.   Commenting
upon the conduct of David towards Saul, he points out how
David is said to have refused to lay his hand on the Lord's
anointed, and even to have repented that he cut off the hem of
his garment.   He takes Saul to stand for an evil ruler, and
David for a good subject, and he interprets David's attitude as
signifying that good subjects will not even criticise rashly or
violently the conduct even of bad rulers : for to resist or
offend against a ruler is to offend against God, who has set him
over men.[2]   And lest we should take this to be an isolated

---

[1] St Gregory the Great, Libri
Moralium in Job, xxv. 16.

[2] St Gregory the Great, Regulæ Pastoralis, iii. 4 : "Admonendi sunt subditi, ne præpositorum suorum vitam
temere iudicent, si quid eos fortasse
agere reprehensibiliter vident : ne unde
mala recte redarguunt, inde per elationis
impulsum in profundiora mergantur.
Admonendi sunt, ne cum culpas præpositorum considerant, contra eis au-
daciores fiant, sed sic si qua valde sunt
eorum prava, apud semetipsos dijudi-
cant, ut tamen divino timore con-
stricti ferre sub eis iugum reverentiæ
non recusent.   Quod melius osten-
dimus, si David factum ad medium
deducamus (1 Sam. xxiv.) . . . Quid
enim per Saul, nisi mali rectores :
quid per David, nisi boni subditi desig-
nantur ? . . . Quem tamen David ferire
metuit, quia piæ subditorum mentes

ab omni se peste obtrectationis absti-
nentes, præpositorum vitam nullo lin-
guæ gladio percutiunt, etiam cum
de imperfectione reprehendunt.   Qui
etsi quando pro infirmitate sese abstinere vix possunt, ut extrema quædam atque exteriora præpositorum mala,
sed tamen humiliter loquantur, quasi
oram chlamidis silenter incidunt : quia
videlicet dum prælatæ dignitati saltem innoxie et latenter derogant, quasi
regis superpositi vestem fœdant ; sed
tamen ad semetipsos redeunt, seque ve-
hementissime vel de tenuissima verbi
laceratione reprehendunt.   Unde bene
et illic scriptum est : "Post hæc David
percussit cor suum, eo quod abscidisset
oram chlamidis Saul."   Facta quippe
præpositorum oris gladio ferienda non
sunt, etiam cum recte reprehendenda iu-
dicantur.   Si quando vero contra eos vel
in minimis lingua labitur, necesse est ut

phrase, it is well to observe that he recurs to the matter in his treatise on the Book of Job,[1] and restates the same view with an equal, perhaps even with slightly greater, emphasis.

There can be no doubt that we have here the doctrine of the sanctity and Divine authority of the ruler in a very strong form : even the seventeenth-century apologists of the Divine Right hardly go further in preaching the necessity of obedience and the wickedness of resistance. It is from the doctrine of St Gregory the Great that the religious theory of the absolute and irresponsible authority of the ruler continually drew its strongest arguments, both in the Middle Ages and later. Other elements, no doubt, both of theory and of actual circumstance, go to produce the later theory, but the authority of St Gregory the Great was a continual protection to those who maintained it.

It may be asked whether the conception of St Gregory the Great was an entirely abstract one, or whether it actually governed his conduct. We think that its influence can be traced, in some degree at least, in his actual relations with the Emperors. Knowing as we do the great force and capacity of Gregory the Great as an administrator, and the energy with which he defended and pushed forward what he considered to be the rights and authority of the Roman See,

per afflictionem pœnitentiæ cor prematur ; quatenus ad semetipsum redeat, et cum præpositæ potestati deliquerit, ejus contra se judicium a quo sibi prælata est, perhorrescat. Nam cum præpositis delinquimus, ejus ordinationi qui eos nobis prætulit obviamus. Unde Moyses quoque cum contra se et Aaron conqueri populum cognovisset, ait : "Nos enim quid sumus ? Nec contra nos murmur vestrum, sed contra Dominum."

[1] St Gregory the Great, Libri Moralium in Job, xxii. 24 : "Qua in re semper sollicita consideratione pensandum est, ne aut hi qui præsunt exempla mali operis subjectis præbeant, eorumque vitam suæ gladio pravitatis exstinguant : aut hi qui alieno regimini subjacent, facile judicare audeant facta rectorum, atque per hoc quod de his qui sibi prælati sunt murmurant, non humano, sed ei qui cuncta disponit divino ordini contradicant. Illis namque dicitur : 'Oves meæ his quæ conculcata pedibus vestris fuerant pascebantur, et quæ pedes vestri turbaverant, hæc bibebant.' Oves enim turbata pedibus bibunt, cum subjecti ea ad exemplum vivendi appetunt quæ prælati quique pravo opere pervertunt. At contra a prælatis hi audiunt : 'Nos enim, quid sumus ? Nec contra nos est murmur vestrum, sed contra Dominum.' Qui enim contra superpositam sibi potestatem murmurat, liquet quod illum redarguit, qui eamdem homini potestatem dedit."

we cannot but be in some measure astonished at the extremely deferential, sometimes almost servile, tone which we find, at least occasionally, in his letters to the Emperors. We may take as an example a letter addressed to Anatolius, the representative of the Roman Church at Constantinople, with regard to the wish of the Emperor that John the Bishop of *Prima Justiniana* should be deposed on account of his bad health. Gregory protests against such action as being wholly contrary to the canons, and unjust, and says therefore that as far as he is concerned he can take no part in such action. But, he concludes, it is in the power of the Emperor to do what he pleases,—he must act according to his judgment: what the Emperor does, if it is canonical, Gregory will follow; if not canonical, he will, so far as he can do so without sin, endure.[1] The tone of the letter is not undignified, but it is a little strange to find Gregory even appearing to acquiesce in an open breach of canonical rule by the Emperor, especially when we remember that there was quite another tradition in the Western Church than this, as we shall presently see.

Another example will be found in a letter written to the Emperor Maurice with regard to a law issued by him, forbidding the reception in monasteries of soldiers and other persons who were responsible to discharge various public duties. Gregory is much distressed about the law, and begs Maurice to consider what emperor ever issued such a regulation. (It appears from Ep. 64 in the same book that Gregory believed that this had been done by Julian.) He urges that for some men salvation is only possible if they leave the world and give themselves wholly to religion, and he warns Maurice that Christ will in the last day demand

---

[1] St Gregory the Great, Epist., Lib. xi. 29, " Gregorius Anatolio Diacono Constantinopolim : " ". . . Et quidem nusquam canones præcipiunt, ut præ ægritudine episcopo succedatur, et omnino injustum est, ut si molestia corporis inruit, honore suo privetur ægrotus. Atque ideo hoc per nos fieri nullatenus potest, ne peccatum in mea anima ex ejus depositione veniat. . . . Quod si hoc petere ille noluerit quod piissimo domno placet, quicquid jubet facere, in ejus potestate est. Sicut novit, ipse provideat ; nos tantummodo in depositione talis viri non faciat permisceri. Quod vero ipse fecerit, si canonicum est, sequimur ; si vero canonicum non est, in quantum sine peccato nostro portamus."

from him an account of his conduct in having withdrawn men from the service of Christ. And yet he concludes the letter by saying that, in obedience to the Emperor's commands, he has caused the law to be sent on to various regions. He has obeyed the Emperor, and has delivered his soul by protesting.[1] It is certainly strange to find Gregory, who feels so strongly the impiety of such a law, still acting as an agent for its promulgation, instead of refusing to do this in the name of the Christian law and his own ecclesiastical position. It is true that we must balance the tone of these letters with that of a later one addressed to Boniface, the representative of the Roman see at Constantinople, with reference to a question

[1] St Gregory the Great, Epist., Lib. iii. 61, "Gregorius Mauritio Augusto:" "Longino viro clarissimo stratore veniente, dominorum legem suscepi, ad quam fatigatus tunc egritudine corporis, respondere nil valui. In qua dominorum pietas sanxit, ut quisquis publicis administrationibus fuerit implicatus, ei ad Ecclesiasticum officium venire non liceat. Quod valde laudavi, evidentissime sciens quia qui secularem habitum deserens, ad Ecclesiastica officia venire festinat, mutare vult seculum, non relinquere. Quod vero in eadem lege dicitur, ut ei in monasterio converti non liceat, omnino miratus sum : . . . In qua lege subiunctum est, ut nulli qui in manu signatus est, converti liceat. Quam constitutionem ego, fateor dominis meis, vehementer expavi. Quia per eam cœlorum via multis clanditur, et quod nuncusque licuit, ne liceat prohibetur. Multi enim sunt, qui possunt religiosam vitam etiam cum sæculari habitu ducere. Et plerique sunt, qui nisi omnia reliquerint, salvari apud Deum nullatenus possunt. Ego vero hæc dominis meis loquens, quid sum nisi pulvis et vermis ? Sed tamen quia contra auctorem omnium Deum hanc intendere constitutionem sentio, dominis tacere non possum. Ad hoc enim potestas super omnes homines,

pietati dominorum meorum cælitus data est, ut qui bona appetunt adjuventur ; ut cœlorum via largus pateat, ut terrestre regnum cœlesti regno famuletur. Et ecce aperta voce dicitur, ut ei, qui semel in terrena militia signatus fuerit, nisi aut expleta militia, aut pro debilitate corporis repulsus, Christo militare non liceat.

Ad hæc ecce per me servum ultimum suum et vestrum respondit Christus, dicens : "Ego te de notario comitem excubitorum, de comite excubitorum cæsarem, de cæsare imperatorem : nec solum hoc, sed etiam patrem imperatorum feci. Sacerdotes meis tuæ manui commisi, et tu a meo servitio milites tuos subtrahis." Responde rogo piissime domine, servo tuo, quid venienti et hæc dicenti responsurus es in judicio Domino tuo ? . . . Requirat rogo dominus meus, quis prior imperator talem legem dederit, et subtilius æstimet, si debuit dari. . . . Ego quidem jussioni subjectus eandem legem per diversas terrarum partes feci transmitti, et quia lex ipsa omnipotenti Deo minime concordet, ecce per suggestionis meæ paginam serenissimis dominis nuntiavi. Utrobique ergo quæ debui exolvi, qui et imperatori obedientiam præbui, et pro Deo quod sensi minime tacui."

of the jurisdiction of the Bishop of Corcyra.   It appears from
this that the Emperor Maurice had given some decision upon
the subject, and Gregory speaks of this as wholly void, as being
"*contra leges et sacras canones.*"   The Bishop of Nicopolis, the
Metropolitan of Corcyra, had given a different judgment, to
which Gregory says he had given his approbation.   But Gregory
adds that, as the Emperor Maurice had given a decision, he had
abstained from publishing his own decision lest he should appear
to act contrary to the imperial command and in contempt of it.
He therefore instructs Boniface to do what he can to persuade
the Emperor to issue an order confirming the judgment of
Gregory.[1]   Gregory's tone is very emphatic about the illegality
and invalidity of the action of Maurice, but it must be observed
that he carefully refrains from publicly denouncing it, and

---

[1] St Gregory the Great, Epist., Lib.
xiv. 8 : ". . . Hoc tamen breviter
indicamus, quia dum Mauricio quondam
imperatori esset in præjudicio Ecclesiæ Corcyritanæ subreptum, nec jus-
sio ejus, quippe quæ contra leges et sacros canones data fuerat, habuisset effec-
tum, et indecisa inter partes contentio
remansisset : aliam illam ad Andream
quondam fratrem nostrum tunc Nico-
politanum metropolitam jussionem de-
disse, ut, quoniam utraque pars ejus
erat jurisdictioni subjecta, ipse hanc
causam cognoscere et finire canonice
debuisset.   Qui metropolita, cognita
causa, prolataque sententia, cujus tibi
exemplaria misimus, prædictum Cassiopi
castrum sub potestate ac jurisdictione
Corcyritani Episcopi cujus et semper fuit
diœcesis, esse distinxit.   Quam nos
sententiam comprobantes, apostolicæ
Sedis auctoritate prævidimus confirman-
dum. . . . Sed quia inter ipsa prim-
ordia serenissimo domno imperatori
subreptum est, atque contra judicatum
Nicopolitani metropolitæ quod ecclesiastica rectitudine et canonica ratione
suffultum est, episcopo Euriæ, quod
nec sine dolore audire vel loqui sine
gemitu possumus, cum majori injuria
episcopi Corcyritani atque clericorum
ejus antefatum Cassiopi castrum traditum memoratur, ut amota, quod dici
grave est, jurisdictione Corcyritanæ Ecclesiæ, ipse illic omnem tamquam prin-
cipalem habeat potestatem, sententiam
nostram nulli dare prævidimus, ne contra
jussionem clementissimi domni imperatoris vel, quod absit in despectu ipsius aliquid facere videremur.   Itaque
dilectio tua pietati ejus cuncta diligenter insinuet, atque constanter astruat
hoc omnino pravum, omnino injustum,
omnino inlicitum, et sacris esse valde
canonibus inimicum : et ideo hujusmodi
peccatum temporibus suis introduci in
Ecclesiæ præjudicium non permittat,
sed quid de hoc negotio judicatum
antefati quondam metropolitæ con-
tineat, vel qualiter a nobis ea quæ ab illo
decreta sunt, confirmata fuerint, sug-
gerat, atque id agere studeat, ut cum
ejus jussione nostra illic sententia trans-
mittatur, quatenus et serenitati ipsius,
sicut dignum est, reservasse et rational-
ibiter correxisse quæ male præsumpta
sunt videamur.   Qua in re omnino
opera danda est ut, si fieri potest,
etiam ipse jussionem tribuat, in qua
ea quæ a nobis definita sunt servari
præcipiat."

setting his own judgment, or that of the Metropolitan, against it; and hopes to gain his point by persuading the Emperor to agree with his judgment and to issue an order expressing this.

In Gregory the Great, then, we find this theory of the sacred character of government so developed as to make the ruler in all his actions the representative of God, not merely the representative of God as embodying the sacred ends for which the government of society exists. The conception is, so far as we have seen, almost peculiar to some Christian writers. We have not observed anything which is really parallel to the conception in the legal writers, and even in Seneca and Pliny we have only indications of an attitude of mind which might be capable of development in this direction. The theory is a somewhat irregular and illogical development of the Christian conception of the divine character of the civil order.

It will naturally be asked, What were the circumstances under which this theory grew up. We think that we can trace the development of this conception to three causes : first, the need of correcting that anarchical tendency in the primitive Church to which we have already referred ; secondly, the relation between the Christian Church and the Emperor after the conversion of Constantine ; and, thirdly, the influence of the Old Testament conception of the position of the King of Israel.

We think that the necessity for counteracting the anarchical tendencies in the primitive Christian societies was probably a very real cause of the tendency to exaggerate or misstate the divine authority of the ruler. We think that the great emphasis laid upon the sacred character of the civil order in the New Testament—an emphasis which is maintained by writers like Clement of Rome and Irenæus—is a very real indication of a danger which menaced the Church, and led naturally to just the same kind of exaggeration as did the parallel phenomena in the sixteenth century. If we add to this the imperious need which lay on the Christian societies to disarm the hostility of the Empire, we shall, it seems to us, find one reasonable explanation of the tendency to overstate the sanctity of authority in the earliest ages of the Church.

With the conversion of the Empire to Christianity no doubt these conditions were greatly altered. But while, as we shall see presently, many of the Christian writers from the fourth to the seventh centuries illustrate conceptions of quite another kind from those which we have just discussed, yet in this period, too, there were continually in operation circumstances which tended to make the attitude of the Church towards the Emperors one of a somewhat servile deference. We may find an extremely good illustration of the influence of these circumstances in that passage from St Optatus [1] which we have already considered. In the case of the Donatist dispute the Empire at last exercised its authority to put down what it considered a schismatical faction. And it is easy to see from the tone of St Optatus that this intervention was unhappily as welcome to many Churchmen as it was distasteful to the Donatists.[2] Donatus urged that the Emperor had nothing to do with Church affairs ; St Optatus bids him remember that the Church is within the Empire, and that the Emperor has no superior save God. The truth is, that with the conversion of Constantine the Emperor became the patron and protector of the Church, and it would be easy enough to trace in many cases the effect of this protectorate on the course of Church disputes. Churchmen would resist the Emperor when he happened to be opposed to their view ; but when he agreed with them, they were only too apt to fall into the habit of regarding his action against their enemies as that of a truly sacred authority. The emancipation of the political theory of the Church from such conceptions as those of Gregory the Great must be traced in large measure to the actual contests between the Church and the Empire.

It is, however, possible that these influences would not alone have been sufficient to produce so rigorous a theory as that of Gregory the Great, had they not been reinforced and confirmed by traditions which the Christian Church inherited from the

[1] See p. 148.
[2] Cf. the temper of St Augustine as illustrated in the passages on the property of the Donatists, which we have already considered. See pp. 140, 141.

religion of Israel. We can hardly doubt that, directly, the theories of St Augustine and St Isidore on the Divine appointment of even wicked rulers, and St Gregory's theory of the duty of submission even to such rulers, are drawn from the Old Testament conception of the position of the king of Israel. According to the tradition of the first Book of Samuel, the monarchy was indeed instituted against the advice of the prophet, who is taken as speaking in the name of God; but the narrative of the same book and of the other historical books makes it very plain that the king, when once appointed, was looked upon as the anointed of the Lord,—that his person and his authority were sacred. There may, indeed, be traces in the Old Testament of other views than this, but this is the normal view of the monarchy in Israel, a view which possessed no doubt a special force with regard to the monarchy of the house of David. Such conceptions with regard to the sanctity of monarchy were probably in no way peculiar to Israel, but belonged to many oriental nations; but it was largely through the Christian Fathers that they came into the West. The passages to which we have referred will make it sufficiently plain that it is in relation to the Old Testament that these views are developed by the Fathers. We may at least reasonably say that the tradition of Israel provided the centre round which such opinions took definite shape and form.

In St Gregory the Great, then, we find in definite and systematic form a theory of the source of authority in Government which is very sharply contrasted with that which we have seen to be characteristic of the legal writers. They trace the source of all authority in the State to its fountainhead in the people. St Gregory traces the authority of rulers directly to God. The history of mediæval political theory is very largely the history of the struggle between these two views, in which, however, for many centuries, the combatants change places. For, at least from the eleventh to the fourteenth century, it is the Imperialist party which defends the theory of the Divine authority of the ruler, it is the ecclesiastical which maintains that his authority is derived from the people. We have to consider how it was that this change took place, and to do

this we shall have to examine in detail the history of the
political ideas especially of the ninth century.

But before we proceed to do this we have still to examine
some other tendencies of thought in the Christian Fathers.
We shall see that besides that tradition which we have so
far been examining, there are others which, as we think,
greatly influenced the political theory of the ninth century.

CHAPTER XIV.

AUTHORITY AND JUSTICE.

So far we have endeavoured to disentangle the history and
significance of a political conception, which, as it appears to
us, was first, in Western thought, developed by the Christian
Fathers,—the conception of the Divine authority of the ruler,
the doctrine that the ruler is absolute relatively to his subjects,
responsible only to God. It would, however, be a great mistake
to suppose that this theory represents the whole contribution of
the Christian Fathers to this portion of political theory. There
are many other elements in their conception of the nature of
authority in the State; one or two of the great Fathers, indeed,
seem to tend in quite another direction, and with regard to
them all it must be recognised that the elements of their theory
on this matter are highly complex, perhaps a little confused.
We must consider some general aspects of their thought,
arranging them as well as we can.

While the Christian Fathers as a rule think that the institution of coercive Government is not primitive or natural, in that
sense, they look upon the institution as being good, inasmuch
as it is a remedy for the confusions and disorder which sin
has brought into the world. It is true, as we have seen, that
they sometimes think of it as being a punishment as well as
a remedy for sin; but, normally, they think of the State as
an instrument for securing and preserving justice, and they
regard it as the chief duty of the king as ruler to benefit his
people by maintaining justice. We have already observed that
St Paul's assertion of the Divine character of the authority of
the State rests upon the assumption that the State rewards

the good and punishes the evil,—that is, that it maintains justice.[1]

In the second century we find Irenæus in very plain terms threatening unjust rulers with the judgment of God, assuring them that God will certainly visit their wickedness upon them;[2] and if we turn to the Alexandrian Fathers, we find Clement defining a king as one who rules according to law, and who is willingly obeyed by his subjects,[3]—that is, if we may so interpret Clement's meaning, a king is one who follows not merely his own caprice or desire, but governs according to those rules of public action which are designed for the attainment and preservation of justice, and whom his subjects willingly obey as representing their own just desires.

When we pass to St Ambrose in the latter part of the fourth century, we find all these conceptions drawn out and developed very clearly and fully. To St Ambrose justice and beneficence form the "ratio" of the State:[4] justice is that which builds up the State, while injustice destroys it.[5] This conception is very significant, especially when we compare it, as we shall have to do presently, with St Augustine's attempt to define the State; and it finds its proper development in the discussion of the relation of the unjust person who discharges an office of Government, to the sacred character of the institution of Government itself. St Ambrose seems to mean that he only is properly the minister of God who uses his authority well:[6] the passage is, indeed, somewhat obscure, but that seems to be his meaning.

---

[1] Rom. xiii. 1, &c.

[2] Irenæus, Adv. Hær., v. 24.

[3] Clement of Alexandria, Stromata, i. 24: "βασιλεὺς τοίνυν ἐστὶν ὁ ἄρχων κατὰ νόμους, ὁ τὴν τοῦ ἄρχειν ἑκόντων ἐπιστήμην ἔχων."

[4] St Ambrose, De Officiis, i. 28: "Justitia ergo ad societatem generis humani, et ad communitatem refertur. Societatis enim ratio dividitur in duas partes, justitiam et beneficentiam, quam eamdem liberalitatem et benignitatem vocant; justitia mihi excelsior videtur, liberalitas gratior."

[5] St Ambrose, De Off., ii. 19:

"Claret ergo quoniam et æquitas imperia confirmet, et injustitia dissolvat."

[6] St Ambrose, Exp. Ev. S. Lucæ iv. 5: "Denique eo usque a Deo ordinatio potestatis; ut Dei minister sit, qui bene utitur potestate. 'Dei' inquit, 'minister est tibi in bonum.' Non ergo muneris aliqua culpa est, sed ministri; nec Dei potest ordinatio displicere, sed administrantis actio. Nam ut de cœlestibus ad terrena derivemus exemplum, dat honorem imperator, et habet laudem. Quod si quis male honore usus fuerit, non imperatoris est culpa, sed judicis."

But this is not all that is worth observing in St Ambrose's theory of the institution of Government. It is interesting to notice that he lays some stress upon the attitude of the ruler towards liberty. In a letter to Theodosius, on the subject of certain demands which had been made upon the Church, and against which St Ambrose protests, he urges the importance of the permission of freedom of speech and remonstrance; and while, no doubt, he is thinking primarily of the freedom óf ecclesiastics in relation to the civil power, he shows some sense of the significance of the conception of liberty in the political order: good rulers, he says, love liberty, while bad rulers love slavery.[1] It would of course be very foolish to lay too much stress on such phrases; but they are at least worth noting, especially as similar phrases are used both by Cassiodorus and by Gregory the Great. Cassiodorus, writing in the name of Athalaric to a certain Ambrose who had just been appointed to the quæstorship, recalls a saying of Trajan, in which he had expressed his wish that his counsellors should freely advise him, rebuking him if necessary.[2] Gregory the Great, in a letter not perhaps very creditable to him, in which he expressed to the Emperor Phocas his joy that he had taken the place of Maurice, hails his accession as promising to restore liberty to the people in his dominions, adding that this is the great difference between the emperors of the Commonwealth and the kings of the nations, that the former are the lords of free men, the latter of slaves.[3]

In later times St Ambrose was frequently quoted as

[1] St Ambrose, Ep. xl. 2: "Sed neque imperiale est libertatem dicendi denegare, neque sacerdotale quod sentias non dicere. Nihil enim in vobis imperatoribus tam popularis et tam amabilis est, quam libertatem etiam in iis diligere, qui obsequio militiæ vobis subditi sunt. Siquidem hoc interest inter bonos et malos principes, quod boni libertatem amant, servitutem improbi. Nihil etiam in sacerdote tam periculosum apud Deum, tam turpe apud homines, quam quod sentiat, non libere denuntiare."

[2] Cassiodorus, Varia, viii. 13: "Renovamus certe dictum illud celeberrimi Trajani; sume dictationem, si bonus fuero, pro republica et me, si malus, pro republica in me."

[3] St Greg. the Great, Ep. xiii. 34: "Reformetur jam singulis sub jugo pii imperii libertas sua. Hoc namque inter reges gentium et reipublicæ imperatores distat, quod reges gentium domini servorum sunt, imperatores vero reipublicæ, domini liberorum." The same phrase occurs in Ep. xi. 4: perhaps it is a quotation.

maintaining that the king or ruler is bound by the laws; and, indeed, there is more than one passage which would seem to have this meaning. In one of his letters he seems to argue that the emperor who makes the laws is also bound to obey them;[1] and in one of his treatises he seems to express an opinion of the same kind.[2] It must, however, be observed that in other places he uses the ordinary legal phrase, that the emperor is *legibus solutus*.[3] It is worth observing that St Augustine also deals with the relation of the ruler to the law in terms analogous[4] to those of St Ambrose, and, in later times, is much quoted with St Ambrose. St Isidore of Seville also urges very strongly upon the prince the propriety of his respecting his own laws. Subjects will learn obedience when they see their rulers observing the laws.[5]

With some parts of St Augustine's theory of the State we have already dealt; but St Augustine's theory has a certain completeness which we do not find in that of the other Fathers, and, at the risk of a little repetition, we think it well to try to consider briefly his theory of law and the State as a whole. We have already seen that in St Augustine's view men were

[1] St Ambrose, Ep. xxi. 9: "Ubi illud constituimus, imperator, quod jam ipse tuum judicium declarasti; immo etiam dedisti leges, nec cui esset liberum aliud judicare? Quod cum prescripsisti aliis, prescripsisti et tibi. Leges enim imperator fert, quas primus ipse custodiat."

[2] St Ambrose, Apol. Alt. Proph. Daniel, iii.: "Quem mihi hujuscemodi reperias virum qui in potestate constitutus non magis peccata sua diligat . . . qui se legibus obstringat suis, et quod per justitiam non licet, nec per potestatem licere agnoscat? Non enim solvit potestas justitiam, sed justitia potestatem; nec legibus rex solutus est, sed leges suo solvit exemplo. An fieri potest, ut qui de aliis judicat, suo ipse sit liber judicio, et in se suscipiat, in quo et alios astringat?"

[3] St Ambrose, Apol. Prophet Daniel, xvi.: "Quamvis rex legibus absolutus";

and in the same work, x.: "Sequitur, 'Tibi soli peccavi,' Rex utique erat, nullis ipse legibus tenebatur, quia liberi sunt reges a vinculis delictorum; neque enim ullis ad pœnam vocantur legibus, tuti sub imperii potestate."

[4] St Aug., De Vera Religione, 31: "Sicut in istis temporalibus legibus, quanquam de his homines iudicent, cum eas instituunt, tamen cum fuerint institutæ atque firmatæ, non licebit judici de ipsis judicare sed secundum ipsas."

[5] St Isidore of Seville, Sent. iii. 51: "Justum est principem legibus obtemperare suis. Tunc enim jura sua ab omnibus custodienda existimet, quando et ipse illis reverentiam præbet. Principes legibus tenere suis, neque in se posse damnare jura quæ in subjectis constituunt. Justa est enim vocis eorum auctoritas, si quod populis prohibent, sibi licere non patiantur."

originally equal, and that the institutions of slavery and government, in which one man is the superior of another, are consequences of man's sin. The subjection of man to man is a punishment and a remedy for sin. It must be remembered, however, that this does not mean that men were by nature solitary. On the contrary, as we have already pointed out, St Augustine definitely maintains that by his own nature man is driven to seek the society of his fellow-men; society is natural and primitive. It is the organised society of the State, with its coercive government and its authority of man over his fellow-men, which is a conventional institution, and it may be regarded partly as punitive, partly as remedial.[1]

It is important, therefore, to consider how St Augustine defines the State and what is its relation to justice. In the second book of the ' De Civitate Dei ' he gives an account of the discussion of the nature of the State in Cicero's ' De Republica,' and quotes the definition of Scipio: "Populum autem non omnem cœtum multitudinis, sed cœtum juris consensu et utilitatis communione sociatum esse determinat,"[2] but postpones the discussion of the definition. We find this discussion in the nineteenth book. Here, after restating Cicero's definition, he explains that this means that there can be no true State without justice: when there is not justice there can be no *jus*. But, he objects, how can you speak of justice among men who do not serve God? What sort of justice is this to take men from the service of God and to subject them to demons? There is no justice in men who do such things, and there can therefore be no justice in a society formed of such men.[3] This definition, then, will not work, and he proceeds to

<hr>

[1] St Aug., De Civ. Dei, xix. 12 and 15. See pp. 125, 126.

[2] St Aug., De Civ. Dei, ii. 21.

[3] St Aug., De Civ. Dei, xix. 21 : "Populum enim esse definivit cœtum multitudinis juris consensu et utilitatis communione sociatum. Quid autem dicat juris consensum, disputando explicat, per hoc ostendens geri sine justitia non posse rem publicam ; ubi ergo justitia vera non est, nec jus pot-

est esse. Quod enim jure fit, profecto juste fit ; quod autem fit injuste, nec jure fieri potest. Non enim jura dicenda sunt vel putanda iniqua hominum constituta, cum illud etiam ipsi jus esse dicant, quod de justitiæ fonte manaverit, falsumque esse, quod a quibusdam non recte sentientibus dici solet, id esse jus, quod ei, qui plus potest, utile est. Quocirca ubi non est vera justitia, juris consensu

search for some other definition which may make it possible to admit that Rome had been a true State. This is given in a later chapter of the same book, and is as follows: "Populus est cœtus multitudinis rationalis rerum quas diligit concordi communione sociatus." A State may be more or less corrupt, but so long as it consists of a multitude of rational beings associated together in the harmonious enjoyment of that which they love, St Augustine thinks it may be regarded as a State or Commonwealth.[1] This is practically Cicero's definition, but with the elements of law and justice left out. No more fundamental difference could very well be imagined, although St Augustine seems to take the matter lightly; for Cicero's whole conception of the State turns upon this principle, that it is a means for attaining and preserving justice.

sociatus cœtus hominum non potest esse, et ideo nec populus juxta illam Scipionis vel Ciceronis definitionem; et si non populus, nec res populi, sed qualiscumque multitudinis, quæ populi nomine non digna est. Ac per hoc, si res publica res est populi, et populus non est, qui consensu non sociatus est juris, non est autem jus, ubi nulla justitia: procul dubio colligitur, ubi justitia non est, non esse rem publicam. Justitia porro ea virtus est, quæ sua cuique distribuit. Quæ igitur justitia est hominis, quæ ipsum hominem Deo vero tollit et immundis dæmonibus subdit? Hocine est sua cuique distribuere. . . . Qua propter ubi homo Deum non servit, quid in eo putandus est esse justitiæ? Quando quidem Deo non serviens nullo modo potest juste animus corpori aut humana ratio vitiis imperare. Et si in homine tali non est ulla justitia, procul dubio nec in hominum cœtu, qui ex hominibus talibus constat. Non est hic ergo juris ille consensus, qui hominum multitudinem populum facit, cujus res dicitur esse respublica." Cf. St Aug., De Civ. Dei, ii. 21, conclusion.

[1] St Aug., De Civ. Dei, xix. 24: "Si autem populus non isto, sed alio definiatur modo, velut si dicatur: 'Populus est cœtus multitudinis rationalis rerum quas diligit concordi communione sociatus,' profecto, ut videatur qualis quisque populus sit, illa sunt intuenda quæ diligit. Quæcumque tamen diligat, si cœtus est multitudinis non pecorum, sed rationalium creaturarum et eorum quæ diligit concordi communione sociatus est, non absurde populus nuncupatur; tanto utique melior, quanto in melioribus, tantoque deterior, quanto est in deterioribus concors. Secundum istam definitionem nostram Romanus populus populus est et res ejus sine dubitatione respublica. Quid autem primis temporibus suis quidve sequentibus populus ille dilexerit et quibus moribus ad cruentissimas seditiones atque inde ad socialia atque civilia bella perveniens ipsam concordiam, quæ salus est quodam modo populi, ruperit atque corruperit, testatur historia; de qua in præcedentibus libris multa posuimus. Nec ideo tamen vel ipsum non esse populum vel ejus rem dixerimus non esse rem publicam, quamdiu manet qualiscumque rationalis multitudinis cœtus, rerum quas diligit concordi communione sociatus."

This definition does not seem to represent a casual or isolated judgment of St Augustine, corrected perhaps at other times. He does not, indeed, so far as we have seen, formally set out to define the nature of the State in any other place, but he alludes to the matter more than once, and always in the same sense. In one letter he says : "What is a State (*civitas*) but a multitude of men, brought together into some bond of agreement?"[1] and again, in another letter, "A State is nothing else but a harmonious multitude of men";[2] and again, in one of his treatises, he urges that every one must recognise the importance of the order of the State, which coerces even sinners into the bond of some earthly peace.[3] These phrases would not, if they stood alone, be sufficient to make clear St Augustine's conception of the State; but when taken with the definition which we have just considered, they seem to indicate that his omissions from Cicero's definition are not accidental, but more or less deliberate and considered.

It must at the same time be recognised that once at least St Augustine uses a phrase which would seem to point in another direction. In the 'De Civitate,' after discussing the comparative advantages of great dominions, and of living in peace and goodwill with one's neighbours, he draws out a comparison between a band of robbers or pirates and a kingdom, and seems to mean that the only point of distinction is that the latter has the quality of justice.[4] Here at least St Augustine expresses himself in the terms of Cicero's conception of the State. And with this passage we may compare a definition which is obviously closely related to that of Cicero,—nothing can be properly called *jus* which is unjust;[5] and an interesting

---

[1] St Aug., Ep. cxxxviii. 2 : "Quid est autem civitas, nisi multitudo hominum in quoddam vinculum redactum concordiæ?"

[2] Id., Ep. clv. 3 : "Cum aliud civitas non sit, quam concors hominum multitudo."

[3] Id., De Genesi ad Litteram, ix. ix : "An vero ita quis cæcus est mente, ut non cernat quanto terris ornamento sit genus humanum, etiam cum a

paucis recte laudabiliterque vivatur; quantumque valeat ordo reipublicæ, in cujusdam pacis terrenæ vinculum coercens etiam peccatores."

[4] Id., De Civ. Dei, iv. 4 : "Remota itaque justitia quid sunt regna nisi magna latrocinia? quia et latrocinia quid sunt nisi parva regna?"

[5] Id., Enarr. in Ps. cxlv. 15 : "Jus et injuria contraria sunt. Jus enim est quod justum est. Neque enim

passage, in which St Augustine describes the characteristics of justice in language taken, in the main, from Cicero's treatise, " De Inventione," but which in part also suggests the definitions of Ulpian.[1] These definitions of justice, however, only show that St Augustine follows the general tradition of the relations of law and justice, and the nature of civil justice.

The first mentioned phrase is, as far as we have seen, isolated, and can hardly be cited in correction of the deliberate and considered omission of the quality of justice in his formal definition of the State.   It must, at the same time, be recognised that St Augustine is compelled to abstract the quality of justice from the definition of the State, not by any course of reflection upon the nature of the State, but by his theological conception of justice,—a conception which might be regarded as true upon his premises, but which can only be understood as related to those premises.

We cannot express a decided judgment upon the very inter-

omne quod jus dicitur, jus est.   Quid si aliquis condat jus iniquum ?   Nec jus dicendum est, si injustum est. Illud ergo verum jus, quod etiam justum est.   Vide quid feceris, non quid patiaris.   Si jus fecisti, injuriam pateris : si injuriam fecisti jus pateris." —Cf. with Cicero in De Civ. Dei, xix. 21.

[1] De Div. Quæst., xxxi : " Justitia est habitus animi, communi utilitate conservata, suam cuique tribuens dignitatem.   Ejus initium est ab natura profectum : deinde quædam in consuetudinem ex utilitatis ratione venerunt : postea res et ab natura profectas et a consuetudine probatas, legum metus et religio sanxit. Natura jus est, quod non opinio genuit, sed quædam innata vis inseruit, ut religionem, pietatem, gratiam, vindicationem, observantiam, veritatem. Religio est quæ superioris cujusdam naturæ, quam divinam vocant, curam ceremoniamque affert.   Pietas, per quam sanguine conjunctis patriæque benevolens officium, et diligens tribui-

tur cultus.   Gratia, in qua amicitiarum et officiorum, alterius memoria, et alterius remunerandi voluntas continetur. Vindicatio, per quam vis aut injuria, et omnino omne quod obfuturum est, defendendo et ulciscendo propulsatur. Observantia, per quam homines aliqua dignitate antecellentes, cultu quodam et honore dignamur.   Veritas per quam immutata ea quæ sunt aut fuerunt aut futura sunt dicuntur. Consuetudine autem jus est quod aut leviter a natura tractum aluit, et majus fecit usus, ut religionem ; et si quid eorum quæ ante diximus a natura profectum, majus factum propter consuetudinem videmus : aut quod in morem vetustas vulgi approbatione perduxit.   Quod genus pactum est, par, lex, judicatum.   Pactum est quod inter aliquos convenit.   Par, quod in omnes æquale est.   Judicatum, de quo alicujus aut aliquorum jam sententiis constitutum est.   Lege jus est, quod in eo scripto, quod populo expositum est ut observet, continetur."

esting question whether St Augustine's definition of the State exercised any great influence upon the course of political speculation. We have not found that this part of his work is often cited; indeed, we have not come across any instance of this in the earlier Middle Ages at all. But it is hardly possible to escape the impression that, however indirectly, this attitude of St Augustine towards the conception of justice in society is related to that conception of the unrestricted authority of the ruler, which, as we have already seen, takes shape about this period, and was drawn out so sharply by St Gregory the Great. As we have already seen, the tendency to confuse between the Divine authority of the institution of government, and the Divine authority of the individual ruler, can be traced back to very early Christian writers, but in St Augustine this tendency is very much developed. We have already quoted one passage from his writings which illustrates this point,[1] but it will be useful to cite some other passages in which he draws out in detail his view that the worst, just as much as the best, kings draw their authority from God Himself.[2] We have already seen that it is out of this judgment that there grows the dogmatic conception of Gregory the Great, that the ruler must not under any circumstances be resisted. The references to the subject in St Augustine are too scanty to enable us to form a very complete theory of the matter; but, so far as they go, we should be inclined to suggest that there is some real connec-

[1] See p. 151.

[2] St Aug., De Civ. Dei, v. 21 : " Quæ cum ita sint, non tribuamus dandi regni atque imperii potestatem nisi Deo vero, qui dat felicitatem in regno cœlorum solis piis ; regnum vero terrarum et piis et impiis, sicut ei placet, cui nihil injuste placet. . . . Sic etiam homini- bus, qui Mario ipse Gaio Cæsari ; qui Augusto, ipse et Neroni ; qui Vespasia- nis, vel patri vel filio, suavissimis imperatoribus, ipse et Domitiano crudelissimo ; et ne per singulos ire necesse sit, qui Constantino Christiano, ipse apostatæ Juliano."

Id., De Natura Boni contra Mani-

chæos, 32 : " ' A Deo esse et ipsam nocendi potestatem.' Item quia etiam nocentium potestas non est nisi a Deo, sic scriptum est, loquente sapientia : ' Per me reges regnant, et tyranni per me tenent terram.' Dicit et apos- tolus : ' Non est potestas nisi a Deo.' Digne autem fieri, in libro Job scrip- tum est : ' qui regnare facit ' inquit ' hominem hypocritam, propter perver- sitatem populi.' Et de populo Israel dicat Deus. ' Dedi eis regem in ira mea.' Injustum enim non est ut im- probis accipientibus nocendi potes- tatem, et bonorum patientia probetur, et malorum iniquitas puniatur."

tion between a theory of the State which deliberately omits the characteristic of justice, and the theory that the ruler, whether just or unjust, must in all cases be looked on as holding God's authority. It would appear, then, that the political theory of St Augustine is materially different in several respects from that of St Ambrose and other Fathers, who represent the ancient tradition that justice is the essential quality, as it is also the end, of the State.

We have still to consider two Christian writers of the fifth and seventh centuries who seem to represent the more normal conception of the subject. The first of these writers, Cassiodorus, does not indeed furnish us with any detailed definition of the nature of the State, and he uses phrases which are sometimes ambiguous, but he does in the main seem to present the same judgment as that of St Ambrose, on the importance of justice in the State. He defines justice very much in the terms of Ulpian, as that habit of mind which renders his own to every man;[1] he recognises that it is this which truly magnifies the ruler, and causes the State to prosper;[2] and he exhorts the ministers of State to just conduct, as that which alone renders them worthy of the name of judge.[3] Law is the true instrument of social progress, the true method of human happiness, and this because law represents justice.[4] He quotes the great passage from St Paul on the authority of the ruler, with an interesting comment, pointing out that it is the ruler whose commands are just who is to be obeyed;[5] and, as we have seen, he describes the character of the good prince as that of one who is always ready to hear those who speak in the name of justice, and who delights in a counsellor who will always speak for the State, even when he has to criticise the ruler to

[1] Cassiodorus, De Anima, 5.
[2] Cass., Varia, iv. 12, and iii. 34.
[3] Cass., Varia, iii. 27.
[4] Cass., Varia, iii. 17, iv. 33, v. 39.
[5] Cass., 'Complexiones, in Epist. Apost.,' Rom. xiii. 1 : " Omnibus potestatibus sublimioribus subditi estote " ; et reliqua. Omnibus potestatibus justitiam præcipientibus dixit esse debere subjectos, quoniam potestas a Deo datur, et Deo videtur velle resistere qui ordinationi judiciariæ nititur obviare, dicens ab eo propter conscientiam rationabiliter formidari, qui in aliquo facinore probatur involvi ; ideo enim et tributa solvimus, quia nos principibus subjectos esse sentimus ; ministri enim Dei sunt, cum crimina commissa distringunt."

his face.[1] The true king is one who can govern and control himself.[2]

On the other hand, Cassiodorus seems to regard the king not only as the source of law, but as one who normally stands above it: the king feels himself bound by his own *pietas* when he is not bound by anything else;[3] and further, the king is only accountable to God—he may transgress against Him, but cannot be said to sin against others, for there is none who can judge him.[4] It is, however, possible to interpret this last passage as merely representing the legal theory as to the ruler being *legibus solutus* and the constitutional conditions which provided no court of justice to which the king was accountable. These phrases of Cassiodorus are interesting, but do not add much to what we have already seen in other Christian writers.

St Isidore of Seville presents us with some of the same ambiguities as Cassiodorus, but his treatment of the subject of the nature of Government is on the whole clear. He gives us very briefly a statement of the beginnings of social life among men.

[1] Cass., Varia, viii. 13. 'Ambrosio, v. i., quæstori Athalaricus Rex' : "Ecce iterum ad quæsturam eminens evenit ingenio. Redde nunc Plinium et sume Trajanum. Habes magna quæ dicas, si et tu simili oratione resplendeas. Fama temporum de legitima atque eloquenti jussione generatur. Omnia si quidem bona cumulat lingua diserta et quod a nobis præcipitur, gratia dictantis ornatur. Esto nobis ad bona suggerenda promptissimus et adversum improbitatem male præsumentium constanter erectus. Dic etiam auribus nostris quod est omnino pro nobis. Bonus princeps ille est, cui licet pro justitia loqui, et contra tyrannicæ feritatis judicium audire nolle constituta veterum sanctionum. Renovamus certe dictum illud celeberrimum Trajani : sume dictationem, si bonus fuero, pro republica et me, si malus, pro republica in me. Sed vide quid a te quæramus, quando nec nobis aliquid injustum licere permittimus. Decreta ergo nostra priscorum resonent consti-

tuta, quæ tantam suavitatem laudis inveniunt, quantum saporem vetustatis assumunt. Præjudicia, quæ nos horremus, in aliis non amamus. Obligamus te certe generalitati, dum absolute præcipimus jura servare. . . . Nam quid tibi conveniat, vides. Vox legum diceris, dum nos jura condamus."

[2] Cass., Exp. in Psalt., Ps. cxxxvii. 5.

[3] Cass., Varia, x. 16 : "Imperiosa nimium res est, patres conscripti, pietas nostra, quando propria voluntate vincimur, qui alienis condicionibus non tenemur. Nam cum deo præstante possimus omnia, sola nobis credimus licere laudanda."

[4] Cass., Exp. in Psalt., Ps. l. 5: "Nunc ad exponenda verba redeamus. De populo si quis erraverit, et Deo peccat, et regi. Nam quando rex delinquit, soli Deo reus est, quia hominem non habet qui ejus facta dijudicet. Merito ergo rex Deo tantum se dixit peccasse, quia solus erat qui ejus potuisset admissa discutere."

In his definition of *oppidum* he says that men were originally
naked and unarmed, defenceless against the inclemency of heat
and cold, and the attacks of wild beasts and of other men.
At last they learned to make for themselves huts in which
they might be sheltered and safe, and these were gradually
collected in towns.[1] But much more important than this is
his definition of the nature of the State. He defines *civitas* as
a multitude of men joined together by the bond of society:[2]
this is ambiguous, and he might be following St Augustine;
but his definition of *populus* makes his meaning plain. *Populus*
he defines as a multitude of men joined together in society by
an agreement of law, and harmonious fellowship.[3] It is both
interesting and important to see that St Isidore, whether intentionally or not, goes back from the position of St Augustine
to that of Cicero, and makes justice an essential part of the
nature of the State.

St Isidore carries out a conception of the same kind in his
definition of the true king and the sharp contrast he draws
between him and the tyrant. The king, he says, derives his
name from his function of ruling, and to rule means to correct:
if the king does what is right he will keep his name, if he does
evil he will lose it. St Isidore quotes an old proverb which
says, "Thou shalt be king if thou do right; if not, thou
shalt not be king," and he defines the chief virtues of a king
as Justice and *Pietas*.[4] With this definition is sharply con-

---

[1] St Isidore of Seville, Etym., xv. 2:
"Oppidum quidam ab oppositione
murorum dixerunt: alii ab opibus
recondendis, eo quod sit munitum:
alii quod sibi in eo conventus habitantium opem det mutuam contra
hostem. Nam primum homines tamquam nudi et inermes, nec contra
beluas præsidia habebant, nec receptacula frigoris et caloris, nec ipsi inter
se homines ab hominibus satis erant
tuti. Tandem naturali solertia speluncis sylvestribusque tegumentis tuguria
sibi et casas virgultis arundinibusque
contexerunt, quo esset vita tutior, ne
his, qui nocere possent, aditus esset.

Hæc est origo oppidorum, quæ quod
opem darent, idcirco oppida nominata
dixerunt."

[2] St Isidore of Seville, Etym., xv.
2: "Civitas est hominum multitudo
societatis vinculo adunata."

[3] St Isidore of Seville, Etym., ix. 4:
"Populus est humanæ multitudinis,
juris consensu, et concordi communione sociatus."

[4] St Isidore of Seville, Etym., ix. 3:
"Reges a regendo vocati. Sicut enim
sacerdos a sacrificando, ita et rex a
regendo. Non autem regit qui non corrigit. Recte igitur faciendo regis nomen
tenetur, peccando amittitur. Unde

trasted that of the tyrant, the wicked ruler who cruelly oppresses his people.[1] He carries out the same conception of kingship in greater detail in his 'Sentences.' In one place he again says that kings are so called from ruling, and lose the name if they transgress.[2] In another passage, which we have already quoted, he explains that the object for which kings and princes were appointed was that the people should be restrained from evil and directed to good.[3] The duty of the ruler is therefore to set forward justice in truth and reality;[4] and he will be guilty of a very great crime if he appoint unjust judges.[5] And finally, in a chapter already cited, which is often referred to in later times, having been embodied by Gratian in the Decretum, he maintains that it is a just thing that a prince should obey his own laws.[6]

It is true that along with these judgments he also maintains with St Augustine that evil kings are sent by God as a judgment upon evil peoples.[7] We have already quoted his words, and have seen that this notion probably assisted in the development of the theory that the ruler was in such a sense the representative of God that he could in no case be resisted. But St Isidore himself does not draw this conclusion; rather he seems in the main to hold that the legitimacy of Government is determined by its character,—that it is only as far as the ruler

---

et apud veteres, tale erat proverbium. 'Rex eris si recte facias, si non facias, non eris.

Regiæ virtutes præcipuæ duæ, justitia et pietas. Plus autem in regibus laudatur pietas; nam justitia per se severa est."

[1] St Isidore of Seville, Etym. ix. 3 : "Tyranni Græce dicuntur. Iidem Latine et reges. Nam apud veteres inter regem et tyrannum nulla discretio erat: ut, 'Pars mihi pacis erit, dextram tetigisse tyranni.' Fortes enim reges tyranni vocabantur. Nam tiro fortis. De quibus Dominus loquitur : ' Per me reges regnant, et tyranni per me tenent terram.' Jam postea in usum accidit, tyrannos vocari pessimos atque improbos reges luxuriosæ dominationis

cupiditatem, et crudelissimam dominationem in populis exercentes."

[2] St Isidore of Seville, Sententiæ, iii. 48.

[3] Id., id., iii. 47. See p. 119.

[4] Id., id., iii. 49.

[5] Id., id., iii. 52.

[6] Id., id., iii. 51 : " Justum est principem legibus obtemperare suis. Tunc enim jura sua ab omnibus custodienda existimet, quando et ipse illis reverentiam præbet. Principem legibus teneri suis, neque in se posse damnare jura, quæ in subjectis constituunt. Justa est enim vocis eorum auctoritas, si, quod populis prohibent, sibi licere non patiantur." Cf. Gratian, Decretum, Dist. ix. 2.

[7] Id., id., iii. 48. See p. 151.

promotes justice that he is to be looked upon as a true ruler at all.

We have endeavoured in this chapter to put together the judgments of the Fathers upon the place of justice in society. We have seen that, with the exception of St Augustine, they seem to show the persistence of the conception that the end of the State is the attainment of justice, and that the quality of justice is essential to the legitimacy of any organisation of society. We think it is important to observe this, for in some measure it seems to counteract that tendency of some of the Christian Fathers towards the theory of the absolute Divine authority of the monarch, and the consequent obligation of unlimited obedience. The truth is, probably, that the Christian Fathers had no clearly and completely developed conception of the nature of civil authority. One or two principles with respect to this were firmly fixed in their minds, but the conclusions which might be more or less legitimately derived from these principles were undefined, and not generally thought out, still less brought into logical coherence with each other. They were convinced of the Divine nature of the authority of the State, they were convinced that disobedience to that authority was in normal cases an offence against God. Some of them drew from this the conclusion that all authority, under all circumstances, was from God, and that even an unjust and oppressive command of the ruler must be obeyed. On the other hand, they were for the most part equally clear that the foundation and end of civil authority was the attainment of justice, and some of them more or less distinctly apprehended, as a consequence of this principle, that an unjust authority was no authority at all. The great principles which they held were of the profoundest and most permanent significance; but they had not drawn out from them a complete and coherent theory of the nature of authority in society.

CHAPTER XV.

THE THEORY OF THE RELATION OF CHURCH AND STATE.

WE have endeavoured to recognise something of the complexity of the patristic conceptions with regard to the nature of authority in the State. We have at least seen that while there is in the Fathers a tendency towards a theory of absolutism in the ruler, which finds its complete expression in St Gregory the Great, there are also other tendencies which seem to counteract this. These tendencies may be said to centre round the conception of justice, in spite of the fact that St Augustine's hold upon this conception is so loose; for in this matter, as in so much of his theology, St Augustine probably represents, not the normal, but a somewhat eccentric though influential, mode of thought. We think it is correct to say that the Fathers tend to think of the principle of justice as of something which lies outside the power of the civil authority—something which it does not create, and to which it is in some measure answerable. We may perhaps justly consider that there is some relation between this conception of a principle of justice outside the civil order and the gradually developing consciousness that while the civil order is itself one manifestation or expression of the principle of justice, this same principle finds expression in another order, the ecclesiastical, which is, properly speaking, not so much within the State as parallel to it. We find in the Fathers the consciousness that the Church has its own laws and principles, its own administrative authority, which is not at all to be regarded as dependent upon the State, but as something which stands beside it and is independent of it; that the relations between the Church and the

State are those of two independent though closely related powers, relations which it becomes necessary, as time goes by, to understand and define more clearly.

Before the conversion of Constantine, indeed, there was little question about the relation between the State and the Church: the Church was not merely separate, but was generally treated by the State as an enemy—an enemy which it would be well, if possible, to destroy. The Church was a voluntary society within the Empire, dependent for every public right that it might enjoy upon the grudging consent of the State. Christians asked for toleration, and maintained that they could not give up their faith and worship at the command of any earthly power; but toleration was all that they asked, and they asked it in the name of humanity, and on the ground that their religion, so far from being hurtful to the State or to good morals, would rather tend to loyalty and good order. The Church was necessarily conscious of its independence, but this independence was a purely spiritual one, and it claimed no rights or properties of a secular kind, except as derived from the sanction and authority of the State.

The conversion of Constantine and the official Christianisation of the Empire brought with them an entirely new set of circumstances; and the Church had to find its true place in these with much difficulty and labour. The change which the conversion of the Empire brought about does not seem to have been at all clearly recognised at first; at least we have been unable to find any source of information as to this in the literature of the time. The actual historical circumstances, however, gradually compelled men to form some sort of theory of the relation of the two societies. The relation of the Church and Church law to the civil authorities was gradually defined; great questions were indeed left outstanding, but we feel that at least some of the Fathers arrived at certain more or less clearly defined conceptions of the relations between Church and State.

We think that, while some of the Fathers use ambiguous phrases, there can be no serious doubt that after the conversion of Constantine, as much as before it, churchmen did normally refuse to recognise any authority of the civil ruler in spiritual matters. Rufinus of Aquileia has preserved in his history a report of a speech which Constantine, as he says, made to the bishops of the Church assembled in the Council of Nice. According to this report, Constantine recognised very clearly the limitations of the imperial authority in relation to Church order. He acknowledges frankly that he has no jurisdiction over bishops in spiritual matters, while they have jurisdiction over all Christians.[1] A little later than the Council of Nice, we find Hosius of Cordova, as quoted by St Athanasius, in spite of his close connection with the imperial court, repudiating in the most emphatic terms the notion that the emperor had any right to interfere in Church affairs. He warns Constantius not to intrude into ecclesiastical affairs: God had granted to him the kingdom, to the churchmen the care of the Church; he should remember that just as any one who should revolt against him would disobey God, so if he presumed to draw Church affairs under his control he would be guilty of a great fault.[2] Hosius's tone is very emphatic, much more so than we should perhaps have expected from the somewhat servile attitude of churchmen like Eusebius of Cæsarea, and it would seem to indicate the presence of a more general appreciation, at that time, of the independence of the Church relatively to the State than has been always recognised. If such language could be attributed to Constantine, and used by a friend of the court like

---

[1] Rufinus, Hist. Eccl., i. 2: "Deus vos constituit sacerdotes, et potestatem vobis dedit de nobis quoque judicandi, et ideo nos a vobis recte judicamur. Vos autem non potestis ab hominibus judicari. Propter quod Dei solius inter vos exspectate judicium, et vestra jurgia quæcumque sunt, ad illud divinum reserventur examen. Vos etenim nobis a Deo dati estis dii, et conveniens non est ut homo judicet Deos, sed ille solus, de quo scriptum est: 'Deus stetit in synagoga deorum; in medio autem deos discernit.'"

How far Rufinus's report is historically correct is a matter on which we express no opinion. We cite the passage not to illustrate the standpoint

of Constantine, but that of a Western churchman like Rufinus.

[2] Hosius of Cordova, letter quoted in St Athanasius, 'Historia Arianorum,' 44: Μὴ τίθει σεαυτὸν εἰς τὰ ἐκκλησιαστικά· μηδὲ σὺ περὶ τούτων ἡμῖν παρακελεύου· ἀλλὰ μᾶλλον παρ' ἡμῶν σὺ μάνθανε ταῦτα. Σοὶ βασιλείαν ὁ θεὸς ἐνεχείρισεν· ἡμῖν τὰ τῆς Ἐκκλησίας ἐπίστευσε. Καὶ ὥσπερ ὁ τὴν σὴν ἀρχὴν ὑποκλέπτων ἀντιλέγει τῷ διαταξαμένῳ θεῷ, οὕτω φοβήθητι μὴ καὶ σύ, τὰ τῆς Ἐκκλησίας εἰς ἑαυτὸν ἕλκων, ὑπεύθυνος ἐγκλήματι μεγάλῳ γένῃ. Ἀπόδοτε, γέγραπται, τὰ Καίσαρος Καίσαρι, καὶ τὰ τοῦ θεοῦ τῷ θεῷ. Οὔτε τοίνυν ἡμῖν ἄρχειν ἐπὶ τῆς γῆς ἔξεστιν, οὔτε σὺ τοῦ θυμιᾶν ἐξουσίαν ἔχεις βασιλεῦ.

Hosius, we need not perhaps be surprised to find a man of the violent temper of Lucifer of Cagliari using language identical in sentiment but somewhat more unqualified in tone, in the height of the contest of the Athanasian party with the Emperor Constantius. Without these phrases of Rufinus and Hosius we should indeed have hesitated as to the genuineness of the work from which we quote. Lucifer indignantly protests that Constantius is no judge of bishops, but rather should obey them and their laws; and he concludes by saying that the emperor is not even a Christian, and appointed by God to rule his people, but only a heretic and a persecutor.[1] Lucifer's tone is like that of the spurious letters of Gregory II. in the eighth century: we might even imagine ourselves in the early stages of the Investiture controversy of the eleventh century.

Against these passages we must no doubt set certain sayings which have a somewhat different character. We have already quoted a passage from the writings of St Optatus of Milevis, in which we find represented a different attitude towards the

---

[1] Lucifer of Cagliari, 'Pro Sancto Athanasio,' i. (in Migne, Patrol. Lat., vol. xiii. p. 826) : "Sed dicis : isto in loco Deo devotissimus Moyses quomodo sacerdotum fecit mentionem, sic et judicis. Proba te super nos factum judicem, proba ad hoc te constitutum imperatorem, ut nos armis tuis ad omnem implendam voluntatem amici tui diaboli perduceres ; cum probare non possis quia præceptum sit tibi, non solum non dominari episcopis, sed et ita eorum obedire statutis, ut si subvertere eorum decreta tentaveris, si fueris in superbia comprehensus, morte mori jussus sis. Quomodo dicere poteris, judicare te posse de episcopis, quibus nisi obedieris, jam, quantum apud Deum, mortis pœna fueris multatus ? Cum hæc ita sint, tu qui es profanus, ad Dei domesticos, quare istam sumis in Dei sacerdotum auctoritatem ? Cum etiam ipsos judices Judæos, tunc quando in lege manebant Dei, ex genere habere permiserit suo. 'Si enim' inquit Moyses 'dixeris, Statuam supra me principem, quomodo et reliquæ gentes . . .' Et subsequitur, cur noluerit alienigenam fieri principem, ne scilicet ad sectam suam traheret alios. Propterea dicit : 'Ne revocet nos in Ægyptum,' hoc est, ad idolorum cultum, quasi dicat : Quis est tu, inquam, qui tibi usurpasti hanc auctoritatem, quam tibi Deus non tradidit, et si traderet, et inter te esse permitteret, primo in loco Christianum te esse oportuerat, quia scelus esset alienigenam Dei servos judicare, inimicum religionis domesticos Dei. Deinde si fuisses Christianus, et te participem censuisset Deus sacerdotibus fieri ad gerendum populum ejus, accipe qualem te esse præceperit in Deuteronomio. 'Et erit cum sederit in principatu suo, scribe hoc in libro ante sacerdotes et levitas, et erit cum ipso. . . .' Quid tu hujusmodi habes, nisi omnia contraria, nisi cuncta, quæ Dei impugnent domum ? Primo es hæreticus, deinde persecutor Dei domesticorum."

State, and its interference with Church matters. Donatus had evidently treated the intervention of the emperor in favour of the Catholic party just as Lucifer of Cagliari had treated his interference against it, and had indignantly argued that the emperor had no right to interfere in Church matters. St Optatus urges in reply that the Church is in the empire, not the empire in the Church, and seems to treat the attitude of Donatus as that of one who set himself over the emperor, while, he urges, there is no one over the emperor but God.[1] Optatus seems to go rather far towards admitting the supremacy of the imperial jurisdiction even in Church matters.

It is natural to conjecture that some such notion lies behind that strange phrase of Ambrosiaster, to which we have already referred. He calls the king the Vicar of God, and says that he has the image of God, and the bishop has that of Christ.[2] The phrase is indeed very difficult of interpretation, but it is at least possible that it is intended to signify some superiority of jurisdiction.

If, then, we find in some of the Christian writers a very clear and explicit declaration of the principle that the State has no jurisdiction in Church matters, we must also recognise that others tend to a more doubtful position. We may in part explain the phrases of the latter as only referring to the power of the State to carry out secular penalties for eccclesiastical offences: no doubt the Catholic Church, when it invoked the arm of the temporal power to put down heretics and schismatics, conceived that its position was secure,—that it was for the Church to judge in spiritual matters, for the secular power to carry out the consequence of its judgments in secular conditions. But actually the policy of persecution did tend to make the State the arbitrator between different religious parties. At the same time, we do not think there can be any doubt as to the normal character of the Church theory with regard to its relation to the State. Indeed, the consideration of the views of these writers is, we think, of importance, mainly as preparing us for the examination of the much more complete treatment of the subject in the work of St Ambrose.

[1] See p. 148.   [2] See p. 148.

In St Ambrose the theory of the relation between the Church and State is more or less clearly defined. He is clear that certain rights of the Church are sacred and inviolable, in the very nature of things, and in accordance with the nature of God's ordinance in the world. He is very clearly conscious that the Church has its own jurisdiction, to which all Christian men, whatever their rank, are subject, and that the jurisdiction of the State does not extend over any strictly ecclesiastical matters.

We have already seen that St Ambrose, like all the Fathers, recognises the divine character of the civil order of society. He insists that the Christian man must render obedience to the civil ruler in virtue of his religion: not even the priest is to act disrespectfully towards the civil ruler, but, on the other hand, if the ruler commits any grave offence, then the priest must reprove him.[1] The ministers of the Church have jurisdiction over all Christian men, and their jurisdiction extends even over the Emperor or other civil ruler.[2] For even the Emperor is the son of the Church, subject to its authority, to its discipline: no title, St Ambrose says, is more honourable than that of son of the Church,—the Emperor is within the Church, not over it.[3] We find it, therefore, very natural that we should hear of St Ambrose exercising the last discipline of the Church, even against so pious and orthodox a ruler as the great Theodosius. The story of the exclusion of Theodosius from the Eucharist is, of course, very familiar, and it is not necessary here to detail the circumstances. For the massacre

---

[1] St Ambrose, Enarr. in Ps. xxxvii. 43 : "Vides ergo quia regibus non temere vel a prophetis Dei, vel a sacerdotibus facienda injuria sit ; si nulla sint graviora peccata, in quibus debeant argui : ubi autem peccata graviora sunt, ibi non videtur a Sacerdote parcendum, ut justis increpationibus corrigantur."

[2] St Ambrose, Ep. xxi. 4 (Ad Valent. II.) : "Quando audisti, clementissime Imperator, in causa fidei laicos de episcopo judicasse. . . . At certe si vel Scripturarum seriem divinarum, vel vetera tempora retractemus, quis est qui abnuat in causa fidei, in causa, inquam, fidei episcopos solere de imperatoribus Christianis, non imperatores de episcopis judicare."

[3] St Ambrose, Sermo contra Auxentium, 36 in Ep. xxi. : "Quod cum honorificentia imperatoris dictum nemo potest negare. Quid enim honorificentius, quam ut imperator Ecclesiæ filius esse dicatur ? Quod cum dicitur, sine peccato dicitur, cum gratia dicitur. Imperator enim intra Ecclesiam, non supra Ecclesiam est ; bonus enim imperator quærit auxilium Ecclesiæ non refutat." Contrast with St Optatus. See p. 148.

in Thessalonica Theodosius was responsible, and St Ambrose excluded him from attendance at the celebration of the Eucharist. It is perhaps worth while to cite some words from St Ambrose's letter to Theodosius, and to observe the mingled deference and firmness with which St Ambrose tells Theodosius that he cannot "offer the sacrifice" if he is present.[1]

It may, perhaps, serve to bring out more clearly the significance of this event, when we observe that this action was not isolated, but that for a much smaller matter, as we learn from a letter to his sister, St Ambrose had been prepared to take almost the same action. Certain Christians had burned down a synagogue of the Jews, and some monks had burned down a church belonging to adherents of the Valentinian heresy. Theodosius, very justly, as we should probably think, ordered the Christians to rebuild the synagogue, and the punishment of the monks. But St Ambrose took another view of the matter, and regarded the action of Theodosius as being contrary to religion. He wrote him a letter on the subject, and then preached on the matter in his presence, and, the sermon ended, demanded of Theodosius an assurance that he would withdraw the obnoxious order, before he would consent to celebrate the Eucharist.[2] Practically, St Ambrose was

[1] St Ambrose, Ep. li. 13 : "Ego certe in omnibus aliis licet debitor pietati tuæ, cui ingratus esse non possum, quam pietatem multis imperatoribus præferebam, uni adæquabam : ego inquam, causam in te contumaciæ nullam habeo, sed habeo timoris ; offerre non audeo sacrificium, si volueris assistere."

[2] St Ambrose (to his sister), Ep. xli. 27 : "Ubi descendi, ait mihi : De nobis proposuisti. Respondi : Hoc tractavi, quod ad utilitatem tuam pertineret. Tunc ait : Re vera de synagoga reparanda ab episcopo durius statueram, sed emendatum est. Monachi multa scelera faciunt. Tunc Timasius magister equitum et peditum cœpit adversum monachos esse vehementior. Respondi ei : Ego cum imperatore ago, ut oportet ; quia novi quod habeat Domini timo-

rem : tecum autem aliter agendum, qui tam dura loqueris.

28. Deinde cum aliquamdiu starem, dico imperatori : Fac me securum pro te offerre, absolve animum meum. Cum assideret, annueretque, non tamen aperte polliceretur, atque ego starem, dixit se emendaturum rescriptum. Statim dicere cœpi, ut omnem cognitionem tolleret ; ne occasione cognitionis comes aliqua Christianos attereret injuria. Promisit futurum. Aio illi : Ago fide tua ; et repetivi. Ago fide tua. Age, inquit, fide mea. Et ita ad altare accessi, non aliter accessurus nisi mihi plene promisisset. Et vere tanta oblationis fuit gratia, ut sentirem etiam ipse eam Deo nostro commendatiorem fuisse gratiam, et divinam præsentiam non defuisse. Omnia itaque ex sententia gesta sunt."

threatening Theodosius with exclusion from attendance at the celebration of the sacrament.

St Ambrose, then, is very clear in his assertion of the principle that the Church exercises jurisdiction over all Christian men, even the most exalted—even over the chief of the State. And at the same time he asserts, with equal emphasis, the principle that in religious matters the civil magistrate has no authority over ecclesiastics. We have cited one of the emphatic passages in which St Ambrose asserts that in matters of faith the layman has no jurisdiction over the priest.[1] He evidently traces this rule to the divine law, and that law, he urges, is greater than the imperial;[2] but he also urges that the principle has been admitted by the imperial legislation. In the letter from which we have just cited St Ambrose urges this point with great persistence. He had been requested to appear before the Imperial Court, and he refuses to comply, on the ground that this was an infringement of a law of Valentinian I.[3] We do not propose to enter into the history of ecclesiastical exemption from secular jurisdiction, a subject of formidable complexity, but it is necessary to observe it as illustrating the development of the position of the Church as being, within its own sphere, independent of the State.

It is not only in relation to the jurisdiction of the Church over the laity in spiritual matters, and its independence

[1] See p. 180, note 2.

[2] St Ambrose, Ep. xxi. 10 (**Ad** Valent. II.) : "Ecce, imperator, legem tuam jam ex parte rescindis : sed utinam non ex parte, sed in universum ! legem enim tuam nollem esse supra Dei legem. Dei lex nos docuit quid sequamur, humanæ leges hoc docere non possunt."

[3] St Ambrose, Ep. xxi. 2 (Ad Valent. II.) : "Cui rei respondeo, ut arbitror, competenter. Nec quisquam contumacem judicare me debet, cum hoc asseram, quod augustæ memoriæ pater tuus non solum sermone respondit, sed etiam legibus suis sanxit. In causa fidei vel ecclesiastici alicujus ordinis eum judicare debere, qui nec munere impar sit, nec jure dissimilis ; hæc enim verba rescripti sunt, hoc est, sacerdotes de sacerdotibus voluit judicare. Quinetiam si alias quoque argueretur episcopus, et morum esset examinanda causa, etiam hæc voluit ad episcopale judicium pertinere. . . .

5. Eris Deo favente, etiam senectutis maturitate provectior, et tunc de hoc censebis qualis ille episcopus sit, qui laicis jus sacerdotale substernit. Pater tuus, Deo favente, vir maturioris ævi, dicebat : non est meum judicare inter episcopos ; tua nunc dicit clementia. Ego debeo judicare. . . ."

of the civil ruler in all such matters, that we can recognise
in St Ambrose the sense of the existence of a power and
law which is altogether outside of the sphere of the civil
ruler. We can see in his writings the beginning of the importance of those questions with regard to Church property,
round which so much of the controversies of later times turned.
We have fortunately a tolerably full account in St Ambrose's
own writings of the position he took up, when the emperor
wished to insist on his giving up one or more of the churches
in his diocese for the use of the Arians. In a letter to his
sister he gives an account of the discussion between himself
and the officials sent to demand this. They insisted that
he should acquiesce promptly, for the emperor was within
his rights, for all things were in his power. He replied that
if the emperor were to demand his private property, he would
not refuse it; but those things which were *divina* were not
subject to the imperial power. Further on, however, he
qualifies this statement by urging that the emperor cannot
lawfully seize a private house, much less the house of God.
When he is again urged to surrender a church, he replies that
it is neither lawful for him to surrender it nor for the emperor
to accept it. The emperor, if he wishes to reign long, must be
subject to God, and obey the rule to give to Cæsar what is
Cæsar's and to God what is God's. Palaces belong to the emperor, churches to the priest, and he cannot surrender a church.[1]

[1] Ep. xx. 8: "Convenior ipse a comitibus et tribunis, ut basilicæ fieret
matura traditio, dicentibus imperatorem jure suo uti, eo quod in potestate ejus essent omnia. Respondi, si
a me peteret, quod meum est, id est,
fundum meum, argentum meum, quid-
vis hujusmodi meum, me non refraga-
turum; quamquam omnia quæ mei
sunt, essent pauperum : verum ea quæ
sunt divina, imperatoriæ potestati non
esse subjecta. . . .

19. Mandatur denique : Trade basilicam. Respondeo : Nec mihi fas est
tradere, nec tibi accipere, Imperator,
expedit. Domum privati nullo potes
jure temerare, domum Dei existimas

auferendam ? Allegatur imperatori
licere omnia, ipsius esse universa.
Respondeo, noli te gravare, Imperator,
ut putes te in ea, quæ divina sunt, imperiale aliquod jus habere. Noli te ex-
tollere, sed si vis diutius imperare, esto
Deo subditus. Scriptum est, quæ Dei
Deo, quæ Cæsaris, Cæsari. Ad imperatorem palatia pertinent, ad sacerdotem
Ecclesiæ. Publicorum tibi mœnium
jus commissum est, non sacrorum. . . .

22. Tradere basilicam non possum
sed pugnare non debeo. . . .

23. Si hæc tyrannidis videntur,
habeo arma, sed in Christi nomine ;
habeo offerendi mei corporis potestatem. Quid moraretur ferire, si tyran-

In the public discourse which St Ambrose delivered upon the same subject he repeats the same observations, but also throws some further light upon the question of what he understood to be the Church property, which was sacred to God. He protests his habitual respect for the emperor, but the demand for a church he cannot comply with. But, he adds, the lands of the Church pay tribute to the emperor; and if the emperor wishes to take these, he will not resist.[1] Evidently he draws a distinction between the churches and other ecclesiastical property. The distinction is one of some importance with regard to later developments of the relation of the State to Church property.

St Ambrose, then, is clear that there are distinct limitations to the imperial authority when the emperor comes into relation with religious matters. The Church has its own position and authority, which is independent of that of the State. We think that it is not unreasonable to judge that there was some relation between these clear convictions of St Ambrose and that tendency which we have already observed in him to limit the absolute authority of the civil ruler, even in secular matters— at least, to conceive of his authority as limited by the principle of justice, and perhaps as limited by the laws of the State.

In the latter part of the fifth century the question of the relation between the authority of the State and that of the Church is discussed very fully, especially in the letters and treatises of Pope Gelasius I.; and these not only show us how clearly the question was then apprehended, but also lay the foundations on which the theory of the ninth century was based. It is true that these discussions and definitions

---

num putaret? Veteri jure a sacerdotibus donata imperia, non usurpata: et vulgo dici quod imperatores sacerdotium magis optaverunt, quam imperium sacerdotes. . . . Addidi quia numquam sacerdotes tyranni fuerunt, sed tyrannos sæpe sunt passi."

[1] St Ambrose, Sermo contra Auxentium, in Ep. xxi.: "Scitis et vos ipsi quod imperatoribus soleam deferre non cedere: suppliciis me libenter offerre, nec metuere quæ parantur. . . .

33. Agri Ecclesiæ solvunt tributum: si agros desiderat imperator, potestatem habet vindicandorum; nemo nostrum intervenit. Potest pauperibus collatio populi redundare: non faciant de agris invidiam, tollant eos, si libitum est imperatori: non dono sed non nego."

go to establish a theory of a strict dualism in society, and they are not therefore in accord with the tendency of those mediæval thinkers who thought of society as organised under the terms of a complete unity. The development of the theory of unity in society is one of the most important of the movements which we shall have to study,—one of the most interesting aspects of mediæval political theory : we are at the same time not certain whether its historical significance has not been to some extent exaggerated,—whether scholars have not sometimes mistaken the formal or superficial tendencies of mediæval political thought for the fundamental. We are not quite sure whether the real importance of the conception of an absolute or formal unity in society, either in mediæval or in modern political theory, is quite what some may imagine. But this is a subject about which we shall have more to say in later volumes. The discussions and definitions of the fifth century belong to a stage in the development of political theory when the conception of dualism in society was taking shape and making itself felt as of importance in practical administration : we can at the same time recognise in them some of the elements out of which, in later times, the theory of the complete unity of society was to be constructed.

The historical circumstances which produced the literature which we have now to examine were of a highly complex kind. The Council of Chalcedon had tried to end the disputes of the Alexandrian and Antiochene schools in the Church by a definition of the doctrine of the union of the human and divine natures in our Lord, which was intended equally to condemn the extreme or so-called monophysite tendency of the Alexandrian and the extreme or so-called Nestorian tendency of the Antiochene school. In the main, while its decisions resulted in the separation from the Church of a certain number of extremists at each end, the decisions of Chalcedon did conclude the historical settlement of the terms of the faith of the Church with regard to our Lord's nature. But it was more than two centuries before the disputes on the subject in the Church were set at rest. The monophysite tendency was so strong, especially in Egypt, that in 482 the Emperor Zeno, with the advice ap-

parently of Acacius, Patriarch of Constantinople, issued a statement known to us as the "Henoticon," in which he tried to
state the doctrine of our Lord's nature in such a way as to
conciliate the Egyptians. In the West, however, and notably
by the Bishops of Rome, these proceedings were looked upon
with the greatest disfavour, and Felix II. finally anathematised
Acacius. It is not clear that Felix or his successor, Gelasius I.,
actually excommunicated either Zeno or any of the other emperors who remained in communion with Acacius, and with
Peter, the Patriarch of Alexandria; but practically all communion with those who held to Acacius was broken off, and
the Emperors and the Bishop of Rome found themselves in
formal opposition to each other.

The circumstances of the time were no doubt favourable
to the development of an independent attitude in the Western
Church, for this was the period during which the Gothic invasions
and occupation had practically destroyed all the power of the
Byzantine emperor in Italy. This may perhaps partly explain
the confidence of the tone adopted by the bishops of Rome towards the emperors, though it would be a mistake to think that
such an attitude towards the civil ruler was unprecedented : we
have indeed seen something of the same kind in the case of
St Ambrose.

We may perhaps with advantage notice some details in the
theory of Felix II. and Gelasius I. with regard to the relations
of the Church and the emperor before we discuss their formal
definitions on this subject. They both assert with great
emphasis the subordination even of the emperor to the Church
in spiritual matters. Felix exhorts Zeno to remember that it is
well for him if he strive to submit his royal will to the priests
of Christ: when the things concerning God are in question,
the king should learn rather than presume to teach.[1] In

---

[1] Felix II., Ep. viii. 5: "Certum est enim, hoc rebus vestris esse salutare, ut cum de causis Dei agitur, et juxta ipsius constitutum regiam voluntatem sacerdotibus Christi studeatis subdere, non præferre, et sacrosancta per eorum præsules discere potius quam docere. Ecclesiæ formam sequi, non huic humanitus sequenda jura præfigere, neque ejus sanctionibus velle dominari, cui Deus voluit clementiam tuam piæ devotionis colla submittere : ne dum mensura cœlestis dispositionis exceditur eatur in contumeliam disponentis."

the tenth letter of Pope Gelasius the same thing is said, with perhaps a little additional precision and a special assertion of the authority of the apostolic see. The secular power should learn, not judge, of divine things from the bishops, and specially from the Vicar of St Peter: not even the most powerful of Christian rulers of the world may draw such things into his hands.[1] The subject is drawn out in greater detail in the first letter attributed to Gelasius, a letter thought to have been written by him in the name of Pope Felix II. to the Eastern bishops. The emperor has no authority, Gelasius urges, to consider the cause of an ecclesiastic or to receive him to communion: this is contrary to all church order. The emperor is the son, not the ruler, of the Church: God gave the authority of ruler in His Church to bishops and priests, not to secular rulers or to the civil law. The emperor has indeed received his authority from God, and should therefore not set himself against the divine order.[2]

[1] Gelasius I., Ep. x. 9 : "Si quantum ad religionem pertinet, non nisi apostolicæ sedi juxta canones debetur summa judicii totius; si quantum ad sæculi potestatem, illa a pontificibus et præcipue a beati Petri vicario debet cognoscere, quæ divina sunt, non ipsa eadem judicare. Nec sibi hoc quisquam potentissimus sæculi, qui tamen Christianus est, vindicare præsumit, nisi religionem forsitan persequens."

[2] Gelasius I., Ep. i. 10, Ad Episcopos Orientales : "An imperator illum discussit atque suscepit ? Constat interim illum ecclesiasticis regulis non receptum : ab ecclesiastica igitur regula receptio ejus omnis aliena est. Quod si dixeris : 'Sed imperator catholicus est'; salva pace ipsius dixerimus, filius est, non præsul Ecclesiæ : quod ad religionem competit, discere ei convenit non docere ; habet privilegia potestatis suæ, quæ administrandis publicis rebus divinitus consecutus est ; et ejus beneficiis non ingratus contra dispositionem cœlestis ordinis nil usurpet. Ad sacerdotes enim Deus voluit, quæ Ecclesiæ dis-

ponenda sunt, pertinere, non ad sæculi potestates ; quæ si fideles sunt, Ecclesiæ suæ et sacerdotibus voluit esse subjectas. Non sibi vindicet alienum jus, et ministerium, quod altero deputatum est ; ne contra eum tendat abrupte, a quo omnia constituta sunt, et contra illius beneficia pugnare videatur, a quo propriam consecutus est potestatem. Non legibus publicis, non a potestatibus sæculi, sed a pontificibus et sacerdotibus omnipotens Deus Christianæ religionis dominos et sacerdotes voluit ordinari, et discuti recipique de errore remeantes. Imperatores Christiani subdere debent exsecutiones suas ecclesiasticis præsulibus, non præferre. Nulla ergo nec certa discussio est, nec manere potest ista susceptio ejus, quem Ecclesia suis legibus nec ordine competenti nec discussit omnino nec communioni restituit. Ideoque potius errori ejus communicavit Acacius catholicamque fidem ei prostituit, quam illum ad communionem catholicam revocavit ; cujus enim non est ordinata receptio, sequitur ut in errore permanserit."

As we have said, we do not find in these letters any trace of
a definite or explicit excommunication of the emperor; but it
is evident from them that they do not look upon the emperor as
in any way exempt from the operation of such general disciplinary measures as they had taken. Felix II. seems to put
before the Emperor Zeno the choice between communion with
St Peter or with Peter of Alexandria;[1] and while Gelasius I.
expresses himself in courteous and friendly terms, and repudiates the notion that he has condemned the emperor, yet
we think that his phrases practically mean that communion
with the excommunicate separates the emperor from the Roman
Church.[2]

The attitude of Felix and Gelasius towards the emperor is
courteous, and even deferential, but it is at the same time
quite firm. It is clear that while they were reluctant to break
with the emperor, to have an open quarrel with him, they had
no hesitation in resisting him. It is, in this connection, therefore, very interesting to find that we have in one of the letters
of Gelasius perhaps the first example of a regular enumeration
of occasions on which churchmen had, as he thinks, been compelled to resist and reprove the secular ruler. Gelasius begins
by referring to the rebuke of David by the prophet Nathan,
and then mentions the public separation of Theodosius from
the communion of the Church by St Ambrose, the rebuke of
Theodosius the younger by St Leo, the action of Pope Hilary

---

[1] Felix II., Ep. viii. 2: "Unde
quoniam adhortationem meam duxistis
onerosam, in vestro relinquo delibera-
tionis arbitrio, utrum beati apostoli
Petri an Alexandrini Petri cuiquam sit
eligenda communio."

[2] Gelasius I., Ep. x. 2: "Quid sibi
vult autem, quod dixerit imperator, a
nobis se irreligiose damnatum, cum
super hac parte et decessor meus non
solum minime nomen ejus attigerit, sed
insuper quando principia adeptus regiæ
potestatis exseruit, in ejus se rescripsit
imperii promotione gaudere: et ego
nulla ipsius unquam scripta percipiens,
honorificis eum, ut nostis, litteris salu-

tare curaverim? Decessores mei sacerdotes, qui prævaricatoribus se communi-
casse propria voce confessi sunt, a
communione apostolica submoverunt.
Si isti placet se miscere damnatis, nobis
non potest imputari: si ab eis velit
abscedere, tanto magis a nobis non
potest esse damnatus, sed potius ad
gratiam sinceræ communionis admissus
Ad senatum vero pertinet Romanum,
ut memor fidei, quam a parentibus se
suscepisse meminit, contagia vitet communionis externæ, ne a communione
hujus sedis apostolicæ, quod absit, red-
datur externus."

against the Emperor Anthemius, and of Pope Simplicius and Pope Felix against the usurper Basiliscus and the legitimate Emperor Zeno.[1] This enumeration of cases in which the authority of the Church had dealt with and rebuked the heads of the civil government serves to furnish us with an interesting view of the circumstances out of which arose the growing consciousness of the existence of an authority in the Church independent of, and in its own sphere superior to, that of the State.

We may again note that Pope Gelasius was concerned not only to assert the authority of the Church in all spiritual matters, but also to establish the principle that the civil power had no jurisdiction over ecclesiastical persons, at least in spiritual matters. We have a letter in which he indignantly protests to the Eastern bishops against their suffering ecclesiastical persons to be tried by secular authorities.[2] We

---

[1] Gelasius I., Ep. xxvi. 11 : "Nathan propheta palam publiceque in facie regi David et commissum pronuntiavit errorem, et ipsum commississe non tacuit, et confessione correctum consequenter absolvit. Beatæ memoriæ Ambrosius, Mediolanensis sacerdos ecclesiæ, majorem Theodosium imperatorem a communione publice palamque suspendit, atque ad pœnitentiam redegit regiam potestatem. Beatæ memoriæ papa Leo, sicut legitur, imperatorem Theodosium juniorem Ephesino latrocinio libere coarguit excedentem. Sanctæ memoriæ quoque papa Hilarius Anthemium imperatorem, quum Philotheus Macedonianus ejus familiaritate suffultus diversarum conciliabula nova sectarum in Urbem vellet inducere, apud beatum Petrum apostolum palam, ne id fieret, clara voce constrinxit in tantum, ut non ea facienda cum interpositione sacramenti idem promitteret imperator. Sanctæ memoriæ nihilominus papa Simplicius, et post eum sanctæ memoriæ papa Felix, non solum Basiliscum tyrannum, sed etiam imperatorem Zenonem pro iisdem ipsis excessibus

auctoritate libera sæpius increpasse noscuntur ; flectique potuisset, nisi Constantinopolitani præsulis accenderetur instinctu, qui particeps externæ communionis effectus, necessario, in quod inciderat, jam fovebat, malens in suæ prævaricationis obstinatione persistere, quam curandus ad salubria remeare, sicut ipse rerum probavit eventus." For a discussion of the authenticity of this passage, we would refer to Thiel's Preface to his edition of these letters.

[2] Gelasius I., Ep. xxvii. 8 : "Cur igitur compassi non estis tantis fratribus vestris. Cur non adiistis imperatorem ? Cur non Ecclesiæ causam et sacerdotii miserabilem decolorationem continuatis vocibus deflevistis ? allegantes ; numquam de pontificibus nisi Ecclesiam judicasse ; non esse humanarum legum de talibus ferre sententiam absque Ecclesiæ principaliter constitutis pontificibus : obsequi solere principes Christianos decretis Ecclesiæ, non suam præponere potestatem, episcopis caput subdere principem solitum, non de eorum capitibus judicare."

are not prepared to express a definite judgment upon the extent of the immunity which Pope Gelasius claims for ecclesiastics : it is enough for our purpose to observe how vigorously he repudiates the idea of the State having any authority over them, in matters, at any rate, belonging to the Church.

The theory of the relation of the two authorities, the Church and the State, is definitely set out in the fourth Tractate and the twelfth letter of Pope Gelasius. Together these furnish us with a statement of the actual spheres of the two powers, and also with some explanation of the cause of their separation. Before the coming of Christ, Gelasius says, there were some who were justly and legitimately both kings and priests, such as Melchizedek ; and Satan imitated this among the unbelievers,—hence it was that the pagan emperors held the office of Pontifex Maximus. The true and perfect king and priest was Christ Himself, and in that sense in which His people are partakers of His nature they may be said to be a royal and priestly race. But Christ, knowing the weakness of human nature, and careful for the welfare of His people, separated the two offices, giving to each its peculiar functions and duties. Thus the Christian emperor needs the ecclesiastic for the attainment of eternal life, and the ecclesiastic depends upon the government of the emperor in temporal things.[1]   There

[1] Gelasius I., Tractatus iv. 11: "Quodsi hæc tentare formidant, nec ad suæ pertinere cognoscunt modulum potestatis, cui tantum de humanis rebus judicare permissum est, non etiam præesse divinis ; quomodo de his, per quos divina ministrantur, judicare præsumunt ? Fuerint hæc ante adventum Christi, ut quidam figuraliter, adhuc tamen in carnalibus actionibus constituti, pariter reges exsisterent et pariter sacerdotes, quod sanctum Melchisedech fuisse sacra prodit historia. Quod in suis quoque diabolus imitatus est, utpote qui semper quæ divino cultui convenirent sibimet tyrannico spiritu vindicare contendit, ut pagani imperatores iidem et maximi pontifices dicerentur. Sed quum ad verum ven-

tum est eumdem regem atque pontificem, ultra sibi nec imperator pontificis nomen imposuit, nec pontifex regale fastigium vindicavit : (quamvis enim membra ipsius, id est, veri regis atque pontificis, secundum participationem naturæ magnificæ utrumque in sacra generositate sumpsisse dicantur, ut simul regale genus et sacerdotale subsistant) : quoniam Christus memor fragilitatis humanæ, quod suorum saluti congrueret, dispensatione magnifica temperavit, sic actionibus propriis dignitatibusque distinctis officia potestates utriusque discrevit, suos volens medicinali humilitate salvari, non humana superbia rursus intercipi : ut et Christiani imperatores pro æterna vita pontificibus indigerent, et pontifices pro

are, then, two authorities by which chiefly the world is ruled,
the sacred authority of the prelates and the royal power;
but the burden laid upon the priests is the heavier, for they
will have to give account in the divine judgment, even for the
kings of men: thus it is that the emperor looks to them for
the means of his salvation, and submits to them and to their
judgment in sacred matters.   The authority of the emperor is
derived from the divine order, and the rulers of religion obey
his laws: he should therefore the more zealously obey them.
If the bishop is silent when he ought to speak for the divine
religion he will run great danger, and so also will he who
contemns this authority instead of obeying it.   If the faithful
owe obedience to all priests, how much more do they owe it to
the bishop of that see which God has set over all priests.[1]

The most important points in these definitions of the character and relation of the two powers are, first, the dogmatic
statement and careful explanation of the fact that in Christian

temporalium cursu rerum imperialibus
dispositionibus uterentur : quatenus
spiritalis actio a carnalibus distaret incursibus, et 'Deo militans minime se
negotiis sæcularibus implicaret,' ac
vicissim non ille rebus divinis præsidere
videretur, qui esset negotiis sæcularibus
implicatus : ut et modestia utriusque
ordinis curaretur, ne extolleretur
utroque suffultus, et competens qualitatibus actionum specialiter professio
aptaretur."

[1] Gelasius I., Ep. xii. 2 : "Pietatem
tuam precor, ne arrogantiam judices
divinæ rationis officium. Absit, quæso,
a Romano principe, ut intimatam suis
sensibus veritatem arbitretur injuriam.
Duo quippe sunt, imperator auguste,
quibus principaliter mundus hic
regitur : auctoritas sacrata pontificum,
et regalis potestas. In quibus tanto
gravius est pondus sacerdotum, quanto
etiam pro ipsis regibus hominum in
divino reddituri sunt examine rationem.
Nosti enim, fili clementissime, quod
licet præsideas humano generi dignitate, rerum tamen præsulibus divinarum devotus colla submittis, atque

ab eis causas tuæ salutis exspectas, inque
sumendis cœlestibus sacramentis eisque
ut competit disponendis, subdi te
debere cognoscis religionis ordine potius
quam præesse, itaque inter hæc ex illorum te pendere judicio, non illos ad
tuam velle redigi voluntatem. Si enim
quantum ad ordinem pertinet publicæ
disciplinæ, cognoscentes imperium tibi
superna dispositione collatum, legibus
tuis ipsi quoque parent religionis antistites, ne vel in rebus mundanis exclusæ
videantur obviare sententiæ ; quo, oro
te, decet affectu eis obedire, qui præ-
rogandis venerabilibus sunt attributi
mysteriis ? Proinde sicut non leve discrimen incumbit pontificibus, siluisse
pro divinitatis cultu, quod congruit ; ita
his, quod absit, non mediocre periculum
est, qui, quum parere debeant, despiciunt. Et si cunctis generaliter sacerdotibus recte divina tractantibus
fidelium convenit corda submitti,
quanto potius sedis illius præsuli consensus est adhibendus, quem cunctis
sacerdotibus et Divinitas summa voluit
præeminere, et subsequens Ecclesiæ
generalis jugiter pietas celebravit ?''

society the spiritual and the temporal powers are intrusted to two different orders, each drawing its authority from God, each supreme in its own sphere, and independent, within its own sphere, of the other. We shall have frequent occasion in later chapters to observe the importance of this conception of a two-fold authority in society—this attempt to divide the whole field of human activity into two separate parts, and to establish an independent authority for each part. We shall see how the ninth-century writers in particular take these statements as the normal expression of their own position, and we shall have to consider how this is related to the theory of the later Middle Ages. But, secondly, it is necessary to observe that Gelasius is also conscious of the fact that while these two authorities are each independent of the other, and supreme in their own spheres, they are also dependent upon each other, and cannot avoid relations with each other ; so that while each is supreme in its own sphere, each is also subordinate in relation to the other sphere. The king is subject to the bishop in spiritual matters, the bishop to the king in temporal matters. Gelasius is conscious of the fact that no division between the two powers can be complete—that we are compelled to recognise the fact that each has, in certain relations, authority over the other ; and, more than this, we may say that Gelasius perhaps feels that the question which is the greater of the two cannot be wholly avoided. He restricts himself, indeed, to arguing that the burden laid upon the ecclesiastics is the heavier; but we can see in his words the beginning of a tendency whose ultimate development we shall have to trace in the scholastic writers. The definitely dualistic theory of authority in society has rarely been more clearly set out than by Gelasius, but his definitions show us the difficulties with which that theory has constantly to contend.

In the Fathers, then, we see clearly the first development of those difficult questions concerning the relations of the temporal and spiritual authorities in society, round which so much of medi-æval political theory was to take shape. There can, we think, be little doubt that in the end nothing contributed so much to emancipate the judgment of theologians from the tendency to recognise an absolute authority in the monarch, as the clearly felt necessity of defending the independence of the Church. It was this, probably more than any other single cause, which compelled the ecclesiastical thinkers to analyse again, and more completely, the source and character of civil authority. There is, indeed, in the Fathers little trace of any very direct connection between the general course of political theory and these questions of the relations of Church and State, though it is noteworthy that St Ambrose, who is the first careful exponent of the independence of the Church, is also that one of the Fathers who seems most conscious of the limitations of the imperial authority even in secular matters. But we think that it is very necessary to take account of the patristic theory of the relations of Church and State; for, however little they may have anticipated the ultimate significance of these questions, we, when we look back from the standpoint of the ninth century or of the later Middle Ages, can see that here are the beginnings of one of the most important elements of the later political theory.

PART IV.

THE POLITICAL THEORY OF THE NINTH CENTURY.

CHAPTER XVI.

NATURAL EQUALITY AND SLAVERY.

WE have examined the history of the political theory of the ancient world in its last stages, and the modifications introduced into this theory by Christianity. It is, we think, necessary for the proper understanding of the course of political theory to keep very clearly before us the fact that the political theory of the Fathers is that of the ancient world, that the modifications introduced by Christianity are to be regarded rather as modifications of detail than as completely or fundamentally changing the conceptions which were already current. Unless we are entirely mistaken, the Fathers take the framework of their political theory whole and ready-made from their predecessors and contemporaries, and do but fit into this framework such conceptions as are to be regarded as in some sense peculiar to themselves. As we have endeavoured to show, their peculiar conceptions are, except in regard to two subjects, not very important in character. The two exceptions to this general principle are to be found, first, in the turn they give to the theory of the sacred character of government, and, second, in their development of the relation between the temporal or civil and the religious or ecclesiastical powers in society. Here, indeed, they present to us the be-

ginnings of modes of thought of the greatest historical significance,—modes of thought whose development and modifications we shall have to trace in considerable detail.

The Christian Fathers cannot be regarded as political philosophers, but their theory is constantly and organically related
to a system of political thought which, whatever its merits
or truth, may be regarded as a philosophical system, the system
which centres in the theory of natural law and the contrast
between the conventional and the natural state. The Fathers
accept these theories, and, as we have endeavoured to show, it
is only in relation to these that their own conceptions become
intelligible.

When we pass to the political theory of the ninth century,
we find ourselves in an atmosphere wholly different. The
elements of public life are altered, the conceptions which
dominate men's minds are in some most important respects
new and strange; we can never forget that the barbarians
have overthrown the old civilisation of the West. They may
sometimes deck themselves in the trappings of the old world,
they are glad to use old names and to claim the titles of ancient
offices, but the world has changed. St Gregory the Great
or St Augustine may have been very different men from the
Roman citizens of the Republic or the Early Empire, but still
they were primarily Romans, members of the ancient commonwealth, sharers in the ancient culture, while the greatest
ecclesiastics of the ninth century, Alcuin, Hincmar of Rheims,
or Hrabanus Maurus, are at bottom men of the new Teutonic
tradition, also no doubt the heirs of what had survived of the
culture of the ancient world, but still primarily men of the
new world. What is true even of the great ecclesiastics is
still more obviously true of the greatest laymen. The great
Charles himself may be the " Augustus," the great and " peaceable " emperor ; but he is really the head of the Franks, the
representative, the repository of the tradition of the greatest
and most powerful of the new Teutonic races; a great man,
great ruler, but still a barbarian.

And the new world is governed by new traditions, new conceptions of life and of law, of the meaning and character of

the social organisation. Not indeed that there is as yet much new theory—the time for that has not yet come—but new traditions, new customs, a new sense of the relations between the different members of the State, these meet us at every turn. The world in which we find ourselves in the ninth century is a new world, is indeed the world as we know it now, for it cannot be seriously pretended that between the ninth century and the twentieth there is such interruption of continuity even as there is between the sixth century and the ninth. When we study the Carolingian writers, we feel at once that we are studying the writings of men whose tradition of society and government is that out of which our own has directly and immediately grown. And yet there are in the social and political theory of the ninth century older elements. There is a great gulf between the Teutonic societies of the Middle Ages and the ancient empire, but there are many relations, many traditions which have been carried over from the one to the other. The new society has its own distinctive traditions, its own individual characteristics; but the men who give expression to these, the articulate representatives of the new society in literature, have inherited from the past traditions and theories which profoundly influence the new society: they have inherited a framework of political theory into which, in the end, they will fit their own independent political and social conceptions. The ninth-century writers are Teutonic politicians, but they are obviously also the disciples of the Western Fathers. Indeed they are always trying to bring their own conceptions into harmony with the theories of the Fathers. They seem instinctively to recognise the fact that they have no formal theory of their own, and constantly fall back upon the Fathers, St Ambrose, St Augustine, St Gelasius, St Gregory, or St Isidore, to find a reasoned expression of their own convictions.

At the same time, their own conceptions are often very different from those of the Fathers, and it is largely to this cause that we may attribute that appearance of incoherence, or even self-contradictoriness, which is perhaps the first characteristic which we notice when we study this literature. The truth is, that some centuries were still to pass before, in the hands of the scholastic writers, the Teutonic traditions and the general principles of the political theory of the Fathers and the Roman Jurists were to be reduced to one coherent whole.

The Fathers, as we have said, may not be political philosophers, but in reading them we feel the presence of a great framework of political theory to which even their most incidental phrases are related. The Schoolmen of the twelfth and thirteenth centuries in their turn produced a complete system of political theory by which we may again interpret even the most paradoxical of their phrases. But the writers of the ninth century are neither original political philosophers nor are they as yet fully conscious of the nature of the theory which lay behind the phrases of the Fathers. They are interested in, they are indeed profoundly concerned with, the solution of the innumerable difficulties which presented themselves to the new civilisation of Europe; they are full of interest, and often exhibit a considerable analytical power in dealing with such questions as the nature of the royal power, the relation of the civil power to the ecclesiastical, the nature of the origin and authority of law, and they eagerly lay hold of any straw of traditional authority, or explanation, in the Fathers, or in the remains of the ancient jurisprudence, which may assist them in the practical solution of their difficulties. But they do not go beyond the practical use of the writings of the Fathers: they are not concerned with, or interested in, the question of a general and systematic philosophy of political and social relations.

We shall therefore find that there is much less of reference in the ninth-century writers to the questions of natural law, the natural condition, the relation between natural and conventional institutions, than in the Fathers. All this we shall find again when we come to discuss the scholastic political theory, but in the ninth century there is comparatively little reference to these matters. Their treatment of political theory is concerned mainly with questions regarding the nature and source of authority, secular and ecclesiastical, and the relations of these authorities to each other. This does not mean that they denied the truth of the conceptions of the earlier writers; on the contrary, as we shall see, so far as they do refer to such general questions as those which we have mentioned, they accept the views, they reproduce the phrases, of the Fathers.

There is only one aspect of the patristic theory of the natural conditions of human nature which has an important place in the ninth-century writings, and that is the theory of the natural equality and liberty of man.   Here it is evident that the ninth-century writers not only reproduce the views of the Fathers, but that they do this with intelligence and conviction.   They find the authority for their view largely in those passages from St Gregory the Great's writings which we have in former chapters had to consider carefully; but it is clear that the view of St Gregory the Great and the other Fathers is one which is firmly held and understood by them as being the foundation of their conception of human nature in society.

One of the most representative passages in the literature of the ninth century dealing with this subject is to be found in Jonas of Orleans' treatise for the instruction of the layman.   He warns his readers lest they should mistake the differences of worldly dignity and wealth for a real difference in nature. Human nature always remains equal in its character, whatever may be the difference of wealth or education.   It is only a foolish and impious pride which causes men to forget these things.   Jonas justifies himself in this view by quoting the famous phrase of St Gregory the Great, " Omnes namque homines natura æquales sumus," and urges masters to treat their slaves with some humanity, quoting from St Paul, and from a sermon attributed to St Augustine, in which he dwells on the brotherhood of Christian men by grace.[1]   The same sentiments are

---

[1] Jonas of Orleans, De Institutione Laicali, ii. 22 : "Cavendum his qui præsunt, ne sibi subjectos, sicut ordine, ita natura inferiores se esse putent ; provida namque dispensatione divina actum est, ut mortalis a mortali, non natura, sed quadam mundana dignitate inferior, ut pote imbecillis a valido pia prælatione et gubernatione tueretur ; ita tamen ut natura semper æqualis agnoscetur.   Quod cum ita sit, multi rebus perituris, et cito præterlabentibus tumentes, tam eos, quibus præsunt, quam etiam eos, quos potentia et honoribus, et divitiis præcedunt, sibi natura æquales non recognoscunt ; et

to be found in another treatise of Jonas, "De Institutione Regia," in which he admonishes the king to appoint such officers as will always remember that the people of Christ over whom they are placed are by nature equal to them.[1]

We find another careful statement and exposition of this conception of the equality of human nature in the writings of Agobard, Archbishop of Lyons. In a letter or short treatise on the baptism of those who were slaves of Jews he protests strongly against some regulations of the Emperor Lewis the Pious, which, as Agobard understood, would have prevented the baptism of such slaves without the consent of their masters, and he does this on the ground that all men are of one race, one descent, one condition.[2] But we shall come back to this passage in dealing with the question of slavery.

Hrabanus Maurus, again, quotes St Gregory the Great, Moralia, xxi. 15, in his Commentary on the Book of Genesis,[3] and Hincmar of Rheims quotes the same passage, and also Moralia, xxvi. 26, which expresses much the same sentiments.[4]

It is interesting to observe that the conviction of the inalien-

si verbis agnoscunt, affectione tamen non agnoscunt. Quod vitium ex fonte superbiæ emanare manifestum est. Cur enim dominus et servus, dives et pauper, natura non sunt æquales, qui unum Deum non acceptorem personarum habent in cœlis."

Jonas then quotes St Paul, Col. iv. 1, and then St Gregory, Moral., xxi. 15 : "Potentibus viris magna est virtus humilitatis, considerata æqualitas conditionis. Omnes namque homines, natura æquales sumus," &c.

He then quotes Pseudo Augustine (a passage to which we have before referred, see p. 116) on the harsh treatment of slaves. Notice especially : "Et quod magis dolendum est, Christianus dominus Christiano in his diebus servo non parcit, minime respiciens, quod si servus est conditione, gratia tamen frater est. Etenim similiter Christum induit, iisdem participat sacramentis, eodem quo et tu utitur Deo Patre, cur te non utaris ut fratre."

Jonas concludes : "His et cæterorum divinorum eloquiorum sententiis, potentes et divites edocti, agnoscant et servos suos, et pauperes sibi natura æquales. Si igitur servi dominis natura æquales sunt, utique quia sunt, non se putent impune domini laturos, dum turbida indignatione et concitanti animi furore adversus errata servorum inflammati, circa eos aut in sævissimis verberibus cædendo, aut in membrorum amputatione debilitando, nimii existunt, quoniam unum Deum habent in cœlis. Eos vero qui in hoc sæculo infirmos abjectosque cultu, et cute et opibus se impares conspiciunt, natura pares et æquales sibi esse prorsus agnoscant."

[1] Jonas of Orleans, De Inst. Reg., v.

[2] M. G. H. Ep., v. ; Agobard of Lyons, Ep. vi.

[3] Hrabanus Maurus, In Genesim II. c. viii.

[4] Hincmar, Opus lv. Capit. xiv.; and De Regis Persona, 3.

able natural equality of human nature has even found a place
in the technical legal documents of the time. In the preface
to a collection of capitularies issued by the Emperor Lewis the
Pious, it is interesting to read a formal recognition by the
emperor of his equality in condition with other men,[1] and in
a collection made from the canons of various councils we have
the same sentiment expressed at greater length and in more
detail, and Christian men, whether lay or clerical, are warned
to behave towards those who are their inferiors with mercy, for
they should remember that they are their brethren, and have
one Father, that is, God, and one Mother, that is, the Holy
Church.[2]

The theory of human equality is treated most fully in
relation to the institution of slavery. In the ninth century
we find again that apparently paradoxical combination of a
theory of equality with an almost universal acquiescence in the
institution of slavery. The explanation is the same in this case
as that which we have already considered in the Fathers,
namely, that slavery is a disciplinary check upon the licence
and disorder of sinful men. There is one writer, indeed, the
author of the 'Via Regia,' Smaragdus, the abbot of St Michael
in the diocese of Verdun, whose attitude to the institution may
be different; but it will be best to leave him till we have considered the general position of the ninth century.

Human nature is recognised by all the writers who refer
to the matter as being equal. We have already quoted

---

[1] M. G. H. Leg., sect. ii. vol. i.
No. 137, Hludowici Proemium Gen.
ad Cap. tam Eccl. quam Mundana:
"Nobis præcipue—qui ceteris mortali-
bus conditione æquales existimus et
dignitate tantum regiminis superem-
inemus."

[2] M. G. H. Leg., sect. ii. vol. i.
No. 154, Cap. e Conciliis Excerpta, 9 :
"Quia ergo constat in æcclesia diversarum conditionum homines esse, ut
sint nobiles et ignobiles, servi, coloni
inquilini et cetera hujuscemodi nomina,
oportet ut quicumque eis prælati sunt
clerici sive laici, clementer erga eos

agant et misericorditer eos tractent,
sive in exigendis ab eis operibus,
sivi in accipiendis tributis et quibusdam debitis ; sciantque eos fratres
suos esse et unum patrem secum habere
Deum, cui clamant ' Pater noster, qui
es in cœlis,' unam matrem sanctam
ecclesiam, quæ eos intemerato sacri
fontis utero gignit. Disciplina igitur
eis misericordissima et gubernatio op-
ortuna adhibenda est ; disciplina, ne
indisciplinate vivendo auctorem suum
offendant ; gubernatio, ne in cotidianis
vitæ commeatibus prælatorum admin-
iculo destituti fatescant." Cf. clause 12.

a passage from Jonas of Orleans [1] which illustrates this, and we may now consider that passage from Agobard of Lyons to which we before referred. In this passage Agobard expresses very clearly both the principle of the equality of the origin and condition of the human race and the justification of slavery as being caused by sin. God is the creator of all mankind, having formed the first man and woman, and from them all men are descended: it is in consequence of men's sins and of the secret judgment of God that some men are exalted and others placed under the yoke of slavery. But while God has thus ordered that men should serve each other with their bodies, He does not allow the inner man to be subject to any one but Himself. The inner man is free.[2] It is for this reason that Agobard protests so strongly against the prohibition of the baptism of slaves without the consent of their masters. Men, that is, are by nature equal, and this equality continues in the soul of man, whatever may be his external condition. Agobard reproduces the view of the Fathers with hardly any change. Slavery is not, as we might say, natural, but is an institution adapted to the actual condition of human nature.[3]

---

[1] See p. 199.

[2] M. G. H. Ep., v.; Agobard of Lyons, Ep. vi. : "Denique et pie considerantibus perspicuum est, quod unus omnipotens Deus, omnium conditor et moderator justissimus, qui primum hominem de limo formavit et de costa ejus adjutorium illi simile sibi fecit, quique ex eis omne genus humanum, quasi ex uno fonte et una radice propagavit, omnes unius conditionis fecerit. Et licet peccatis exigentibus justissimo et occultissimo ejus judicio, alii diversis honoribus sublimati, alii servitutis jugo depressi sunt, ita tamen a servis corporale ministerium dominis exhiberi ordinaverit, ut interiorem hominem ad imaginem suam conditum nulli hominum, nulli angelorum, nulli omnino creaturæ, sed sibi soli voluerit esse subjectum. Unde in lege sua de hac

mentis servitute, quæ illi tantum debetur, mandavit : 'Dominum Deum tuum timebis et illi soli servies.' Et apostolus eumdem interiorem hominem ab omni sexu diversitate, ab omni conditionis et generis distantia liberum esse demonstrans ita docet" (quotes Col. iii. 9, 11). "Cum ergo hi qui ad baptismum veniunt per agnitionem creatoris in interiore homine, qui ab omni servitutis conditione liber est, renoventur, quæ ratio esse potest, ut id servi absque permissione dominorum suorum consequi prohibeantur, nec servire eis Deo liceat, nisi licentiam ab hominibus impetraverint ?"

[3] Cf. M. G. H. Ep., v.; Agobard of Lyons, Ep. iv.; "De qua re ego quidem talem teneo rationem : omnem profecto hominem creaturam Dei esse, et in unoquoque homine, quamvis servo, majorem portionem habere dominum

Alcuin and Hrabanus Maurus contrast the primitive domination of man over the irrational animals with the later rule of
man over man, and trace slavery either to iniquity or adversity,
and cite the legal explanation of the condition of the slave, *servus*,
as that of one who might have been slain, but has been spared
(*servatus*).[1] It is necessary to observe that Hrabanus Maurus

Deum, qui in utero creavit, ad lucem
hujus vitæ produxit, concessam vitam
custodivit, sanitatem servavit, quam
illum qui viginti aut triginta solidis
datis fruitur corporis ejus servitio. Nec
est qui dubitet quod unusquisque servus, membrorum corporis opera carnali
domino debens, mentis religionem soli
debeat creatori. Propter quod omnes
sancti prædicatores, socii apostolorum
. . . omnes baptizaverunt, omnes
in uno corpore redigerunt, omnesque
fratres et filios Dei esse docuerunt,
ita tamen ut unusquisque in quo
vocatus est, in hoc permaneret, non
studio sed necessitate. Sed et si
qui possent liberi fieri, magis uterentur. Im-promptu est etiam ratione
colligere si qui ethnicorum ad Christum fugiunt, et non recolligimus sed
repudiamus propter carnales dominos,
esse impium et crudele cum humanæ
animæ nullus esse possit dominus nisi
conditor."

[1] Alcuin, Inter. et Resp. in Librum
Geneseos, Inter. 273 : "Filii Jacob
interrogati quid operis haberent,
responderunt : Pastores ovium sumus,
sicut et patres nostri. Quare Pat-
riarchos primos, pastores ovium et
non Reges gentium fuisse legimus ?
R. Quia sine ulla dubitatione justa
servitus, et justa est dominatio, cum
pecora homini serviunt ; et homo
pecoribus dominatur. Sic enim dictum
est homini cum crearetur. 'Faciamus
hominem ad imaginem et similitudinem
nostram, et habeat potestatem . . .
omnium quæ sunt super terram.'
Ubi insinuatur rationem debere dominari irrationali vitæ. Servum autem
hominem vel iniquitas fecit vel adver-

sitas. Iniquitas quidem sicut dictum
est : "Maledictus Chanaan, erit servus
fratribus suis." Adversitas vero, sicut
accidit ipsi Joseph, ut venditus a fratribus servus alienigenæ fieret. Itaque
primos servos, quibus hoc nomen in
Latina lingua inductum est, bella
fecerunt ; cum enim homo ab homine
superatus, jure belli possit occidi, quia
servatus est, servus est appellatus.
Inde et mancipia, quia sunt manu
capta."

Hrabanus Maurus, In Genesim IV.
cap. ix. : "Commendatur in patri-
archis, quod pecorum nutritores erant
a pueritia sua, et parentibus suis, et
merito. Nam hæc est sine ulla dubitatione justa servitus et justa dominatio, cum pecora homini serviunt, et
homo pecoribus dominatur. Sic enim
dictum est cum crearetur : 'Faciamus
hominem ad imaginem et similitudinem nostram, et habeat potestatem
piscium maris et volatilium cœli et
omnium pecorum quæ sunt super
terram.' Ubi insinuatur, rationem
debere dominari irrationabili vitæ.
Servum autem hominem homini vel
iniquitas, vel adversitas fecit. Iniquitas
quidem, sicut dictum est : 'Maledictus
Chanaan ; erit servus fratribus suis.'
Adversitas vero, sicut accidit ipsi
Joseph, ut venditus a fratribus, servus
alienigenæ fieret, itaque primos servos
quibus hoc nomen inditum est in
Latina lingua, bella fecerunt. Qui
enim homo ab homine superatus jure
belli posset occidi, quia servatus est
servus appellatus est. Inde et mancipia, quasi manu capti sunt. Est etiam
ordo naturalis in hominibus ut serviant viris feminæ, et filii parentibus,

in this passage also gives an explanation of slavery, which is obviously related to the Aristotelian theory, that slavery is the natural and justifiable result of the superiority of some men in reason over others. It will perhaps be remembered that in Cicero[1] there are traces of the survival of this theory alongside of the doctrine of natural equality. Hrabanus recognises, indeed, that the actual facts of slavery are not always in accordance with this rational order, and exhorts the pious to submit in view of the rationally ordered and eternal felicity which awaits them. The two views are not wholly inconsistent with each other, the natural and fundamental equality does not exclude differences of capacity and intelligence. But this is not the usual line of thought of the Fathers or the ninth-century writers. It may be well to compare this with the parallel theory of a natural hierarchy of order in government, stated by St Gregory the Great,[2] while in his general view government, or at least coercive government, is a consequence of sin.

Slavery, then, is just and lawful under the actual conditions of human nature. But this does not adequately represent the sanction given by the Church of the ninth century to the institution of slavery. A letter of Hrabanus to a certain Reginbaldus shows us that it was maintained that it was an irreligious as well as unlawful thing for a slave to attempt to escape from his master. Reginbaldus had asked Hrabanus whether it was lawful to say mass for a slave who died while escaping from his master. Hrabanus replies that he does not find any reason against this, and orders prayers for the slave unless he has committed some other crime. At the same time he admits that it is a grave sin to fly from one's master. He quotes the canon of the Council of Gangræ in which those who teach slaves to despise their masters and to fly from them are

quia et illic hæc justitia est ut infirmior ratio serviat fortiori. Hæc igitur dominationibus et servitutibus clara justitia est, ut qui excellunt ratione, excellant dominatione. Quod cum in hoc seculo per iniquitatem hominum perturbatur, vel per natur-

arum carnalium diversitatem, ferunt justi temporalem perversitatem, in fine habituri ordinatissimam et sempiternam felicitatem."

[1] See p. 11.
[2] See p. 117.

anathematised, and admits that he must be still more deserving of anathema who actually escapes from his master. But he also urges that the degree of the sin depends upon the reason of his flight, whether it is due to mere pride or to the cruelty of his master. The fugitive slave should be exhorted to return to his master, as Hagar did to Sarah, and Onesimus to Philemon.[1] We have already dealt with this canon[2] of Gangræ in our discussion of the Patristic theory of slavery, and it may be said in explanation of it that, considering the fact that the Church gave its sanction to the institution of slavery as a disciplinary institution, such a condemnation of those who incited slaves to fly was at least logically proper. But the letter of Hrabanus seems to indicate the presence among Christian men in the ninth century of a much harsher view. The question of Reginbaldus clearly shows that it was held by some Christians that a slave who fled from his master was guilty of a mortal sin, and Hrabanus's answer makes it plain that though he thought that the precise degree or quality of

---

[1] M. G. H. Ep., v. ; Hrabanus Maurus, Ep. 30 :—

"V. De servo autem qui fugerit dominum suum, interrogabas, si ille in ipsa fuga mortuus fuerit, utrum liceret pro eo missas cantare aut psalmodias. Hoc in divinis libris non invenimus prohibitum, sed tamen scimus ab apostolis fortissime præceptum, ut servi subditi sint in omni timore dominis, non tantum bonis et modestis, sed etiam discolis, et obedientes illis fiant in omnibus.

In canone autem Gangrensis concilii ita scriptum est : 'Si quis servum sub pretextu divini cultus doceat dominum contempnere proprium, ut discedat ab ejus obsequio, nec ei cum benevolentia et omni honore deserviat, anathema sit.' Unde datur intelligi quod si ille anathema meruit, qui docet servum proprium dominum contempnere, et ab ejus obsequio recedere, quanto magis ille, qui dominum suum spernit et ejus servitio subdi noluerit ?

Sed tamen distantia est inter eum, qui propter superbiam et illum, qui propter necessitatem fugit, coactus crudelitate domini sui. Nam Agar famula Saræ fugam iniit, affligente eam domina sua, sed angelo ammonente, ut reverteretur et fieret subjecta dominatrici suæ, reversa est ad dominam suam. Sic et Honesimus servus Philemonis effugit a domino suo, sed Paulo apostolo docente credidit Christo et baptizatus est et sic per patrocinium apostoli restitutus est proprio domino.

Ammonendus est enim servus quilibet fugitivus per fideles Christi doctores, ubicumque fuerit inventus, ut revertatur ad dominum suum et fiat ei subjectus, ne forte contempnens præceptum domini, perpetuo anathemate percutiatur. Attamen si in ipsa fuga obierit, orandum est pro eo, nisi forte aliquo crimine majore implicetur aut in perfidiam devolvatur, unde fructuosa pro eo non possit esse oratio."

[2] See p. 121.

the sin depended upon the motive prompting the slave's escape, yet such an attempt was in itself sinful.

We may again find illustrations of the ecclesiastical view of slavery in the legislation of the Church as well as of the State with regard to the qualifications of those who were to be admitted to ordination. We could quote a series of enactments from the Council of Frankfurt in 794 to the Council of Tribur in 895 by which the ordination of a slave is prohibited except with the consent of his master.[1]

The Council of Frankfurt requires the permission of the master,[2] but does not say whether the slave must be emancipated, but in all the other passages we cite it is laid down that the slave should only be ordained when he has been handed over by his master to the bishops to be free for the rest of his life, and in one passage the master is warned that he will then lose all rights over the slave.[3] It is perhaps worth noticing, also, that in a letter or precept of Lewis the Pious the slave thus emancipated is warned that in the event of his sinning against the sacred orders which he has received, he will be obliged to return to his former slavery.[4]

According to one set of regulations, if a slave procures his ordination by fraud he is to be handed over to his master, or if he was ordained in ignorance of the fact that he was a slave, he may be retained in his office if his master consents, or his master may reclaim him as a slave.[5]

[1] M. G. H. Leg., sect. ii. 28, 112, 114, 138, 173, 252 ; M. G. H. Ep., v., Ep. var. 8. Cf. also Pseudo Isidore, Stephen, Dec. II.

[2] M. G. H. Leg., sect. ii. vol. i. No. 28, Synod Franc. : " De servis alienis : ut a nemine recipiantur neque ab episcopis sacrentur sine licentia dominorum."

[3] M. G. H. Leg., sect. ii. vol. i. No. 112, Statuta Rhispacensia, &c., 31.

[4] M. G. H. Ep., v. ; Ep. Var. 8 : " Proinde has nostræ imperialis et regiæ auctoritatis litteras tuæ sanctitati dandas decrevimus, per quas tibi et successoribus tuis talem concessam noveris potestatem, ut servum ecclesiasticum tam de tua parochia quam de suffraga-

neorum tuorum necnon et de jure monasteriorum, quæ in tua diocœsi constituta sunt, ad præsbiteratus ordinem electum coram clero et plebe, præsente et consentiente eo, cujus dominatui idem servus usque in id temporis erat addictus, a jugo servitutis absolvas et perpetuo liberum efficias, ea tamen conditione, ut noverit se is qui libertate donatur in pristinam servitutis conditionem relapsurum, si sacri ordinis quem susceperit prævaricator fuerit conprobatus."

[5] M. G. H. Leg., sect. ii. vol. i. No. 138, 6 : " Et si quilibet servus dominum suum fugiens, aut latitans aut adhibitis testibus munere conductis vel corruptis aut qualibet calliditate

It is perhaps deserving of notice that we find it alleged as a reason for such regulations, that it is improper that the service of God should be conducted by men of ignoble position. We have an excellent commentary on such a view in the very interesting account which Jonas of Orleans and Agobard of Lyons give of the common attitude of the wealthy and noble persons of their time towards the inferior clergy. Their observations illustrate what seems to have been a real difficulty of the time—a difficulty which alone would have compelled the Church to enforce very strict rules about the condition of those who were to be admitted to orders. Jonas of Orleans gives us a very gloomy picture of the social condition of many of the clergy. They were often employed by wealthy laymen as their stewards, and were considered unfit to be their companions at table.[1] Agobard is equally gloomy, and even more vivid, in his picture. All great men, he says, have a domestic priest, not that they may obey him, but simply that he may be useful to them in performing religious services and in discharging any secular function to suit their convenience. When they want a domestic chaplain, he says, they bring to the bishop some slave whom they have brought up in their house or bought, and demand his ordination.[2]

vel fraude, ad gradus ecclesiastices pervenerit, decretum est ut deponatur, et dominus ejus eum recipiat. Si vero avus vel pater ab alia patria in aliam migrans in eadem provincia filium genuerit, et ipse filius ibidem educatus et ad gradus ecclesiasticos promotus fuerit et utrum servus sit ignoraverit, et postea veniens dominus illius legibus eum adquisiverit, sancitum est ut, si dominus ejus illi libertatem dare voluerit, in gradu suo permaneat; si vero eum catena servitutis a castris dominicis extrahere voluerit, ut gradum amittat; quia juxta sacros canones vilis persona manens sacerdotii dignitate fungi non potest." Cf. St Gelasius, Ep. 21. See p. 122.

[1] Jonas of Orleans, De Inst. Laicali, ii. 20: "Sunt etiam quidam sacerdotes divitiis et honoribus mundi carentes, qui adeo contemptui a quibusdam laicis habentur, ut eos non solum administratores et procuratores rerum suarum faciant, sed etiam sibi more laicorum servire compellant, eosque convivas mensæ suæ habere dedignentur ; qui videlicet habere sacerdotes nomine tenus sibi videri gestiunt, re autem ipsa propter quam habendi sunt, nolunt, talesque intercessores apud Deum habere volunt, quales esse prorsus despiciunt."

[2] M. G. H. Ep., v.; Agobard, Ep. 11 : "Unde et contumeliose eos nominantes, quando volunt illos ordinari præsbiteros, rogant nos aut jubent, dicentes : 'Habeo unum clericionem, quem mihi nutrivi de servis meis propriis aut beneficialibus sive pagensibus, aut obtinui ab illo vel illo homine, sive de illo vel illo pago, volo ut ordines eum mihi præsbiterum."

The Church of the ninth century acquiesced in the existence of slavery, and adapted its own legislation to this. It is well, however, also to observe that the influence of the Church seems still, as in the period of the later Empire, to tend towards a mitigation of the condition of slavery. The Church still continued to impose its own penalties upon those who killed the slave. We find a Council of Maintz in 847 A.D. renewing the canons of the Councils of Agde and of Elliberis, which imposed the penalty of excommunication for certain periods upon those who killed their slaves intentionally or by accident.[1] We have already considered that passage from the writings of Jonas of Orleans in which he protests against the harsh treatment of slaves.[2] It is also interesting to find in the " Edictum Pistense " of 864 a revival of a regulation contained in a novel of Valentinian, by which those who sold themselves or their children, because of their great poverty or in time of famine, could be redeemed at a price slightly higher than that for which they had sold themselves or their children.[3]

There is, as we have said, one writer in the ninth century who goes beyond this in his attitude to slavery, and who may even desire its abolition. This writer, Smaragdus, is the author of a little treatise or handbook, the 'Via Regia,' on the character and duty of the good king. We shall have occasion to refer to him again in connection with the theory of the royal power, though there is in this portion of his work little that is very different from other treatises.

[1] M. G. H. Leg., sect. ii. vol. ii. No. 248, 22.

[2] See p. 199.

[3] M. G. H. Leg., sect. ii. vol. ii. No. 273, c. 34. "Tamen illud capitulum, quod cum sanctis ecclesiasticis regulis ex maxima parte concordari invenimus, hic ponere necessarium duximus in quo dicit : Ut quicumque ingenui filios suos, quod et de ipsis liberis hominibus, qui se vendunt, observari volumus, qualibet necessitate seu famis tempore vendiderint ipsa necessitate compulsi, emptor, si quinque solidis emit sex recipiat ; si decem, duo-decim solidos similiter recipiat ; aut si amplius, secundum suprascriptam rationem augmentum pretii consequatur. . . . Et si quis dixerit, quia non vult aut tempore famis aut pro alia necessitate pretium suum dare pro libero homine, si semper illum servum habere non debet, adtendat quid ei Dominus per apostolum suum dicat : 'Qui habuerit,' inquiens, 'substantiam hujus mundi et viderit fratrem suum necesse habere et clauserit viscera sua ab eo, non manet caritas Dei in eo.' Cf. Nov. Valent., iii. Tit. xi., Interpretatio.

With regard to slavery the position of the treatise is different. The author quotes a passage from Ecclesiasticus, which enjoins that a slave should be treated as one's own soul, as a brother,[1] and entreats the king to forbid the making of slaves in the kingdom—that is, we suppose, he desires to prevent any of the subjects of the king from being enslaved by their fellow-subjects. Then, after quoting a number of passages from the canonical and apocryphal Scriptures of the Old Testament, on the subject of slavery, he urges that the Christian man should set his slaves at liberty, considering that it is not nature but sin that subjected men to each other, seeing that we were all created equal. He concludes by urging the king to honour God with his riches and slaves, by giving alms of the former and by setting the latter at liberty.[2]

We think that the author of the treatise feels that there is something unchristian in the slavery at least of Christian men, and that he would like to see this ended. He does not, indeed, actually ask the king to abolish the institution, though he does ask him to forbid the enslavement of any of his subjects; but he does look upon it as being the true mode of honouring God, to set the slave at liberty. It is certainly interesting to find this view held in the ninth century, but we must not make any mistake: this view is hardly the normal one; the premisses of Smaragdus are the same as those of the other ninth-century writers, but the conclusions deduced by him from them are different. The theory of slavery in the ninth century is the same as that of the Fathers: slavery is not natural or primitive, but is a just punishment of man's sin, and a remedial discipline by which his vicious inclinations may be restrained.

[1] Smaragdus Abbas, Via Regia, 1.
[2] Smaragdus Abbas, Via Regia, 30; "Prohibe ergo clementissime rex; ne in regno tuo captivitas fiat. . . . Vere obedire debet homo Deo et ejus præcepta in quantum ille possibilitatem dederit, obedire. Et inter alia præcepta salutaria, et opera recta, propter nimiam illius charitatem unusquisque liberos debet dimittere servos, consid-erans quia non illi eos natura subegit, sed culpa; conditione enim æqualiter creati sumus, sed aliis alii culpa subacti. . . . Honorifica ergo, justissime ac piissime rex, pro omnibus Deum tuum, quia ut scriptum est, 'Pro omnibus honorificavit te,' sive in servis tibi subactis, sive in divitiis tibi concessis, ex illis liberos faciendo, et ex istis eleemosynas tribuendo, præceptis illius obedire non cesses."

CHAPTER XVII.

THE DIVINE AUTHORITY OF THE KING.

WE have seen that the ninth-century writers maintain the tradition of the natural equality of human nature—an equality which, in a certain sense, is permanent and inalienable; but we have seen that this is not inconsistent with their maintaining that slavery is a necessary and wholesome discipline. It is so also with government; in one sense it might seem that this is incompatible with the theory of the natural equality of man, but these writers look upon it as a necessary discipline by means of which life is preserved and order is maintained. The State is a divine institution; its coercive discipline may indeed be a consequence of the Fall, but it is the divine remedy for the Fall, and as such it must be respected and obeyed by all men. We have seen that in some of the Fathers this conception is developed into a theory that the person and authority of the ruler is so sacred that disobedience to him or resistance to his commands is equivalent to disobedience and resistance to God Himself. By some of the Fathers the divine authority of the State is transferred whole and entire to the particular ruler.

This view is in the ninth century formally held by many, perhaps indeed by all writers. But the actual conditions of the political life of the time often came into conflict with this view, and while the writers of the time may have continued to maintain it in form, they were in fact often compelled to adopt quite another attitude towards the head of the State. We also begin to find in them the influence of a tradition which does not descend from the ancient world. The ninth-century writers are for the most part ecclesiastics,

CHAP. XVII.]   THE DIVINE AUTHORITY OF THE KING.   211

but they are also, at least in Northern Europe, men of the Teutonic tradition. And the Teutonic tradition of the authority of the king is not the same as that of the Latin Fathers.

The conflict of these ideas is the cause of much apparent incoherence and inconsistency: we find the same man speaking at one time as though the divine authority of the king could never be resisted, at another time as if his authority were limited and restricted. The difficulty also of defining the limits of the authority of the ecclesiastical and the civil powers produced a constant friction, which tended to destroy any unqualified theory of the absolute authority of the State.

We find but little speculation or theory as to the beginnings of society and the State, and what little there is, is obviously second-hand and borrowed from earlier writers. In a treatise attributed to Alcuin, 'De Rhetorica et Virtutibus,' there is an interesting passage on the primitive conditions of human life, drawn, as the author says, from ancient sources, in which man is represented as having originally lived like the beasts, wandering about in the fields, without any rational or moral principle or rule of life. A great and wise man at last appears, and, recognising the qualities and capacities of human nature, gathers men together into one place, and thus brings them to live a peaceable and humane life.[1]

[1] Alcuin, 'Dialogus De Rhetorica et Virtutibus:' "Carolus. Primum mihi, magister, hujus artis (vel studii) initium pande.

"Alb. Pandam juxta auctoritatem veterum. Nam fuit, ut fertur, quoddam tempus, cum in agris homines passim bestiarum more vagabantur, nec ratione animi quidquam, sed pleraque viribus corporis administrabant. Nondum divina religio nondum humani officii ratio colebatur, sed cæca et temeraria (dominatrix) cupiditas ad se explendam viribus corporis abutebatur. Quo tempore quidam vir magnus et sapiens cognovit quæ materia et quanta ad maximas res opportunitas animis inesset hominum, si quis eam posset elicere et præcipiendo meliorem reddere. Qui dispersos homines in agris et in tectis sylvestribus abditos ratione quadam compulit in unum locum, et congregavit eos in unum, aliquam quietem inducens utilem atque honestam; primo propter insolentiam reclamantes, deinde propter rationem atque orationem studiosius audientes, ex feris et immanibus mites reddidit et mansuetos. Ac mihi quidem videtur, domine mi rex, hoc nec tacita, nec inops dicendi sapientia perficere potuisse, ut homines a consuetudine subito converteret et ad diversas vitæ rationes traduceret."

We find a very similar account of the primitive condition of man in Hrabanus Maurus's 'De Universo,' taken from St Isidore of Seville.   Under the definition of "oppidum" he tells us that in the earliest times men were naked and unarmed and had no protection against the wild beasts, no shelter against the heat or cold, no safety against each other.   As time went on they learned to make houses in which they could dwell in safety, and in this way towns began to spring up.[1]

We can scarcely found any conclusions on such scanty and incidental references to the beginnings of society; it is evident that both the author of the 'De Rhetorica' and Hrabanus Maurus are simply writing down fragments of ancient descriptions of society, which they accept, but upon which they are not reasoning.   In themselves these statements are both too vague and too commonplace to enable us to fix very definitely the philosophic tradition to which we might say they belong.   We can hardly go further than this, that they represent a tradition which held that behind the period of the organised society of men there lay a time when there was no fixed order among mankind.   It is a state of nature, but not, so far as these passages go, a good or ideal state, but rather one of disorder and misery.   It would agree well enough with the conditions of human life, as they might be pictured after sin and vice had come into the world, and before the great institutions, by which sin is controlled and checked, had been developed.

We have seen that the ninth-century writers maintain the primitive or natural equality of men ; but they recognise that the actual conditions of life demand government, as they justify slavery.   This is well expressed in a treatise of Hincmar of Rheims.   God has set diverse orders in the world, as is shown

---

[1] Hrabanus Maurus, De Universo, xiv. 1. "Oppidum quidam ab oppositione murorum dixerunt : alii ab opibus recondendis, eo quod sit munitum : quod sit conventus in eo habitantium, et opem ferat mutuam contra hostem. Nam primum homines, tanquam nudi et inermes, nec contra belluas præsidia habebant, nec receptacula frigoris et caloris, nec ipsi inter se homines ab

hominibus satis erant tuti. Tandem naturali sollertia speluncis silvestribusque tegumentis tuguria sibi et casas virgultis arundinibusque contexuerunt, quo esset vita tutior, ne his, qui nocere possent aditus esset. Hæc est origo oppidorum, quæ, eo quod opem darent, idcirco oppida nominata dixerunt." See p. 172.

by the apostolic exhortation to obey kings and rulers for God's sake; for although, as St Gregory says, nature brought forth all men equal, sin has put some below others, and this by God's dispensation, who has ordained that one man should be ruled by another.[1] Indeed the writers of the ninth century reproduce the strongest phrases of the Fathers with reference to the divine nature of the civil power. In the middle of the century we find this enunciated with great force in the 'Capitula Pistensia.' These lament the disturbances and discord in the kingdom, and complain that some men will not endure subjection to the king. They forget that, as St Paul says, all power is from God, and that he who resists the power resists the ordinance of God. God is indeed the true King of kings and Lord of lords, but He has ordained that the ruler is to be a true king and lord in God's place (*vice sua*) on the earth. The devil fell from heaven because he would not accept his subjection to his Creator; and so he who will not recognise the power ordained by God in the world, makes himself the servant of the devil and the enemy of God.[2]

---

[1] Hincmar of Rheims, Opus lv. Capit. xiv.: "Ad quod instar sunt ordines in sæculo Dei ordinatione distincti, sicut monstrat apostolus, dicens : 'Subjecti estote omni humanæ creaturæ propter Deum, sive regi tanquam præcellenti, sive ducibus tanquam ab eo missis' (1 Pet. ii. 13). 'Liquet,' inquit beatus Gregorius (Moral., lib. xxi. c. 15), 'quod omnes homines natura æquales genuit sed variante meritorum ordine, alios aliis culpa postponit. Ipsa autem diversitas, quæ accessit ex vitio, divino judicio dispensatur, ut quia omnis homo æque stare non valet, alter regatur ab altero.'"

[2] M. G. H. Leg., sect. ii. vol. ii. No. 272, Capitula Pistensia, i.: "Quia per discordiam et regnum istud temporale imminuitur et pene desertum et æternum regnum perditum habemus, quia nec omnes reges esse possumus nec regem super nos a Deo constitutum —quia, sicut scriptum est, 'imposuit homines super capita nostra,'—'habere sustinemus, non attendentes, quia,' sicut dicit apostolus, 'non est potestas nisi a Deo, et qui potestati resistit, Dei ordinationi resistit'; quoniam Deus qui essentialiter est 'rex regum et dominus dominantium,' participatione nominis et numinis Dei, id est potestatis suæ, voluit et esse et vocari regem et dominum pro honore et vice sua regem in terris. Et sicut archangelus, qui nunc est diabolus, cum suis sequacibus, quia per humilitatis subjectionem conditori suo subditus esse noluit et per æqualitatem caritatis coangelis suis socius esse despexit, de cœlo cecidit, ita et illi, qui potestati a Deo constitutæ propter Deum et in Deo subjecti esse nolunt et pares vel coæquales in regno habere non sufferunt, per quam debitam subjectionem et parilem æqualitatem Dei amici et angelorum consortes esse poterant, subjecti diabolo et Dei inimici constituuntur."

These phrases can be paralleled over and over again in the Capitularies [1] and in the writers of the time,—Smaragdus, Sedulius Scotus, Jonas of Orleans, Hrabanus Maurus, Hincmar of Rheims, Cathulfus.[2] They represent the accepted view that temporal authority is derived from God, and that all men must obey the authority for the sake of God.

It is this conception which is embodied in the phrases used by Charles the Great and his successors: " Karolus gratia Dei rex "; " Karolus serenissimus augustus, a Deo coronatus magnus pacificus imperator, Romanum gubernans imperium, qui et per misericordiam Dei Rex Francorum atque Longobardorum"; " Hludowicus, divina ordinante providentia imperator augustus"; " Hludowicus divino nutu coronatus." [3] These phrases serve to express the conception that it is God who is the ultimate source of all authority. This is also, we venture to think, the conception which was ultimately conceived to be expressed in the consecration of the king or emperor at his coronation. We shall have a good deal to say about this later, for the mediæval interpretations of the rite and of the part taken in it by the clergy are of considerable importance. For the present it is enough to observe that the introduction of a religious element into the solemn appointment of a king or emperor, while at first it probably meant little more than that the blessing of God was being invoked upon the monarch, was very soon taken to be symbolical of the fact that it is from God that authority came.[4]

[1] M. G. H. Leg., sect. ii. Nos. 5, 290, 293, 302.

[2] E.g., Smaragdus Abbas, Via Regia, 18 ; Sedulius Scotus, De Rectoribus Christianis, 1 and 19 ; Jonas of Orleans, De Inst. Regia, 7, 8 ; Hrabanus Maurus, M. G. H. Ep., v. 15, iii. ; Hincmar of Rheims, De Regis Persona, 1, 8 ; M. G. H. Ep., iv. Var. Car. Mag. Regn. 7.

[3] M. G. H. Leg., sect. ii. vol. i. Nos. 19, 45, 132, 134.

[4] From the time of the coronation of Leo II. as emperor in the year 473 A.D., the appointment of the emperor in the East was accompanied by some religious

rites. How far back this may have gone in the West we do not know: the earliest coronation with religious service of which there is trustworthy evidence is that of Pippin in 752, and the earliest form of coronation service in the West is that contained in the Pontifical of Egbert, which it is thought may have been in use in the first half of the eighth century.

We would refer the reader to the articles by the Rev. J. E. Brightman, on the Byzantine Imperial Coronations, and by the Rev. H. A. Wilson, on the English Coronation Order, in the

The writers of the ninth century, then, maintain the tradition of the Fathers, that the State is a religious institution, that the authority of the civil government is sacred, and that all Christian men should obey it, as representing the authority of God Himself. But they go much further than this. We have just considered a passage from the 'Capitula Pistensia,' and we must now observe that the king is here spoken of as standing in God's place (*vice sua*) in the world. Smaragdus uses an almost exactly similar phrase when he speaks of the king acting "pro vice Christi."[1] Sedulius Scotus calls the king the "Vicar of God."[2] It is true that Sedulius calls him God's vicar in the government of the Church, a statement which we shall have to consider again in connection with the relations of the ecclesiastical and civil powers,—but probably he includes the State in the Church.

A writer called Cathulfus, of whom little is known, and who is represented in literature only by a letter or short treatise, addressed to Charles the Great, uses a similar phrase. He bids the king remember God always with fear and love, for he stands in His place over all His members, to guard them and reign over them. The bishop is said to stand in the second place, to represent Christ.[3] Our readers may remember that the writer known as Ambrosiaster expresses a similar thought when he says that the king, whom he calls the Vicar of God, has the "image of God," and the bishop has the "image of Christ."[4] Whether Cathulfus draws the phrase from Am-

'Journal of Theological Studies' for April and July 1901, for a detailed discussion of the exact character and significance of the ecclesiastical ceremony.

[1] Smaragdus Abbas, Via Regia, 18: " Fac quidquid potes pro persona quam gestas, pro ministerio regali quod portas, pro nomine Christiani quod habes, pro vice Christi qua fungeris."

[2] Sedulius Scotus, De Rectoribus Christianis, 19: " Oportet enim Deo amabilem regnatorem, quem divina ordinatio tanquam vicarium suum in regimine Ecclesiæ suæ esse voluit, et potestatem ei super utrumque ordinem prælatorum et subditorum tribuit, ut singulis personis et quæ justa sunt decernat, et sub sua dispositione prior ordo devote obediendo fideliter subditus fiat."

[3] M. G. H. Ep., iv. Variorum Carolo Magno Regnante Scriptæ, 7 : " Memor esto ergo semper, rex mi, Dei regis tui cum timore et amore, quod tu es in vice illius super omnia membra ejus custodire et regere, et rationem reddere in die judicii, etiam per te. Et episcopus est in secundo loco, in vice Christi tantum est."

[4] See p. 149.

brosiaster we cannot tell,—it is at least possible that it is
from him that the phrases which speak of the king acting in
God's place come; but it is also possible that this method of
speaking was traditional among Christians, though it has not
come down to us in any patristic writer of the West, except
Ambrosiaster. It is important to observe the phrase the
"Vicar of God." We shall presently have to consider its
meaning in these writers in relation to the Church: in a later
volume we shall see that it came to mean a great deal in
the controversy between Church and State. It is significant
for us for the moment as representing in the most terse
form the universal judgment of the time that the king is
the representative of God,—that it is from God that he
draws his authority.

The king thus stands in God's place, is His representative on
earth, and the writers of the ninth century use very strong
phrases to express their condemnation of rebellion against his
authority. The Council of Maintz in 847 inserts in its decrees
a very strong condemnation of conspiracy and rebellion against
the lawful authorities in Church and State, and threatens those
guilty of such acts with excommunication.[1] Some of the manu-
scripts which contain the documents of this council say that
these sentences come from an epistle of Hrabanus Maurus.
In one of his letters, written some years earlier, he speaks
very strongly on the wickedness of revolt, and enforces this
by a number of quotations from the Old and New Testa-
ments, citing especially the conduct of David, who would not
raise his hand against the Lord's anointed, and recounting

[1] M. G. H. Leg., sect. ii. vol. ii.
No. 248, Concilium Moguntinum. 5.
De conspiratione: "Si vero pax et
concordia summum inter homines et
maxime Christianos bonum judicatur
et præmio summo remunerandum, id
est, ut ejus merito filii Dei vocemur,
nonne, e contrario discordiæ et dissen-
sionis summum est malum et summa
pœna plectendum? Ita ut sapiens
dicat animam Domini illum detestari,
qui inter fratres discordiam seminat
atque ideo filius diaboli non immerito

nominetur. Unde statuimus atque
auctoritate ecclesiastica confirmamus
eos, qui contra regem vel ecclesiasticas
dignitates sive reipublicæ potestates
in unoquoque ordine legitima dispositione constitutas conjurationes et
conspirationes rebellionis et repug-
nantiæ faciunt, a communione et
consortio catholicorum veram pacem
amantium summovendos et, nisi per
pœnitentiam et emendationem paci se
ecclesiasticæ incorpaverint, ab omnibus
filiis pacis sancimus extorres."

the judgments that overtook several of those who in later times rose in insurrection against their legitimate lords.[1]

Hincmar of Rheims uses equally strong phrases on the necessity of obedience. In his treatise, 'De Fide Carolo Rege Servanda,' he also cites the example of David's conduct towards Saul as the true model of right conduct,[2] and then quotes those very strong words of St Gregory the Great on which we commented in a former chapter, in which he warns subjects that if they transgress against their rulers, they transgress against God, who set them over men.[3] In one of his letters he speaks more directly and strongly still. Nothing, he says, is done in the world except by God, or by His just permission. When kings, therefore, reign by God's appointment (*ex illo*) it is the work of God's mercy, that their people may be safe. When they rule, not by his appointment (*non ex illo*), but by His permission, it is God's punishment on a sinful people. The true believers do not resist the power, which is either given or permitted by God, but, humbling themselves under God's hand, give thanks to Him

[1] M. G. H. Ep., v.; Hrabanus Maurus, Ep. 15, iii.: "Quod autem regiæ dignitati honor sit a subditis offerendus, et quod Deo displiceat contumatia subditorum, ostendit scriptura divina tam in sententiis quam etiam in exemplis. Nam in Exodo scriptum est: 'Diis non detrahes et principi populi tui non maledices.' . . .

"Horum ergo casum atque ruinam pertimescens David unctus jam rex non ausus est levare manum suam contra Saul regem, sed viris illis, qui eum persuaserunt, ut Saul quasi sibi traditum in deserto Engathi vel in deserto Ciph percuteret atque interimeret, respondit dicens, 'Propitius sit mihi Dominus, ne faciam hanc rem domino meo Christo Domini, ut mittam manum meam in eum, quoniam Christus Domini est.' Et item: 'Quis inquit, extendit manum suam in Christum Domini et innocens erit? Vivit Dominus, quia nisi Dominus percusserit eum, aut dies ejus venerit ut moriatur, aut in prœlium descendens perierit, propitius sit mihi Dominus, ne ex-

tendam manum meam in Christum Domini.' . . . Nam tyranni, qui contra dominos legitimos subita insolentia se ærexerant, non impuniti evaserant, sed justo judicio Dei dampnati pœnas condignas luebant. Cujus rei inditia sunt bella famosissima gloriosissimi et fidelissimi imperatoris Theodosii, quæ gessit contra Maximum tyrannum Gratiani domini sui interfectorem fratrisque ejus Valentiniani de regno expulsorem, quem sola fide major, universa autem apparatus belli comparatione minor, sine dolo et sine controversia Theodosius clausit, cœpit, occidit. Similiter et contra Arbogastem atque Eugenium infestissimos tyrannos . . . quos utique christianissimus imperator, potentia Dei, non fiducia hominis fretus, magis orationibus quam armis subegit."

[2] Hincmar of Rheims, De Fide Carolo Rege Servanda, xxxiii.

[3] Hincmar, De Fid. Car. Reg. Serv., xxxiv: "Nam cum in præpositis delinquimus, ejus ordinationi qui eos nobis prætulit obviamus." See p. 152.

for good princes, and rejoice even while they groan under those who are permitted by God to reign for their chastisement. They do indeed resist wicked works and commands, but they endure patiently, for God's sake, the evils which are brought upon them by wicked princes.[1] This passage is the more noticeable that the general purpose of the letter is to protest against infractions of the privileges of the clergy by the king.

These passages will be sufficient to show how strongly the doctrine of the divine authority of the civil government, and the duty of obedience to it, was held in the ninth century. It might seem as though these writers were still wholly under the influence of the extreme position of St Gregory the Great. We can indeed understand how they came to this view. God is the source of all authority; the king as ruler derives his power from God, the evil king as much as the good; the former indeed, as we have seen, in the last passage quoted from Hincmar, holds his power by God's permission rather than by His appointment, but still he holds it by God's permission for the chastisement and correction of evil. Therefore, they say, we must always obey the king, and submit to him, even when unreasonable and unjust, lest we should be found to be resisting God. These writers think that their principles are the same as those of Gregory the Great. We must now consider other aspects of their theory of government, and we shall be led to recognise that while they repeat these patristic phrases with sincerity, their own final judgment is influenced also by considerations of quite another kind.

---

[1] Hincmar of Rheims, Ep. xv. Ad Carolum Regem : " Quia nihil fit in mundo, nisi quod aut Deus misericorditer facit, aut fieri juste permittit. Cum itaque reges ex illo regnant, misericordia illius est, ut salventur populi eis commissi : cum vero non ex illo, sed permittente justo ipsius judicio reges regnare videntur, vindicta est peccatoris populi et regnantis cumulus pœnæ. Sed fideles quique potestati aut a Deo collatæ aut a Deo permissæ non resistunt, cum juxta Petri vocem : 'Sub manu Dei humiliantur, et de bonis principibus gratias referunt ; et de his qui ad purgationem suam a Deo regnare permissi sunt, gementes exsultant; sicut scriptum est 'Exsultaverunt filiæ Judæ in omnibus judiciis tuis, Domine.' Sicque non resistunt ordinationi Dei, qui novit, non mala facere, sed ordinare. Resistunt autem iniquis iniquorum operibus et mandatis. Unde scriptum est : 'Verba sapientium quasi stimuli, et quasi claves in altum defixi,' quia nesciunt culpas palpare, sed pungere, et tolerant patienter propter Dominum illata mala sibi a principibus malis."

CHAPTER XVIII.

THE THEORY OF THE KING AND JUSTICE.

So far as we have gone in our examination of the political theory of the writers of the ninth century, we have recognised the influence of the theories of St Gregory the Great as to the duty of an unlimited obedience to the civil ruler; for in the main it is his sentiments and phrases which they are reproducing. No doubt they reproduce these with honesty and sincerity; no doubt they imagined that they really held just the same opinions as St Gregory. But when we examine their writings further, we discover at once that we have here only one aspect of their view of the nature and source of the authority of government.

The truth is, that while the writers of the ninth century are most anxious to express themselves in the language of the Fathers, most anxious to be faithful to the traditions which they had inherited from them, their own standpoint is really in many ways a very different one from that of St Gregory the Great. The situation of the ninth century was, in fact, a very different one from that of the sixth century. The whole Western Church must probably have been influenced by the violent rupture between the Bishop of Rome and the iconoclastic emperors. Italy had risen in revolt against the attempt to suppress the use of images, and the Bishops of Rome, though they had tried to moderate the violence of the revolt,[1] yet had necessarily been compelled by their own convictions to approve the Italian resistance to the impious wishes of the iconoclastic emperors; and such armed resistance must have tended to neutralise the tradition of St Gregory the Great.

[1] Liber Pontificalis : Gregory II., xvii. and xx.

The transference of the empire from the Byzantine to the Frank, and the fact that the Western ecclesiastics had in the ninth century to do, not with the civilised chiefs of the ancient Roman civilisation, but with the half-barbarous Teutonic kings and emperors, must have exercised an even greater influence upon the temper of the great churchmen. They might express themselves in the most deferential terms to their rulers, but actually they were civilised men,—at least they had the tradition of civilisation,—while the rulers were for the most part uneducated and half-barbarous. It must have become very difficult for the churchmen to think of an unqualified obedience to men who in some very important matters were their inferiors. And there was yet a third circumstance which profoundly affected the political conceptions of churchmen and laymen alike. They might, as Christians, desire to be faithful to the traditions of the Christian Fathers, like Gregory the Great, but actually and necessarily they were still more powerfully influenced by the traditions of their own race. We shall have to examine the Teutonic tradition of Government presently in more detail: for the moment it is enough to say that the Teutonic tradition knew nothing of an unlimited authority in the ruler, but a great deal of the relation of the king to his great or wise men, and even to the nation as a whole; and for the most part the churchmen outside of Italy, and even to a large extent in Italy, were men of the Teutonic race or tradition.

The situation of the ninth century was wholly different from that of the sixth; and while, as we have seen, the writers of the ninth century, in their anxiety to be faithful to the tradition of the earlier Christian writers, constantly repeat such phrases as these of St Gregory the Great, they are also continually and quite clearly governed by other traditions and give expression to other principles. In this and the following chapters we have to consider these. We begin by examining their conceptions of the relation of government and justice. We have seen that the writers of the ninth century look upon the king as the representative of God, and sometimes speak as though this were true, whether he is good or bad, just or unjust. This does not, however, mean that they are blind to the difference between the just

king and the unjust, whom they do not hesitate to call a tyrant.
It is true that some of the Fathers had spoken as though this
made no difference in the duty of the subject, and we have seen
that St Augustine actually omits the characteristic of justice
from his definition of the State; but, as we have also seen,
other Fathers represent another tendency, and the influence of
one of these is very strong in the ninth century.

We have in a previous chapter mentioned the definitions of
civitas and *populus* given by St Isidore of Seville. Hrabanus
Maurus reproduces them,[1] and it is perhaps worth noticing that
in doing this he follows St Isidore in his reproduction of Cicero's
definition of the State as against St Augustine. We cannot,
indeed, argue from this that he intends to repudiate St Augustine's definition; but the fact may serve to illustrate what we
have already said, that St Augustine's definition of the State
does not seem to have exercised any considerable influence
in the Middle Ages.

We have also in a previous chapter mentioned the definition
of the king given by St Isidore of Seville. Kings, he says, are
so called from ruling, but he does not rule who does not correct:
if the ruler acts rightly, he will keep the name of king; if he
transgresses, he will lose it. There is an ancient proverb,
" Thou shalt be king, if thou doest rightly; if not, thou shalt
not be king."[2] His definition is constantly referred to by the
writers of the ninth century. Hrabanus Maurus reproduces it
verbatim in his 'De Universo,'[3] and it is more or less exactly
cited by Sedulius Scotus,[4] by Jonas of Orleans,[5] by Cathulfus,[6]

[1] Hrabanus Maurus, De Universo,
xiv. 1 : "Civitas est hominum multitudo societatis vinculo adunata ; dicta
a civibus, id est, ab ipsis incolis urbis.
Nam urbs ipsa mœnia sunt ; civitas
autem non saxa, sed habitatores vocantur." Id., id., xvi. 4: "Populus
est coetus humanæ multitudinis
juris consensu concordi communione
sociatus."

[2] St Isidore of Seville, Etym., ix. 3 :
"Reges a regendo vocati. Sicut enim
sacerdos a sacrificando, ita et rex
a regendo. Non autem regit qui non

corrigit. Recte igitur faciendo regis
nomen tenetur, peccando amittitur
Unde et apud veteres, tale erat
proverbium : ' Rex eris si recte facias,
si non facias non eris.' "

[3] De Universo, xvi. 3.

[4] De Rectoribus Christianis, 2.

[5] De Instit. Regia, 3 : "Rex a recte
regendo vocatur ; si enim pie, et juste,
et misericorditer regit, merito rex
appellatur ; si his caruerit nomen regis
amittit."

[6] M. G. H. Ep., iv. Var. Car. Mag
Regn., 7.

and by Hincmar of Rheims.[1] In itself this definition might mean much or little, but it obtains a very considerable significance when we observe again how sharply the "king" is contrasted with the "tyrant." St Isidore, in the same place where he defines the meaning of "king," also defines the meaning of "tyrant." This name, he says, had formerly been used as equivalent to that of king, but in later time was used to denote a wicked and cruel ruler.[2] This definition, again, is reproduced exactly by Hrabanus Maurus,[3] less precisely by Jonas of Orleans;[4] and Hincmar of Rheims seems to have it in his mind when he says that without clemency, patience, and love a man may become a tyrant, but cannot well attain to the kingdom.[5] St Isidore of Seville adds to his definition of the king the observation that the principal royal virtues are *justitia* and *pietas*.[6] Hrabanus Maurus[7] and Hincmar of Rheims reproduce his phrase.[8]

The ninth-century writers are also strongly influenced by a work of uncertain date, which some of them seem to have regarded as being by St Cyprian, though it was also at various times attributed to Origen, St Augustine, or other Fathers. It seems clear that the work is of a much later time than any of these, and it has been contended that it belongs to the

---

[1] Ad Episcopos de Institutione Carolomanni, 16.

[2] St Isidore of Seville, Etym., ix. 3: "Tyranni Græce dicuntur. Idem Latine et reges. Nam apud veteres inter regem et tyrannum nulla discretio erat; ut 'Pars mihi pacis erat dextram tetigisse tyranni.' Fortes enim reges tyranni vocabantur. Nam tiro fortis. De quibus Dominus loquitur: 'Per me reges regnant, et tyranni tenent terram.' Jam postea in usum accidit tyrannos vocari pessimos atque inprobos reges, luxuriosæ dominationis cupiditatem et crudelissimam dominationem in populis exercentes."

[3] De Universo, xvi. 3.

[4] De Instit. Regia, 3: "Antiqui autem omnes reges tyrannos vocabant;

sed postea pie, et juste, et misericorditer regentes regis nomen sunt adepti; impie vel injuste, crudeliterque principantibus, non regis sed tyrannicum aptatum est nomen."

[5] De Divortio Lotharii et Tetbergæ, Præf.: "Et licet sint aliæ virtutes sine quibus ad regnum non pervenitur æternum, tamen sine his tribus quas posuimus, tyrannus fieri potest, regnum autem salubriter nemo potest obtinere terrenum, id est sine mansuetudine . . . sine patientia . . . sine vera dilectione."

[6] Etym., ix. 3: "Regiæ virtutes præcipuæ duæ, justitia et pietas: plus autem in regibus laudatur pietas; nam justitia per se severa est."

[7] De Universo, xvi. 3.

[8] Ad Episc. de Inst. Carol., 17.

seventh century.[1] This treatise, 'De Duodecim Abusivis
Sæculi,' which is of much value and interest throughout as a
criticism of the condition of society in the period, whatever
that may precisely be, to which it belongs, has one chapter
which is specially important in relation to the conception of
justice in the State. The ninth chapter deals with the unjust
king, and declares that the king must not be unjust, but
must restrain the unjust: it is the proper purpose of his
office to rule, but how can he rule and correct others unless
he first corrects himself? Justice in the king means to
oppress no man unjustly, to judge righteously between men,
to defend the weak, to punish the wicked, to protect the
Church, to put just rulers over the kingdom, to live in God
and the Catholic faith, and to keep his children from evil.
The king who does not rule according to these principles
will bring many evils and disasters on his country and his
descendants. The king should remember that as he has the
greatest station among men, so also he will suffer the greatest
punishment if he does not do justice.[2] This chapter is quoted

---

[1] It has been argued with great
force by S. Hellmann, in his admirable
edition, 1908, that this work is of
Irish origin, and belongs to the seventh
century.

[2] De Duodecim Abusivis Sæculi, 9:
"Nonus abusionis gradus est rex in-
iquus. Quem cum correctorem iniquorum esse oportet, licet in semet
ipso nominis sui dignitatem non
custodit. Nomen enim regis intellectu-
aliter hoc retinet, ut subjectis omnibus
rectoris officium procuret. Sed qualiter
alios corrigere poterit qui proprios
mores ne iniqui sint non corrigit?
Quoniam in justitia regis exaltatur
solium et in veritate solidantur
gubernacula populorum. Justitia vero
regis est neminem injuste per potentiam opprimere, sine acceptione personarum inter virum et proximum
suum judicare, advenis et pupillis
et viduis defensorem esse, furta
cohibere, adulteria purire, iniquos non
exaltare . . . ecclesias defendere,

pauperes elemosynis alere, justos
super regni negotia constituere, senes
et sapientes et sobrios consiliarios
habere . . . iracundiam differre,
patriam fortiter et juste contra ad-
versarios defendere, per omnia in
Deo confidere, prosperitatibus animum
non elevare cuncta advsersaria
patienter ferre, fidem Catholicam in
Deum habere, filios suos non sinere
impie agere, certis horis orationibus
insistere, ante horas congruas non
gustare cibum. . . . Qui vero regnum
secundum hanc legem non dispensat,
multas nimirum adversitates imperii
tolerat. Idcirco enim sæpe pax
populorum rumpitur et offendicula
etiam de regno suscitantur, terrarum
quoque fructus diminuuntur et servitia populorum præpediuntur, multi
et varii dolores prosperitatem regni
inficiunt. . . . Ecce quantum justitia
regis sæculo valet, intuentibus per-
spicue patet. Pax populorum est,
tutamen patriæ, munitas plebis,

by Jonas of Orleans[1] and by Hincmar of Rheims[2] in their treatises dealing with the nature of the royal authority.

The formal treatises on kingship in the ninth century are indeed very largely made up of admonitions to the king to follow after justice and mercy, to seek wisdom and to fear God. Smaragdus bids the king to love justice and judgment, the royal way trodden in older times by former kings. He admonishes him to do justice to the poor and the orphan, if he desire that God should establish his throne.[3] Alcuin in his letters continually urges upon the various rulers to whom these are addressed the same principle, that their chief duty is to do justice and mercy to their people.[4] Sedulius Scotus, in his treatise on the nature of the Christian ruler, lays much stress on the same points.[5] He and Cathulfus have a very interesting enumeration of the eight qualities which are

munimentum gentis, cura languorum, gaudium hominum, temperies æris, serenitas maris, terræ fecunditas, solacium pauperum, hereditas filiorum et sibimet ipsi spes futuræ beatitudinis. Attamen sciat rex quod sicut in throno hominum primus constitutus est, sic et in pœnis, si justitiam non fecerit, primatum habiturus est. Omnes namque quoscumque peccatores sub se in præsenti habuit, supra se modo plagali in illa pœna habebit."

[1] De Inst. Regia, 3.

[2] Ad Episc. de Inst. Carol., 7, and De Regis Persona, 25.

[3] Via Regia, 8 and 9 : "Dilige ergo, rex, justitiam et judicium, quæ est via regia, et a prioribus regibus antiquitus trita. . . . Sed tempera justitiam et crudelitatem solliciter cave sinistram. . . . Si vis ergo, O rex, ut thronus tuus a Domino firmetur, non cesses justificare pauperem et pupillum."

[4] M. G. H. Ep., iv. ; Alcuin, Ep. 18 : "Illorum est, id est, Sacerdotum, verba Dei non tacere. Vestrum est, o Principes, humiliter obœdire, diligenter implere. Regis est, omnes iniquitates pietatis suæ potentia obprimere ; justum esse in judiciis,

pronum in misericordia — secundum quod ille miseretur subjectis, miserebitur ei Deus — sobrium in moribus, veridicum in verbis, largum in donis, providum in consiliis : consiliarios habere prudentes, Deum timentes, honestis moribus ornatos. . . . Legimus quoque, quod Regis bonitas totius est gentis prosperitas, victoria exercitus. . . . Magnum est totam regere gentem. A regendo vero Rex dicitur : et qui bene regit subjectum sibi populum, bonam habet a Deo retributionem, regnum scilicet cœleste. Valde feliciter regnat in terra, qui de terreno regno merebitur cœleste. Orationibus vero et vigiliis eo instantius ad Deum insistere debet, quo non pro se solummodo, sed et pro totius gentis prosperitate Deum deprecari debet. Similiter Principes et Judices populi in justitia et pietate populo præsint. Viduis, pupillis et miseris sint quasi patres ; quia æquitas Principum populi est exultatio. Ecclesiarum Christi sint defensores et tutores ; ut servorum Dei orationibus longa vivant prosperitate." Cf. Ep. 30, 64, 217.

[5] De Rect. Christ., 2, 3, &c.

the most firm supports of a just king.[1] Jonas of Orleans, as we have already mentioned, cites St Isidore's definition of the king and the tyrant, and also the ninth chapter of the treatise 'De Duodecim Abusivis Sæculi,' and himself urges with much vigour on the king the duty of doing justice. The king's chief duty, he says, is to govern the people of God with equity and justice, and to strive that they may have peace and concord. He is to prevent all injustice and to appoint fit persons to administer the State under him, for he will be responsible if they are unjust. Such ministers must learn that the people of Christ are by nature their equals, and that they must rule them justly, and not lord it over them or ill-treat them, thinking that they belong to them, or are put under them for the glory of the rulers. Such notions belong to tyranny and unjust power, and not to justice.[2]

[1] M. G. H. Ep., vol. iv. ; Ep. Var. Car. Mag. Regn. Script., 7 : "Sunt autem octo columnæ regis justi propriæ. . . . Prima est veritas in rebus regalibus ; secunda pacientia in omni negotio ; tertia largitas in muneribus ; quarta persuadibilitas in verbis ; quinta malorum correptio et constrictio ; sexta bonorum elevatio et exaltatio, septima levitas tributi in populo, octava æquitas judicii inter divitem et pauperem." Cf. Sedulius Scotus, De Rect. Christ., 10.

[2] De Inst. Regia, 4 : "Regale ministerium specialiter est populum Dei gubernare et regere cum æquitate et justitia, et ut pacem et concordiam habeant studere. Ipse enim debet primo defensor esse ecclesiarum et servorum Dei. Ipsorum etiam officium est saluti et ministerio sacerdotum solerter prospicere, eorumque armis et protectione Ecclesia Christi debet tueri : viduarum, orphanorum, cæterorumque pauperum, necnon et omnium indigentium inopia defendi. Ipsius enim terror ac studium hujuscemodi, in quantum possibile est, esse debet : primo ut nulla injustitia fiat ; deinde, si evenerit, ut nullo modo eam sub-

sistere permittat, nec spem delitescendi, sive audaciam male agendi cuiquam relinquat ; sed sciant omnes quoniam si ad ipsius notitiam pervenerit quidquam mali quod admiserint, nequaquam incorreptum aut inultum remanebit : sed juxta facti qualitatem erit et modus justæ correptionis. Quapropter hoc in throno regiminis positus est ad judicia recta peragenda, ut ipse per se provideat et perquirat, ne in judicio aliquis a veritate et æquitate declinet. Scire etiam debet quod causa, quam juxta ministerium sibi commissum administrat, non hominum sed Dei causa existit, cui pro ministerio quod suscepit, in examinis tremendi die rationem redditurus est. Et ideo oportet ut ipse, qui judex est judicum, causam pauperum ad se ingredi faciat, et diligenter inquirat, ne forte illi qui ab eo constituti sunt, et vicem ejus agere debent in populo, injuste aut negligenter pauperes oppressiones pati permittant. . . .

" 5. His quæ præmissa sunt declaratur quod hi qui post regem populum Dei regere debent, id est duces et comites, necesse est ut tales

In another passage of the same treatise Jonas urges that justice preserves a kingdom, while injustice causes its ruin ;[1] and he
prefixes to another chapter, in which he urges on subjects the
religious obligations of obedience to the king, the observation
that the duty of the royal office is to care for the wellbeing of
the subjects, and that therefore, as they desire that the king
should aid them, they should obey and serve him.[2] Hincmar
of Rheims, as we have already seen, cites St Isidore's definition
of the king and the tyrant, and the treatise 'De Duodecim
Abusivis Sæculi' on the unjust king, and he repeats Jonas of
Orleans' observations on the duty of kings' ministers.[3]

We find Jonas' statement of the nature of the true king
and of his chief duties reproduced in the address presented by
the bishops to Lewis the Pious in the year 829. In this they
first cite passages from the writings of St Isidore of Seville, St
Gregory the Great, and Fulgentius of Ruspe, to illustrate the
difference between the tyrant and the king, and the true character of the king, and then urge upon him to remember that
his chief duty is to govern with equity and justice, to defend
Churches and the servants of God, the widows, orphans, and
all other poor and needy people. His duty is to prevent all
injustice, if possible, and if it does occur, to put it down. He
should therefore be always ready himself to hear the cause of
the poor, lest any of his ministers should act unjustly, or suffer
the poor to be oppressed. Men of every rank must remember

ad constituendum provideantur, qui
sine periculo ejus, a quo constituuntur,
constitui possint, scientes se ad hoc
positos esse ut plebem Christi sibi
natura æqualem recognoscant, eamque
clementer salvent, et juste regant, non
ut dominentur et affligant, neque ut
populum suum æstiment, aut ad suam
gloriam sibi illum subjiciant: quod non
pertinet ad justitiam, sed potius ad
tyrannidem et iniquam potestatem."

[1] De Inst. Reg., 6. Cf. De Inst.
Laicali, ii. 24.

[2] De Inst. Reg., 8: "Constat regalem potestatem omnibus sibi subjectis secundum æquitatis ordinem

consultum ferre debere; et idcirco
oportet ut omnes subjecti fideliter,
et utiliter, atque obedienter eidem
pareant potestati : quoniam qui potestati a Deo ordinatæ resistit, Dei
utique ordinationi, juxta apostoli docu-
mentum, resistit. Sicut enim subjecti
a rege sibi volunt pie et juste opitu-
lari, ita specialiter ei primum ad salutem animæ suæ procurandam, deinde
generaliter ad honestatem et utilitatem
regni secundum Dei voluntatem dis-
ponendam atque administrandam, in-
dissimulanter atque irretractibiliter solatium opportunum debent exhibere."

[3] Ad Ep. de Inst. Carol., 14.

that if they will have to answer for every idle word, much more will they have to give account to God for the office which He has intrusted to them.[1]

Hincmar of Rheims and Sedulius Scotus seem to express these conceptions in stronger terms than any others. Hincmar quotes, without comment indeed, but no great comment was

[1] M. G. H. Leg., sect. ii. vol. ii. No. 196, Episcoporum ad Hludovicum Imperatorem Relatio, 56 : "Ut quid rex dictus sit; Ysidorus in libro Sententiarum scribit : 'Rex enim,' inquit, 'a recte agendo vocatur : si enim pie et juste et misericorditer regit, merito rex appellatur : si his caruerit, non rex sed tyrannus est.' Antiqui autem ut idem Isidorus in libro Ethimologiarum scribit, omnes reges tyrannos vocabant. Sed postea pie et misericorditer regentibus regis nomen adeptis, impie vero, injuste, crudeliterque principantibus non regis, sed tyrannicum aptatum est nomen. Unde et beatus Gregorius ait in Moralibus : 'Viros namque sanctos proinde reges vocari in sacris suis eloquiis didicimus, eo quod recte agant sensusque proprios bene regant et motus resistentes sibi rationabili discretione componant. Recte igitur illi reges vocantur qui tam semet ipsos, quam subjectos bene gerendo pacificare noverunt.' Ad quid etiam constitutus sit imperator, Fulgentius in libro de veritate predestinationis et gratiæ, scribit : 'Clementissimus quoque imperator non ideo est vas misericordiæ preparatum in gloriam, quia apicem terreni principatus accipit, sed si in imperiali culmine recta fide vivat et vera cordis humilitate preditus culmen regiæ dignitatis sanctæ religioni subjiciat : si magis in timore servire Deo, quam in timore dominari populo delectetur, si in eo lenitas iracundiam mitiget, ornet benignitas potestatem, si se magis diligendum, quam metuendum cunctis exibeat, si subjectis salubriter consulat, si justitiam sic teneat, ut misericordiam non relinquat, si pre omnibus ita se sanctæ matris ecclesiæ catholicæ meminerit filium, ut ejus paci atque tranquillitati per universum mundum prodesse suum faciat principatus. Magis enim christianum regitur imperium, dum ecclesiastico statui per omnem terram consulitur, quam cum in parte quacunque terrarum pro temporali securitate pugnatur.'"

It is important to notice the way in which the bishops understand the authors whom they quote. They continue to enforce the same ideas in the words of Jonas of Orleans : "Regale namque ministerium specialiter est, populum Dei gubernare et regere cum equitate et justitia et, ut pacem et concordiam habeant, studere. Ipse enim debet primo defensor esse ecclesiarum et servorum Dei, viduarum, orfanorum ceterorumque pauperum necnon et omnium indigentium. Ipsius enim terror et studium hujuscemodi, in quantum possibile est, esse debet, primo, ut nulla injustitia fiat, deinde, si evenerit, ut nullo modo eam subsistere permittat, nec spem delitescendi sive audatiam male agendi cuiquam relinquat. . . . Unde oportet, ut ipse, qui judex est judicum causam pauperum ad se ingredi faciat et diligenter inquirat, ne forte aliqui, qui ab eo constituti sunt et vicem ejus agere debent in populo, injuste aut negligenter pauperes oppressiones pati permittant. Scire autem unumquemque cujuslibet sit ordinis, oportet, quia si de ocioso sermone Deo rationem redditurus est, multo magis de ministerio sibi divinitus commisso."

needed by him, a phrase of St Augustine's to which we have referred in an earlier chapter : " Remota itaque justitia, quid sint regna nisi magna latrocinia." [1]   And Sedulius Scotus, warning evil rulers of the ruin which impends over them, of the judgment of God which awaits them both in this world and the next, exclaims : " What are impious kings but the greater robbers of the earth, fierce as lions, ravening like wolves ; but they are great to-day and perish to-morrow, and of them God has said, ' They reigned, but not by Me ; they arose as princes, but I knew it not.' " [2]   The evil ruler or tyrant is no true king; he is only, as Cicero indeed had called him, a wild beast, the most terrible and loathsome known to the world.

The writers of the ninth century, then, while they reproduce the phrases of St Gregory the Great with regard to the divine authority of the ruler, and speak at times as though he must under all circumstances be obeyed as the representative of God, are also clearly and strongly influenced by other considerations, partly founded, no doubt, upon the authority of other Fathers like St Isidore of Seville, but also in large measure related to their own experience and traditions.   They no doubt felt really and profoundly the truth which lay behind St Gregory's phrases, the truth that authority in the State is sacred ; they had ample experience of the consequences of discord and civil strife.   But, on the other hand, they had no mind to submit to injustice or tyranny ; they were probably clearly enough conscious of the fact that many of the kings whom they had known were capricious and fallible rulers.

We must turn to the actual conditions of the government of the time, not to discuss the intricacies of the Frankish or other Teutonic constitutions, but that we may recognise some of the principles which lay behind the constitutional machinery and practice of those times, and that we may more completely understand the forces which were moulding the theory of the State.

[1] De Regis Persona, 6. Cf. p. 167.
[2] De Rect. Chris., 8: "Quid sunt autem impii reges, nisi majores ter- rarum latrones, feroces ut leones, rabidi ut ursi ?"

CHAPTER XIX.

THE KING AND THE LAW.

WE have seen that the writers of the ninth century look upon
justice as something essential to the character of the true ruler.
Without justice he is a tyrant and no king. The conception of
justice was indeed no more clear in the ninth century than
in the present day, or in ancient times; but we think that
justice, relatively to the ruler, had a meaning in the ninth
century whose importance is very great indeed. No king is
just who does not observe and respect the law; the law is
at least one standard of justice, clear, distinct, constantly
appealed to.

We have seen in earlier chapters that in the theory of the
Roman jurists the emperor is the source of law. Justinian
even speaks of him as the sole "legis lator." [1] It is true that, as
we have also seen, this power is his only because the Roman
people have chosen to confer their authority upon him; the
people is the only ultimate source of law. But still the emperor is the actual source of law. And the emperor is "legibus
solutus," a phrase whose significance it is not easy to define. It
may indeed be doubted whether it can be clearly defined. Perhaps it only expresses a conception whose history can be traced
in such a constitutional form as that of the dispensing power of
the English Crown,—a power which seems to represent the consciousness present, however vaguely, to any more developed
reflection upon law and the State, that there must be a power
in the State itself which can, if necessary, interfere to prevent
the harsh or inequitable operation of the law in particular cases;

[1] Cod. i. 14. 12.

a power which, being in its nature administrative rather than legislative, must be intrusted to the head of the State as administrator. It is the influence, perhaps, partly of this consciousness, partly of the revived study of the Roman jurisprudence, which leads the more systematic political thinkers of the thirteenth century like St Thomas Aquinas to observe that the prince cannot properly be said to be under the law, for he must have the power of dispensing with it.[1]

In the ninth century, however, the king is not the sole source of law, but only has his part in the national relation to it, and he is not usually thought of as above the law, or outside of it, but as bound to carry it out. The ninth-century theory of the relation of the king to justice may be reasonably connected with the theory of his relation to law. Lothair, Lewis, and Charles, at their meeting at Mersen in 851, put out a declaration promising their faithful subjects that for the future they would not condemn, or dishonour, or oppress any man against the law and justice.[2] And when Lewis at Coblentz in 860 repeats the promises of Mersen, he adds an emphatic assurance that his faithful subjects shall enjoy the ancient law, and that all shall receive justice and law.[3] Justice, when translated into constitutional tradition, means, in the first place, the observation of the national law: the king is just when he sees that this is carried out, unjust when he acts in contradiction to it.

In the treatise of Hincmar of Rheims on the divorce of Lothair and Tetburga we find a formal discussion of the nature and source of the royal authority, to which we shall have to return later, for it contains much which is important. For the

[1] St Thom. Aquin., Summa 1, 2, Q. xcvi. 5 ; and Sum. 2, 2, Q. lxvii. 4. Cf. article by R. W. Carlyle in 'Scottish Review,' Jan. 1896, "The Political Theories of St Thomas Aquinas."

[2] M. G. H. Leg., sect. ii. vol. ii. 205. 6 : "Ut nostri fideles, unusquisque in suo ordine et statu, veraciter sint de nobis securi, quia nullum adhinc in ante contra legem et justitiam vel auctoritatem ac justam rationem aut damnabimus aut dehonorabimus aut opprimemus vel indebitis machinationibus affligemus," &c.

[3] M. G. H. Leg., sect. ii. vol. ii. 242. 5 : "Et volumus, ut vos et ceteri homines fideles nostri talem legem et rectitudinem et tale salvamentum in regnis nostris habeatis, sicut antecessores vestri tempore antecessorum nostrorum habuerint . . . et justitia et lex omnibus conservetur."

moment we look at it only to see how he deals with the relation
of the king to law. It is contended, he says, by some wise
men that the prince is a king, and that the king is subject to
the laws and judgment of none save God alone. This is true in
one sense, he replies—that is, if he is a true king, for the king
is so called from ruling; and if he governs himself according to
God's will, and directs the good into the right way, and corrects
the wicked so as to drive them from the evil way to the good
and right one, then he is a king indeed, and subject to the laws
and judgments of none save God. Whosoever, then, is a king
in the true sense, is not subject to law, for law is set not for
the just but for the unjust, for wicked men and for sinners; and
he who rules himself and others according to the fruits of the
spirit is not subject to law, for "against such there is no law."
But the adulterer, murderer, unjust man, the ravisher, and the
man guilty of other vices, whoever he may be, will be judged
by the priest.[1] Hincmar's treatment of the question seems to
indicate that he was in some measure conscious of the difficulty
of defining in precise terms the relation of the king to law; but

[1] Hincmar of Rheims, De Div. Loth.
et Tetb., Quæstio vi.: "Dicunt quoque
etiam aliqui sapientes, quia iste princeps rex est, et nullorum legibus vel
judiciis subjacet, nisi solius Dei. . . .
  "Resp. . . . Quod dicitur, quia rex
nullorum legibus vel judiciis subjacet,
nisi solius Dei, verum dicitur si rex
est sicuti nominatur. Rex enim a
regendo dicitur, et si seipsum secundum
voluntatem Dei regit, et bonos in viam
rectam dirigit, malos autem de via
prava ad rectam corrigit, tunc rex est,
et nullorum legibus vel judiciis nisi
solius Dei subjacet: quoniam arbitria
possunt dici, leges autem non sunt,
nisi illæ quæ Dei sunt per quem reges
regnant, et conditores legem justam
decernunt. Et quicunque rex veraciter
rex est, legi non subjacet, quia lex
non est posita justo, sed injustis et
non subditis, impiis et peccatoribus,
sceleratis, contaminatis, parricidis et
matricidis, . . . et si quid aliud sanæ

doctrinæ adversatur, et his qui operibus carnis serviunt, de quibus dicit
Apostolus [quotes Gal. v. 19-21]. . . .
Qui autem se et alios secundum
fructus Spiritus regit [quotes Gal. v.
22, 23] . . . legi non subjacet quia
'adversus hujusmodi non est lex.'
Sed solo judicio Christi subjacet a
quo et remunerabitur cujus est qui
carnem suam crucifigit cum vitiis
et concupiscentiis. Alioquin adulter,
homicida, injustus, raptor, et aliorum
vitiorum obnoxius quilibet, vel secrete,
vel publice, judicabitur a sacerdotibus,
qui sunt throni Dei, in quibus Deus
sedet, et per quos sua decernit judicia,
quibus et in apostolis suis quorum
locum in Ecclesia tenent, Dominus
dixit 'Si peccaverit frater . . .
(Matt. xviii. 15, 16).' Et ne quis in
hoc sacerdotem parvipendat adjunxit
Dominus [quotes Matt. xviii. 18]. . . .
Et item dicit 'qui vos audit me audit,
et qui vos spernit, me spernit.'"

it is fairly explicit as indicating that whatever might be the relation of the true ruler to the law which he is justly administering, the evil ruler who sets at nought the moral law is liable to correction at least by the Church.   We shall have to return to this particular aspect of the question later.

If in this passage Hincmar seems to express himself in the most cautious fashion, we find him speaking in more unqualified terms in other places on the principle that it is the duty of the ruler to observe and obey the law.   In another part of the same treatise he quotes a phrase of St Ambrose which we have already discussed, "Leges enim imperator fert, quas primus ipse custodiat," and warns the king that if he breaks the laws he may find himself condemned by the apostle's words, "Thou that preachest a man should not steal, dost thou steal?"[1] We have considered the meaning which may be attached to this phrase as it is used by St Ambrose; Hincmar of Rheims' comment on it makes it fairly clear that he understands it in a somewhat strict sense.   Hincmar also quotes the passage from St Augustine's treatise 'De Vera Religione' which we have already discussed: the citation occurs as part of a discussion of the action of Charles the Bald in summoning Hincmar, Bishop of Laon, to appear before a secular court, and passing some sort of judgment on him in his absence.   Hincmar argues that this action is contrary not only to the canons, but also to laws of the emperors from Constantine downwards, and to the promises made by Charles himself to observe the canons.   Therefore he concludes, in a phrase of St Gregory the Great, "It must be so, that whatever is contrary to the laws has no force," and then quotes St Augustine as saying that when men make laws they judge what is good, but when they have once been made, the magistrate cannot judge the laws, but can only act in accordance

---

[1] Hincmar of Rheims, De Div. Loth. et Tetb., Quæstio v. : Resp. : "Capitula sunt legalia imperatorum et regum prædecessorum suorum, quid sustinere debeat qui post bannum latronem receperit, et in chirographo regum nostrorum hinc expresse decernitur, cujus ministerium est agere ut illa observentur, sicut sanctus Ambrosius ad Valentinianum scribit. 'Leges enim imperator ferat, quas primus ipse custodiat,' quas si ipse fregerit, timendum est ne audiat ab apostolo, 'Qui prædicas non furandum, furaris, qui abominaris idola sacrilegium facis.'" See p. 164.

with them.[1] It is clear that Hincmar uses St Augustine's phrase
to confirm his opinion that the king cannot violate the laws
which had long been in force as to the relation of the ecclesiastical and secular courts.   In the 'De Regis Persona' Hincmar
quotes the first part of the same saying of St Augustine, and
then concludes that just laws which have been promulgated
must be enforced by the prince.[2]

But the strongest and most noteworthy statement of the
same view is to be found in Hincmar's treatise called 'De
Ordine Palatii.'   In the eighth chapter of this work we have
an exceedingly important statement of the writer's conception
of the relation of the king to the law, and of the source of
the authority of the latter.   He begins by a reference to the
rule that no priest must be ignorant of the canons, and then
proceeds to say that in like manner the sacred laws—that is,
the Roman laws in the 'Lex Romana Visigothorum'—decree
that no one may be ignorant of the law or despise its decrees.
This includes persons of every worldly rank.   Kings, therefore,
and the ministers of the commonwealth, have laws by which
they must rule the inhabitants of every province; they have
the capitularies of the Christian kings, their ancestors, which

---

[1] Hincmar of Rheims, Pro. Eccl. Lib.
Def. i. : "Unde legalis sententia, quam
ut prædecessores illius, B. Gregorius
in commonitorio Joanni dato decrevit
esse canonicam, dicit: 'Necesse est
quod contra leges est actum firmitatem
non habeat.'   Et S. Augustinus in
libro, 'De Vera Religione,' dicit, 'In
istis temporalibus legibus quanquam
de his homines judicent, cum eas
instituunt: tamen cum fuerint institutæ atque firmatæ non licebit judici
de ipsis judicare, sed secundum ipsas.
Conditor tamen legum temporalium si
vir bonus et sapiens est, illam ipsam
consulit æternam, de qua nulli animæ
judicare datum est, ut secundum ejus
incommutabiles regulas quid sit pro
tempore jubendum vitandumque dis-
cernat. Æternam igitur legem mun-
dis animis fas est cognoscere, nefas

est judicare.'   De qua B. Prosper
dicit :—

'Lex æterna Dei stabili regit omnia nutu
Nec mutat vario tempore consilium.'

Nam si imperatores Romanorum suam
legem æternam, vel perpetuam appel-
laverunt, multo magis lex illa æterna
est, quæ est Sancto Spiritu pro-
mulgata."

[2] Hincmar of Rheims, De Reg. Per.,
27 : "Sanctus Augustinus in libro 'De
Vera Religione' leges principum ser-
vandas ostendit.   'In istis,' inquiens,
'temporalibus legibus quanquam de his
homines judicent cum eas instituunt,
tamen cum fuerint institutæ atque
firmatæ non licebit judici de ipsis judicare, sed secundum ipsas.' Igitur aut a
populo promulgatæ justæ leges ser-
vandæ, aut a principe juste ac rationabiliter sunt in quolibet vindicandæ."

were lawfully promulgated with the universal consent of their faithful subjects. And he then again quotes St Augustine's sentence that men judge the laws when they make them, but when they are once made, the judge cannot judge them, but must act in accordance with them.[1] We cannot here mistake Hincmar's meaning; the king's duty is to govern according to the laws; he is no more entitled than any private person to ignore the law or to violate it. His duty is to carry out the law, not to act contrary to it.

In Hincmar's words we find not only a strong statement of the normal subordination of the prince to the law, but a suggestion of one important cause of this subordination. We think that the words which describe the "capitula" which the king is to carry out, as having been made *generali consensu fidelium*, are extremely significant, and indicate one of the strongest grounds for Hincmar's judgment that he must keep the law. The law is not merely his law, nor is it merely by his will that it has been made. So far as laws have been made, they proceed from the whole State, they have been made with the general consent of the faithful subjects of the king. It requires but little reflection to observe how far this conception is from that of the Roman jurists. The relation of the Roman emperor to laws when promulgated may be a little obscure, perhaps a little doubtful. Ulpian's "legibus solutus,"[2] and Theodosius' and Valentinian's "Digna vox majestate regnantis legibus alligatum se principem profiteri,"[3] may represent two different tendencies of thought, but at least the emperor was normally in his own person the direct source of law. To the ninth-century writers

---

[1] M. G. H. Leg., sect. ii. vol. ii., Hincmar, De Ordine Palatii, 8 : "Et sicut dictum est de legibus ecclesiasticis, quod nulli sacerdoti suos liceat canones ignorare nec quicquam facere, quod patrum possit regulis obviare, ita legibus sacris decretum est, ut leges nescire nulli liceat aut quæ sunt statuta contemnere ? Cum enim dicitur, 'Nulli liceat leges nescire vel quæ sunt statuta contemnere,' nulla persona in quocumque ordine mundano excipitur, quæ hac sententia non constringatur. Habent enim reges et

reipublicæ ministri leges, quibus in quacumque provincia degentes regere debent, habent capitula christianorum regum ac progenitorum suorum, quæ generali consensu fidelium suorum tenere legaliter promulgaverunt. De quibus beatus Augustinus dicit, quia, 'licet homines de his judicent cum eas instituunt, tamen cum fuerint institutæ atque firmatæ, non licebit judicibus de ipsis judicare, sed secundum ipsas.'"

[2] Dig. i. 3. 31.

[3] Cod. i. 14. 4.

the king had his part in making law, so far as law is made, but he has only one part out of many. Other voices have been heard besides his, the consent of others has to be given before anything can become the national law. This conception is one of the very greatest importance in the development of mediæval political thought, and we must proceed to examine the legislation of the ninth century to make ourselves quite clear upon the matter.

We must observe in passing that the legal system of the ninth century has a very different character from that which we should attribute to modern law. The great mass of the law of the early Middle Ages was not, so far as the consciousness of men went, made at all. It was a part of the national or tribal life; it had grown with the tribe, changing, no doubt, but the people or tribe were hardly conscious of the changes. Such traditional law is contained in most of the early mediæval codes, and its authority was like that of nature. But in the ninth century there was already developed, perhaps prematurely, the conception that law needs deliberate adaptation, or at least addition, and therefore, while much of the legislation of the time is nothing but the formal reiteration of what is supposed to be immemorial custom, other parts of it represent conscious and deliberate attempts to improve or add to the traditional customs of the nation.

There are three bodies of secular law to which the ruler of the Teutonic States was related: first, the traditional tribal law, which varied considerably within such extended dominions as those of the Frankish Empire; secondly, the legislation of the ancient Roman Empire, which obtained in many districts, mainly in the form of different editions of the Theodosian code, a system of laws over which the Frankish king or emperor had little control, which are usually referred to by the writers of this time as the "leges sacræ"; and, thirdly, the actual new laws, or additions to old laws, which the king or emperor might issue, but only with the consent and counsel of some or all of his subjects.

The relation of the king or emperor of the ninth century to the secular law is thus very different from that of the Roman emperors of antiquity. We are only repeating the judgment of the great majority of historical scholars, and would refer to

the work of Stubbs[1] and Waitz[2] among the older writers, and
to Richter and Kohl[3] and Viollet[4] among the more recent.   It
is true that Fustel de Coulanges has argued with much learning
and ingenuity against this view, or at least in favour of a
considerable modification of it, but we do not think that he
has succeeded in establishing his case.   The matter is, however,
of such great importance in the history of the development of
political theory that we think it well to illustrate it briefly
from the legal documents of the ninth century.

We may begin by observing the method of promulgation of a
series of " capitula," to be added to the " leges," issued by Charles
the Great in the year 803.   One manuscript contains an account
of the method of promulgating these in Paris.   They were sent
to Stephen the Count, who was to cause them to be read in the
" mallus publicus " in the presence of all the " scabinei."   When
this had been done, and they all agreed that they would for the
future observe the laws, the " scabinei," bishops, abbots, and
counts, affixed their signatures.[5]   This statement, it is true,
only refers to one place, but a comparison with sect. 19 of the
" Capitulare Missorum " of the same year makes it fairly plain
that something like this was the normal mode of promulgating
these new laws.   We learn that the " missi " were to inquire of
the " populus " about the " capitula " which were to be added to
the laws, and to see that, when all had consented, their signature
or other authentication was appended to the " capitula."[6]

We can now compare with this the formula with which

---

[1] Stubbs, Const. Hist. of Eng. (ed.
1891), vol. i. p. 141, &c.

[2] Waitz, Deutsche Verfassung's
Geschichte (ed. 1883), vol. iii. p.
601, &c.

[3] Richter and Kohl, "Annalen des
Fränkischen Reiches," II. Abtheilung,
p. 586, &c.

[4] P. Viollet, "Histoire des Institutions Politiques et Administratives de
la France," vol. i. p. 197, &c.

[5] M. G. H. Leg., sect. ii. vol. i. No.
39 : "Sub ipso anno hæc capitula facta
sunt et consignata Stephano Comiti,
ut hæc manifesta fecisset in civitate

Parisiis mallo pubplico et ipsa legere
fecisset coram illis scabineis ; quod ita
et fecit.   Et omnes in uno consenserunt, quod ipsi voluissent omni
tempore observare usque in posterum ; etiam omnes scabinei, episcopi,
abbatis, comitis manu propria subter
firmaverunt."

[6] M. G. H. Leg., sect. ii. vol. i. No.
40, c. 19 : "Ut populus interrogetur
de capitulis quæ in lege noviter
addita sunt ; et postquam omnes con-
senserint,   subscriptiones et manu-
firmationes suas in ipsis capitulis
faciant."

Charles the Great issues the "Capitulare Aquisgranense." Charles does this with the consent of his bishops, abbots, counts, and all his faithful subjects.[1] We find yet another very noteworthy illustration of this conception of the mode of public administration and legislation in the 'Ordinatio Imperii' of Lewis the Pious in 817, the document which provides for the partition of his dominions between his sons. These regulations are made in a sacred assembly and "generalitas" of the whole people, held after the wonted manner. After a fast of three days his eldest son (Lothair) was elected by Lewis and the whole people to be his colleague in the empire. Then with the common counsel it was decided to give the younger sons, Pippin and Lewis, the title of kings, and to allot to them certain lands by definite "capitula." These were considered and then confirmed by Lewis and all his faithful subjects, so that what was done by all might by all be held inviolable.[2] (This

---

[1] M. G. H. Leg., sect. ii. vol. i. No. 77 : " Karolus serenissimus imperator Augustus, a Deo coronatus, magnus et pacificus, cum episcopis, abbatibus, comitibus, ducibus, omnibusque fidelibus Christianæ ecclesiæ cum consensu consilioque constituit ex lege Salica, Romana atque Gombata capitula ista in palatio Aquis, ut unusquisque fidelis justitias ita faceret qui et ipse manu propria firmavit capitula ista, ut omnes fideles manu roborare studuissent."

[2] M. G. H. Leg., sect. ii. vol. i. No. 136 : " Cum nos in Dei nomine anno incarnationis Domini octingentesimo septimo decimo, indictione decima annoque imperii nostri quarto, mense Julio, Aquisgrani palatio nostro more solito sacrum conventum et generalitatem populi nostri propter ecclesiasticas vel totius imperii nostri utilitates pertractandas congregassemus et in his studeremus, subito divina inspiratione actum est, ut nos fideles nostri ammonerent, quatenus manente nostra incolumitate et pace undique a Deo concessa de statu totius regni et de filiorum nostrorum causa more parentum nostrorum tractaremus.　. . Quibus (jejuniis orationibus elemosinarum largitionibus) rite per triduum celebratis, nutu omnipotentis Dei, ut credimus, actum est ut et nostra et totius populi nostri in dilecti primogeniti nostri Hlutharii electione vota concurrerent. Itaque taliter divina dispensatione manifestatum placuit et nobis et omni populo nostro, more solemni imperiali diademate coronatum nobis et consortem et successorem imperii, si Dominus ita voluerit, communi voto constitui. Ceteros vero fratres ejus, Pippinum videlicet et Hludowicum æquivocum nostrum, communi consilio placuit regiis insigniri nominibus, et loca inferius denominata constituere, in quibus post decessum nostrum sub seniore fratre regali potestate potiantur juxta inferius adnotata capitula, quibus, quam inter eos constituimus, conditio continetur. Quæ capitula propter utilitatem imperii et perpetuam inter eos pacem conservandam et totius ecclesiæ tutamen cum omnibus fidelibus nostris considerare placuit et considerata conscribere et conscripta propriis

last phrase is perhaps specially worthy of notice.) We may compare with these the terms of the "Proemium" to the "Capitularia tam Ecclesiastica quam Mundana" of 818, 819; sect. 29 of the "Capitulare Ecclesiasticum"; the phrases of the "Cap. Legi Salicæ Addita" of 819; and the "Cap. de Functionibus Publicis" of 820.[1]

But it is hardly necessary to multiply citations to establish a judgment which is almost universally accepted as to the constitutional theory of the Teutonic States,—namely, that the king does not make laws by his own authority, but requires the consent and advice of his wise men, and, in some more or less vague sense, of the whole nation.[2] It is this tradition or theory which at last finds something like a formal and explicit definition in the famous phrase of the "Edictum Pistense" of 864, "Quoniam lex consensu populi et constitutione regis fit," [3]— a phrase which, no doubt, like so many of the *obiter dicta* of the Middle Ages, must not be interpreted under the terms of what we consider our clear-cut modern conceptions, but which is full of significance for the development of the theory of law, when it is taken in its proper connection with the general tendencies of the ninth century and of the Teutonic traditions.

manibus firmare, ut, Deo opem ferente, sicut ab omnibus communi voto actum est, ita communi devotione a cunctis inviolabiliter conserventur ad illorum et totius populi Christiani perpetuam pacem ; salva in omnibus nostra imperiali potestate super filios et populum nostrum, cum omni subjectione quæ patri a filiis et imperatori ac regi a suis populis exhibetur."

[1] M. G. H. Leg., sect. ii. 137 ; 138, c. 29 ; 142, c. 2, 3, 6, 8 ; 143, c. 5. Cf. also Nos. 215 and 221.

[2] We do not mean by this that the emperor or king did not exercise a great and perhaps almost independent authority in issuing administrative ordinances, and many of these belong to the category of what would in later times have been regarded as laws.

[3] M. G. H. Leg., sect. ii. vol. ii. 273 ; Edict. Pist., 864 ; Jun. 25. "Karolus

gratia Dei rex. Notum esse volumus omnibus Dei et nostris fidelibus, quoniam hæc, quæ sequuntur, capitula nunc in isto placito nostro, anno ab incarnatione domini nostri Jesu Christi DCCCLXIV., anno videlicet regni nostri ipso propitio xxv., indictione xii. vii. Kalend. Julias in hoc loco, qui dicitur Pistis, una cum fidelium nostrorum consensu atque consilio constituimus et cunctis sine ulla refragatione per regnum nostrum observanda mandamus. . . .

"6. Et quoniam lex consensu populi et constitutione regis fit, Franci jurare debent, quia secundum regium mandatum nostrum ad justitiam reddendam vel faciendam legibus bannitus vel mannitus fuit ; et sic ipsæ res illi judicio scabiniorum in bannum mittantur, et, si necesse fuerit, ipse in forbannum mittatur, qui ad justitiam reddendam venire noluerit."

This phrase represents the common tradition of the Teutonic States, and we can see no reason to think that the transformation of the Frankish kingdom into the empire made any change whatever in these constitutional conceptions.   We see no reason to think that even Charles the Great dreamed of claiming the position of the ancient Roman emperors as the sole legislator. It is true, indeed, that Charles the Great and Pippin issue laws in Italy under another form than that which is customary elsewhere, and that in these there is usually no mention of the council and consent of the great men,[1] but we think that this must be understood as arising out of their position in Lombardy as conquerors.

We think, then, that the political theory of the ninth century regarded the ruler as being bound by the laws of the nation, not as superior to them.   The king had his part in making and promulgating law, but others had a part also, and in some vague sense even the whole nation.   We think that this is clear, but it is no doubt also true to say that the historical circumstances of the Frankish States in the ninth century probably tended to give this tradition rather more reality than it may have had before, or in other Teutonic States.   The history of the century is the history of a perpetual series of revolts and civil wars, and as a result of these the royal authority was certainly dwindling, so that as the century advances we perhaps find a more and more frank assertion of the limited and even conditional nature of the royal authority.

[1] M. H. G. Leg., sect. ii. vol. i. Nos. 88, 92, 93, 94, 95, 97, 98.

CHAPTER XX.

THE THEORY OF THE SOURCE AND CONDITIONS OF AUTHORITY
IN THE STATE.

WE have so far considered the source of the authority of law, and its relation to the king or other ruler. We must now examine the immediate source of the authority of the ruler.

It would be a grave mistake, we think, to conceive of the ninth-century writers as having any such definite theory of the delegation of the popular authority to one man as that which obtained among the Roman Jurists. The theory of the ninth century is much vaguer than this: the divine appointment, the custom of hereditary succession, the election by the great men and the people,—all these elements go to constitute the conception of a legitimate claim to the throne. In a document concerning the election of Charles the Bald to the kingdom of the Eastern Franks in 869 we have a good statement of all the grounds of succession—the right of the legitimate heir, the appointment of God, and the election of the nation.[1]

The custom of hereditary succession—that is, of succession within one family—was among the Franks, as generally among the Teutonic tribes, accepted as normal; but it is also true that among the Franks as elsewhere, in order that a succession

---

[1] M. G. H. Leg., sect. ii. vol. ii. 276, Electionis Karoli Capitula in Regno Hlotharii Factæ, 869, Sept. 9.

2. "Quia denique voluntatem Dei, qui voluntatem timentium se facit et deprecationes eorum exaudit, in concordi unanimitate nostra videmus hunc regni hujus heredem esse legitimum, cui nos sponte commisimus, domnum videlicet praesentem regem ac principem nostrum Karolum, ut nobis praesit et prosit, videtur nobis, si vobis placet, ut, sicut post illius verba vobis manifestabimus, signo certissimo demonstremus, quia illum a Deo electum et nobis datum principem credimus et eidem largitori Deo ex suis beneficiis non simus ingrati."

should be valid, it should be confirmed by some national election or recognition. We are not here concerned with the constitutional question of the organisation of the council of the great men or wise men of the kingdom,—that their election was in some sense considered as the election of the nation will hardly be doubted, we think, by any one. The question in which we are now interested is the fact of the elective character of the monarchy of the ninth century rather than its method.

In order to make the matter clear we think it is desirable to consider certain elections as illustrating this principle. There is, indeed, one instance of the appointment of rulers in the Frankish Empire of the ninth century which might seem at first sight to furnish an example of a strictly personal appointment without the sanction of the nation. This is to be found in the statement of the division of his dominions by Charles the Great in 806. In this he makes no mention of the counsel or consent of any one, but seems to determine all the questions concerning the appointment of his sons as colleagues to himself during his lifetime, and the division of his dominions among them after his death, by his own will and authority.[1] It should, however, be observed that Einhard in his Annuals for the year 806 relates how this settlement was made by Charles at a meeting of the *primores* and *optimates* of the Franks, and that it was confirmed by the oath of the Frankish *optimates* and sent to Pope Leo to be subscribed by his hand.[2] It is perhaps also worth noting that even if Charles might be thought to claim the right of nominating his successor, he clearly enough conceives of a return, after his death, to the custom of election. In the fifth clause of the "Divisio Regnorum" he provides that if one of his sons should die leaving

---

[1] M. G. H. Leg., sect. ii. vol. i. No. 45, Divisio Regnorum.

[2] Einhardi Annales, a. 806, M. G. H. Script., vol. i. : " Illisque absolutis, conventum habuit imperator cum primoribus et optimatibus Francorum de pace constituenda et conservanda inter filios suos, et divisione regni facienda in tres partes, ut sciret unusquisque illorum, quam partem tueri et regere debuisset, si superstes illi deveniret. De hac partitione et testamentum factum, et jurejurando ab optimatibus Francorum confirmatum, et constitutiones pacis conservandæ causa factæ, atque hæc omnia litteris mandata sunt, et Leoni papæ, ut his sua manu subscriberet, per Einhardum missa."

a son, he should, if the people elect him, reign in his father's place.[1] If, however, it should be contended that the relation of the action of Charles the Great to the principle of election is a little ambiguous, there can be no doubt about the matter when we turn to the successors of Charles the Great.

We have already considered the settlement of the empire in 817 by Lewis the Pious,[2] and we need only here draw attention to the very explicit terms in which is expressed the consent of the whole people to the election of Lothair, the eldest son, as colleague to his father in the empire, and to the elevation of the younger sons to the dignity and title of kings and to authority in the several portions of the empire,[3] and to the provision for the election by the people of their successors.[4]

We pass on to the later part of the century, and we find not only that the principle of election is very clearly retained, but that we can trace the gradual development of the custom of stating the conditions on which the elections are made. In the documents concerning the succession of Charles the Bald to the kingdom of Italy in 876 we have a very clear statement of the election by the bishops, abbots, counts, and others, and we have also the record of the mutual promises made by subjects and king to each other. The bishops and counts swear obedience, counsel, help, and fidelity, while Charles swears to give law, justice, honour, and mercy to all.[5]

---

[1] M. G. H. Leg., sect. ii. vol. i. No. 45, 5 : " Quod si talis filius cuilibet istorum trium fratrum natus fuerit, quem populus eligere velit ut patri suo in regni hereditate succedat, volumus ut hoc consentiant patrui ipsius pueri, et regnare permittant filium fratris sui in portione regni quam pater ejus, frater eorum habuit."

[2] See p. 237.

[3] M. G. H. Leg., sect. ii. vol. i. No. 136, Ordinatio Imperii : "Actum est, ut et nostra et totius populi nostri in dilecti primogeniti nostri electione vota concurrerent," and " Ceteros vero fratres ejus, Pippinum videlicet et Hlodowicum æquivocum nostrum, communi consilio placuit regiis insigniri

nominibus, et loca inferius denominata constituere, in quibus post decessum nostrum sub seniore fratre regali potestate potiantur."

[4] M. G. H. Leg., sect. ii. vol. i. No. 136, c. 14.

[5] M. G. H. Leg., sect. ii. vol. ii. No. 220, Kar. II. Imp. Electio., 876 Febr. : " Gloriosissimo et a Deo coronato, magno et pacifico imperatori, domino nostro Karolo perpetuo augusto nos quidem Ansbertus cum omnibus episcopis, abbatibus, comitibus ac reliquis . . . perpetuam optamus prosperitatem et pacem.

" Jam quia divina pietas vos beatorum principum apostolorum Petri et Pauli interventione per vicarium ip-

When Charles the Bald died Lewis the Stammerer finally came to the throne, with the consent of the bishops, the abbots, the *primores* of the kingdom, and others, and was consecrated and crowned by Hincmar, Archbishop of Rheims.[1] We have

sorum, domnum videlicet Johannem summum pontificem et universalem papam spiritalemque patrem vestrum, ad profectum sanctæ Dei ecclesiæ nostrorumque omnium incitavit et ad imperiale culmen sancti Spiritus judicio provexit, nos unanimiter vos protectorem, dominum ac defensorem omnium nostrum et Italici regni regem eligimus, cui et gaudenter toto cordis affectu subdi gaudemus, et omnia, quæ nobiscum ad profectum totius sanctæ Dei ecclesiæ nostrorumque omnium salutem decernitis et sancitis, totis viribus annuente Christo concordi mente et prompta voluntate observare promittimus.

"Anspertus, sanctæ Mediolanensis archiepiscopus subscripsi," &c.

"Sic promitto ego, quia de isto die in antea isti seniori meo, quamdiu vixero, fidelis et obediens et adjutor, quantumcumque plus et melius sciero et potuero, et consilio et auxilio secundum meum ministerium in omnibus ero absque fraude et malo ingenio et absque ulla dolositate vel seductione seu deceptione et absque respectu alicujus personæ, et neque per me neque per missum neque per literas . . . contra suum honorem et suam ac ecclesiæ atque regni sibi commissi quietem et tranquillitatem atque soliditatem machinabo, . . . neque aliquod umquam scandalum movebo, quod illius præsenti vel futuræ saluti contraria vel nociva esse possit. Sic me Deus adjuvet et ista sanctorum patrocinia."

"Et ego, quantum sciero et rationabiliter potuero, Domino adjuvante te, sanctissime ac reverentissime archiepiscope, et unumquemque ves-

trum secundum suum ordinem et personam honorabo, et salvabo, et honoratum et salvatum absque ullo dolo ac damnatione vel deceptione conservabo, et unicuique competentem legem ac justitiam conservabo, et qui illam necesse habuerint et rationabiliter petierit, rationabilem misericordiam exhibebo, sicut fidelis rex suos fideles per rectum honorare et salvare et unicuique competentem legem et justitiam in unoquoque ordine conservare et indigentibus et rationabiliter petentibus rationabilem misericordiam debet impendere. Et pro nullo homine ab hoc, quantum dimittit humana fragilitas, per studium aut malevolentiam vel alicujus indebitum hortamentum deviabo, quantum mihi Deus intellectum et possibilitatem (donaverit) ; et si per fragilitatem contra hoc mihi surreptum fuerit, cum recognovero, voluntarie illud emendare studebo, sic," &c.

[1] M. G. H. Script., vol. i. Hincm. Rem. Annales, ad ann. 877. The *primores* were indignant because Lewis had granted *honores* to certain persons "sine illorum consensu." The *primores* then, with Richildis, "conventum suum ad Montem-Witmari condixerunt," and from there negotiated with Lewis. Finally Richildis and the *primores* go to him at Compiègne, and Richildis "attulit ei præceptum per quod pater suus illi regnum ante mortem suam tradiderat, et spatam quæ vocatur Sancti Petri, per quam eum de regno revestiret, sed et regium vestimentum et coronam ac fustem ex auro et gemmis. Et discurrentibus legatis inter Ludovicum et regni primores, et pactis honoribus singulis quos petierunt, 6 Idus Decembris consensu omnium tam episcoporum et

the promises which he made at the time, and in these we find both a very frank recognition of the fact that he is appointed king by the mercy of God and the election of the people, and very emphatic assurances that he will observe the ecclesiastical rules and the national laws.[1]

We may compare the tone in which Hincmar addresses Lewis III. While protesting his humility, Hincmar says that he may very well say to him (the king) that it was not he who elected Hincmar to his office in the Church, but Hincmar and his colleagues, with the other faithful subjects of God and his forefathers, who elected him to be ruler in the kingdom, on the condition of his keeping the laws.[2]

If we find such strong pledges of good government given by the kings and emperors of the regular line, we need hardly be surprised to find that these become almost stronger in the case of the election of those who were not so near the direct succession. In the documents concerning the election of Boso to the kingdom of Arles in 879, we find something very like a formal statement of conditions of election. The synod or assembly sends to Boso inquiring whether he will grant law and justice to all his subjects, great and small, and will listen to all intercession, and freely hearken to all good counsel, seeking rather to make himself useful than merely to be chief. Boso replies that he is but little equal to such a charge as

abbatum, quam regni primorum ceterorumque qui adfuerunt, consecratus et coronatus est in regem Ludovicus ab Hincmaro Remorum episcopo."

[1] M. G. H. Leg., sect. ii. vol. ii. No. 283 (A.) : Professio istius Hlodowici filii Karoli : " Ego Hlodowicus, misericordia domini Dei nostri et electione populi rex constitutus, promitto teste ecclesia Dei omnibus ordinibus, episcoporum videlicet, sacerdotum, monachorum, canonicorum atque sanctimonialium, regulas a patribus conscriptas et apostolicis adtestationibus roboratas ex hoc et in futurum tempus me illis ex integro servaturum. Polliceor etiam me servaturum leges et statuta populo, qui mihi ad regen-

dum misericordia Dei committitur, pro communi consilio fidelium nostrorum, secundum quod prædecessores mei imperatores et reges gestis inseruerunt et omnino inviolabiliter tenenda et observanda decreverunt. Ego igitur Hlodowicus rectitudinis et justitiæ amore hanc spontaneam promissionem meam relegens manu propria firmavi."

[2] Hincmar of Rheims, Ep. xx. : . . . "ita et ego juxta modulum meum humili corde ac voce dicere possum : Non vos me elegistis in prælatione Ecclesiæ, sed ego cum collegis meis et ceteris Dei ac progenitorum vestrorum fidelibus, vos elegi ad regimen regni, sub conditione debitas leges servandi."

that offered, and would have refused it had they not been unanimous, and promises that he will maintain law and justice, and will strive to follow the example of the former good princes, and to maintain equity both to the clergy and to his other faithful men.[1]   We feel that this is something like a compact between the ruler about to be elected and his subjects.

This is almost more clearly still expressed in the capitularies of the election of Guido as King of Italy by the bishops met at Pavia in 889.   The formal document of the election recalls the disastrous confusions that had followed the death of the Emperor Charles, and then proceeds to state how they have met at Pavia to consider the common welfare of the kingdom, and have elected Guido, inasmuch as the divine aid has enabled him to triumph over his enemies, and inasmuch as he promises to love and honour the holy Roman Church and to obey the ecclesiastical laws, and to maintain their own laws to all his subjects, to put down rapine and establish and maintain peace throughout his kingdom.   They report that for all these and many other indications of his goodwill they have elected him to the kingdom.[2]

[1] M. G. H. Leg., sect. ii. vol. ii. No. 284, Convent. Mantalensis, 879, Oct. 15 (A). Synodi ad Bosonem regem designatum legatio : "Si vultis omnibus, sicut boni principes . . . legem, justitiam et rectum concedere et servare, tenentes humilitatem, quæ est fundamentum virtutum . . . qui sitis accessibiles omnibus recte suggerentibus et pro aliis intercedentibus, quærentes magis prodesse, quam præesse . . . justus patricius vestris majoribus et minoribus apparentes . . . salubre consilium libenter audientes . . . ut neque eadem sancta synodus et primates vestri cum ea sentientes nunc de vobis in bonitate maledicantur vel detrahantur in futuro neque sacro vestro principatui nobis, ut credimus, profuturo juste derogetur. . . ."

(B.) Bosoni regis electi ad synodum responsio—

" Ego autem conscius meæ con-

ditionis et figmenti fragilis imparem me judicans tanto negotio omnimodis abnuissem, nisi per Dei nutum vobis cor unum datum et animam unam in unum consensum advertissem. . . . Omnibus ut monuistis, legem, justitiam, et rectum momburgium auxiliante Deo conservabo et impendere curabo ; quo sequens præcedentium bonorum principum vestigia tam sacris ordinibus quam vobis nostris fidelibus consulere certem æquitatem servando."

[2] M. G. H. Leg., sect. ii. vol. ii. No. 222, Widonis Capitulatio Electionis. Electionis Decretum : "Post obitum recordandæ memoriæ domni Karoli, gloriosi imperatoris et senioris nostri, quot quantaque pericula huic Italico regno usque in præsens tempus supervenirent, nec lingua potest evolvere nec calamus explicare. . . . Sed quia illi supervenienti perspicuo principe Widone bis jam fuga lapsi ut fumus

It is, however, not only at the time of the election or appointment of a king that we can see something very like a bargain or agreement between people and ruler. More than once we find the emperors or kings trying to bring back confidence and order by solemn assurances that they will maintain law and justice if their subjects on their side will render them true help and obedience. In 851 Lothair, Lewis, and Charles met at Mersen, and issued a document in which they assure their faithful subjects of all ranks and conditions that they may be fully secure that for the future they will not condemn or dishonour or oppress any one in violation of law and justice or right authority and reason, and that they will, with the common council of their faithful subjects, set forward the restoration of holy Church, and the whole state of the kingdom, in the assurance that their subjects on their part will be faithful and obedient, and true helpers to them, with such counsel and aid as is due from every subject to his prince.[1] This assurance or agreement we find repeated

evanuerunt nosque in ambiguo reliquerunt tamquam oves non habentes pastorem, necessarium duximus ad mutuum colloquium Papie in aula regia convenire. Ibique de communi salute et statu hujus regni solliciti pertractantes decrevimus uno animo eademque sententia præfatum magnanimum principem Widonem ad protegendum et regaliter gubernandum nos in regem et seniorem nobis eligere et in regni fastigium Deo miserante prefigere pro eo, quod isdem magnificus rex divino, ut credimus, protectus auxilio de hostibus potenter triumphavit et hoc non sue virtutis, sed totum divinæ miserationis providentiæ adtribuit, in super etiam sanctam Romanam ecclesiam ex corde se diligere, et exaltare et ecclesiastica jura in omnibus observare, et leges proprias singulis quibusque sub sua ditione positis concedere et rapinas de suo regno penitus extirpare, et pacem reformare et custodire se velle Deo teste professus est. Pro his ergo et

aliis multis ejus bonæ voluntatis inditiis ipsum, ut prelibavimus, ad regni hujus gubernacula ascivimus, eique toto mentis nisu adhesimus seniorem, piissimum et regem excellentissimum pari consensu ex hinc et in posterum decernentes.''

[1] M. G. H. Leg., sect. ii. vol. ii. No. 205, Hloth., Hlud., et Karoli Conventus apud Marsnam Secundus, 851 : 6. ''Ut nostri fideles, unusquisque in suo ordine et statu, veraciter sint de nobis securi, quia nullum abhinc inante contra legem et justitiam vel auctoritatem ac justam rationem aut damnabimus aut dehonorabimus aut opprimemus vel indebitis machinationibus affligemus, et illorum, scilicet veraciter nobis fidelium, communi consilio secundum Dei voluntatem et commune salvamentum ad restitutionem sanctæ Dei ecclesiæ et statum regni et ad honorem regium, atque pacem populi commissi nobis pertinenti adsensum præbebimus in hoc, ut illi non solum non sint nobis

at Coblentz in 860 in almost identical terms,[1] and again by Charles the Bald in the "Capitula Pistensia" of 869.[2] We have also the form in which these promises were issued after the meeting at Coblentz by Lewis, and it is perhaps worth while looking at this, as it exhibits almost more clearly the character of an agreement or mutual promise.[3]

In the "Capitula Pistensia" of 862 we have another statement of the same principle of mutual obligation. These begin with a very solemn acknowledgment of the faults which have brought the present distress upon the country: the king laments that by his own evil deeds he has driven away

contradicentes et resistentes ad ista exsequenda, verum etiam sic sint nobis fideles et obœdientes ac veri adjutores atque co-operatores vero consilio et sincero auxilio ad ista peragenda quæ præmisimus, sicut per rectum unusquisque in suo ordine et statu suo principi et suo seniori esse debet."

[1] M. G. H. Leg., sect. ii. vol. ii. No. 242, Hlud., Kar., and Hloth. II., Conventus apud Confluentes, clause 10.

[2] M. G. H. Leg., sect. ii. vol. ii. No. 275 : "3. Ut omnes nostri fideles, veraciter sint de nobis securi, quia, quantum sciero et juste ac rationabiliter potuero, Domino adjuvante unumquemque secundum sui ordinis dignitatem et personam honorare, et salvare et honoratum ac salvatum conservare volo, et unicuique eorum in suo ordine secundum sibi competentes leges tam mundanas quam ecclesiasticas rectam rationem et justitiam conservabo, et nullum fidelium nostrorum contra legem et justitiam vel auctoritatem ac justam rationem aut damnabo aut dehonorabo aut opprimam aut indebitis machinationibus affligam ; et legem ut prædiximus, unicuique competentem, sicut antecessores sui tempore antecessorum meorum habuerunt, in omni dignitate et ordine adjuvante Deo conservaturum perdono, cuilibet duntaxat ex eis, qui mihi fideles et obœdientes ac veri adjutores atque

co-operatores juxta suum ministerium et personam consilio et auxilio secundum suum scire et posse et secundum Deum ac secundum seculum fuerint, sicut per rectum unusquisque in suo ordine et statu regi suo et suo seniori esse debet."

[3] M. G. H. Leg., sect. ii. vol. ii. No. 242, Hlud., Kar., Hloth. II., Conventus apud Confluentes, 860, Jun. Adnuntiatio domini Hludowici regis apud Confluentes lingua Theodisca, 5 : "Et volumus, ut vos et ceteri homines fideles nostri talem legem et rectitudinem et tale salvamentum in regnis nostris habeatis, sicut antecessores vestri tempore antecessorum nostrorum habuerunt, et nos talem honorem et rectam potestatem in nostro regio nomine apud vos habeamus, sicut nostri antecessores apud vestros antecessores habuerunt ; et justitia et lex omnibus conservetur ; et pauperes homines talem defensionem habeant, sicut tempore antecessorum nostrorum lex et consuetudo fuit, et sicut hic fideles nostri communiter consenserunt et scripto nobis demonstraverunt et nos cum illorum consilio consentimus et observari communiter volumus. Et si aliquis hoc perturbare voluerit, a nullo nostrum recipiatur, nisi ut aut ad rectam rationem aut ad rationabilem indulgentiæ concessionem deducatur."

the Holy Spirit, which was given to him by the imposition of hands of the bishops at his consecration. Then there follows a passage, which we have already quoted, on the divine nature and authority of government on earth, and this again is followed by an exhortation to all to strive together for justice; and the capitulary concludes by saying that by common consent it has been decreed to sign this, remembering that as all men of all ranks expect that the king shall maintain their proper and lawful rights, so all men of all ranks must observe the proper and lawful honour and obedience due to the king.[1]

We have seen that the principle of the joint action of the king and the nation in making law finds a formal expression in the "Edictum Pistense"; we may find a good illustration of the significance of the promises of justice and obedience on the part of kings and subjects in another document of this time, the "Capitula ad Francos et Aquitanos Missa de Carisiaco" of 856. A large part of his kingdom was in revolt against Charles the Bald, and these Capitula were drawn up with the view of pacifying the revolters, and present us with a very clear statement of the conception that just as his subjects were bound by certain obligations to the king, so he on his part was bound by very distinct obligations to them: they even speak of these mutual obligations as constituting a *pactum*. What is more than this, the capitula are drawn in the form

---

[1] M. G. H. Leg., sect. ii. vol. ii. No. 272, Capitula Pistensia, 862: "1. Quia illum Spiritum Sanctum, qui requievit super adjutorem in oportunitatibus, in tribulatione, Christum dominum nostrum, et quem per impositionem manus episcopalis in consignatione accepimus, contristatum malignis operibus a nobis effugavimus. . . .

"4. Quoniam nisi communiter certaverimus, ut in omnibus justitia omnibus conservetur, nec rex pater patriæ nec episcopi propitiatores et reconciliatores populi ad salutem æternam nec, qui participatione nominis Christi christiani vocantur, hoc, quod humano ore dicimus, in divinis oculis esse valemus. Ut autem hæc, quæ observanda supra scripsimus ac prænominavimus, nunc et de cetero certius et expressius a nobis atque a successoribus nostris inconvulsa serventur, propriis manibus his subscribere communi consensu decrevimus ea conditione servata, ut, quia omnes in cunctis ordinibus a regia ditione sibi expetunt competentia legis jura servari, regiæ quoque potestati in cunctis ordinibus lex juris debiti et honor ab omnibus obedienter et fideliter cooperante Domino conservetur." See p. 213.

of an address from the loyal subjects of Charles to the revolters, and while they urge them to come back to their allegiance, and intimate plainly that they will in the future compel obedience to the just judgments of the king, on the other hand they intimate just as clearly that if the king, "juxta humanam fragilitatem," should do anything contrary to the *pactum*, they will, reverently and honourably, admonish him of his duty ; and they assure the rebels that if, when he is thus admonished, he should wish to do injustice, the king will be unable to carry out his will.[1]   The document exhibits

[1] M. G. H. Leg., sect. ii. vol. ii. No. 262, Cap. ad Francos et Aquitanos Missa de Carisiaco, 856, Jul. 7 : "Hæc, quæ secuntur, capitula misit dominus rex Karolus ad Francos et Aquitanos, qui ab eo desciverant, anno incarnationis dominicæ DCCCLVI. Nonis Julii de palatio Carisiaco per fideles missos suos Adalardum abbatem, Rodulfum, Richuinum, Adalgarium et Berengarium."

"10. Et sciatis, quia sic est adunatus cum omnibus suis fidelibus in omni ordine et statu et nos omnes sui fideles de omni ordine et statu, ut, si ille juxta humanam fragilitatem aliquid contra tale pactum fecerit, illum honeste et cum reverentia, sicut seniorem decet, ammonemus, ut ille hoc corrigat et emendet et unicuique in suo ordine debitam legem conservet. Et si aliquis de nobis in quocunque ordine contra istum pactum incontra illum fecerit, si talis est, ut ille inde enim ammonere voleat, ut emendet, faciat ; et si talis est causa, ut ille illum familiariter non debeat ammonere, et ante suos pares illum in rectam rationem mittat, et ille, qui debitum pactum et rectam legem et debitam seniori reverentiam non vult exhibere et observare, justum justitiæ judicium sustineat. Et si sustinere non voluerit et contumax et rebellis exititerit et converti non potuerit, a nostra omnium societate et regno ab omnibus expellatur. Et

si senior noster legem unicuique debitam et a se et a suis antecessoribus nobis et nostris antecessoribus perdonatam per rectam rationem vel misericordiam competentem unicuique in suo ordine conservare non voluerit et ammonitus a suis fidelibus suam intentionem non voluerit, sciatis, quia sic est ille nobiscum et nos cum illo adunati et sic sumus omnes per illius voluntatem et consensum confirmati, episcopi atque abbates cum laicis et laici cum viris ecclesiasticis, ut nullus suum parem dimittat, ut contra suam legem et rectam rationem et justum judicium, etiamsi voluerit, quod absit, rex noster alicui facere non possit. . . .

"12. Et sciatis, quia vult senior noster et nos ac cœteri fideles illius, ut, si vos, qui illius fideles et consiliarii esse debetis, volueritis, sicut vobis diximus, ad illius præsentiam et fidelitatem atque servitium venire et nobiscum in ista societate esse, quia et ipse et nos quæ voluntarie volemus, ut cum nobis hoc et quæratis et inveniatis et statuatis et confirmetis atque conservetis et nos cum vobis similiter : et vobis aliis omnibus, sicut et nobis, debitam legem et rectam rationem dehinc inante, sicut rectum est, vult conservare, sicut sui antecessores, qui hoc melius et rationabilius fecerunt, nostris et vestris antecessoribus in omni ordine conservaverunt."

not only the conception of a mutual agreement made, at his election or otherwise, between the king and the people, but also the conception that the subjects have the same right to compel the king to observe his agreement as he has to compel them to observe theirs.

The circumstances of the ninth century tended thus to favour the development of the conception that the ruler holds his place in virtue of the election of the nation, and of his fulfilment of the promises on which that election was based; and there were not wanting in the century circumstances which tended towards the further conclusion, that if the king failed to discharge the obligations which he had undertaken, he might not improperly be deposed. The deposition of the unhappy Lewis the Pious serves to illustrate this tendency, and probably also helped materially to develop it. We cannot here discuss either the general circumstances or the constitutional conditions of the deposition or abdication of Lewis the Pious. But it is for our purpose extremely important to observe the terms in which the deposition of Lewis is alluded to. It was at Compiègne in the year 833 that Lewis was compelled to abdicate, and the bishops, there assembled, published a statement in which they set forth the great faults that Lewis had committed,—how he had neglected his charge, and done many things displeasing to God and men; and they relate how they had exhorted him to repentance, inasmuch as he had been deprived of his earthly power in accordance with the counsel of God and the ecclesiastical authority.[1] In the next chapter we must consider the significance of this reference to the

[1] M. G. H. Leg., sect. ii. vol. ii. No. 197, Episc. de Pœn. quam Hlud. Imp. professus est, Relatio Compendiensis, 833 : " Sed quia idem princeps ministerium sibi commissum negligenter tractaverit et multa, quæ Deo et hominibus displicebant, et fecerit et facere compulerit vel fieri permiserit et in multis nefandis consiliis Deum irritaverit et sanctam ecclesiam scandalizaverit . . . et ab eo divino justoque judicio subito imperialis sit subtracta potestas, nos tamen memores præceptorum Dei, ministeriique nostri atque beneficiorum ejus dignum duximus, ut per licentiam memorati principis Lotharii legationem ad illum ex auctoritate sacri conventus mitteremus, quæ eum de suis reatibus admoneat, quatenus certum consilium suæ salutis caperet, ut, quia potestate privatus erat terrena juxta divinum consilium et ecclesiasticam auctoritatem, ne suam animam perderet, elaborare in extremis positus totis viribus studeret."

action of the ecclesiastical authority in the deposition of Lewis. In the meanwhile we are only concerned to observe that the bishops look upon the deposition as lawful.

It is in this same sense that Hincmar of Rheims appears to refer to the subject in his treatise on the divorce of Lothair and Tetburga, in a passage to which we have already referred. He is arguing against those who maintained that the king was subject to no laws or judgments, and pointing out that kings like David were rebuked by the prophets, Theodosius by St Ambrose, goes on to say that in his own time the pious Emperor Lewis had been cast down from his kingship, and was restored to it " post satisfactionem " by the bishops with the consent of the people.[1] Hincmar seems to mean that the deposition had been unwise, but he does not suggest that in itself there was anything improper in the action; indeed the general context would suggest that he regarded such action as being under certain circumstances proper and right.

It is true that in that letter or treatise of Hrabanus Maurus which we have already cited, Hrabanus, referring to the deposition of Lewis, speaks very emphatically about the honour due from sons to their parents, and the honour and obedience which all men are to give to the royal authority, and illustrates the right attitude of the subject by the classical example of David and Saul, and from more recent historical examples shows the judgment which overtakes those who rise against their legitimate princes. We have already cited the letter as illustrating the persistence of the characteristic mode of thought of Gregory the Great in the ninth century, and there is nothing to surprise us in the fact that those who disapproved of the revolt against Lewis the Pious should have appealed to these principles.[2]

Perhaps the strongest illustration of the tendency to conceive of the deposition of the king as being under certain circumstances justifiable is to be found in a document or proclamation

[1] Hincmar of Rheims, De Div. Loth. et Tet., Quest. vi. Resp. : "Nostra aetate pium Augustum Ludovicum a regno dejectum, post satisfactionem episcopalis unanimitas, saniore consilio, cum populi consensu, et Ecclesiæ et regno restituit."

[2] Hrabanus Maurus, Epist. 15, in M. G. H. Ep., v. See p. 216.

issued in 859 by Charles the Bald against those who wished to depose him. In this document, after appealing to his claim of hereditary succession from the Emperor Lewis, he argues that he was elected with the will, consent, and acclamation of the bishops and other faithful men of the kingdom, and was consecrated, anointed, and crowned by Wenilo, Bishop of Orleans, and that from the office in which he was then placed he cannot be cast out, at least without the judgment of the bishops by whom he was then consecrated. "They are," he says, "the thrones of God," among whom God sits, and by whom he decrees judgments, and to their paternal correction and chastisement he is willing to submit, and does submit.[1]

We shall have to consider this passage again in discussing the relation of the ecclesiastical and secular powers, but in the meanwhile it is worthy of note, as indicating in a very forcible way that the deposition of a king, who was held to have failed to discharge his obligations, was a thing not wholly improper in the minds of the men of the ninth century. We may very well recall those phrases concerning the distinction between the king and the tyrant which we considered in a previous chapter, and we shall feel that the conception of the character of the king, as depending upon his respecting and maintaining justice, was not a mere piece of abstract sentiment, but was tending to have a more or less practical and effective influence on public life.

[1] M. G. H. Leg., sect. ii. vol. ii. No. 300, Libellus proclamationis adversus Wenilonem, c. 3 : "Sed et post hoc electione sua aliorumque episcoporum ac ceterorum fidelium regni nostri voluntate, consensu et acclamatione cum aliis archiepiscopis et episcopis Wenilo in diocesi sua apud Aurelianis civitatem in basilica sanctæ crucis me secundum traditionem ecclesiasticam regem consecravit et in regni regimine chrismate sacro perunxit et diademate atque regni sceptro in regni solio sublimavit. A qua consecratione vel regni sublimitate subplantari vel proici a nullo debueram, saltem sine audientia et judicio episcoporum, quorum ministerio in regem sum consecratus et qui throni Dei sunt dicti, in quibus Deus sedet, et per quos sua decernit judicia; quorum paternis correptionibus et castigatoriis judiciis me subdere fui paratus et in præsenti sum subditus."

CHAPTER XXI.

THE RELATION OF THE AUTHORITIES OF CHURCH AND STATE.

WE must now resume the consideration of the theory of the relations of the secular and ecclesiastical authorities. No student of the history of the Middle Ages will doubt that the theoretical and actual relations of the two great powers in society continually exercised a very strong influence upon the theory of the State and the theory of the origin and nature of political authority.

To the political theorists of the ninth century, however great their reverence for the king and the secular authority, there is obviously always present the consideration that alongside of the law of the State there stands a law which the nation has not made, a law which is more majestic and authoritative than that of any secular society—the law of the Christian Church; and that alongside of the secular organisation and institutions there stand the organisation and institutions of the Church. If the ruler is bound to respect the law of the nation, much more is he bound to respect and obey the law of the Church; and while the great organisation of the Catholic Church may admit him to some share in its councils, may look to him for assistance in enforcing its decrees, yet the Church is not only independent of him in religion but looks upon him as its subject in spiritual matters.

We have seen that the patristic theory of the relation of the two powers, the ecclesiastical and the civil, finds its completest statement and definition in the letters and tractates of Gelasius I. These may also be said to furnish us with the best starting-point for examining the theory of the ninth century. The bishops of the empire, in a long and important statement on the condition of Church and State and the nature of ecclesiastical and civil authority, addressed in the year 829 to the Emperor Lewis the Pious, quote and comment on the words of Gelasius' twelfth letter, in which he had said that there are two authorities by which alone all the world is governed—the sacred authority of the bishop and the power of the sovereign.[1] The same passage is quoted by Jonas of Orleans in the first chapter of his work 'De Institutione Regia,'[2] while Hincmar of Rheims cites the words of this letter and also those of Gelasius' fourth tractate.[3]

[1] M. G. H. Leg., sect. ii. vol. ii. No. 196, Episcoporum ad Hlud. Imp. Relatio, 3 : "Quod ejusdem æcclesiæ corpus in duabus principaliter dividatur eximiis personis. Principaliter itaque totius sanctæ Dei ecclesiæ corpus in duas eximias personas, in sacerdotalem videlicet et regalem, sicut a sanctis patribus traditum accepimus, divisum esse novimus ; de qua re Gelasius Romanæ sedis venerabilis episcopus ad Anastasium imperatorem ita scribit : ' Duæ sunt quippe,' inquit, 'imperator auguste quibus principaliter mundus hic regitur, auctoritas sacrata pontificum et regalis potestas ; in quibus tanto gravius pondus est sacerdotum, quanto etiam pro ipsis regibus hominum in divino reddituri sunt examine rationem.' Fulgentius quoque in libro de Veritate Prædestinationis et Gratia ita scribit : ' Quantum pertinet,' inquit, 'ad hujus temporis vitam, in æcclesia nemo pontifice potior, et in sæclo christiano nemo imperatore celsior invenitur.' "

[2] Jonas of Orleans, De Instit. Reg., cap. i. : "Sciendum omnibus fidelibus est quia universalis Ecclesia corpus est Christi et ejus caput idem est Christus, et in ea duæ principaliter exstant eximiæ personæ, sacerdotalis videlicet et regalis, tantoque est præstantior sacerdotalis, quanto pro ipsis

regibus Deo est rationem redditurus. Unde Gelasius Romanæ Ecclesiæ venerabilis pontifex ad Anastasium imperatorem scribens, ' Duo quippe . . . examine rationem reddituri.' Fulgentius quoque in libro de Veritate Prædestinationis et Gratiae ita scribit : ' Quantum attinet ad hujus temporis vitam, in Ecclesia nemo pontifice potior et in sæculo Christiano imperatore nemo celsior invenitur.' Ergo quia tantæ auctoritatis, imo tanti discriminis est ministerium sacerdotum, ut de ipsis etiam regibus Deo sint rationem reddituri, oportet et valde necesse est, ut de vestra salute semper simus solliciti, vosque ne a voluntate Dei, quod absit, aut a ministerio quod vobis commisit, erretis, vigilanter admoneamus, et si, quod absit, ab eo aliquo modo exorbitaveritis, pontificali studio humiliter admonendo, et salubriter procurando, opportunum consultum saluti vestræ conferamus, ut non de silentio taciturnitatis nostræ damnemur, sed magis de solertissima cura et admonitione salutifera remunerari a Christo mereamur."

[3] Hincmar of Rheims, Ad Episc. De Inst. Carol. cap. i. : "Hincmarus episcopus ac plebis Dei famulus. Doctrina est Christiana, secundum sanctarum scripturarum tramitem, prædicationemque majorum, qua Deo ac Domino nostro Jesu Christu con-

It is important to observe not only the fact that these passages are quoted, but the character of the comments which are made on them. The bishops in 829 preface their quotation by the statement that the body of the Church of God is divided chiefly between two exalted persons, the priestly and the royal. Jonas of Orleans puts the same view more clearly when he tells us that all faithful men should know that the universal Church is the body of Christ, and that Christ is the head of the body, and in this body there are two persons of chief authority, the priest and the king. While Gelasius thinks of these two authorities as existing in the world, the bishops and Jonas conceive of them as being both within the Church.

It is also worth noting that while the bishops simply quote the words of Gelasius, "In quibus tanto gravius pondus est

ditore et redemptore nostro, qui simul solus rex et sacerdos fieri potuit, in cujus nomine omne genuflectitur, cœlestium, terrestrium et infernorum, disponente, sicut beatus Gelasius papa ad Anastasium imperatorem dicit, et in gestis quæ nuper apud martyrium sanctæ Macræ in synodo gesta sunt partim continetur, duo sunt, quibus principaliter, una cum specialiter cujuscumque curæ subjectis, mundus hic regitur, auctoritas sacra pontificum, et regalis potestas ; in quibus personis, sicut ordine sunt divisa vocabula, ita sunt et divisa in unoquoque ordine ac professione ordinationum officia. Quamvis enim membra veri regis atque pontificis secundum participationem naturæ, magnifice utrumque in sacra generositate sumpsisse dicantur, ut simul regale genus et sacerdotale subsistant, memor tamen Christus fragilitatis humanæ, quod suorum salute congrueret, dispensatione magnifica temperans, sic actionibus propriis, dignitatibusque distinctis officia potestatis utriusque discrevit, suos volens medicinali humilitate salvari, non humana superbia rursus (ut ante adventum ejus in carnem pagani imperatores, qui iidem et maxime ponti-

fices dicebantur), intercipi, ut et Christiani reges pro æterna vita pontificibus indigerent, et pontifices pro temporalium cursu rerum imperialibus dispositionibus uterentur ; quatenus spiritalis actio a carnalibus distaret incursibus, et ideo militans Deo minime se negotiis sæcularibus implicaret, ac vicissim non ille rebus divinis præsidere videretur qui esset negotiis sæcularibus implicatus, ut et modestia utriusque ordinis curaretur, ne extolleretur utroque suffultus, et competens qualitatibus actionum specialiter professio aptaretur.

"Cap. ii. Sed tanto gravius pondus est sacerdotum, quanto etiam pro ipsis regibus hominum in divino reddituri sunt examine rationem ; et tanto est dignitas pontificum major quam regum, quia reges in culmen regium sacrantur a pontificibus, pontifices autem a regibus consecrari non possunt ; et tanto in humanis rebus regum cura est propensior quam sacerdotum, quanto pro honore et defensione et quiete sanctæ Ecclesiæ, ac rectorum et ministrorum ipsius, et leges promulgando, ac militando, a Rege regum est eis curæ onus impositum."

sacerdotum," Jonas, in his introduction, calls the priestly person *præstantior*, and in applying this conception he urges that the priest must always anxiously care for the salvation of the king and carefully admonish him lest he should turn aside from the will of God or neglect the charge which God has committed to him. While Gelasius, that is, insists only upon the obedience which the king should render to the priests in religious matters, and the priest to the king in secular matters, Jonas also thinks that the priest is in some measure responsible to see that the king does his duty even in secular affairs.

Hincmar embodies large parts of the tenth letter and of the fourth tractate of Gelasius. Christ is the only person who was both king and priest, and although there is a sense in which Christians may be called a royal and priestly race, yet Christ, mindful of the infirmity of human nature, has allotted to each authority its own duties, so that Christian kings require the bishops for eternal life, and the bishops require the king for temporal things, and therefore the clergy should keep themselves clear of secular business, and the secular person should not interfere in spiritual matters. So far Hincmar does little more than follow Gelasius, but his development of the principle " Tanto gravius est pondus sacerdotum," &c., is different and noteworthy. The burden of the priest is greater, because he will have to give account, in the judgment, even for kings, and the dignity of the bishop is greater than that of the king, because kings are consecrated to their office by the bishop, while the bishop cannot be consecrated by kings.

In three important points, then, we see that some ninth-century writers have developed the position of Gelasius,—the first, that both the secular and the spiritual powers are within the Church; the second, that in some measure the priest is responsible to see that the secular ruler does his duty; and the third, that the dignity of the ecclesiastical person is greater, for it is by him that the king is consecrated: and each of these principles has importance in the ninth-century conception of the relation between the spiritual and the temporal powers. In the main it is clear that the ninth century simply carries on from the sixth the principle of the two authorities in society—two authorities which are theoretically independent of each other in their own spheres; but the experience of the ninth century tended to bring out the difficulties of this position, and to develop the tendency towards the assertion of the priority of one or other of the two. The conditions of the time are indeed so complex that we could easily quote phrases from the legal documents and the general authors of the period to support almost any theory of the relations of the two powers. It would be easy to produce evidence to show that the temporal power was really superior even in ecclesiastical matters; to show that the consent of the king or emperor was necessary for ecclesiastical action, and that it was the secular power which controlled all ecclesiastical appointments. On the other hand, it would be quite as easy to produce evidence to show that the Church was actually superior to the State; that the king was absolutely under the canonical law, liable to excommunication like any private person; that it was the Church which really conferred the royal authority, and that the Church could take it away again.

A century or two later we shall find views of this kind set out in open contradiction to each other; we shall find Europe filled with the clamour of the great struggle for supremacy between the Church and the Empire. But it is the characteristic of the ninth century that these apparently divergent tendencies of thought can often be traced in the same person; that we find the same person using language which in later times would mark him clearly as a papalist, and the next moment using phrases which became the catchwords of the imperialist.

It is possible, no doubt, to maintain that in the early years of the ninth century the authority of the State relatively to the Church was at its highest point, and that the opposed conception develops throughout the century till it culminates in the pseudo-Isidorian literature. But we think that the safest judgment which we can form on the whole character of the ninth century is this, that men were convinced that each power had its own appropriate sphere, but that they were also keenly alive to the fact that in practical life the two spheres intersected, and that no general principle could enable them to determine, with regard to many questions, what exactly was the sphere of the State and what the sphere of the Church.

We may find a very good illustration of the complexity of the situation and the ambiguities of theory in the position of that writer to whom we have already so often referred, Sedulius Scotus, whose work seems to belong to the middle of the century. He does not seem to have had the same practical experience of affairs as Hincmar of Rheims, and there are therefore some points on which Hincmar is his superior; but he shows a considerable power of putting together his views, so that, in spite of a certain incoherence of detail, they really form an organic whole. At any rate, it may be useful to consider for a moment what are his views as to the position of the emperor or king relatively to the Church.

He begins his treatise by urging the prince to remember that he should give thanks to God and honour to His Church. The whole commonwealth flourishes when the king fears and honours God and provides carefully for the wellbeing of the Church.[1] The charge of the king, then, is not to be thought of as merely secular. The work of the king is to set forward such conditions as will further the cause of religion as well as the temporal wellbeing of the State. If his heart is not set upon God's service, God may take the kingdom from him.[2] He has therefore great responsibilities in Church matters as well as in secular. He must prefer the wellbeing of the Church to his own personal advantage, and must help and protect all those who work in God's service.[3] We have here simply the common mediæval conception of the duty of the ruler of the State to do what he can to further the work of the Church. Sedulius evidently did not imagine that the State could stand aside and refuse to take a part in the service of religion. But this is not all. The good ruler, he says, will set forward the wellbeing of the Church in

---

[1] Sedulius Scotus, De Rectoribus Christianis, 1.

[2] Id. 3.

[3] Id. 11.

all ways, and he must remember that God has set him as His vicar in the government of the Church, and has given him power over both orders of rulers and subjects,[1] and therefore he is especially admonished to see to the holding of synods every year.[2] We have in an earlier chapter referred to this title of the Vicar of God as applied to the secular ruler. Certainly as used by Sedulius it seems clearly to imply a large measure of authority even over the Church.

So far we have one aspect of the theory of Sedulius. But if we now turn back to the eleventh chapter of his treatise we shall see the other side of the matter. Here also the king is admonished to provide diligently for the meeting of synods, inasmuch as these are of great benefit to the Church. But then, abruptly and somewhat sharply, he is warned that he must not interfere recklessly in ecclesiastical affairs; he must show himself humble and very cautious, and beware lest he should take upon himself to judge of any ecclesiastical affair before he has learnt the decrees of the synods. The pious ruler will carefully hear what is just and lawful according to the canonical decision of the holy bishops, and will then give his consent and authority to what is just and true. He will in no way form any *præjudicium* on such matters, lest haply, falling into error, he should find himself guilty of some fault hateful in the sight of God. Sedulius enforces this with a story of how Valentinian, when he was invited by the bishops to take part in some doctrinal discussion, said that he was in no way worthy to take part in such matters, but that this belonged to the priests.[3] Sedulius follows

---

[1] Sedulius Scotus, De Rectoribus Christianis, 19 : "Oportet enim Deo amabilem regnatorem, quem divina ordinatio tanquam vicarium suum in regimine Ecclesiæ suæ esse voluit, et potestatem ei super utrumque ordinem prælatorum et subditorum tribuit, ut singulis personis et quæ justa sunt decernat, et sub sua dispensatione prior ordo devote obediendo fideliter subditus fiat."

[2] Id. id.

[3] Id. 11 : "Unde cautum et humilem et valde circumspectum oportet esse

regem : nec quidquam de negotiis ecclesiasticis judicare præsumat, antequam synodalia statuta cognoscat. . . . Pius itaque rector tanquam luminosa pupilla primo quod justum et legitimum est secundum canonicas sanctorum episcoporum sanctiones perspicaciter attendat ; dehinc consensum atque auctoritatis adminiculum his quæ sunt vera et justa adhibeat. Per se vero nullatenus de talibus præjudicium faciat, ne forte errando ante conspectum domini culpam aliquam detestabilem incurrat. Unde venera-

this up in the next chapter by urging the ruler to make himself an example of humility and obedience. If he is reproved by wise men he should repent; and Sedulius cites the examples of David and Nathan, of Theodosius and Ambrose.[1]

If, then, in the title of Vicar of God in the government of His Church Sedulius expresses something of the authority of the king even over churchmen, in his treatment of his relation to the synods and their decisions he gives us the other side of the matter. It must be noticed, however, that even here the king has his own place, at least in the execution of Church law. After he has heard the judgment of the bishops, it still remains for him to give his consent and authority to what has been decreed.

We have before cited the letter of Cathulfus on the nature of the royal authority. He states, even more emphatically than Sedulius, that the king is the representative of God, and he certainly seems to imply that the position of the bishop is secondary. He bids the king remember God always with fear and love, for he is in God's place, to watch over and govern all God's members, and will have to give account for these in the day of judgment. The bishop is, in the second place, "in vice Christi tantum." The king must therefore carefully see that he establishes the law of God over the people of God, whose place he holds, "cujus vicem tenes." He must, with his bishops, superintend the life of the monks and nuns, but he must do this through spiritual pastors, not through laymen, for that would be wickedness.[2] We should judge that the position of

bilis memoriæ Valentinianus Imperator cum a sanctis episcopis rogaretur quatenus dignaretur ad emendationem sacri dogmatis interesse, 'Mihi,' inquit, 'cum minimus de populo sim, fas non est talia perscrutari, verum sacerdotes quibus hæc cura est, apud semetipsos congregentur ubi voluerint.'"

[1] Sedulius Scotus, De Rectoribus Christianis, 12.

[2] M. G. H. Ep., iv. "Epistolæ Variorum Carolo Magno Regnante Scriptæ," 7: "Cathuulfus Carolo I. Francorum Regi prosperitatem gratu-

latur eumque ad virtutem sequendam admonet." "Memor esto ergo semper, rex mi, Dei regis tui cum timore et amore, quod tu es in vice illius super omnia membra ejus custodire et regere, et rationem reddere in die judicii, etiam per te. Et episcopus est in secundo loco, in vice Christi tantum est. Ergo considerate inter vos diligenter legem Dei constituere super populum Dei, quod Deus tuus dixit tibi, cujus vicem tenes, in psalmo: 'Et nunc reges intelligite,' et reliqua; item: 'Servite Domino in timore,' et

Cathulfus was practically the same as that of Sedulius, though undoubtedly he is more emphatic in his assertion of a certain priority of the royal power. The letter is, however, too brief, and the discussion too incomplete, to enable us to form a very definite decision upon the subject.[1]

The conception of the separate provinces of the secular and the spiritual powers is so well defined in the fifth century, and so carefully restated in the ninth, that we cannot doubt that all parties, lay or clerical, would have, in theory, held that the powers were co-ordinate, and, in their own spheres, independent of each other. But, as a matter of fact, circumstances were too strong for theory, and not only did the definition and delimitation of the boundaries of the province of each power prove a task of insuperable difficulty, but each power in turn found itself compelled to trench in some measure upon the province of the other. We begin by considering some of the many points in which, in spite of the theory of the independence and authority of the Church, the State did actually trench upon its prerogatives.

We have seen how Sedulius and Cathulfus speak of the king or emperor as the vicar of God in the government of His Church; that is, they conceive that it is part of the duty of the civil ruler to maintain good order and piety in the Church. We find the same principle very strongly declared by Smaragdus. He urges upon the king that if he sees anything wrong in the Church of Christ it is his duty to reprove and correct it. If he sees any person in the Church of God running into luxury or drunkenness, he is to forbid, to terrify him. He is to put

reliqua; item 'Adprehendite disciplinam ne quando irascatur Dominus,' et reliqua. . . . 'Sponsam Christi vestire cum ornamentis super omnia, id est ecclesiarum privilegia constituere maxima. Monachorum vitam et canonicorum cum episcopis tuis simul virginum monasteriorum regere. Non per laicos, quod scelus . . . sed per spiritales pastores emendare, super omnia Deum timentes, sicut scriptum (est) in lege.'"

[1] The letter of Cathulfus belongs probably to the last years of the eighth century,—that is, to a time when the papacy was under a cloud and the authority of Charles the Great in relation to the Church was at its highest point; and the letter cannot therefore be taken as properly representative of the general standpoint of the ninth century, except so far as its statements are found to be confirmed by later writers.

down all pride and anger with threats and sharp reproofs. He
is to do what he can as a king, as a Christian, and as the representative of Christ ("pro vice Christi qua fungeris").[1] We can
find illustrations of this conception of the duty of the civil
ruler to maintain good order and discipline in the Church in
the proceedings of Charles the Great, of Lewis the Pious, and of
Charles the Bald. In the "Capitula de Causis cum Episcopis
et Abbatibus Tractandis" of 811 we have a list of topics on
which the bishops and abbots are to be interrogated, and
certainly the tone of the questions indicates clearly enough
that Charles the Great thought it his duty to look very sharply
into the conduct of the clergy even in purely religious matters.[2]
In the "Admonitio ad omnes regni ordines," issued by Lewis
the Pious in 823-5, Lewis lays down very explicitly the principle that it is his duty to admonish men of all orders as to
the discharge of their duties, and frames regulations for a
very comprehensive inquiry which is to be made by taking
the evidence of the bishops about the conduct of the counts
in administering justice, and that of the counts as to the
conduct of the bishops in their life and teaching.[3] In the

[1] Smaragdus Abbas, Via Regia, 8 :
"Si quid forte perversum in Ecclesia
videris Christi, satage corripere, et
emendare non cesses. Si videris aliquem in domo Dei, quæ est Ecclesia,
currere ad luxuriam ad ebrietatem,
prohibe, veta, terre, si zelus domus
Dei comedit te. Si videris superbia
inflatum, aut iracundia sævum, . . .
reprime omnes, minare omnibus, et
refrena severissime omnes. Fac quicquid potes pro persona quam gestas,
pro ministerio regali quod portas, pro
nomine Christiani quod habes, pro
vice Christi qua fungeris."

[2] M. G. H. Leg., sect. ii. vol. i.
No. 72, Capitula de Causis cum
Episcopis et Abbatibus Tractandis.

[3] M. G. H. Leg., sect. ii. vol. i.
No. 150 : "3. Sed quamquam summa
hujus ministerii in nostra persona
consistere videatur, tamen et divina
auctoritate et humana ordinatione ita

per partes divisum esse cognoscitur,
ut unusquisque vestrum in suo loco
et ordine partem nostri ministerii
habere cognoscatur ; unde apparet,
quod ego omnium vestrum admonitor
esse debeo, et omnes vos nostri
adjutores esse debetis. . . .

"14. Volumus studere . . . et per
commune testimonium, id est episcoporum de comitibus, comitum de
episcopis, comperire, qualiter scilicet
comites justitiam diligant et faciant,
et quam religiose episcopi conver-
sentur et prædicent, et amborum
relatu de aliorum fidelium in suis
ministeriis consistentium æquitate
et pace atque concordia cognoscere.
Similiter etiam volumus, ut omnes
illis et illi omnibus de communi
societate et statu a nobis interrogati,
verum testimonium sibi mutuo per-
hibere possint."

"Capitulare Septimanicum apud Tolosam datum" of 844 we find Charles the Bald strictly forbidding the bishops to take action against those priests who had appealed to him for protection against the oppression of the bishops, and warning them that they must obey his injunctions, and see that every one obeys the Canons.[1] In 853 we find the same Charles sending round his "missi" to hold inquiries and correct abuses in all cities and monasteries along with the bishop of each diocese.[2]

There are even indications in the literature and history of the times that the responsibility of the emperor for the conduct of the Church extended to the condition of the papacy itself. We do not wish to enter into any discussion of the exact character of the purgation of Pope Leo III. in the year 800, but at least it is clear that Charles the Great had been gravely concerned with regard to the charges brought against the Pope. Leo III. was very careful, in purging himself by oath of the crimes laid to his charge, to make it quite clear that he did this of his own free will, and not as one amenable to the judgment of any man, and to guard against his action being taken as a precedent for his successors; but his own statement makes it clear that Charles had come to Rome, in part at least, to inquire into the matter.[3] And in spite of

---

[1] M. G. H. Leg., sect. ii. vol. ii. No. 255: "1. Ut episcopi nullum inquietudinem sive exprobationem presbyteris aut aperte ingerendo aut alia qualibet occasione machinando pro eo, quod se ad nos hac vice reclamare venerunt, inferant; quia longa oppressio hujusmodi itineris eos fecit subire laborem. . . .

"8. Ut episcopi sub occasione, quasi auctoritatem habeant canonum, his constitutis excellentiæ nostræ nequaquam resultent aut neglegant, sed potius canones, ut intelligendi sunt, intelligere et in cunctis observare procurent; quia si aliter fecerint, omnimodis et qualiter canones fidelium decimis agendum statuant et qualiter intellegi ac observari cum mansuetudinis nostræ decreto debeant, synodali dijudicatione et nostra regia auctoritate docebuntur."

[2] M. G. H. Leg., sect. ii. vol. ii. No. 259, Cap. Missorum Suessionense: "1. Ut missi nostri per civitates et singula monasteria, tam canonicorum quam monachorum sive sanctimonialium, una cum episcopo parochiæ uniuscujusque, in qua consistunt, cum consilio et consensu ipsius, qui monasterium retinet vitam ibi degentium et conversationem inquirant, et ubi necesse est corrigant," &c.

[3] M. G. H. Ep., v. Ep. Select. Pont. Rom., 6. 800 A.D. Dec. 23. "Sacramentum quod Leo Papa juravit. 'Auditum, fratres karissimi, et divulgatum est per multa loca, qualiter homines mali adversus me insurrexerunt, et debilitare voluerunt, et miser-

the care Leo III. had taken to guard against his action becoming a precedent, we cannot help feeling that Pope Leo IV. was following in Leo III.'s steps, and was even going somewhat further, when, in his letter to the Emperor Lewis II. of about 853, he expressed his willingness that the emperor and his "missi" should inquire into the charges which had been made against him, and his readiness to amend everything according to their judgment.[1]

We think that all this will serve to show sufficiently clearly that the civil ruler in the ninth century was thought of, and was recognised in fact, as having some real responsibility for the good order and conduct of the Church. He was not only the protector of the Church against external enemies, but was, at least in some measure, responsible to guard it against corruption and decay. How exactly this responsibility was to be carried out into practice was a very uncertain matter, and one upon which, when put to the test of practical action, men in the ninth century would probably have differed greatly; but there

---

unt super me gravia crimina. Propter quam causam audiendam iste clementissimus ac serenissimus dominus rex Carolus una cum sacerdotibus et optimatibus suis istam pervenit ad urbem. Quam ob rem ego Leo pontifex sanctæ Romanæ ecclesiæ, a nemine judicatus neque coactus, sed spontanea mea voluntate purifico et purgo me in conspectu vestro coram Deo et angelis suis, qui conscientiam meam novit, et beato Petro principe apostolorum in cujus basilica consistimus : quia istas criminosas et sceleratas res, quas illi mihi obiciunt, nec perpetravi nec perpetrare jussi ; testis mihi est Deus, in cujus judicium venturi sumus et in cujus conspectu consistimus. Et hoc propter suspitiones tollendas mea spontanea voluntate facio ; non quasi in canonibus inventum sit, aut quasi ego hanc consuetudinem aut decretum in sancta ecclesia successoribus meis necnon et fratribus et coepiscopis nostris imponam.'"

[1] M. G. H. Ep., v. Ep. Select. Leonis IV., 40, c. 853 : "Nos si aliquid incompetenter egimus, et in subditis justæ legis tramitem non conservavimus, vestro ac vestrorum missorum cuncta volumus emendare judicio quoniam si nos qui aliena debemus corrigere, pejora committimus, certe non veritatis discipuli, sed quod dolentes dicimus, erimus pre cæteris erroris magistri. Inde magnitudinis vestræ magnopere clemenciam imploramus, ut tales ad hæc quæ diximus perquirenda missos in his partibus dirigatis, qui Deum per omnia timeant, et cuncta quemadmodum si vestra præsens imperialis gloria fuisset, examussim diligenter exquirant, et non tantum hæc quæ superius diximus exagitent, sed sive minora sive etiam majora illis sint de nobis indicata negotia, ita eorum cuncta legitimo terminentur examine, quatenus in posterum nichil sit, quod ex eis indiscussum vel indiffinitum remaneat."

seems no doubt that this conception of the responsibility of the king was held very commonly, if not universally.

It is partly at least from this standpoint that we may most usefully consider the relation of the civil ruler of the time to the synodical and legislative organisation of the Church. We do not think that any one doubted the independent legislative and administrative authority of the synods of the Church, but yet we find that the synods are constantly spoken of as being called together by the emperor or king as well as by the ecclesiastical chiefs, and that the decrees, administrative or legislative, of the synods, are issued with the co-operation of the royal power.

We may take as our first example of this condition of things the Capitulare of Karlmann of 742. Here we find Karlmann, with the counsel of the bishops, presbyters, and chief men of the kingdom, decreeing that a council and synod should be held to advise him how religion and the law of God might be restored, and then, with the bishops and great men, ordering that synods should be held every year, at which the king should be present, and by which the canons and laws of the Church should be restored.[1] We find parallels in Charles the Great's Capitulary of 769,[2] in the "Capitulare Haristallense" of 779,[3] and in the "Admonitio Generalis" of 789.[4] We are specially told that Charles the Great was present at the Synod of Frankfort in 794, and he is said to have pre-

---

[1] M. G. H. Leg., sect. ii. vol. i. No. 10 : "In nomine Domini nostri Jesu Christi. Ego Karlmannus, dux et princeps Francorum, anno ab incarnatione Christi septingentesimo quadragesimo secundo, xi Kalendas Maias, cum concilio servorum Dei et optimatum meorum episcopos qui in regno meo sunt cum presbyteris et concilium et synodum pro timore Christi congregavi, id est Bonifatium archiepiscopum et Burghardum . . . cum presbiteris eorum, ut mihi consilium dedissent, quamodo lex Dei et æcclesiastica religio recuperetur, quæ in diebus præteritorum principum dissipata corruit, et qualiter populus Christianus ad salutem animæ per-

venire possit et per falsos sacerdotes deceptus non pereat.

"1. Et per consilium sacerdotum et optimatum meorum ordinavimus per civitates episcopos, et constituimus super eos archiepiscopum Bonifatium qui est missus sancti Petri. Statuimus per annos singulos synodum congregare, ut nobis præsentibus canonum decreta et æcclesiæ jura restaurentur et relegio Christiana emendetur."

[2] M. G. H. Leg., sect. ii. vol. i. No. 19.

[3] M. G. H. Leg., sect. ii. vol. i. No. 20.

[4] M. G. H. Leg., sect. ii. vol. i. No. 22.

sided.[1] The synod, we are told, was called together by the
apostolic authority and by that of Charles the Great.[2] Perhaps the most marked recognition of the imperial share in
such ecclesiastical business is to be found in the Epilogue to
the decrees of the Council of Arles of 813. In this we find
the decrees presented to the emperor, and he is asked to add
anything which may have been omitted, to correct anything
that may be wrong, and to aid in carrying into effect whatever may have been rightly decreed.[3]

It may perhaps be urged that these examples are all taken
from the time of Charles the Great himself, and that his relation to the Church was wholly exceptional; but we can find some
parallels at least later in the century. In 818-19 Lewis the
Pious issued a number of capitula on ecclesiastical and secular
matters, and it is worthy of note that the form in which this
is done is very much the same as that in the earlier cases.
Lewis calls together his bishops, abbots, and great men, and
with their advice issues the Capitula which are to be observed
by ecclesiastics and laymen alike.[4] The proceedings of the

[1] Synodica concilii Franconofurt.
Mansi Councils, vol. xiii. p. 884: "Præ-
cipiente et præsidente piisimo et gloriosissimo domno nostro Carolo rege."

[2] M. G. H. Leg., sect. ii. vol. i.
No. 28, Synodus Franconofurtensis:
"Conjungentibus, Deo favente, apostolica auctoritate atque piissimi domini
nostri Karoli regni anno xxvi. principatus sui, cunctis regni Francorum seu
Italiæ, Aquitaniæ, Provintiæ, episcopis
ac sacerdotibus synodali concilio, inter
quos ipse mitissimus sancto interfuit
conventui."

[3] Mansi, Councils, vol. xiv. p. 62:
" Hæc igitur . . . quam brevissime
annotavimus, et domino imperatori
præsentanda decrevimus, poscentes ejus
clementiam, ut si quid hic minus est,
ejus prudentia suppleatur: si quid secus
quam se ratio habet, ejus judicio emendetur, si quid rationabiliter taxatum
est, ejus adjutorio divina opitulante
clementia perficiatur."

[4] M. G. H. Leg., sect. ii. vol. i. No.

137, "Prœmium Generale ad Cap.
Tam. Eccl. quam Mundana": . . .
" Quinto anno imperii nostri, accersitis
nonnullis episcopis, abbatibus, canonicis
et monachis et fidelibus optimatibus
nostris, studuimus eorum consultu
sagacissima investigare inquisitione,
qualiter unicuique ordini, canonicorum
videlicet, monachorum et laicorum
juxta quod ratio dictabat et facultas
suppetebat, Deo opem ferente consul-
eremus. . . . Sed qualiter de his divina
co-operante gratia consultu fidelium
pro viribus et temporis brevitate, licet
non quantum debuimus et voluimus
sed quantum a Deo posse accepimus,
egerimus et quid unicuique ordini
communi voto communique consensu
consulere studuerimus, ita ut quid canonicis proprie de his, quidve monachis
observandis, quid etiam in legibus mundanis addenda, quid quoque in capitulis inserenda forent, adnotaverimus
et singulis singula observanda contra-
deremus," &c.

Synod of Ponthion in 876 seem to show that the principle that synods should be summoned by the king or emperor, and that he might preside at them, was still accepted. The Emperor Charles the Bald is said to have presided at this synod, and it is spoken of as having been called together by the Pope and the Emperor.[1]

The history of the century seems to illustrate very exactly the theory as we have seen it in Sedulius and Smaragdus or Cathulfus. The king is responsible for the good order of the Church, and at least has his share in the calling together of the synods of the Church and the promulgation of their decrees.

There is yet one further point of Church order in which the influence of the secular power is very great—that is, in the appointment of ecclesiastics. We do not wish to enter upon a discussion of the many and intricate questions connected with this subject, but we must deal with it so far as is necessary to bring out the fact that here again the theory of a separation of the two powers was found impossible of literal application to the actual circumstances of the time. The emperor or king did as a matter of fact exercise a most powerful influence over all appointments of the greater ecclesiastics, and the propriety of this is not denied by any writer of the ninth century.

The bishops, in their address to Lewis the Pious of 829, quite frankly recognise this, and exhort him to see that the greatest care is exercised in appointing pastors and rulers in the Church of God.[2] Hincmar of Rheims is quite as frank in recognising the authority of the secular ruler in the appointment of bishops. In his treatise, "De Institutione Carolo-

[1] M. G. H. Leg., sect. ii. vol. ii. No. 279, Synodus Pontigonensis: "E. Ideoque, quia imperialem excellentiam vestram synodo præesse, et vicarios sedis apostolicæ præsto nobis adesse gaudemus, &c. G. Sancta synodus, quæ in nomine Domini vocatione domini Johannis ter beatissimi, ac universalis papæ et jussione domini Karoli perpetui augusti congregata est in loco qui vocatur Pontigonis," &c.

[2] M. G. H. Leg., sect. ii. vol. ii. No. 196, Episcoporum ad Hlud. Imp. Relatio: "57. Iterum monendo magnitudini vestræ suppliciter suggerimus, ut deinceps in bonis pastoribus, rectoribusque in ecclesiis Dei constituendis magnum studium atque sollertissimam adhibeatis curam."

manni," he very clearly reckons the consent of the prince, and the election of the clergy and people, as the proper elements in an appointment to ecclesiastical rule;[1] and in a letter to Lewis III., occasioned by some dispute about the appointment of a Bishop of Beauvais, he again admits very frankly that the consent of the prince is a necessary part of the appointment to such an office. This is the more noticeable, as the general purpose of the letter is to condemn and correct what Hincmar clearly thought was an exaggerated conception of the royal authority with regard to ecclesiastical appointments. We must indeed notice how emphatically Hincmar condemns the notion that the appointment of a bishop was a matter in the arbitrary power of the prince, attributing this to the suggestion of the devil himself, and that he wholly denies that the prince can order the election of whomsoever he pleases. A bishop, Hincmar seems to mean, should be elected by the other bishops of the province, with the consent of the people and clergy of the diocese, and when the prince has given his consent he is to be taken to the metropolitan for consecration.[2] We do not enter into any discussion of Hincmar's

---

[1] Hincmar of Rheims, De Institutione Carolomanni, 5 : " Qualiter autem consensu principis terræ, qui res ecclesiasticas divino judicio ad tuendas et defensandas suscepit, electione cleri ac plebis quisque ad ecclesiasticum regimen absque ulla venalitate provehi debeat, et Dominus in Evangelio, et sacri canones aperte demonstrant dicente Domino : ' Qui non intrat per ostium in ovile ovium, sed ascendit aliunde, ille fur est et latro.' "

[2] Hincmar of Rheims, Ep. xix. : c. i. " ' Ut sicut sacræ leges et regulæ præcipiunt, archiepiscopis et episcopis collimitanearum diœceseon electionem concedere dignemini, ut undecunque, secundum formam regularem electionis, episcopi talem eligant, qui et sanctæ Ecclesiæ utilis, et regno proficuus, et vobis fidelis ac devotus co-operator existat : et consentientibus clero et plebe eum vobis adducant, ut secundum

ministerium vestrum res et facultates Ecclesiæ, quas ad defendendum et tuendum vobis Dominus commendavit, suæ dispositioni committatis, et cum consensu ac letteris vestris eum ad metropolitanum episcopum ac coepiscopos ipsius dioceseos qui eum ordinare debent, transmittatis, et sic sine scandali macula ad sanctum sacerdotium provehatur.' . . .

" c. iii. Nam si quod a quibusdam dicitur, ut audivi, quando petitam apud vos electionem conceditis, illum debent episcopi, et clerus, ac plebs eligere, quem vos vultis, et quem jubetis (quæ non est divinæ legis electio, sed humanæ potestatis extorsio), si ita est, ut dici a quibusdam audivi, ille malignus spiritus, qui per serpentem primos parentes nostros in paradiso decepit et inde illos ejecit, per tales adulatores in aures vestras hæc sibilat ; quia hoc in Scriptura tam

position with regard to the part of the metropolitan and the other bishops of the province in the election of a bishop: it is enough for us to observe that Hincmar clearly admits the place of the secular ruler, but as clearly also is anxious that this should be defined and limited.

A position very similar to that of Hincmar is represented by the little treatise "De Electionibus Episcoporum," written by Florus Diaconus, a writer of the ninth century. Here also it is candidly admitted that in certain kingdoms the custom prevailed that a bishop should be consecrated after the prince had been consulted, and Florus admits that this custom tends to peace and tranquillity, but he emphatically denies that it is necessary to a proper consecration.[1] Florus maintains that

veteris quam Novi Testamenti non continetur, neque in catholicorum dictis, vel sacris canonibus, nec etiam in legibus a Christianis imperatoribus et regibus promulgatis hoc scriptum vel decretum invenitur, sed talia dicta infernus evomuit. Christus enim per apostolum loquens, talem jubet eligere: 'qui potens sit exhortari in doctrina sacra et iis qui contradicunt revincere.' Et si quis contra hoc loquitur, iniquitatem contra Dominum loquitur et inter blasphemos a Sancto Spiritu computatur. Sic enim atavus vester Carolus et abavus Ludovicus imperatores intellexerunt, et ideo in primo libro capitulorum suorum promulgaverunt scribentes. 'Sacrorum,' inquiunt, 'canonum non ignari, ut in Dei nomine sancta Ecclesia suo liberius potiatur honore, assensum ordini ecclesiastico præbemus, ut scilicet episcopi per electionem cleri et populi secundum statuta canonum, de propria diœcesi, remota personarum et munerum acceptione ob vitæ meritum et sapientiæ donum eligantur, ut exemplo et verbo sibi subjectis usquequaque prodesse valeant.' . . . Et sacri canones dicunt, 'Primum enim illi (quin clerici uniuscujusque Ecclesiæ) reprobandi sunt, ut aliqui de alienis Ecclesiis merito præferantur.' Et

item, 'Ut episcopi, judicio metropolitanorum et eorum episcoporum qui circumcirca sunt, provehantur ad ecclesiasticam potestatem ; hi, videlicet qui plurimo tempore probantur tam verbo fidei quam rectæ conversationis exemplo.' Attendendum est igitur qualiter hoc imperiale capitulum sacris regulis et antiquorum imperatorum legibus congruat, ostendens quoniam, sicut et leges et regulæ dicunt, in electione episcopi assensio regis sit, non electio, in episcoporum vero exsecutione sit electio, sicut et ordinatio."

[1] Florus Diaconus, De Electionibus Episcoporum iv. : "Quod vero in quibusdam regnis postea consuetudo obtinuit, ut consultu principis ordinatio fieret episcopalis, valet utique ad cumulum fraternitatis, propter pacem et concordiam mundanæ potestatis ; non tamen ad complendam veritatem vel auctoritatem sacræ ordinationis, quæ nequaquam regio potentatu, sed solo Dei nutu, et Ecclesiæ fidelium consensu, cuique conferri potest. . . . Unde graviter quilibet princeps delinquit, si hoc suo beneficio largiri posse existimat, quod sola divina gratia dispensat ; cum ministerium suæ potestatis in hujusmodi negotium peragendo adjungere debeat, non præferre. . . . "vii. Quæ omnia non ideo dicimus,

the true requirements for a proper appointment are the election of the clergy and the whole people of the diocese, and consecration by the lawful number of bishops;[1] and he urges that for nearly four hundred years from the time of the apostles no consent was asked from the secular power, and that even after the emperor was Christian this liberty for the most part continued.[2]

The position of Hincmar and Florus is not quite identical. Hincmar looks upon the consent of the prince as normally necessary for the appointment of a bishop; Florus considers this as a legitimate custom of some kingdoms, but not as being a universal custom, and still less does he admit it to be of universal obligation. But they agree in admitting that, as a matter of fact, the secular ruler has a considerable power with regard to ecclesiastical appointments, while they are both concerned to correct any exaggerated conception of this.

quasi potestatem principum in aliquo minuendam putemus, vel contra religiosum morem regni aliquid sentiendum persuadeamus ; sed ut clarissime demonstretur, in re hujusmodi divinam gratiam sufficere, humanam vero potentiam nisi illi consonet, nihil valere. Quapropter in sacris canonibus Patrum, ubi plurimæ causæ commemorantur sine quibus episcopalis ordinatio irrita habenda est, de hac re nihil invenitur insertum."

[1] Id., i.: "Manifestum est omnibus qui in Ecclesia Dei sacerdotale officium administrant, quæ sunt illa quæ in ordinatione episcopali, et sacrorum canonorum auctoritas, et consuetudo ecclesiastica, juxta dispositionem divinæ legis et traditionem apostolicam jubeat observari. Videlicet ut pastore defuncto, et sede vacante, unus de clero Ecclesiæ, quem communis et concors ejusdem cleri et totius plebis consensus elegerit, et publico decreto celebriter ac solemniter designaverit, legitimo episcoporum numero consecratus, locum decedentis antistitis rite valeat ob-

tinere ; nec dubitetur divino judicio et dispositione firmatum, quod ab Ecclesia Dei tam sancto ordine et legitima observatione fuerit celebratum."

[2] Id., iii. : "Juxta hæc verba beati Cypriani, ordinatos fuisse constat, et legitime præfuisse universo populo deinceps omnes Ecclesiarum Dei antistites, absque ullo consultu mundanæ potestatis, a temporibus apostolorum, et postea per annos fere quadringentos. Ex quo autem Christiani principes esse cœperunt, eamdem episcoporum ordinationibus ecclesiasticam libertatem ex parte maxima permansisse, manifesta ratio declarat. Neque enim fieri potuit, cum unus Imperator orbis terræ monarchiam obtineret, ut ex omnibus latissimis mundi partibus, Asiæ videlicet, Europæ et Africæ, omnes qui ordinandi erant Episcopi ad ejus cognitionem deducerentur. Sed fuit semper integra et rata ordinatio, quam sancta Ecclesia juxta traditionem apostolicam et religiosæ observationis formam celebravit."

It is perhaps necessary to say a word about the theory of the relation of the emperor to the papal elections. We may begin by observing that Florus Diaconus assumes that the consent of the civil power is never asked for in this case.[1] Whether such a statement can be taken as accurately representing the relations of the emperor to the papal elections in the ninth century is doubtful. The "Pactum Hludowici Pii cum Paschali Pontifice" of 817 does, indeed, agree with this in its careful provision that no one is to interfere with the election of a Pope, but that it is to be left in the hands of the Romans, and that they are freely to elect him whom the divine inspiration and the intercession of St Peter suggest. Only after the consecration is an ambassador to be sent to Lewis or his successor to arrange for the continuance of friendship and peace between the Emperor and the Pope.[2] The terms of Lothair's "Constitutio Romana" of 824 are so far in agreement with this. It reiterates the provision of the Pactum, that no one is to take part in the election of a Pope except the Romans themselves.[3] There is in existence,

[1] Id. vi. : "Sed et in Romana Ecclesia usque in præsentem diem cernimus absque interrogatione Principis solo dispositionis judicio et fidelium suffragio, legitime pontifices consecrari; qui etiam omnium regionum et civitatum quæ illi subjectæ sunt, juxta antiquum morem, eadem libertate ordinant atque constituunt sacerdotes ; nec adeo quisquam absurdus est, ut putet minorem illic sanctificationis divinam esse gratiam, eo quod nulla mundanæ potestatis comitetur auctoritas."

[2] M. G. H. Leg., sect. ii. vol. i. No. 172: "Et quando divina vocatione hujus sacratissimæ sedis pontifex de hoc mundo migraverit, nullus ex regno nostro, aut Francus aut Longobardus aut de qualibet gente homo sub nostra potestate constitutus, licentiam habeat contra Romanos, aut publice aut private veniendi vel electionem faciendi ; nullusque in civitatibus vel territoriis ad ecclesiæ beati Petri apostoli potestatem pertinentibus aliquod malum propter

hoc facere presumat. Sed liceat Romanis cum omni veneratione et sine qualibet perturbatione honorificam suo pontifici exibere sepulturam, et eum quem divina inspiratione et beati Petri intercessione omnes Romani uno consilio atque concordia sine aliqua promissione ad pontificatus ordinem elegerint sine qualibet ambiguitate vel contradictione more canonico consecrari. Et dum consecratus fuerit, legati ad nos vel ad successores nostros reges Francorum dirigantur, qui inter nos et illos amicitiam et caritatem ac pacem socient, sicut temporibus pie recordationis domni Karoli attavi nostri, seu domni Pipini avi nostri vel etiam domni Karoli imperatoris genitoris nostri consuetudo erat faciendi."

[3] M. G. H. Leg., sect. ii. vol. i. No. 161 : "3. Volumus ut in electione pontificis nullus præsumat venire, neque liber neque servus, qui aliquod impedimentum faciat illis solummodo

however, a form of oath, supposed to be of this time, required of all those who were to take part in the papal election : this not only makes the electors swear allegiance and fidelity to the emperor, but also includes a provision that he who is elected is not to be consecrated until he has taken such an oath in the presence of the "missus" of the emperor as that taken by Pope Eugenius.   From a passage in Einhard's Annals for 827, it would appear that on the death of Valentinus, his successor, Gregory IV., was elected, but not consecrated until the ambassador of the emperor had come and examined into the character of the election.[1]   It must, however, be noticed that these documents, and especially the "Pactum," while they are probably genuine in substance, are probably not all authentic in detail.

Our examination of these matters will, we think, have served to bring out sufficiently clearly the fact that, whatever might be the theory of the division of functions between the secular and the spiritual powers, the secular power did in practice certainly tend to exercise a very considerable authority even in the strictly spiritual sphere.   We may say that the foundation of the whole situation, as far as theory is concerned, lies in this, that it is the duty of the civil ruler to care for the

---

Romanis, quibus antiquitus fuit consuetudo concessa per constitutionem sanctorum patrum eligendi pontificem. Quod si quis contra hanc jussionem nostram facere præsumpserit, exilio tradatur."

[1] M. G. H. Leg., sect. ii. vol. i. No. 161.   Form of oath to the emperor to be taken by electors to the Papacy, which seems to belong to the time of Pope Eugenius : " Promitto ego ille per Deum omnipotentem et per ista sacra quattuor evangelia et per hanc crucem domini nostri Jesu Christi et per corpus beatissimi Petri principis apostolorum, quod ab hac die in futurum fidelis ero dominis nostris imperatoribus Hludowico et Hlothario diebus vitæ meæ, juxta vires et intellectum meum, sine fraude atque malo ingenio, salva fide

quam repromisi domino apostolico ; et quod non consentiam ut aliter in hac sede Romana fiat electio pontificis nisi canonice et juste, secundum vires et intellectum meum ; et ille qui electus fuerit me consentiente consecratus pontifex non fiat, priusquam tale sacramentum faciat in præsentia missi domini imperatoris et populi, cum juramento, quale dominus Eugenius papa, sponte pro conservatione omnium factum habet per scriptum."

The editor cites, to illustrate this, from Einhard's Annals for 827 : "2. . . . quo defuncto (i.e., Pope Valentinus) Gregorius (IV.) electus, sed non prius ordinatus est quam legatus imperatoris Romam venit et electionem populi qualis esset examinavit."

wellbeing of the Church, and to interfere when he sees that the Church is, for any reason, being badly administered or falling into corruption. We can see how this conception naturally gives rise to the theory that it is the king's duty to see to the regular meeting of synods, and thus gives him necessarily a share in the legislative, as well as the administrative, control of the Church. It is easy also to see how this conception of the responsibility lying upon the king to see that justice and righteousness prevailed in the Church as well as elsewhere, might lead to a considerable ambiguity in his relation to the discipline of the Church. The relations of the empire to the Papacy in the cases of Leo III. and Leo IV. are but the final examples of a tendency to look to the civil power to set things right in the Church, when there was no one else who could act. And, finally, the tendency to subject ecclesiastical appointments to some control on the part of the civil ruler, while it has many other political and social relations, may also be regarded in part at least as illustrating the same conception, that the secular power has its own responsibility for the good order of the Church, and has therefore necessarily something to say with regard to the persons to whom the government of the Church is to be intrusted.

We have said enough, we think, to make it clear that in the ninth century the theory of a strict duality of authority in society does not prevent the civil power from acting very frequently in the sphere of the ecclesiastical, and that this intervention is not only tolerated in practice, but is to a considerable extent justified in theory.

We must now consider the other side of the subject, the extent to which the ecclesiastical authority intervened in civil affairs, and the character and conditions of this interference. We may begin by observing that if the king or emperor is by some writers styled the Vicar of God, the same title is also claimed for the bishops.[1] Hrabanus Maurus calls the priests or bishops the vicars of the prince of shepherds in

---

[1] M. G. H. Leg., sect. ii. vol. ii. No. 293, Concilium Meldense Parisiense, 83 : "Nos autem Dei judicio sui ab illo vicarii constituti," &c.

the Church of God, and warns them to be determined against the proud and contumacious, to be careful that no earthly power terrifies them in their rule of souls, and no worldly blandishments soften their rigour.[1]

What is more important than this title of Vicar of God, it is certain that the people of the ninth century were perfectly clear that the ecclesiastic is bound to correct and reprove persons of every rank and degree,—to use against them, if necessary, the severest penalties of the Church. A very strong phrase is used by a synod held in 859, which expresses this very directly and forcibly: the bishops are exhorted to be united in their ministry and holy authority, and with mutual counsel and help to rule over and correct kings and the great ones of the earth, and the whole people committed to them in the Lord.[2] The same view is very strongly expressed by many writers. Alcuin exhorts the priest to declare the Word of God, and the prince to obey.[3] Jonas of Orleans quotes that passage from the history of Rufinus, discussed in an earlier chapter, in which Constantine is represented as saying to the bishops that God has made them the judges of all, and that they cannot be judged by any.[4] The same passage is quoted by the bishops in that address to Lewis the Pious which we have already frequently cited.[5] There is, therefore, nothing that we should regard as new, when we find the pseudo-Isidorian Decretals using very strong language about the subjection of

[1] M. G. H. Ep., v., Epistolarum Fuldensium Fragmenta, 20, C. iv. : "Rabanus inquit : Quomodo in Christi sacerdotibus discreta debet esse pietas erga condigne pœnitentes, ita debet et fortis esse constantia contra superbos atque contumaces. Nec debet ulla terrena potestas terrere rectorem animarum nec mollire secularibus blandimentis rigorem Christi pontificum, qui vicarii principis pastorum in ecclesia Dei esse videntur. . . . In Epistola ad Humbertum episcopum."

[2] M. G. H. Leg., sect. ii. vol. ii. No. 299, Synodus apud Saponarias habita, 2 : "Episcopi namque secundum illorum ministerium ac sacram auctori-

tatem uniti sint et mutuo consilio atque auxilio reges regnorumque primores, atque populum sibi commissum in Domino regant et corrigant."

[3] M. G. H. Ep., iv., Alcuin, Ep. 18 : "Illorum est, id est, sacerdotum, verba Dei non tacere. Vestrum est, o principes, humiliter obœdire, diligenter implere." Cf. Ep. 108 : "Et sis obediens servis Dei, qui te de mandatis ejus ammoneant."

[4] Jonas of Orleans, "De Instit., Laic.," ii. 20. See p. 177.

[5] M. G. H. Leg., sect. ii. vol. ii. No. 196, Episcop. ad Hlud. Imp. Relatio, 22.

princes to bishops. In his 39th Decretal letter Clement is represented as saying that all princes of the earth are to obey the bishops, to submit to them and help them, and that those who oppose them, unless they repent, are to be put out of the Church.[1]

The political theory of the ninth century, then, very clearly recognises that there is an authority in the Church which extends over all persons, even the most exalted in society. It will be useful to consider more closely the relation of the civil order and the civil rulers to the law and discipline of the Church. We have already examined the treatment in Hincmar's work, 'De Ordine Palatii,' of the relation of the king to the law of the State; we have seen that Hincmar expresses the general view of the ninth century when he maintains that these laws are binding upon the king.[2] Hincmar goes on to say that much more must the king obey the divine laws.[3] There is a system of divine law in the Church to which all men owe their obedience. We do not wish to enter into so complicated a subject as that of the gradual formation of the body of Church law: to do so would take us very far away from our proper topic. It will here suffice if we point out that by the ninth century there were in existence and circulation in Western Europe collections of Church regulations on doctrine and discipline, and these regulations were looked upon as having in some sense a divine authority. There are some words in Hincmar's treatise 'Pro Ecclesiæ Libertatum Defensione' which may very well be taken as representative of the attitude of the ninth century towards these laws. This is the treatise written by Hincmar in the early stages of the quarrel between Charles the Bald and Hincmar's nephew, Hincmar, Bishop of Laon. Hincmar at first sided wholly with

---

[1] Pseudo - Isidore, Clement, Dec. xxxix. : "Omnes principes terræ et cunctos homines eis obædire et capita sua submittere eorumque adjutores existere præcipiebat. . . . Omnes ergo qui eis contradicent, ita damnatos et infames usque ad satisfactionem monstrabat, et nisi converterentur a liminibus ecclesiæ alienos esse præcipiebat."

[2] See p. 233.

[3] M. G. H. Leg., sect. ii. vol. ii. Hincmar of Rheims, De Ordine Palatii, 9 : "Multo minus autem regi, vel cuilibet in quocunque ordine contra leges divinas licet agere per contemptum."

his nephew, and wrote this treatise to protest against the royal action, which at first he looked upon as an outrageous interference with ecclesiastical prerogative.   A vassal of the Bishop of Laon had complained to Charles of his treatment by the bishop, and Charles had summoned the bishop to appear and to answer before his courts.   When he did not appear, Charles put his property under the ban.   Hincmar of Rheims protests against such action as being wholly improper and even scandalous, and quite contrary to the canons and the laws.   He quotes St Leo as saying that the canons were enacted by the Spirit of God, and confirmed by the reverence of the whole world, and were established by men who now reign with God in heaven and still work miracles on the earth.[1]

We think that these words are highly characteristic of the general attitude of men in the ninth century towards Church law.   No one, we think, doubted that in some sense all men of all ranks were bound to obey it.   Earlier in the century Agobard of Lyons had used phrases similar to those of Hincmar. Agobard is writing of the proceedings of the bishops at Attigny and Compiègne, and represents himself as making a speech in which he discussed the nature and authority of the canons of the Church.   In former times, he said, the holy bishops had come together and decreed that the canons must be preserved inviolate, inasmuch as they had been confirmed by the Spirit of God, the consent of the whole world, the obedience of princes, the agreement of Scripture, and that from that time it had been an accepted doctrine that any action against the canons was an action against God Himself, and against His universal Church, and that they could not be violated without danger to religion.[2]   A little earlier in date still we find a letter

---

[1] Hincmar of Rheims, Pro Eccl. Lib. Defen., i. : "Et quis oculum simplicem, id est, rectam intentionem, quam in vobis nescit, putabit : ubi factum Domino contrarium, et inimicum sacris canonibus, sicut beatus Leo scribit, 'Spiritu Dei conditis et totius mundi reverentia consecratis, quorum conditores in cœlo cum Deo regnantes, et in terris miraculis coruscantes, adhuc nobiscum in constitutionibus vivant' : sed et legibus, quibus una cum eisdem sacris canonibus moderatur Ecclesia, constat adversum ? "

[2] M. G. H. Ep., v. ; Agobard, Ep., v. c. 4 : " Convenerunt episcopi, viri sancti, quibus tunc habundabat ecclesia, statuerunt inlibatos conservari debere sacros canones, qui firmati sunt spiritu Dei, consensu totius mundi, obœdientia

by Siegwald, Bishop of Aquileia, mutilated unfortunately and only partly comprehensible, in which we have a very emphatic exhortation to Charles the Great on the duty of obeying the canons. In spite of the fragmentary state in which it has come to us, we can make out fairly clearly the emphatic terms in which Charles is admonished to observe and enforce obedience to the canons.[1]

There is, then, a body of law in the Church which all men must obey and to which all other laws must conform themselves. Hincmar considers the question of a possible collision between the national system of law and the divine law, and is perfectly clear that in such a case the human laws must be altered and made conformable to the divine;[2] and in another treatise written by Hincmar we have an exposition of the superiority of the divine law, and men are reminded that they may now justify themselves in their actions by appealing to human laws and customs, but in the day of judgment they will have to answer, not to the Roman, or Salic, or Gundobadian laws, but to the divine and apostolic laws. Hincmar urges that in a Christian kingdom even the public laws should be in accordance with the principles of Christianity.[3]

principum, consonantia scripturarum. Ex quo tempore acceptum et receptum est non aliud esse agere cuiquam adversus canones quam adversus Deum, et adversus ejus universalem ecclesiam, neque sensum est umquam a quibusque fidelibus, ut talia statuta absque periculo religionis violarentur."

[1] M. G. H. Ep., iv.; Ep. var. Carolo Magno Regnante, 8 : "Vestra est . . . [sac]rorum canonum inviolabiles sanctiones salubriter promulgatas nullo quolibet usurpationis ti[tulo] . . . mutilare, dicente scriptura : Terminos patrum tuorum ne transgredieris presertim cum sere . . . vestræ mansuetudo decrevit omnium ecclesiarum præsules divinis legibus subjacere et pri . . . secum . . . [irrep]rehensibilia documenta sancto dilucidante Spiritu prælibata modis omnibus custodire."

[2] M. G. H. Leg., sect. ii. vol. ii.

De Ordine Palatii, 21 : "Si quid vero tale esset, quod leges mundanæ hoc in suis diffinitionibus statutum non haberent aut secundum gentilium consuetudinem crudelius sancitum esset, quam Christianitatis rectitudo vel sancta auctoritas merito non consentiret, hoc ad regis moderationem perduceretur, ut ipse cum his, qui utramque legem nossent et Dei magis quam humanarum legum statuta metuerent, ita decerneret, ita statueret, ut, ubi utrumque servari posset, utrumque servaretur, sin autem, lex sæculi merito comprimeretur, justitia Dei conservaretur."

[3] Hincmar of Rheims, De Raptu Viduarum, etc., c. xii. : "Defendant se quantum volunt qui hujusmodi sunt, sive per leges, si ullæ sunt, mundanas, sive per consuetudines humanas, tamen si Christiani sunt, sciant se in die

There is again, therefore, nothing new in the strong phrases in which the Pseudo-Isidorian Decretals express the principle that no emperor or other potentate may do anything contrary to the divine commands: if the judges, at the king's desire, should command anything unjust or contrary to the evangelical, or prophetic, or apostolic doctrines, such commands have no authority.[1]

The secular ruler, then, must, like other persons, obey the divine law, and if he refuses to do this he is subject to the discipline of the Church. It is indeed clear that there were some in the ninth century who doubted or denied that the authority of the Church extended so far as to the excommunication of the king or emperor. From that section of Hincmar's treatise on the divorce of Lothair and Tetburga, to which we have so often referred, it is clear that there were some who denied that the king was liable to the judgment of the bishops of his own dominions, or to that of any other bishops. Some wise men, says Hincmar, maintained that the king is subject to no laws or judgments but those of God alone, who made him king; and that, as he should not be excommunicated by his own bishops, whatever he may do, so he cannot be judged by other bishops. Hincmar, indeed, makes short work of this contention, describing it concisely as blasphemous and full of the spirit of the devil, and then shows by a series of examples, drawn from the Old Testament and Church history, that kings were reproved by the prophets and separated from the Church by bishops;[2] and at the end

judicii nec Romanis, nec Salicis, nec Gundobadis, sed divinis et apostolicis legibus judicandos. Quanquam in regno Christiano etiam ipsas leges publicas oporteat esse Christianas, convenientes videlicet et consonantes Christianitati."

[1] Pseudo-Isidore, Marcellinus, Dec. iv.: "Non licet ergo imperatori vel cuiquam pietatem custodienti aliquid contra mandata divina praesumere nec quicquam quod evangelicis propheticisque et apostolicis regulis obviatur agere. Injustum enim juditium et definitio injusta regis metu vel jussu

a judicibus ordinata non valeat, nec quicquam quod contra evangelicae vel propheticae aut apostolicae doctrinae constitutionem successorum patrum actum fuerit, stabit. Et quod ab infidelibus aut hereticis factum fuerit omnino cassabitur."

[2] Hincmar of Rheims, De Div. Loth. et Tetb. Quæstio 6. "Dicunt quoque etiam aliqui sapientes, quia iste princeps rex est, et nullorum legibus vel judiciis subjacet nisi solius Dei, qui eum in regno, quod suus pater illi dimisit, regem constituit, et si voluerit pro hac vel alia causa ibit ad placitum,

of this section of the treatise he lays it down that the synods of the Church know no respect of persons.[1]

Hincmar's judgment is clear, and we do not doubt that almost all ecclesiastics in the ninth century would have agreed with him. That the Popes may have been unwilling to go the length of directly and explictly excommunicating the emperors of the fifth and sixth centuries, we have seen in former chapters. But in their relations to the Frankish rulers the Popes were not so restrained. As early as 770 we find Stephen III. threatening to excommunicate Charles and Carloman if they neglected his injunctions against a marriage with the daughter of the Lombard king Desiderius;[2] and in regard to this very question on which Hincmar writes we find that Pope Nicholas threatened at last to excommunicate Lothair unless he would take back Tetburga.[3]

vel ad synodum, et si noluerit, libere et licenter dimittet : et sicut a suis episcopis, quidquid egerit, non debet excommunicari, ita ab aliis episcopis non potest judicari, quoniam solius Dei principatui debet subjici, a quo solo potuit in principatu constitui ; et quod facit, et qualis est in regimine, divino sit nutu, sicut scriptum est : 'Cor regis in manu Dei, quocunque voluerit vertet illud.'"

Responsio. "Hæc vox non est catholici Christiani, sed nimium blasphemi, et spiritu diabolico pleni." He cites David's reproof by Nathan, Saul's by Samuel, Rehoboam's by the prophet, and proceeds : "Quando peccaverunt reges, et filii Israel, et traditi sunt in manus gentium, sicut Manasses et Sedechias, vel timuerunt a facie Domini sicut Ezechias, per prophetas vel iram a Domino susceperunt, vel misericordiam meruerunt. Et in Deuteronomio scriptum est (Deut. xvii. 8-13). Per sacerdotes enim dicit Dominus (Ps. ii. 10-12). Et apostolica auctoritas commonet, ut et reges etiam obediant præpositis suis in Domino, qui pro animabus eorum invigilant, ut non cum tristitia hoc faciant. Et beatus Gelasius papa ad

Anastasium imperatorem scribit : 'Quia duæ sunt personæ, quibus principaliter hic regitur mundus, scilicet pontificalis auctoritas, et regia dignitas, et tanto majus est pondus pontificum quanto de ipsis etiam regibus reddituri sunt Domino rationem.' Ambrosius Theodosium imperatorem ab ecclesia culpis exigentibus segregavit et per pœnitentiam revocavit."

[1] Hincmar of Rheims, De Div. Loth. et Tetb. *Quæst.* 6, *Responsio.* "De eo quod dicitur, Quia Rex, si noluerit venire ad synodum, libere etiam compellatus dimittet : sancta Scriptura, sacrique canones monstrant, in judicio personam non debere accipere, sed causæ qualitatem discernere."

[2] M. G. H. Ep., iii. Codex Carolinus, 45 : "Et si quis, quod non optamus, contra hujusmodi nostræ adjurationis atque exhortationis seriem agere præsumserit, sciat se auctoritate domini mei, beati Petri apostolorum principis, anathematis vinculo esse innodatum et a regno Dei alienum atque cum diabolo et ejus atrocissimis pompis et ceteris impiis æternis incendiis concremandum deputatum."

[3] M. G. H. Scriptorum, vol. i. Ann. Bert. ad. a. 865.

It must at the same time be noticed that we may find a partial explanation of the existence of such views as those which Hincmar condemns, in the tone of some letters of Pope Leo IV. in reference to a threat of Hincmar to excommunicate the Emperor Lothair. He complains of the pride of Hincmar, which had led him to threaten with excommunication the emperor whom Pope Paschal had consecrated with the oil of benediction, thus violating every divine and earthly law.[1] Leo IV.'s phrases are no doubt related to such a question as whether it was competent for any one except the Pope himself to excommunicate kings and emperors, and must not be construed as meaning that Leo would not have claimed that authority for himself: they belong to the question of the relation of the authority of bishops and metropolitans to that of the Pope. But it is easy to see that such phrases might tend to encourage the judgment that within his own dominion the ruler was not amenable to the jurisdiction of Church courts. There were clearly certain ambiguities and uncertainties in regard to the relation of the discipline of the Church to the monarch in the ninth century; but no doubt, also, the Church was very clear that it had spiritual authority over even the highest in station.

No doubt these claims, that the church should exercise jurisdiction even over the most exalted persons in the State,

[1] M. G. H. Ep., v. Ep. Select. Pont. Rom. Leo IV., 36 : " Ita ut, quem imperatorem princeps sacerdotum et primus sanctæ recordationis predecessor noster dominus Pascalis papa oleo benedictionis unctum consecraverat more predecessorum apostolicorum, una cum fratre Carolo rege et uxoribus ac filiis, anathemate injurasset, nostrum et ejusdem magni imperatoris ministerium parvipendens et transgressus divinas pariter et humanas constitutiones."

Leo IV., 37 : " Nec illum etiam canonice possumus collaudare, quod superstite præsule sedem ejus invasit, qui etiam, cum debuerat de jactura honoris proprii valde esse perterritus, in unctum Domini, quem sedis apostolica benedictionis oleo publice consecravit sibique proprium fecit heredem, anathematis jaculum contra omnem, non solum divinam, immo mundanam institutionem inferre presumpsit.

" Item. Unum pro culpe suæ malicia censura sedis apostolicæ communiter mandamus, ut neque de sua unquam præsumptione valeat gloriari, neque contra vos, quem Deus sibi principem et imperatorem elegit, et per manus summi et apostolici pontificis sanctificatum benedictionis oleum super vestrum caput effudit, clam vel publice audeat aliquam quocumque tempore anathematis vel aliam injurie inferre jacturam."

are to be interpreted as referring to spiritual matters. But
it was not easy to draw a clear line between things which
were to be regarded as spiritual and those which belonged to
the secular sphere. We have already noticed that Jonas
of Orleans, in commenting on the twelfth letter of Gelasius,
urges that as the priests will have to render account to God
for kings as well as for private persons, it is their duty
carefully to admonish them lest they depart from the will
of God, or from the proper discharge of the office which was
committed to them.[1] The ecclesiastical order was in
some measure responsible for the just administration of
the State, just as we have seen that the king was responsible
for the good order of the Church. It is interesting to see
that this principle finds expression in some of the formal
documents of these times. In the " Præceptio " of Chlothar II.,
of about the end of the sixth century or the beginning of the
seventh, we find it provided, that if any judge should condemn
a man unjustly in the absence of the king, the bishop is to
reprove him.[2] Again, in the documents concerning the election
of Guido in 889 we find a provision that the common people
are to have their own laws, and are not to be burdened
further than the laws allow: the count is to see to this, but
if he neglect his duty, or allow injustice to be done, he is
to be excommunicated by the bishop of the place till he has
rendered satisfaction.[3] Again, therefore, we find nothing
strictly new in the emphatic assertion of the Pseudo-Isidorian

---

[1] Jonas of Orleans, De Instit. Reg.,
cap. i. : " Ergo quia tantæ auctoritatis,
imo tanti discriminis est ministerium
sacerdotum, ut de ipsis etiam regibus
Deo sint rationem reddituri, oportet
et valde necesse est, ut de vestra
salute semper simus solliciti, vosque
ne a voluntate Dei, quod absit, aut
a ministerio quod vobis commisit,
erretis, vigilanter admoneamus."

[2] M. G. H. Leg., sect. ii. vol. i.
No. 8, Chlotarii II. Præceptio, 6 :
" Si judex aliquem contra legem injuste damnaverit, in nostri absentia
ab episcopo castigetur, ut quod perpere

judicavit versatim melius discussione
habeta emendare procuret."

[3] M. G. H. Leg., sect. ii. vol. ii.
No. 222, " Widonis Capitulatio Electionis," 5 : " Plebei homines et universi
ecclesiæ filii libere suis utantur legibus ;
ex parte publica ultra, quam legibus
sancitum est, ab eis non exigatur, nec
violenter opprimantur ; quodsi factum
fuerit, legaliter per comitem ipsius loci
emendetur, si suo voluerit deinceps pot-
iri honore ; si vero ipse neglexerit vel
fecerit aut facienti assensum prebuerit,
a loci episcopo usque dignam satisfactionem excommunicatus habeatur."

Decretals, that any one who is oppressed should freely be allowed to appeal to the priest.[1]

The intervention of the bishops for the protection of the oppressed has, indeed, a long and complex history. As early as the time of Justinian we find the Imperial Government laying upon the bishops a great deal of responsibility for the supervision of the expenditure of money left for public charities and other public purposes; and we even find them given a considerable power of intervention, to protect the citizens against attempts on the part of the magistrates to impose improper exactions.[2] It may be doubted whether such powers were originally given to them on account of their spiritual authority, or because of the position occupied by the bishops as prominent citizens in their dioceses: the truth probably is that both their secular and their ecclesiastical position contributed to bring about such arrangements. However this may be, it is clear that in the ninth century the Church, through the bishops, exercised a very considerable authority in the control of even the secular affairs of society, altogether apart from that authority which the bishops possessed as being among the great men of the kingdom or empire.

The Pope and the bishops of the church exercised a considerable authority in the appointment and in the deposition of kings and emperors. We do not wish to discuss the question which in later times was often raised, as to the nature of the authority by which Charles the Great was elected to the empire. In later times men on the one side maintained that this was done by the Pope,—that he in the plenitude of his power conferred the empire on Charles; while on the other side it was held that the action of the Pope was simply that of one who recognised his accession, and by consecration invoked on it the divine blessing. We do not know that there is any reason to suppose that at the time the theory of the matter occupied men's minds to any serious extent at all.

---

[1] Pseud. - Isidore, Anaclètus Dec. xvi.: "Omnis enim oppressus libere sacerdotum, si voluerit, appellet juditium et a nullo prohibeatur, sed ab his fulciatur et liberetur."

[2] Cf. esp. Justinian Codex, i. 3. 45, and i. 4. 26.

The Franks had come to Italy on the urgent invitation of the Popes as their protectors against the Lombard power, and later on against the Greek power.   Pope Stephen II. had recognised Pippin as king of the Franks, and had afterwards crowned him, and finally Pope Leo III. had crowned Charles the Great as emperor.   We doubt whether at the time it occurred to any one to consider what precise authority lay behind these acts.   There is no doubt, however, that in the ninth century we find clear traces of the rapid development of a theory that the Pope had some very distinct share in the appointment of emperors or kings, and that the consecration by him was regarded as something more than the mere solemn recognition of a proper election or succession, and the invocation of the divine blessing.   And so also with the position of the bishops in the appointment and consecration of kings, there are very clear traces of the conception that they had a great deal to say in elections, and that their consecration was looked upon as a very important matter.

It is here again difficult to say how much of the authority of the Pope or the bishops is to be attributed to the political importance of their position among the most important magnates of the empire, and how much to their religious authority.   We must be prepared to recognise that each has its real influence, while these two elements of their authority are often fused to such an extent that it is exceedingly difficult to separate them.   When, for instance, we find that the provisions for the partition of his dominions by Charles the Great, after they had been considered and sworn to by the magnates of the empire, were sent to Pope Leo that he might subscribe them,[1] we can hardly say whether this is to be taken as a recognition of some right in the head of the spiritual power as such to take his part in these arrangements, or whether it is to be interpreted as due to the sense of the great political influence

---

[1] M. G. H. Scriptorum, vol. i., Einhard, "Annals" for 806 : "De hac partitione et testamentum factum, et jurejurando ab optimatibus Francorum confirmatum, et constitutiones pacis conservandæ causa factæ atque hæc omnia litteris mandata sunt, et Leoni papæ, ut his sua manu subscriberet, per Einhardum missa."

which the Pope had exercised and was still exercising in Western Europe, and especially in Italy.

Whatever may be the exact meaning which we are to attach to such a recognition of the authority of the Pope, there is no doubt of the importance of his position later in the century. In the 'Chronicon Salernitanum' there is preserved a letter of the Emperor Lewis II. written to the Emperor Basil of Constantinople in 867. It appears that Basil had expressed his indignation that Lewis should call himself "Imperator Augustus." Lewis defends his use of the title on the ground largely that he had been anointed and consecrated by the Pope, and says that those Frankish princes were called first kings and then emperors who were anointed with the holy oil by the Pope.[1] It has been suggested that this letter is spurious—that it is impossible to think that any Frankish emperor would have spoken in such terms. It seems to us that such a line of argument is exceedingly unsafe, for, apart from this letter, there is considerable evidence that at least in the latter part of the eighth century it was frequently recognised that the Pope had a very important part in the appointment and consecration of kings and emperors. In a former chapter we have referred to the terms of the document concerning the election of Charles the Bald to the kingdom of Italy at Pavia in 876; we must now notice in this document the reference to the elevation of Charles, a few months earlier, to the empire as being the work of the Pope. The bishops and other magnates of Italy elect Charles as king in view of the fact that God had raised him to the imperial throne by means of the vicar of the blessed prince of the apostles Peter and Paul, Pope John.[2] It might, perhaps,

[1] M. G. H. Scriptorum, vol. iii., 'Chronicon Salernitanum,' p. 522: "Invenimus præsertim, cum et ipsi patrui nostri, gloriosi reges, absque invidia imperatorem nos vocitent et imperatorem esse procul dubio fatentur, non profecto ad ætatem, qua nobis majores sunt, attendentes, sed ad unctionem et sacrationem, qua per summi pontificis manus, impositione et oratione divinitus ad hoc sumus cul-

men provecti, et ad Romani principatus imperium, quod superno nutu potimur, aspicientes."

P. 523. "Nam Francorum principes primo reges, deinde vero imperatores dicti sunt, hii dumtaxat, qui a Romano pontifice ad hoc oleo sancto perfusi sunt."

[2] M. G. H. Leg., sect. ii. vol. ii. No. 220, Kar. II. Imp. Electio: "Jam quia divina pietas vos beatorum

be suggested that this is only an Italian view of the appointment of Charles the Bald, but the same conception is expressed
in the proceedings of the synod of Ponthion, which was held in
June and July 876. We learn that at this synod the proceedings of the Italian magnates at Pavia were read and confirmed :
the part of the Pope in the election of Charles to the empire
seems as clearly recognised at Ponthion as it had been at Pavia.[1]
We find similar references to the influence of the Pope in the
election of kings in the separate kingdoms which made up the
empire, while here we also find a similar authority attributed to
the bishops. In the proceedings of the synod held at Quierzy
in 858 we find some very significant phrases on the subject.
The synod sent a letter, which is thought to have been
composed by Hincmar of Rheims, to Lewis of Germany, protesting against his invasion of the territories of Charles, and
addressing a special remonstrance to those archbishops and
bishops who had themselves, with the consent of the people,
anointed Charles to be king, while the Holy See had afterwards
honoured and confirmed him, by letters, as king. The synod
evidently attaches great importance to the unction, and speaks
of him who faithlessly and contumaciously lifts his hand
against the Lord's anointed, as of one who despises Christ,
and who will, therefore, perish by the spiritual sword.[2] Again,

principum apostolorum Petri et Pauli
interventione per vicarium ipsorum,
domnum videlicet Johannem summum pontificem et universalem papam
spiritalemque patrem vestrum, ad profectum sanctæ Dei ecclesiæ nostrorumque omnium incitavit et ad
imperiale culmen Sancti Spiritus
judicio provexit, nos unanimiter vos
. . . Italici regni regem elegimus."
[1] M. G. H. Leg., sect. ii. vol. ii.
No. 279 (B.) : " Sicut domnus Johannes
apostolicus et universalis papa primo
Romæ elegit atque sacra unctione constituit omnesque Italici regni episcopi,
abbates, comites et reliqui omnes, qui
cum illis convenerunt, domnum nostrum gloriosum imperatorem Karolum
augustum unanimi devotione elegerunt

sibi protectorem ac defensorem esse,
ita et nos qui de Francia, Burgundia,
Aquitania, Septimania, Neustria ac
Provincia pridie Kalendas Julii in loco,
qui dicitur Pontigonis, anno xxxvii. in
Francia ac imperii primo, jussu ejusdem
domni et gloriosi augusti convenimus,
pari consensu ac concordi devotione
eligimus et confirmamus."
[2] M. G. H. Leg., sect. ii. vol. ii.
No. 297, "Epist. Synodi. Carisiacensis
ad Hlud. Reg. Germ. Directa," 15 :
"Maxime autem nobis necesse est loqui
cum illis archiepiscopis et episcopis,
qui consensu et voluntate populi regni
istius domnum nostrum fratrem vestrum unxerunt in regem sacro chrismate divina traditione quemque sancta
sedes apostolica mater nostra litteris

we find the archbishops and the bishops of the kingdom of
Arles electing Lewis, the son of Boso, to follow his father in
that kingdom, and they do this partly on the ground that
the Holy See had approved of such an election.[1]

We find the strongest and most remarkable assertion of the
importance of the consecration and unction by the bishops in
another document, which refers to the election of Charles the
Bald as King of the Neustrian Franks. This is a proclamation
issued in the name of Charles the Bald himself in 859 : he
recounts how, after his election by the bishops and other
faithful men of the kingdom, he had been consecrated and
anointed with the holy chrism, and had received the crown
and sceptre, and he urges that after this consecration he
cannot be cast down from the kingdom by any, at least
without the judgment of the bishops by whose ministry he
had been consecrated king : they are, he says, the thrones
of God, among whom God is seated, and by whom he decrees
his judgments, and to their paternal reproofs and chastise-
ments he had been and still was prepared to submit.[2] We
may perhaps suitably recall the phrases in which the bishops
describe the deposition of Lewis the Pious,[3] and the words of

apostolicis ut regem honorare studuit
et confirmare." The letter then cites
examples of the reverence shown to
the Lord's anointed in the Old Testament, and continues : " Sic et qui
infideliter et contumaciter in unctum
qualemcunque Domini manum mittit,
dominum christorum Christum con-
temnit, et in anima procul dubio
spiritualis gladii animadversione perit."
[1] M. G. H. Leg., sect. ii. vol. ii.
No. 289, "Hludowici Regis Arelatensis
Electio," 890 : " Cum igitur diligenter
conperissemus, quod assensus sanctæ
catholicæ et apostolicæ matris nostræ
huic faveret electioni, simul convenimus in civitatem Valentiam (i.e., Archbishop of Lyons, Archbishop of Arles,
Archbishop of Embrun, Archbishop of
Vienne, with other bishops), . . . atque secundum Dei voluntatem quæ-
situri exploravimus, si hunc digne et

rationibiliter secundum monita dominii
apostolici, cujus scripta præ manibus
habebantur, super nos regem constituere deberemus."
[2] M. G. H. Leg., sect. ii. vol. ii.
No. 300, " Libellus Proclamationis adversus Wenilonem " : " A qua consecratione vel regni sublimitate subplantari
vel proici a nullo debueram saltem
sine audientia et judicio episcoporum,
quorum ministerio in regem sum consecratus, et qui throni Dei sunt dicti,
in quibus Deus sedit et per quos sua
decernit judicia ; quorum paternis correptionibus et castigatoriis judiciis me
subdere fui paratus et in præsenti
sum subditus." See p. 252.
[3] M. G. H. Leg., sect. ii. vol. ii.
No. 197, " . . . quia potestate privatus erat juxta divinum consilium
et ecclesiasticam auctoritatem." See
p. 250.

Hincmar in referring to the same event, and to the restoration of Lewis by the bishops with the consent of the people.[1]

The importance of this conception of the authority of the Pope and the bishops in relation to the appointment and the deposition of emperors and kings is very obvious. As we have said, it is very difficult, perhaps impossible, to disentangle the relative importance of their spiritual and their secular position in the matter. The fact that they are great persons in Western Europe, or in a particular kingdom, has obviously much to do with it, but there are already clear traces of a theory that, as spiritual rulers, they have some, though it may be a somewhat indefinable, authority over the secular power.

We have endeavoured to bring out as clearly as possible two facts with regard to the theory of the relation of the authorities of Church and State in the ninth century. First, that in the ninth, just as in the fifth century, men believed firmly that the two authorities were separate and independent, each sacred and supreme in its own sphere—that the ecclesiastic owed allegiance to the king in secular matters, and that the king owed allegiance to the Church in spiritual matters. But also, secondly, that the practical experience of the ninth century made it clear that it was very difficult to distinguish the two spheres by any hard-and-fast line. Still, we think that the writers of the ninth century held to the theory of a dual authority in society; we think that they would have repudiated any other conception.

It is true that there is one work which belongs to this period, which in the later middle ages was interpreted as expressing quite another theory—the theory, that is, of the supremacy of the spiritual power over the temporal. This document is the famous "Donation" of Constantine. We have hitherto left this document out of account for two reasons—first, because it is almost certain that the later interpretation of the docu-

---

[1] Hincmar of Rheims, De Div. Loth. et Tetb., Qu. vi. Resp. : "Nostra ætate pium Augustum Ludovicum a regno dejectum, post satisfactionem episco- palis unanimitas, saniore consilio, cum populi consensu et Ecclesiæ et regno restituit."

ment was incorrect; and, secondly, because, whatever its meaning and purpose may have been, it exercised no appreciable influence in the ninth century on the theory of the relations of Church and State.

From our point of view the important phrases of the "Donation" are those which deal with the grant of authority to the Pope, and the transference of the seat of imperial authority from Rome to Byzantium.[1] The exact meaning of these phrases has been discussed by a number of scholars, and it is generally agreed that the interpretation given to them in the later middle ages can hardly be that which was in the mind of the compiler. In later times they were understood to signify that Constantine granted to the Popes a complete temporal authority over the West, and it is not disputed that the words might have this meaning; but it is now generally agreed that they must be interpreted as referring to a grant of temporal authority in Italy. Most historical critics think that the purpose of the document was to assist the Roman See in securing the reversion of the Byzantine territories in Italy, and especially of the Exarchate. It seems possible that the "Donation" was built up in part on traditions which may have been long current in Italy, and that the circumstances of the eighth century, when the Bishops of Rome came to be the actual representatives of the Roman *res publica* in Italy, and its principal defence against the Lombards, may have tended to give these traditions a new significance, and to sug-

---

[1] Pseudo-Isidore, 'Exemplar Domini Imperatoris Constantini.' "Unde ut non pontificalis apex vilescat, sed magis amplius quam terreni imperii dignitas et gloriæ potentia decoretur, ecce tam palatium nostrum, ut prælatum est, quamque Romane urbis et omnes Italiæ seu occidentalium regionum provincias, loca et civitates sepe fato beatissimo pontifici nostro Silvestro universali papæ contradentes atque relinquentes ejus vel successorum ipsius pontificum potestati et dictione firma imperiali censura per hanc nostram divalem sacram et pragmaticum constitutum decernimus disponendum, atque juræ sanctæ Romanæ ecclesiæ concedimus permansurum. Unde congruum prospeximus nostrum imperium et regni potestatem orientalibus transferri ac transmutari regionibus et in Bizantiæ provintia in obtimo loco nomini nostro civitatem ædificari et nostrum illic constitui imperium, quoniam ubi principatus sacerdotum et christiane religionis caput ab imperatore cœlesti constitutum est, justum non est ut illic imperator terrenus habeat potestatem."

gest to the author their reduction to a definite and coherent form. We are not here concerned with the growth of the temporal states of the Bishop of Rome, but it seems to us that so far from looking upon this as the result of an unreasonable greed for secular power, it should be recognised that nothing was more natural than that the Popes, finding themselves to be the actual chiefs of what survived of the ancient Roman State in Italy, should have desired to maintain and even extend their authority. Any one who studies the papal correspondence and the 'Liber Pontificalis' in the eighth century will, we think, feel that the leadership of the Roman *res publica* in the West was forced upon them rather than deliberately sought. It was only slowly and reluctantly that they drew away from the Byzantine authority, for after all, as civilised members of the Roman State, they preferred the Byzantine to the barbarian; and when circumstances had practically destroyed the Byzantine power in Italy, it was natural that they should seek to hold together, or to recover from the barbarian, even though, like the Frank, he was a friendly barbarian, some fragments of the ancient commonwealth of civilisation. It is of course true that once they had broken with the Byzantine power, they had no inclination for reunion with it, but this again, considering the history of the eighth century, was not unnatural.

It is then generally thought that the purpose of the "Donation" was to assist the Bishops of Rome in establishing a claim to the reversion of the Byzantine authority in Italy. Other conjectures, such as that of Grauert,[1] that it was intended to support the Frankish empire against the criticism of the Byzantines, though they have been urged with much learning and ingenuity, seem too far-fetched. It must at the same time be recognised that the problem of the date and place of origin of the document is surrounded with perplexities. The "Donation" cannot be later than the ninth century, as it is contained in a manuscript of that time, and is embodied in the Pseudo-Isidorian decretals. How long before that it may have existed is a question of great complexity. In a letter of Pope Hadrian I. of 778 there are phrases which, it

---

[1] 'Historisches Jahrbuch der Görresgesellschaft,' 3, 4, 5.

is urged, imply a knowledge of the "Donation," but the text cannot be said to render this certain.[1] Hadrian evidently refers to some tradition of great grants of authority by the Emperor Constantine, but whether he is referring to this document is another question. In a letter of the same Pope to Constantine and Irene, of 785, he describes a vision of Constantine, which suggests the tradition which is embodied in the "Donation," but this does not at all necessarily prove that he was acquainted with the "Donation" itself.[2] The first writers of whom it can be said with any degree of confidence that they are acquainted with this document are Ado of Vienne[3] and Hincmar of Rheims,[4] in the ninth century. It is certainly perplexing that there should be no certain evidence that the document was known in Italy until the latter part of the tenth century.[5] At the same time the more recent investigations into its phraseology, and especially those of Scheffer-Boichorst,[6] seem to make it fairly clear that the work was compiled in Italy, and in the latter part of the eighth century.

In later volumes we shall have to consider what importance this document may have had in the scholastic period. For the present it is enough to say that it produced no appreciable effect upon the political theory of the ninth century. The theorists of the following centuries may have tried to reduce to a complete unity the elements of authority in society; the ninth century writers knew nothing of this.

If we now look back over the political theory of the ninth century, we can lay down certain general propositions about its

[1] M. G. H., Epist. iii., Codex Carolinus, 60 : "Et sicut temporibus beati Silvestri Romani pontificis a sanctæ recordationis piissimo Constantino, magno imperatore, per ejus largitatem sancta Dei catholica et apostolica Romana ecclesia elevata atque exaltata est et potestatem in his Hesperiæ partibus largiri dignatus."
[2] Pope Hadrian I. ; Ep. lvi. Migne Patr. Lat., vol. 96, p. 1220.

[3] Ado of Vienne, Chronicon ; Migne Patr. Lat., vol. 123, p. 92.
[4] M. G. H. Leg., sect. ii. vol. ii. Hincmar of Rheims, "De Ordine Palatii," 13.
[5] M. G. H., Diplomatum ii. Otto III., No. 389.
[6] "Mittheilungen des Instituts für Oesterreichische Geschichtsforschung," 10 and 11.

character. It is, we think, in the first place, clear that there did not exist in this time and among these writers any general philosophical system of political theory.   Certain great and important conceptions the men of this period apprehended and developed with force; but in the main it is true to say that they are concerned much more with the practical circumstances of the life of their time than with the attempt to construct a system of political thought, We have pointed out the fact that their statements are often incoherent, sometimes almost self-contradictory; this is the direct consequence of the fact that they are not conscious of any systematic theory as lying behind their practical judgments. We think that when we have recognised this, and if we very carefully keep it in mind, we may still with justice say that their treatment of the character and the foundation of the organised life of society turns upon three great conceptions.

In the first place, they clearly held, and in some measure understood, that conception of the equality of human nature, whose history we have studied from the time of Cicero. They not only reproduced the phrases of the Fathers, but they clearly also understood their point of view. This implies, indeed, something more than the fact that they held to the theory of equality; it also means that they understood and approved the conception of the difference between the primitive condition of man and the actual condition of human society. They held that it was not nature but man's faults which had brought into existence the conventional institutions of society. It is quite true that, except with regard to the institution of slavery, the subject does not greatly occupy their minds; but it is important, especially with reference to the developed mediæval theory of society, to recognise that this conception was always alive.

Secondly, they held very firmly to the conviction of the sacred character of the organised structure of society in government. They follow the New Testament and the Fathers in the doctrine that the civil order of society is necessary, and that it is sacred. Indeed it is the very firmness with which they hold this that causes them to adopt the extreme language in which St Gregory the Great had expressed the conception,

and sometimes to speak as though any resistance to the actions
of those who represented the sacred authority were a thing
unlawful and irreligious. The disorders of the time were so
great, the necessity of delivering western Europe from the
confusions which followed the downfall of the ancient empire
in the West was so obvious, that we cannot wonder if at times
they exaggerate the principle of obedience to authority.

But, in the third place, the theory of the ninth century
recognised with equal clearness the necessity of checking the
unjust and tyrannical use of authority. If the Fathers like
St Ambrose and St Isidore lay much stress on the limitation
of authority by its end—namely, the establishment and maintenance of justice—the ninth-century writers assert this conception with even greater clearness, and, under the influence
of the traditions of the Teutonic races, find a practical application of the theory of justice in the conception of the supremacy
of law, and of the limited and conditioned character of the
authority of the ruler. The emperor or king is bound by the
national law, and derives his authority, ultimately no doubt
from God, but immediately from the nation, and holds this
authority on the condition of his setting forward righteousness
and justice in the State.

4578

INDEX.

Distinction between churches and other property of the Church, 184.
Possible relation between his view of independence of Church and his conception of limitations of secular authority of civil ruler, 184.

Ambrosiaster—
Relation of law of nature to law of Moses, 104.
Question of identity with author of 'Quæstiones Veteris et Novi Testamenti,' 104, note 4.
Full discussion of origin of slavery and its relation to equality of human nature, 113.
God made men free, 113.
Slavery a consequence of sin, 113.
Slavery extends to body only: God alone is master of the soul, 113.
Masters must be just to their slaves, who are also their equals, 113.
Almsgiving an act of justice, for God gives all things in common to all men, 137.
The king the Vicar of God, 149, 179, 215.
The king has the image of God, as the bishop has that of Christ, 149, 179, 215.
Relation of David to Saul : the divine character of royal office cannot be lost by misconduct, 150.
Obscure passage as to evil form of government, which is not from God, 150.
His writings the possible source of the phrase " Vicar of God," spoken of the king, in ninth century, 215, 216.

Anarchism in primitive Church, 93-97.
Anthemius, Emperor, 189.
Antoninus Pius, rescript for protection of slaves, 49.
Apocalypse, its evidence in regard to relation of Christians to Roman Government, 93.

Aristotle—
Difference between his ideas and those of Roman Lawyers, 2.
His theory of inequality of human nature, 7.
Relation of inequality to government and slavery, 7.
His conceptions related to circumstances of Greek civilisation, 7, 8, 45.
Contrast between his view and that of Cicero and Seneca, 8, 45.
Influence on Cicero's view of slavery, 12.
Conception of just form of government in relation to Cicero's, 15.
Relation of this to views of Stoics, 30.
Relation of his theory of inequality to the theory of Lawyers, 45, 46.

His theory of political society as related to St Paul's, 98.
Contrast of his view of slavery with that of Fathers', 145.

Athanasius, St, quotes letter of Hosius of Cordova in which he warns Emperor Constantine that he has no right to interfere in Church affairs, 177.

Augustine, Pseudo—
Protests against severity to Christian slaves, 115.
Slave a brother, in grace, of master, 116.
Slaves should love and obey masters, 121.
God made masters and slaves, 121.

Augustine, St—
Interpretation of St Paul on natural law, 83, 105.
Definition of natural law, 106.
God made men free, 114.
Slavery a consequence of, a punishment or remedy for sin, imposed by just sentence of God, 118.
Christ makes men good slaves, 121.
Christian slaves must not claim emancipation on precedent of Jewish slaves, 121.
Masters should treat slaves like children with respect to their spiritual wellbeing, 123.
Man is by nature sociable, 125, 165.
Government of man over man not natural and primitive, 126, 128.
Government made necessary by sin, a divine remedy, 130.
Community of goods the more perfect way, 135.
Private property lawful, 135.
His theory of property, 139-142.
A defence of confiscation of Donatists' property by Imperial Government, 139, 140.
By divine law all things belong to God or the saints, 140.
Private property an institution of human and positive law, 140, 141.
Contrast between his theory of property and that of Roman Lawyers, 141.
Refuses to recognise Donatist argument that their property should not be confiscated because it was the result of their labour, 141.
Right of property limited by its just use, 140-142.
Relation of this theory to that of Ambrose and other Fathers and the mediæval theory of right of private property, 142.
Authority of wicked as of good rulers drawn from God, 151.
His view on this drawn from Old Testament, 159.
Contrast between his conception of the State and St Ambrose's, 162.

Theory of Institutes and of Isidore on *jus naturale, gentium,* and *civile,* 106-110.

Limitation of rights of property, 142.

Irenæus, St—
Origin of coercive government, 128, 129.
Authority derived from God, 129.
Coercive government made necessary by sin, 128, 130.
Evil rulers sent by God as a punishment on their people, 148.
Threatens unjust rulers with God's judgment, 162.

Isaiah, his universalism, 85.

Isidore, St, of Seville—
Defines *jus naturale* and *jus gentium,* 42.
On law of nature, 106.
His position in development of political theory, 107.
Character of 'Etymologies,' 107.
On tripartite character of law, 108.
Distinguishes *jus naturale* from *jus gentium,* 108.
Natural law common to all nations, 108.
Defines *jus gentium* and *jus civile,* 109.
Distinction between *jus naturale* and *jus gentium* and theory of state of nature, 109, 110.
Under natural law, "omnium una libertas," 114.
Slavery a punishment and remedy for sin, 118, 119.
Slavery a discipline, 119.
Government a remedy for wickedness, 130, 131.
"Communis omnium possessio" belongs to *jus naturale,* 142-144.
Uncertainty as to meaning of phrase, 143.
Interpretation of phrase in Middle Ages, 143.
Comparison of Isidore's statement with those of Roman Lawyers, 143.
Wicked and good rulers alike derive authority from God, 151.
Wicked ruler a divine punishment, 151.
Urges princes to respect their own laws, 164, 173.
On beginnings of social life, 171, 172.
Defines *civitas* and *populus,* 172.
Agrees with Cicero, not with Augustine, in definition of State, 172.
Defines king and tyrant, 172, 173.
Civil authority must promote justice, 173.
Hrabanus Maurus's definition of *oppidum* taken from Isidore, 212.
Influence of his definition of State in ninth century, 221.

Influence of his definitions of king and tyrant in ninth century, 221, 222.

Isidore, Pseudo—
Possible to maintain that the ninth-century theory of authority of the Church culminates in these writings, but doubtful whether this is correct, 257.
All princes must submit to bishops, 275.
No emperor or ruler may decree anything which is contrary to the divine commands, 278.
Any one who is oppressed may appeal to the priest, 282.
"Donation of Constantine" embodied in Pseudo-Isidore, 289.

James, St—
Freedom, 94.
The poor and the rich, 100, 101.

Jerome, St—
On natural law, 105.
Community of goods belongs to the perfect life, 135.

Jerusalem, communism in Church of, 98-101.

Jesus Christ—
Universalism and its relation to the idea of equality, 83, 84.
Teaching of Christ on relation of Jews to Roman Government, 92.
Contrast of spirit of worldly rule with spirit of disciples, 96, 97.
Justin Martyr holds that Christ teaches Christians to serve their rulers, 129.
Christ alone is truly King and Priest, according to Gelasius, 190.

Jonas of Orleans—
Equality of human nature, 199.
Low social position of inferior clergy in ninth century, 207.
Divine authority of the king, 214.
Influenced by St Isidore's definition of king and tyrant, 221, 222.
Quotes "De Duodecim Abusivis Sæculi" on justice in king, 225.
Chief duty of king is to do justice, 225.
Jonas' statements reproduced by bishops in address to Lewis the Pious, 226, 227.
Quotes Gelasius on Church and State, 254.
Comments on theory of Gelasius, 255, 256.
Priests must urge king to discharge his duty, 255, 256, 281.
Quotes from Rufinus the report that Constantine said God made bishops judges of all, and that they cannot be judged by any, 274.

THE END

PRINTED BY WILLIAM BLACKWOOD & SONS LTD.